Asian-American Education

HISTORICAL BACKGROUND AND CURRENT REALITIES

Sociocultural, Political, and Historical Studies in Education

Joel Spring, Editor

Asian-American Education

HISTORICAL BACKGROUND AND CURRENT REALITIES

Meyer Weinberg

PROFESSOR EMERITUS

University of Massachusetts, Amherst

 LAWRENCE ERLBAUM ASSOCIATES, PUBLISHERS

1997   Mahwah, New Jersey   London

Lawrence Erlbaum Associates, Inc., Publishers
10 Industrial Avenue
Mahwah, New Jersey 07430

A complete bibliography of all works cited in endnotes in each chapter of this volume
may be found on the Internet at http://www.erlbaum.com/wein.htm

LIBRARY OF CONGRESS CATALOGING-IN-PUBLICATION DATA

Weinberg, Meyer, 1920–
      Asian-American education : historical background and current realities / Meyer Weinberg.
      p.   cm.
      Includes bibliographical references and index.
      ISBN 0–8058–2775–7 (cloth : alk. paper). — ISBN 0–8058–2776–5 (pbk. : alk. paper)
      1. Asian Americans—Education—History   I. Title.
   LC2632.W45   1997
   371.82995'073—dc21   97–8974
                                                                                      CIP

Books published by Lawrence Erlbaum Associates are printed on acid-free paper,
and their bindings are chosen for strength and durability.

Printed in the United States of America
10 9 8 7 6 5 4 3 2 1

To Erica

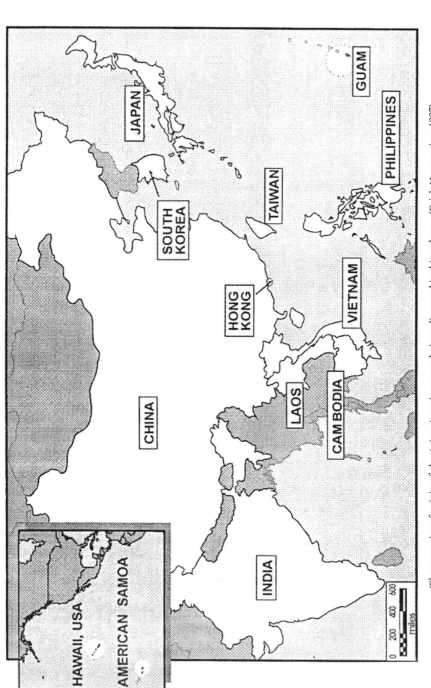

The countries of origin of the Asian-American populations discussed in this volume. (Erick Howenstine, 1997)

Contents

A complete bibliography of all works cited in endnotes in each chapter of this volume may be found on the Internet at http://www.erlbaum.com/wein.htm

Preface

This is the first general history of Asian-American education. During the 1960s and 1970s, when I edited *Integrated Education* magazine, standard educational journals were almost entirely ignoring the rising numbers of Asian-American children. *Integrated Education* took it on itself to publish more articles on the subject than all other educational journals combined. Early in the 1970s, I proposed to write a two-volume history of the education of minorities in the United States, including a chapter each on Chinese Americans and Japanese Americans. No funding agency cared to finance such a large work. Finally, the Field Foundation agreed to facilitate the writing of a single volume, which required the halving of the coverage. The Asian-American material was dropped, along with a number of other significant topics. Meanwhile, I continued to include Asian-American materials in various book-length bibliographies I compiled in the past 20 years. The present work is far more comprehensive than anything I could have written in the mid-1970s about Asian-Americans. Yet, it is not meant as a final word. The time is much too soon for that.

I wish to thank the librarians at the University of Massachusetts, Amherst; the California State University, Long Beach; and the University of Chicago for their unstinting help. Not any less, I am grateful to the people who operate the indispensable Inter-Library Loan System for the thoroughness and dispatch with which they responded to my cascading requests for hard-to-obtain books. Mealedey Seng and Ken Cheng, my research assistants at CSULB during 1992 to 1994, carried loads of books and reports and duplicated numerous journal articles as well as transported gallons of coffee for me. As the initial occupant of the Veffie Milstead Jones endowed chair at CSULB, I met with numerous students, teachers, and others throughout Southern California. Once more, Betty Craker has done a splendid job of translating my handwriting into a clearly typed manuscript. Most rewarding were numerous discussions with Professor Terrence G. Wiley on a broad range of issues, many of them directly concerned with this book-in-process. Staff members at Lawrence Erlbaum Associates were most cooperative and helpful: Naomi Silverman, Senior Editor; Kathryn M. Scornavacca, Book Production Editor; and Susan Helene Gottfried, Copy Editor. Nan Bodgett compiled the index and Erick Howenstine drew the map.

I am deeply indebted to all these. Wherever possible, I have quoted students, teachers, parents, and others directly concerned with educational experiences.

I wish also to express my special thanks to an anonymous publisher's reader who made numerous well-taken comments and suggestions, many of which I adopted.

—Meyer Weinberg
Chicago

CHAPTER ONE

Introduction

In the world of educational research and writing, Asian-American students occupy little more than the margins. Histories of American education simply omit them. Discussions of current educational problems slight their importance when they deign to take note of them at all. The U.S. Education Department is by no means in the forefront of attention to Asian-American students. When, early in 1992, the U.S. Commission on Civil Rights released an outstanding study—*Civil Rights Issues Facing Asian Americans in the 1990s*—that contained two solid chapters on higher and lower education, university-based journals of education ignored it. Even though the report contained evidence of widespread violations of educational equal opportunity, no federal agency, including the Education Department, made public acknowledgement of these. In early autumn days, the press can be expected to carry stories about rising enrollments of Asian-Americans at elite colleges and universities, giving the misimpression that Asian-Americans can be found only or principally at such institutions.

Asian-American students, as a consequence, rarely appear in more familiar roles as students of community colleges, obscure or less than front-rank colleges or universities, or even as high-school dropouts who never made it into higher education. Nor can average Asian-American students recognize themselves as the stereotypical model minority world-beaters they encounter in mass media. Vietnamese children in three Michigan schools told a researcher, "I wish my teachers understood more about my homeland and culture and the experience I've been through."[1]

This book aims to provide a more dependable view of Asian-American

TABLE 1.1
The Asian Pacific American Population of the United States, 1990

Ethnicity	1990 Population	Percent of A/PI Population	Percent of Total U.S. Population
Chinese	1,645,472	22.6	0.7
Filipino	1,406,770	19.3	0.6
Japanese	847,562	11.7	0.3
Asian Indian	815,447	11.2	0.3
Korean	798,849	11.0	0.3
Vietnamese	614,547	8.4	0.2
Hawaiian	211,014	2.9	0.1
Laotian	149,014	2.0	0.1
Cambodian	147,411	2.0	0.1
Thai	91,275	1.3	*
Hmong	90,082	1.2	*
Samoan	62,964	0.9	*
Guamanian	49,345	0.7	*
Tongan	17,606	0.2	*
Other A/PI	326,304	4.5	0.1
Total	7,273,662	100.0	2.9

Note. A/PI = Asian Pacific Islander
*Less than one tenth of one percent
Source: U.S. Bureau of the Census, 1990 Summary Tape File 1C.
Reprinted with permission.

students. Each chapter deals with the kind of education received in the home country, how widely available it was, how equal or unequal the society was, and what were the circumstances under which the emigration of children like these occurred. The latter part of each chapter, on the other hand, deals with the education the children have received in the United States. Also throughout the book, instead of dwelling on a relatively narrow range of children who perform spectacularly well, I try to discover the educational situation among the more ordinary children.

The countries and regions covered are listed in the table of contents. In 1990, people from these places plus their children who were born here numbered nearly 7.3 million (see Table 1.1). By 1996, the figure had reached 9 million. Other countries who had sent few immigrants are not dealt with. Nor are those for which little information exists in English. (These include Burma, Indonesia, Thailand, Malaysia, Sri Lanka, and several countries such as Ladakh and Sikkim.)

The order of the chapters is roughly chronological in terms of when the first sizable numbers of immigrants came from a specific country. As a result of the great increase in Asian immigration since 1965 (see Table 1.2), most Asian-Americans are presently immigrants. Following are the percentages of each group who were immigrants in 1990:[2]

TABLE 1.2
Immigration by Decade and in Recent Years of Asian Groups, 1820–1994

Period	From Asia	Total Immigration	Asian % of Total Immigration	Chinese	Asian Japanese	Indian	Korean	Filipino	Vietnamese
1820	6	8,385	0.1	1	—	1	—	—	—
1821–1830	30	143,439	0.0	2	—	8	—	—	—
1831–1840	55	599,125	0.0	8	—	39	—	—	—
1841–1850	141	1,713,251	0.0	35	—	36	—	—	—
1851–1860	41,571	2,598,214	1.6	41,397	—	43	—	—	—
1861–1870	64,815	2,314,824	2.8	64,301	186	69	—	—	—
1871–1880	123,736	2,812,191	4.4	123,201	149	163	—	—	—
1881–1890	68,206	5,246,613	1.3	61,711	2,270	269	—	—	—
1891–1900	73,751	3,687,564	2.0	14,799	25,942	68	—	—	—
1901–1910	325,430	8,795,386	3.7	20,605	129,797	4,713	7,697	—	—
1911–1920	246,640	5,735,811	4.3	21,278	83,837	2,082	1,049	869	—
1921–1930	110,895	4,107,209	2.7	29,907	33,462	1,886	598	54,747	—
1931–1940	15,853	528,431	3.0	4,928	1,948	496	60	6,159	—
1941–1950	32,086	1,035,039	3.1	16,709	1,555	1,761	—	4,691	—
1951–1960	153,444	2,515,479	6.1	25,201	46,250	1,973	6,231	19,307	—
1961–1970	428,496	3,321,677	12.9	109,771	39,988	27,189	34,526	98,376	3,788
1971–1980	1,586,140	4,493,314	35.3	237,793	49,775	164,134	271,956	360,216	179,681
1981–1990	2,817,391	7,338,062	38.4	446,000	44,800	261,900	338,800	495,300	401,400
1991–1994	1,356,447	4,316,210	31.4	282,900	28,995	154,587	79,435	239,465	233,992

Sources: All data derived from U.S. Immigration and Naturalization Service and its predecessors. Figures for 1981–1990 are rounded to the nearest hundredth. According to INS definition, Asia includes Southwest Asia, e.g., Iraq, Israel, Syria, Turkey, etc.

Source: Larry Hajime Shinagawa, "The Impact of Immigration on the Demography of Asian Pacific Americans," pp. 86 and 88 in *The State of Asian Pacific America: Reframing the Immigration Debate. A Public Policy Report*, edited by Bill Ong Hing and Ronald Lee (LEAP Asian Pacific American Public Policy Institute and UCLA Asian American Studies Center, 1996). Reprinted with permission.

82 Koreans	70 Chinese
82 Vietnamese	68 Filipinos
80 Laotians	67 Hmong
79 Cambodians	35 Japanese
77 Asian Indians	26 Pacific Islanders

The comparative recency of this immigration means that the educational history of these groups is quite abbreviated. A consequence is that relatively little material may be available for the latter half of certain chapters. On the other hand, this did not turn out to be the case for the Hmong. In addition, the sources used do not distinguish between schooling in the United States of children from China, Hong Kong, or Taiwan although all but a handful are undoubtedly Chinese. I have retained the sections of the chapters that deal with schooling in Hong Kong and Taiwan because they provide important background information. Because Pacific Islanders make up only 5% of all Asian-Americans, they are frequently omitted from any extended treatments. I have preferred to devote two entire chapters to their schooling.

The most plentiful material about Asian-American schooling consists of standardized test scores, and there is a temptation to use only what is most available. Unfortunately, however, the scores are much too global—that is, instead of being based on the experience of individual schools, they are national or regional tests and tell us little about learning experiences where they are enacted. In the chapters that follow, much more stress is laid on academics on the level of individual schools or colleges and universities. It is on such levels that learning flourishes or founders. Few studies of this kind are available for this book to utilize.

Another problem with national or regional test scores is their cloaking effect. The scores are generally grouped around a very broad ethnic category that appears to explain more than they actually do. When the category is simply *Asians,* we still do not know whether these are children from Hmong or Japanese families. (It is as though we referred to *Europeans* without knowing whether Albanians or Swedes are meant.) The material in Tables 1.3 and 1.4 demonstrate how global ethnic classifications may hide important economic differences within single groups. Time of arrival may also be significant. The class composition of Vietnamese immigrants differs sharply between 1975 and 1990 through 1993. Among those who arrived earlier were representatives of a small, well-to-do, former ruling class and middle class whereas over 95% of the later group consisted of working-class persons. The differences in educational background were considerable (see Table 1.5).

At a number of places in this book, the issue of academic difficulties is discussed. Asian-American college students, as a group, have grave problems in passing English-language exams within the California State University system, the University of Minnesota, the University of Massachusetts, Boston, and elsewhere (see Table 1.6). In a number of cases, this failure has led to college drop-

TABLE 1.3
Occupational Attainment of Asian Pacific Americans*

Native Born

Occupational Category	Asian Indian	Cambodian	Chinese	Filipino	Hmong	Japanese	Korean	Laotian	Pacific Islander	Vietnamese
Professional	19%	8%	23%	9%	0%	19%	15%	12%	9%	10%
Executive/Management	9%	0%	16%	10%	3%	15%	11%	0%	10%	9%
Technical/Sales	44%	40%	40%	40%	10%	37%	45%	22%	32%	35%
Craft	5%	30%	6%	11%	50%	12%	6%	24%	14%	11%
Service	14%	10%	9%	17%	9%	9%	15%	8%	20%	21%
Operative/Laborer	9%	12%	6%	12%	28%	8%	8%	34%	15%	14%
Total	100%	100%	100%	100%	100%	100%	100%	100%	100%	100%

Immigrant

Occupational Category	Asian Indian	Cambodian	Chinese	Filipino	Hmong	Japanese	Korean	Laotian	Pacific Islander	Vietnamese
Professional	28%	5%	19%	16%	7%	19%	13%	4%	6%	10%
Executive/Management	13%	4%	13%	10%	4%	18%	11%	1%	7%	6%
Technical/Sales	35%	23%	31%	36%	17%	30%	37%	16%	31%	29%
Craft	6%	18%	6%	9%	18%	7%	9%	21%	16%	17%
Service	8%	18%	19%	18%	24%	18%	17%	17%	22%	16%
Operative/Laborer	10%	32%	12%	11%	30%	8%	13%	41%	18%	22%
Total	100%	100%	100%	100%	100%	100%	100%	100%	100%	100%

*Persons 16 years or older who last worked 1985 or later.
Source: Information generated from 1990 Census of the Population, five percent Public Use Microdata Sample (PUMS). Reprinted with permission.

5

TABLE 1.4
Economic Status of Asian Pacific Americans
Labor Force Participation, Unemployment, Poverty, Public Assistance Payments, & Income

Native Born

Economic Status Variable	Asian Indian	Cambodian	Chinese	Filipino	Hmong	Japanese	Korean	Laotian	Pacific Islander	Vietnamese
In the Labor Force (%)*	48%	63%	68%	72%	20%	69%	56%	51%	70%	58%
Unemployed (%)**	4%	16%	3%	4%	—	2%	3%	2%	5%	6%
In Poverty (%)*	8%	43%	8%	7%	63%	4%	12%	40%	16%	6%
Receiving Public Assistance Payments	2%	8%	2%	3%	25%	2%	2%	15%	6%	14%
Poor Receiving Public Assistance Payments	6%	9%	4%	12%	38%	6%	4%	25%	21%	14%
Mean Total Income, 1989 (× $1,000)***	30	12	36	25	13	33	30	19	23	21

Immigrant

Economic Status Variable	Asian Indian	Cambodian	Chinese	Filipino	Hmong	Japanese	Korean	Laotian	Pacific Islander	Vietnamese
In the Labor Force (%)*	74%	48%	65%	76%	29%	55%	64%	58%	69%	65%
Unemployed (%)**	4%	4%	3%	4%	5%	2%	3%	5%	6%	5%
In Poverty (%)*	10%	40%	16%	6%	63%	12%	14%	33%	22%	25%
Receiving Public Assistance Payments	2%	27%	5%	4%	36%	1%	4%	19%	5%	11%
Poor Receiving Public Assistance Payments	6%	40%	9%	8%	40%	2%	7%	32%	11%	23%
Mean Total Income, 1989 (× $1,000)***	35	17	27	25	14	36	25	16	20	21

*Percent of population   **Percent of labor force   ***Persons 25 or older in the civilian labor force

SOURCE: Robert M. Jiobu, "Recent Asian Pacific Immigrants. The Demographic Background," pp. 52 and 53 in Bill Ong Hing and Ronald Lee, eds., *The State of Asian Pacific America: Reframing the Immigration Debate. A Public Policy Report* (LEAP Asian Pacific American Public Policy Institute and UCLA Asian American Studies Center, 1996). Reprinted with permission.

TABLE 1.5
Educational Attainment Among Asian Pacific Americans
Persons 25 Years or Older

Native Born

Educational Attainment	Asian Indian	Cambodian	Chinese	Filipino	Hmong	Japanese	Korean	Laotian	Pacific Islander	Vietnamese
Less than High School	19%	46%	8%	16%	58%	12%	12%	48%	22%	30%
High School Diploma	17%	13%	16%	28%	15%	26%	24%	16%	38%	29%
Some College	19%	32%	25%	35%	23%	28%	27%	11%	29%	23%
Bachelors Degree	24%	9%	33%	16%	4%	24%	22%	12%	8%	11%
Masters Degree	11%	0%	11%	3%	0%	6%	9%	5%	2%	5%
Doctorate or Professional	10%	0%	7%	2%	0%	4%	6%	8%	1%	2%
Total	100%	100%	100%	100%	100%	100%	100%	100%	100%	100%

Immigrant

Educational Attainment	Asian Indian	Cambodian	Chinese	Filipino	Hmong	Japanese	Korean	Laotian	Pacific Islander	Vietnamese
Less than High School	15%	64%	29%	18%	13%	13%	20%	60%	32%	39%
High School Diploma	12%	12%	15%	14%	27%	27%	25%	19%	31%	18%
Some College	14%	17%	17%	26%	24%	24%	20%	14%	29%	26%
Bachelors Degree	25%	5%	20%	34%	25%	25%	22%	5%	6%	12%
Masters Degree	20%	1%	13%	3%	7%	7%	8%	1%	1%	3%
Doctorate or Professional	14%	1%	6%	5%	4%	4%	5%	1%	1%	2%
Total	100%	100%	100%	100%	100%	100%	100%	100%	100%	100%

Source: Information generated from 1990 Census of the Population, five percent Public Use Microdata Sample (PUMS). Reprinted with permission.

TABLE 1.6
English Proficiency Among Asian Pacific Americans

Native Born

English Proficiency	Asian Indian	Cambodian	Chinese	Filipino	Hmong	Japanese	Korean	Laotian	Pacific Islander	Vietnamese
Very Well	43%	33%	37%	15%	22%	13%	39%	35%	11%	45%
Well	7%	27%	10%	3%	34%	6%	9%	31%	2%	24%
Not Well	3%	25%	4%	1%	35%	3%	6%	23%	1%	12%
Not at All	1%	3%	1%	1%	6%	0%	1%	3%	1%	1%
Speak only English	46%	12%	48%	80%	3%	78%	45%	8%	85%	18%
Total	100%	100%	100%	100%	100%	100%	100%	100%	100%	100%

Immigrant

English Proficiency	Asian Indian	Cambodian	Chinese	Filipino	Hmong	Japanese	Korean	Laotian	Pacific Islander	Vietnamese
Very Well	57%	24%	32%	55%	20%	28%	29%	28%	43%	31%
Well	18%	31%	32%	24%	29%	31%	28%	30%	20%	35%
Not Well	7%	32%	22%	6%	32%	21%	23%	31%	10%	24%
Not at All	2%	10%	9%	1%	17%	3%	5%	9%	2%	5%
Speak only English	16%	3%	5%	14%	2%	17%	15%	2%	25%	5%
Total	100%	100%	100%	100%	100%	100%	100%	100%	100%	100%

Source: Information generated from 1990 Census of the Population, five percent Public Use Microdata Sample (PUMS).
SOURCE: Robert M. Jiobu, "Recent Asian Pacific Immigrants. The Demographic Background," pp. 52 and 53 in Bill Ong Hing and Ronald Lee, eds., *The State of Asian Pacific America: Reframing the Immigration Debate. A Public Policy Report* (LEAP Asian Pacific American Public Policy Institute and UCLA Asian American Studies Center, 1996). Reprinted with permission.

outs. Institutions have been reluctant to invest in trained personnel to help students sufficiently to overcome this widespread problem. Asian-American students at many institutions complain of feelings of isolation on campuses and of active racism aimed at them. Exceedingly few colleges or universities have acted preventively in such matters. Customarily, actions follow only after sensational incidents occur and public notice threatens. Even then, long delays follow referrals to languid hearings and related procedures that often culminate only because of further student protests. Specific examples are cited whenever available but it should be noted that this procedural defect characterizes institutional responses to racist incidents involving African-Americans and Hispanics, as well as Asian-Americans.[3]

Examples abound of elementary and secondary schools that do not provide Asian-American students with a productive educational experience. Discussions of these can be found in chapter 2 (Chinese Americans) as well as in chapter 12 (Samoan Americans) and elsewhere in the book. Inadequate programs for language-minority children are common, indeed, more common for Asian-Americans than for Hispanic children. An appearance of accomplishment is maintained by careful classification of children into various ability tracks who then receive devalued letter grades that are less meaningful for attempted entry into college later on. (See, for example, the example of Hmong students, discussed in chapter 8.) Far-reaching use of English-as-a-Second Language (ESL) classes also involves the award of letter grades that are less representative of academic achievement in various subject matters.

Historically, Asian education was profoundly political. Ancient China organized its first schools and colleges to supply bureaucrats of various sorts who would support the emperor's rule and counterbalance regional and aristocratic competitors of the centralizing imperial order. This practice was also adopted by Japan, Korea, Vietnam, and India. Educational institutions thereby had a personal character; they were ultimately aimed at helping consolidate the royal regime rather than attain some broadly based national purpose. By endowing the educated with privileges of political and economic precedence, the established order gained a sense of security. Because there were no other ways of gaining such an education, it was all the clearer that the emperor was the sole source of power and affluence. The rulers were not averse to popular education in principle. Nongovernmental schools were organized in numerous villages, but these offered only minimal instruction that did not lead to advanced schooling.

In none of the countries—except for the Philippines—did there exist widespread literacy based on truly public education in the early phase of their history. The Spanish colonialists promptly eradicated this feature of indigenous culture. The archive of native writings was destroyed and teaching of the indigenous script forbidden. Within a few generations, the script was merely a memory. In other countries, including Korea and Vietnam, a national language evolved over the centuries that was subordinated to classical Chinese. After both countries became outright colonies—of Japan and France—the native tongue was outlawed for certain purposes.

During the 20th century, public and private schooling came to exist in a curious combination. At best, Asian governments preferred to build elementary rather than secondary and higher educational institutions. The publicly financed universities tended to become the terrain of elite sections of the population. Commoners and the poor were left with private colleges and universities, many of which were more or less disguised for-profit businesses. Although the tendency was for such institutions to multiply, this was not a mark of educational vitality. Instead, it was simply a means whereby the burden on public finance was shifted onto the shoulders of parents. There was, of course, no actual transfer of burden because this had never been a government responsibility in the first place. Only as economic expansion clearly required a broadened higher educational structure did government start to invest heavily in the area.[4] Nevertheless, higher education even then cannot be said to have become plentiful in terms of students qualified for it.

In the United States, many parents who arrived from Hong Kong, Taiwan, and Korea were confronted by an abundance of colleges and universities. Unlike their home countries, in the United States, low-cost, high-quality public universities were open to their children, including their daughters. Elite institutions, both public and private, were accessible to many young people who, back home, could not have hoped for acceptance. Unquestionably, had the same opportunities been available there, emigration would probably have been reduced appreciably.

Among the immigrant Asian-American children were three groups who formed the core of successful students in U.S. schools:

1. Middle- and upper class children who as refugees could no longer remain in their homeland and therefore were deprived of any further opportunity to attend elite schools there. Refugees from China, Vietnam, Cambodia, and Laos were the principal sources of these refugees.

2. Middle- and upper class immigrants who chose to leave their homeland even though they could have remained and had their children attend elite schools there. Many of these came from India, the Philippines, Japan, Korea, Taiwan, and Hong Kong.

3. Lower middle- and working-class refugees, many of whose children had no schools to attend or had experienced schooling interrupted by wars and revolutions. The profusion of public schooling in the United States was a palpable sign of renewed opportunity to such children.

The advent of all three types of children in many American schools during a relatively short time gave rise to a misimpression that Asian children were superior students enveloped in a powerful tide of excellence. Because they were almost wholly unaware of the home-country background of the children involved, teachers in particular believed this. Lacking a realistic alternative explanation, the academic excellence was explained by spongy concepts such as cultural traits. Undoubtedly, a number of immigrant Asian-American children truly yearned for learning, but so had many generations of immigrant children from a broad range of cultures. As time went on, experienced teachers observed increasingly that there was a leveling-off of Asian-American academic performance. Many parents feared the same outcome. Overlooked amid all this academic change were large numbers of Asian-American children who were poorly served by the schools, as were many more children from other ethnic groups. In the forthcoming chapters, we become more closely acquainted with such students.

NOTES

[1] See p. 147.

[2] Robert M. Jiobu, "Recent Asian Pacific Immigrants. The Demographic Background," p. 54 in Bill Ong Hing and Ronald Lee, eds., *The State of Asian Pacific America: Reframing the Immigration Debate. A Public Policy Report* (LEAP Asian Pacific American Public Policy Institute and UCLA Asian American Studies Center, 1996).

[3] For an extended account of the notorious series of events at the University of Connecticut, see David Morse, "Prejudiced Studies: One Astounding Lesson for the University of Connecticut," pp. 339–357 in Don T. Nakanishi and Tina Yamano Nishida, eds., *The Asian American Educational Experience. A Source Book for Teachers and Students* (Routledge, 1995). More broadly, see Meyer Weinberg, *A Chance to Learn*, 2nd edition (The University Press, California State University, Long Beach, 1995), pp. 392–395.

[4] For a summary of this process in Hong Kong, Taiwan, S. Korea, and Singapore, see Paul Morris, "Asia's Four Little Tigers: A Comparison of the Role of Education in their Development," *Comparative Education*, 32 (1996), pp. 95–109.

CHAPTER TWO

China

Formal education entered Chinese society as an adjunct to imperial power. For over 1,000 years dating from the Han Dynasty (202 B.C.–A.D. 220), emperors built a system of selection whereby aspirants passed examinations to attain high official positions. The Examination System tested knowledge of Chinese literary classics rather than technical information of practical use in governing. It also created a dependable corps of loyal defenders of the emperor.

Architects of the system created a complex progression of steps that might be ascended successfully over several decades into middle age. The number of official posts to be filled did not grow greatly. Between 1585 and 1850, for example, China's population more than doubled from 200 million to 425 million but only about 20,000 posts were available.[1] Many more passed the examinations than for whom posts could be found. This larger number of degree holders constituted a reservoir for assignments in local and regional governments. Elderly degree holders could retire to their home village and take up teaching duties in the local school.

The Examination System fed on the same social elite that it helped to perpetuate and expand. To garner the literary knowledge necessary for success on the tests required long years of study, and this was not possible without extensive leisure. Accordingly, as Eberhard observed, "the examination system cannot be expected to have contributed much to upward social mobility."[2] The Sung Dynasty (A.D. 960–1279) was the first in Chinese history to experience a mature Examination System. "The number of degree holders at any given time during and after the Sung had always been minuscule," wrote Lee, "constituting, for example in the early 12th century, only about 0.005% of the total population; the social inequality was thus enormous. . . . Their influence on local and national affairs was tremendous."[3]

Highly exclusive private and imperial institutions were established to prepare students for examinations. Women were barred from these as they were from the examinations themselves. On the other hand, "it was a policy of the Sung to give special favors to border and comparatively backward areas."[4] The principle of merit was, however, sweepingly violated in a number of dynasties. Degrees, especially of a lower ranking, were sold to wealthy persons. "Bribery, favoritism, nepotism, and all kinds of gift giving and tipping were endemic in Chinese bureaucracy."[5]

Whatever its admirers contended, however, the Examination System was not a process whereby politics and imperial interests were subordinated to philosopher-kings or merely to the highest scoring candidates. The System produced only a fraction of imperial office holders at any given time; its operations were most palpable on the lower reaches of officialdom. During the Sui (A.D. 581–618) and T'ang (A.D. 618–906) Dynasties, only 15% of imperial bureaucrats were degree holders.[6] During the middle and latter years of Sung, from one fifth to one half were successful aspirants.[7] Alongside the Examination System, officials continued to be chosen in other ways. Thus, office holders were frequently accorded the right to designate their children or other relatives as successors. These designates were not required to qualify as degree holders. Aristocratic lineages usually succeeded in extending their representation in officialdom.

Beneath the levels of imperial court and the aristocracy lay the gentry, the upper class that combined—at its pinnacle—land owning and degree holding. (The latter feature gained it the alternative description of *literati*.) Although the gentry was a nationwide class, its gravity was distinctly local inasmuch as the land was necessarily local. A community of interests arose on the foundation of the gentry's local economic power and the bureaucracy's regional and municipal political power.

The peasantry lay entirely outside the ambit of the Examination System, although they made up by far the great majority of the population. The imperial Chinese state took no responsibility for schooling the peasantry because the practical uselessness of a classical education behind the plow made the mere suggestion appear chimerical.[8] Almost all sources agree on the prevailing illiteracy among the peasants. As Johnson wrote, "Truly poor youths who acquired classical educations . . . must have been as rare as saints."[9] Literate peasants were less scarce, if not downright plentiful.

Schooling in the villages was provided by clans or local communities. Charity schools were open to very poor children. Few of these village institutions, however, embraced all who wished to attend. Many clans, for example, were dominated by the wealthiest and most highly educated members who tended to control policy making. Clans boasted of the academic success of their schools when an alumnus later succeeded in attaining a degree. Some lineages even rewrote their genealogies to exclude the poorest members from benefits.[10]

Rawski estimated national literacy during the end of the 19th century as "perhaps 30 to 45 percent of males and only 2 to 10 percent of females possessing some ability to read and write."[11] Very poor urban dwellers failed to reach such modest levels. In Tianjin, the country's third largest city (after Shanghai and Beijing), many children worked in the numerous factories early in the 20th century. Hershatter, in describing the city's underclass, wrote that "they [could not] have spared their children from collecting scrap coal or junk to let them go to school even if there had been public schools in the area."[12]

Early in the present century, Chinese education underwent two significant changes: In 1905, the Examination System was abolished and the curricula of schools and colleges were modernized. Neither change affected the great majority of people. Higher education had always been beyond their reach and this continued to be the case. And the main beneficiaries of the modernized institutions were male middle- and upper-class children and youth: "Girl students occupied between 1 and 2 percent of the total student body in the new schools. In 1909, 13,489 girls attended schools—roughly 7 of every 100,000 women."[13] That same year, in two provinces—Chili and Szechuan—the proportion of the school-age population attending school ranged from one fortieth to one fiftieth.[14] Clearly, the poor were all but excluded.

Some 30 years later, the situation was unchanged or further entrenched. In two counties in Jiangou Province, along the Yellow Sea, only about 10% of eligible students were enrolled in schools. Chauncey observed that "students in the local western-style schools were from the families of a broadly defined social elite which represented commercial and landed interests."[15] As tax burdens on farmers rose to meet school expenses, they mounted attacks on the schools.[16]

The bitterness that greeted modern education was a great deal more than simple hankering for the past. Rather, it arose from a resentment at the class preferences that had already dominated traditional schooling structures. As Curran put it, "The new schools were essentially elite institutions serving the interests of the landowning establishment and the urban bourgeoisie. . . . The impact of modern education upon Chinese society was probably divisive. . . . The new structure tended to polarize Chinese society."[17]

The great universities in Shanghai and Beijing swelled with students of newly privileged sectors of society. Yeh described these as "the new intellectuals, professionals, financiers, industrialists, engineers, and other members of the educated elite."[18] On the eve of World War II, they constituted an elite for a new China.

A new China arose in 1949 as the Communist Party took control. Education was a major area of action since Party theorists had criticized the failure of the old order in this regard. For the first time in Chinese history, more than 9 out of 10 school-age children entered the elementary schools. The "world's largest poor country"[19] outdistanced the rest of the world's poor countries in education. At the same time, however, the successful revolution tested the Party's devotion to the principle of equalitarianism with variable results. Three periods are discernible: 1949 to 1965; 1966 to 1976; and since 1977.

A socialist educational structure took form during the early postrevolutionary years. Higher education, which had always been the most restricted area, was expanded to allow many poorer youth to attend. As early as 1952, government grants were available to all college students to cover tuition, housing, and living allowances.[20] Three years later, the grants became available only to persons in need but tuition and housing were still available to all. In 1977, the availability of grants was extended to institutions other than universities. By 1983, most students were no longer eligible for food and living allowances although exceptions could be made in cases where students came from poor families. A student-loan system was begun in 1987 under which up to 30% of students could get loans. Grants were available but scholarships were rare. Although the loans were interest free, they had to be repaid within 6 years after graduation. (If an employer failed to collect the loan payments from employees, the employer became responsible for the debt.) Unpaid balances could be cancelled by the borrower agreeing to teach in disadvantaged communities. Having begun in 1952 with an across-the-board system of student aid, 35 years later the system had been severely curtailed. What changes in China underlay the educational transformation?

During the 1950s and early 1960s, Fairbank explained:

> Two types of students vied for top standing and entrance to university from middle school. One group was composed of children from intellectual families, who had a head start in their education at home and were capable of doing high academic work. They gained merit on examinations that could not be denied. The other group was composed of children of the new ruling class of party members, officials, and cadres, whose class background was considered revolutionary and first rate. . . . Their level of scholarship, though, was not as high as that of the children of intellectuals.[21]

In the Communist Party, a trend of thought led by Mao Tse-tung was increasingly disillusioned with the elitist cast of education that had space for children of intellectuals and party leaders but very little for workers' children.

The Cultural Revolution (1966–1977) embodied this viewpoint. Wide-ranging changes were implemented. College entrance no longer depended on the passing of examinations but on recommendations from one's place of work as well as on the political fealty of applicants. Under that level, tracking and ability grouping were abolished. Also outlawed were elitist schools dependent on high-scoring applicants and/or schools for children of cadres. Children simply attended the nearest school. In parts of the country where many children lacked schooling opportunities, these were provided. As a result of the changes, by 1976 some 150 million school-age children, or 95% of the total, were attending schools.[22]

In 1977, 1 year after Mao's death, the Cultural Revolution was over. Almost immediately, the Party—whose leaders had been the target of many changes—undertook to reverse them. National college entrance examinations were revived. Elitist schools—the keypoint schools—were reopened even more lavishly than earlier. Perhaps most startling were the sharp cuts in enrollment enforced on all levels of education that the Cultural Revolution had brought. Especially drastic were the reductions enforced in secondary schools. In 1980, for example, over 20,000 were closed.[23] In 1981 and 1982, the number of students in senior secondary schools had been reduced by two thirds from 1978 levels.[24] Enrollments in junior secondary schools fell by nearly one sixth between 1979 and 1982.[25] Another way of putting the matter is that a smaller secondary enrollment ensured a similar trend in higher education.

By 1989, according to Schoenhals, "less than half the middle-school-age population in China attends middle school, with 10 percent or less of the senior-middle-school age population in senior middle school."[26] Interestingly, beginning in 1988, children seeking to enter junior middle school were assigned by residence rather than test scores.[27] This procedure was a small-scale reminder of Cultural Revolution practices.

Otherwise, however, the elitist trend remains in command. In one elite middle school—a national key school—three quarters of the students regularly pass the national college-entrance test, whereas nationally only one fourth pass. The school therefore attracts not only high-scoring children who pay no tuition but also mainly children of cadres who pay tuition but are not as academically advanced. The result is a school that is highly unrepresentative of the city in which it is located: Only 15 to 20% are children of workers, over half are children of professors or engineers, and about one fourth are children of officials.[28]

In Tianjin, a large industrial city, education grew greatly in importance in recent years. As in the country as a whole, jobs are provided to graduates of universities and vocational schools. University graduates are especially concentrated in state sector jobs, whether these are centrally or locally operated. The state sector is favored by the government not only in appropriations but in pay scales, living accommodations, and educational facilities. Leading elementary schools, elite institutions, are deliberately located in neighborhoods in which employees of academic institutions are likely to live.[29]

Since 1978, China has undergone enormous economic change. Both in agriculture and industry, a socialist market economy has been created. Critics of the changes, which were engineered by the Communist Party, have attacked the growing privatization of community services including education.

In many rural areas, school attendance was said to be declining as farmers kept their children on the farm to meet output goals established by contracts with the state. Farming collectives were disestablished with some of their property being used in individual transactions. In one such case, Hinton reported, "people came and dismantled whatever belonged to them jointly, including the . . .

school. . . . They took window frames out, doors off, and the beams out of the roof."[30] In September 1993, teachers were owed 164 million dollars in salary that school authorities had neglected to pay.[31] The *Los Angeles Times* reported:

> According to the State Education Commission, more than 20,000 private schools and kindergartens had been opened in China by the end of 1993. Many of these schools have impressive facilities, including computers and classroom televisions. However, tuition fees of up to $1,200 per semester for an elite private middle school in Beijing are beyond the reach of most Chinese. Parents of public-school children in Beijing pay an average of $25 a semester in activity and book fees.[32]

Throughout the country, payment of fees was increasingly demanded at public schools.

For a school or university or other institution to become self-sufficient meant that it would have to find a substitute for state-budget appropriations. A former Western teacher at Fudan University in Shanghai described one of the practices: "Students in the art and music academies, instead of experimenting and practicing, are now sent out by their schools to engage in money-making activities at the five-star hotels, painting and performing for tourist dollars that then go, not to them, but to the schools."[33] To counter the growing tendency toward charging of fees and the consequent exclusion of poor children from rural schools especially, a Hope Project was created to help those families keep their children in school.[34]

Equalitarian values were increasingly honored in the breach. Indeed, laws and regulations provided again and again for privileges to be conferred on those deemed more productive. In the name of socialism, sweeping rewards were conferred on those nearest the seats of power.

TO THE UNITED STATES

During the mid-19th century, Chinese immigrants first started arriving in considerable numbers. The educational system they encountered little resembled the one in the old country. Most states had already enacted into law tax-supported public schools, encouraged by gifts of federally owned lands. Racist restrictions were widespread in most southern states, as African-American slaves were forbidden to learn to read or write. In a number of northern states, public schooling was open only to white children. Even when free African-Americans paid school taxes, their own children were frequently excluded from schools partly financed by these taxes. Children of certain racial or ethnic groups were compelled by law to attend segregated schools.

Chinese American students were subjected to some of these very same discriminatory practices.

Outside the schools, in the larger society, discrimination was the prevailing pattern in Chinese American communities. An early racist law passed by Congress in 1790 provided that a foreigner could become a naturalized citizen only if he or she was White. Nearly a century later, the U.S. Supreme Court ruled that Chinese Americans did not qualify for naturalization. Federal, state, and local laws aimed at Chinese Americans were written to apply to aliens ineligible to citizenship, thus discriminating without naming the group targeted. For many years, this rhetorical device was used successfully to deny Chinese Americans—and other Asian-Americans—the right to own land in California and other Western states.

For many years, a special circumstance minimized the number of Chinese American children who could benefit from schooling: Few women accompanied their husbands from China and thus family formation was retarded. These immigrants were valued for their labor power and little else. No other immigrant group was subjected to such a rule by American authorities.

Following is an historical review of the schooling experience of Chinese Americans since the mid-1850s. Special emphasis is on San Francisco and California as a whole.

SAN FRANCISCO

In 1857, Chinese community leaders asked the school board to admit their children to public school inasmuch as they paid school taxes, but the request was rejected. The next year, the board relented and said the students might enroll in the African-American school. The Chinese refused, saying, "they would choose not to attend a public school, unless it were either integrated or segregated for the Chinese." [35] For more than a decade after, the school board conducted an on-again-off-again campaign of opening and closing temporary quarters for the Chinese school. Community leaders complained in 1878 to the state legislature that their children should not be denied the same school privileges that children of White immigrants received. [36]

American governmental authorities ignored these and related arguments. The Burlingame Treaty of 1868 between China and the United States required that public educational rights of citizens of both countries be respected while those citizens resided in the other country. The United States, of course, did not enforce this provision (Article 7). Twelve years later, the Treaty was modified to reaffirm "the responsibility of the United States to protect all Chinese subjects from abuse and mistreatment." [37] Once more, no practical effect resulted.

State authorities reached the pinnacle of their campaign against Chinese schooling in 1871, when the state school law omitted all mention of them whether they were immigrants or born in the United States. For the next 13 years, the omission was continued so that Chinese American children in San Francisco had no legal claim to a public education from 1871 through 1884.

In 1885, a legal landmark, *Tape v. Hurley*, was decided in a San Francisco state court. The state Supreme Court then affirmed the decision. Mamie Tape, the daughter of a Chinese American father and a White mother, sued to compel the city's board of education to admit Mamie into the public schools and thus to end the long period of exclusion. Judge Maguire ruled on the basis of the Fourteenth Amendment that mandated equal treatment under the law. He pointed especially to the school tax Chinese parents paid but whose benefits they were denied. The school board had no alternative but to follow Judge Maguire's order. Instead of admitting Mamie to an ongoing school, however, the board created a segregated school for her.

Mamie's mother, who was White, wrote an angry letter to the school board:

> Dear sirs, Will you please tell me! Is it a disgrace to be Born a Chinese? Didn't God make us all!!! What right!. . . . You had better come and see for yourselves. See if the Tape's is not the same as other Caucasians, except in features. It seems no matter how a Chinese may live and dress so long as you know they Chinese. Then they are hated as one. There is not any right or justice for them. . . . May you Mr. Moulder [the superintendent], never be persecuted like the way you have persecuted little Mamie Tape. Mamie Tape will never attend any of the Chinese schools of your making. Never!!! I will let the world see sir What justice there is When it is govern by the Race prejudice men! . . . Just because she is decended of Chinese parents I guess she is more of a American than a good many of you that is going to prewent [sic] her being Educated.[38]

The board of education would not change its position.

Only grades 1 through 5 were offered at the segregated Chinese Primary School. When students completed the span, however, the school board announced they would have to remain there even though the school had no adequate high school course of study. When some Chinese students persisted in transferring themselves to regular high schools, the board ordered them to return to the elementary school. Instead, Chinese parents warned that they would withdraw all their elementary students if the board continued its plans. Such a move would disorganize the entire school system. The board withdrew its order.[39]

The Oriental School, as the segregated facility was known, opened in 1885 and by the next year enrolled only 24 pupils.[40] Chinese parents were suspicious of the school's intentions and many withheld their children. By 1900, enrollment had risen to 130 and by 1916 to 695.[41] A new school building had opened in 1915. After repeated requests by community representatives, in 1924 the school was renamed the Commodore Stockton School. Presumably, this ended the practice of assigning schools enrolling Asian students an ethnic designation rather than a (White) person's name. Further, as the number of Chinese American students grew, it became necessary to permit the overflow to enroll in nearby non-Chinese schools. Earlier in the century, a federal court rejected a claim that Chinese children had an equal right to attend the nearest school; that is, the neighborhood school.[42] By the late 1920s, however, even the school board yielded to enrollment pressures.

What was the character of the education received by Chinese American students, both in the old Oriental School and its rebuilt and renamed successor? Sensitivity to the special needs of these students was rare on the part of administrators. John Pelton, who served a brief stint as superintendent from 1865 to 1867, said, "the school needed a teacher who could speak both languages or two teachers—one American and one Chinese."[43] In fact, the first Chinese-speaking teacher was not employed until 1926, followed by two more in 1928 and 1930; all three were American-born.

Alice Fong Yu was the pioneer teacher. Later, when asked whether she had used Chinese in the classroom, she replied, "To put across all kinds of ideas, not to teach. We weren't supposed to talk Chinese in the class, and I was so afraid to put it in Chinese. They told me specifically not to use it."[44] An observer reported, "Playing marbles, spinning tops, on their way to the American school, their chatter will be in the language of their fathers."[45] At Francisco Junior High School, in Chinatown, nearly 7 out of 10 students were Chinese Americans. The principal wrote, "For many years English has been our foreign language. Standard tests . . . have revealed a high degree of retardation in every school activity involving the use of English."[46] Students were barred from speaking Chinese in the school or on the playground.

Early in the 1920s, a special English teacher spent 1 hour a week in every elementary school enrolling a considerable number of Chinese-speakers. Eighth graders in each school were divided into four sections where assistance in pronunciation was given for 15 minutes.[47] This may have been the entirety of the formally correct English students ever heard in the school, aside from speech by teachers. The school was far more effective in forbidding Chinese than in promoting English. Indeed, the former was frequently confused with the latter. Students paid a high price for the school's failure because academic-achievement tests showed substandard performance in all but one of the following: spelling, arithmetic, grammar, vocabulary, and reading.

Victor Low, a Chinese American teacher and administrator, who as a child attended Commodore Stockton School, characterized the teaching staff as follows:

> Either old timers set in their culturally biased ways or . . . ineffective teachers shunted to their assignment of last resort. With the emphasis on reading and writing in those early days, the white teaching staff in the "Chinatown schools" failed to improve the oral English skills of the Chinese American students.[48]

(Further material on teaching problems after World War II can be found on pages 23–29.)

The San Francisco earthquake of 1906 resolved one set of school problems. Because of deed restrictions that limited where Chinese could live, Chinatown was rebuilt on its historic site. School segregation rules were enforced more strictly than ever. Thousands of Chinese Americans moved to nearby Oakland where the schools were not segregated.[49] Most remained there and one of their cardinal complaints was thereby resolved.

The public schools of Chinatown paid little heed to traditional Chinese culture. Denigration rather than celebration marked their efforts. Where unavoidable, the schools acknowledged what they could not eliminate, so long as there was no substantial interference with the schools' official educational doctrine.

Thus, when a child brought his or her own abacus to school, little objection was made, especially when mastery of arithmetic resulted more readily.[50] During 2 weeks of Chinese New Year's celebration, few students bothered to come to school. Low observed: "The school solved this problem by joining in the festivities—the staff visited nearly 200 families."[51] It also learned to live with the community habit of breakfast at 10:30 in the morning. Speaking Chinese in school, however, was uniformly condemned for its presumed interference with learning English. The record is bare of efforts by teachers to make educational use of the historical experience of the home country. Writing in 1921, Lee observed, "If Americanization is to be brought about, the two races must mingle more with each other. Were the Chinese lacking in civilization, culture and education there might be difficulties, but the Chinese have a perfectly good civilization of their own."[52] But the schools of California were more receptive to cultures of other immigrant groups.

During the 1860s, for example, a Cosmopolitan public school was organized in San Francisco, to be followed soon by two more. Instruction was given in three languages: English, French, and German. By 1871, one out of every three elementary students was enrolled in what a historian calls "the multilingual courses."[53] State education law required instruction in English and so the Cosmopolitan schools were in violation of that provision. In the original Cosmopolitan school, English was taught as a second language. In the three schools as a whole in 1867, 30% were of a German background, 20% were French, and half were presumably native-born Americans. At that same time:

> The teachers in the Cosmopolitan Schools were required to speak at least two languages fluently and the City Superintendent reported that half of these teachers were immigrants. Such teachers shared both the language and the cultural backgrounds of their students.[54]

The first phase of this history ended in the 1870s when French and German became available only in private instruction and the multilingual approach was stopped.

During 1907 to 1909, the second phase began when the Italian community in San Francisco succeeded in bringing about a revival of foreign-language instruction. In 1909, the legislature extended a mandatory program to San Francisco and other big cities in the state. Italian, German, French, and—later—Spanish were specified. San Francisco superintendent Roncovieri "authorized Italian children to say the pledge of allegiance to the American flag in their native tongue in the North Beach schools."[55]

Cosmopolitan schooling thrived during some of the years when Chinese children had no legal right even to attend public schools in California. Nor was the Chinese language accorded equal treatment to that of German, French, or Spanish in the school curriculum. Unlike Chinese, school authorities did not view the European languages as impediments to the learning of English. Nor did they refuse to employ European immigrants as teachers, which was unthinkable in the case of Chinese. As we have seen, the first American-born Chinese American teacher was not employed until 1926. Many more European immigrant teachers had taught in the Cosmopolitan schools half a century earlier.

Lack of regard for the Chinese easily slipped into open racism. In 1859, a school board member heard his colleagues "classifying Chinese with baboons and monkeys. . . ."[56] A superintendent denied he favored segregation of Chinese students for racial reasons: "It was a question of demoralization of one high race by a lower."[57] As pointed out earlier, Chinese students who completed the fifth grade were not permitted to enter regular high schools, simply for reasons of their ethnicity or race. One Chinese American applicant for a teaching position was asked about her dreams. Interviewers hoped to discover that she dreamed in Chinese and thereby did not merit a position teaching in English.[58] As recently as the late 1960s, administrative applicants were subjected to racial discrimination.[59] In the 1870s, the superintendent reprinted in his annual report various expressions of anti-Chinese sentiment by first- and second-graders as exemplary.[60] The state legislature year after year refused to provide schooling opportunities to Chinese children while providing in each case for White children. (Other minority children were also subjected to similar treatment.) The crowning insult came when Chinese American graduates of junior high school and high school sought jobs for which they had prepared in school. As one commentator noted in the mid-1930s, "In spite of a lip-service affection which all San Franciscans indulge in when they speak of the Chinese, they will not open their working ranks to receive them."[61]

School officials rarely resisted openly racist policies and practices. A number of principals who presided over heavily White schools in cities and the countryside occasionally admitted an individual Chinese student, especially when White parents did not object. In 1906, a state-wide convention of superintendents defeated a resolution endorsing the creation of segregated schools for Asian students.[62] Nevertheless, in most cases, school administrators enforced the racist order in schooling.

Until the outbreak of World War II in the late 1930s, Chinese American youngsters witnessed first-hand a broad range of racist hurts. Although these experiences apparently never became part of the school curriculum, they were common knowledge in Chinese American circles. Parental efforts to breach the boundaries of segregated-school attendance areas were widespread and well-known. Each attempt was another reminder of the larger society's contempt. Tales of bright graduates who were denied jobs for which they had trained were legion. Physical attacks on Chinese Americans were everyday realities. Because community-wide protests were frequently organized against legal (and illegal) oppressions, Chinese American children were well-acquainted with the subjects of such events. These ranged from persistent refusals of the city to clean the streets of Chinatown to efforts by municipal authorities to compel the people of Chinatown to use experimental medicine to head off an alleged epidemic of bubonic plague.

Few persons outside Chinatown were aware of class differences within the area. The tendency was to regard the population as homogeneous or even monolithic. Chang wrote in 1936, "Great prejudice at first existed between these merchants and the poorer class of Chinese who attend the school. They would not sit on the same bench with them, and shrugged their shoulders as they looked upon them. . . ."[63] After a time, the prejudice wore off.

A number of wealthy Chinese in San Francisco established academies and schools in the 1880s and 1890s that prepared their sons to compete for degrees and honors in the imperial examinations. Although few of these organizers were members of the homeland gentry, they nevertheless wished to align themselves with the Ch'ing court.[64] (They were quite tardy, however. In 1905, the historic Examination System was dismantled.) According to Pomerantz, perhaps 100 boys were involved in the San Francisco schools. These schools were separate from the more numerous Chinese-language schools that aimed at creating a modest level of competence in the language among less affluent youth.

The economic and academic status of Chinese Americans changed importantly during World War II. Before that time, Chang wrote, "Asian Pacific Americans shared with other minorities of color roughly the same low social position in American society."[65] Thus, in 1940, Chinese American workers were employed in low-skilled jobs 13 times more frequently than in high-skilled jobs. The former constituted 37.3% and the latter 2.8% of all employed Chinese Americans.[66] In that same year, Whites had a median of 8.7 years of schooling whereas the median figure for Chinese Americans was but 5.5 years.[67] Chinese Americans were only half as likely to complete high school or college as White Americans. A substantial portion of these disparities was directly attributable to various forms of anti-Chinese discrimination. This included defective and segregated schooling and refusals to hire university-trained students. The existence of large numbers of elder persons who were illiterate in English reflected a continuing failure to develop adult education.

Institutional barriers to employment started to fall early in World War II when racial discrimination in government jobs impinging on national defense was outlawed. The way was opened for Chinese Americans (and others) to be hired in war industries as technicians and blue-collar workers.

The Civil Rights movement intensified and focused this development during the 1950s, 1960s, and 1970s. Chinese Americans became beneficiaries of affirmative-action policies as they formed organizations to promote the adoption of these policies in public and private employment. Some opponents of the same policies lauded the consequent progress of Chinese Americans while not dwelling on the affirmative-action foundations of that progress.

More important, however, than civil rights were developments in immigration policy in changing the condition and status of Chinese Americans. Historically, immigration in the United States has generally operated beneficially. Through immigration, a labor supply has materialized when needed, and in the requisite numbers. Yet the American economy did not have to pay any of the costs of producing the labor supply: initial housing, health, and education costs, for example. In this sense, immigration could be likened to an economic transfer at the cost of one society to the benefit of another. As Neal and Uselding put it, "The international flow of human beings to America was responsible for the formation of a large portion of the capital base of the economy and quickened the pace of development."[68]

In 1948, around 9 million Chinese lived outside China; 35 years later, the number exceeded 26 million.[69] Nine out of 10 of the larger number resided in Asia; some 60% of the remainder—or around one and a half million—lived in the United States and Canada. When the Chinese Revolution triumphed in 1949, a number of wealthy Chinese left the country, but most of them settled in other Asian countries. The number going to the United States increased moderately during the next 15 years. Various ad hoc changes in immigration law made this possible.

A very major change occurred in 1965. The Immigration Act of that year established a new set of priorities. Instead of continuing high annual quotas for certain favored countries in western and northern Europe, all countries were given comparable quotas. Persons in some occupations were given high quotas as were persons in the United States who were citizens or permanent residents and wanted members of their immediate family to come here. Another set of laws was enacted to enable refugees—that is, those who left their home country under duress—to emigrate to the United States without respect to the occupation of family members. The great majority of Chinese who came to the United States under these various measures arrived from Hong Kong and Taiwan. A growing minority came directly from Mainland China.

Immigration laws regulate the entry of persons into the social structure as well as into occupations, educational and other institutions, and new personal vistas. Throughout American history, relatively few immigrants were arrivals from any but the lower and medium reaches of sending societies. It was otherwise with the Chinese after 1965. Thus, as Chang noted: "From 1965 to 1979, the total number of Chinese immigrants 25 years and older was 227,680. Of these immigrants, 122,264 or 53.7 percent had [a] college education."[70] (All came either from Hong Kong or Taiwan.) These immigrants made up two thirds of all Chinese American professionals. It was as though a whole class had moved overseas. As a consequence, much of the Chinese American middle class can be said to have been imported.

The impact of the educated immigrants on Chinese American social structure cannot be denied, but it can be exaggerated. One must not forget that however difficult it was to build a native-born, Chinese American middle class, the deed was done on a very slender basis, as can be seen from a review of Kwoh's study of 1947. She analyzed a sample of Chinese Americans who graduated from the University of California, Berkeley, between the years 1920 and 1942. The 1940 Census had shown there were 606 native-born Chinese Americans aged 25 years and over who had completed 4 or more years of college. This fact alone made it highly untypical in the Chinese American community. The cases studied by Kwoh (337 in number) comprised more than half of the national total and was highly representative of the total graduates. Kwoh summarized, "These graduates . . . come from rather select families in the Chinese population. Two thirds of their fathers are business or professional men, very few of whom are in the traditional restaurant or laundry work. . . ."[71] Of 124 graduates, 101 were now professionals, but only 20 were businessmen. Graduate sons of professionals overwhelmingly became professionals whereas barely one fifth of the sons of businessmen themselves became businessmen. Kwoh found that most of the men graduates worked for White organizations or for themselves. Among the older graduates, many more had begun their careers working within the Chinese community.

By 1980, immigration was introducing many more college graduates into the Chinese American communities than had been created by graduation a generation earlier from American institutions such as Berkeley. The expanding Chinese American middle class was a product of both sources.

The Chinese American working class also grew as a result of immigration. Between 1940 and 1980, the national trends were as follows for employed Chinese American workers, by skill group:[72]

	High Skilled		Low Skilled	
	#	%	#	%
1940	1,021	2.8	13,597	37.3
1950	3,437	7.1	16,023	33.1
1960	17,682	17.9	20,843	21.1
1970	48,015	26.5	41,130	22.7
1980	103,883	26.0	81,701	20.4

Many of these workers were employed in low-paid, dead-end jobs in restaurants and garment shops. Children from such families attended schools that were especially inadequate. This issue barely entered public discussion, leaving the impression that Chinese American students were uniformly successful in school. Let us examine this matter.

In 1969, some 85% of Chinatown's people had never attended high school; in Boston and New York, the figures were also correspondingly high.[73] A decade earlier, in San Francisco's Chinatown, "the median education of persons over 25 years was 1.7 years, compared with the citywide median of 12 years. . . ."[74] The city school system had reported about the same time that some 2,800 Chinese students needed special help with English before they could make normal progress. A close observer of the city's schools criticized teachers "who delight in publicly ridiculing and humiliating students speaking English with a slight Chinese accent." He observed that such an attitude "causes severe psychological damage to the students and greatly inhibits students from active participation in classroom activities."[75] Also noted was an inflexibility of White teachers toward students. At Galileo High School during 1969 and 1970, although Chinese Americans made up 64.5% of enrollment, only 3% of teachers and staff were of the same ethnicity.[76] Chin spoke of widespread stereotypes against Chinese teachers: "Chinese are not good teachers because they have an accent, they lack initiative, they are too soft-spoken, bilingual teachers are not effective in any subject."[77]

From 1948 to 1959, children who needed special aid in English language study were officially described as English-handicapped. According to Low, they were placed "in opportunity Classes at the Elementary schools or in the Americanization Department at the secondary schools. It was basically a sink-or-swim approach. . . . [This procedure engendered] community divisiveness between . . . new immigrant and the American born."[78] This largely ineffective approach was aggravated during the 1960s as immigrants greatly increased in number. Simmering discontent expressed itself in many ways. Over the years 1964 to 1969, for example, police arrests and citations of Chinese American juveniles rose by 600%.[79]

A more startling manifestation of discontent occurred on February 26, 1969:

> In an educational forum held at Commodore Stockton School by Superintendent Robert Jenkins, the image of the obedient Chinese student was shattered. Youths, frustrated by empty promises by the [school] district to provide more Chinese-American teachers, counselors, classrooms and curriculum materials, ended the meeting by throwing cherry bombs at the school staff.[80]

This project did not resolve any of the major issues.

Segregation had been abolished in all of the state's schools in 1947 by legislative action. Later federal laws and court rulings placed the subject on the current agenda. Certain informal segregative arrangements were enforced nevertheless, as the following indicates. Reference is to Marilyn Lew, a high-school senior, who was chosen as Miss Chinatown USA of 1967: "[She described George Washington High School as] divided by floors—Caucasians, Orientals and Negroes—with 'inhabitants' abiding by an unwritten 'to his each floor by his own' law. . . ."[81] Students engaged in the practice as administrators looked the other way. During the late 1960s, San Francisco civil rights advocates charged that the board of education had deliberately established and maintained a system of segregated schools. In 1971, a federal district court found the school system to be unconstitutionally segregated and ordered that a desegregation plan be drawn up and implemented.

The leading political group in Chinatown, the Six Companies, consisted primarily of the most influential businessmen in the area; it had strong ties with the Chiang Kai Shek regime that had been defeated by the Communists in China and was now housed in Taiwan. Controlled by the Six Companies, the Chinese-language press voiced extreme displeasure with the desegregation plan and especially the busing feature that would transport children away from the nearest neighborhood school.[82]

As early as 1967, a White organization—Mothers for Neighborhood Schools (MNS)—had begun a campaign in Chinatown against the possibility of desegregation. Schools and other community institutions were visited, leaflets distributed, and consultations held with conservative Chinese groups. The last-named activity led to Chinese-language newspaper stories that "played heavily on the harsher conditions in black sections of the city and in black ghetto schools, hinting darkly of classroom brawls, petty thievery, [and] foul language."[83]

People from outside Chinatown allied with MNS and like-minded others encouraged Chinese Americans not to send their children to the desegregated school. Instead, organizers founded a series of Freedom Schools ironically named after the ad hoc schools set up by African-American civil rights activists throughout the country in protest against discriminatory segregated schools. Followers of the extreme rightist group, the John Birch Society, could be found among MNS members and were strong supporters of Freedom Schools. In the early stages, the leading antisemitic and racist organization in the United States—the Liberty Lobby—helped rally support for the Freedom Schools.[84]

A number of close observers asserted that Chinese opposition to desegregation was to some extent based on anti-African-American racism.[85] On the other hand, there is no evidence to establish that such a sentiment swept the mass of Chinese American parents to oppose desegregation. Thus, although nearly 13,500 Chinese American students were enrolled in the city's schools (in 1970), only about 1,500 children attended the Freedom Schools, even at their peak.[86] A boycott of the regular schools did not prove popular among Chinatown parents. On the first day of the boycott, some 90% of Chinese American students stayed home. About 8 weeks later, Yee estimated that "at least two thirds" had left the Freedom schools and returned to the desegregated schools.[87]

One reason for the large-scale defection was disillusionment with the curriculum and activities of the Freedom Schools. Organizers had promised originally that the Freedom Schools would confront three problem areas:

1. Failure of the public schools to teach Chinese children to read and write; in particular, the Chinatown schools' bilingual classes and the Chinese Education Center [which] did not teach the necessary basic skills. 2. Failure of sixth-grade pupils at the Commodore Stockton Elementary School to achieve sixth-grade norms in standardized tests administered district-wide to all students. 3. Failure of Chinese

youngsters to achieve at grade level at Marina Junior High School, which, along with the Francisco Junior High School, receives a large number of Chinese pupils from Chinatown.[88]

In addition, there was some community concern that desegregation might endanger the fledgling bilingual–bicultural programs in Chinatown.

Lum summarized carefully:

> The curriculum of the Freedom Schools offered the most convincing proof that culture and language were not the main reason for the establishment of the competing system. Their meager resources allowed for only half-day sessions at the schools, and the Freedom Schools therefore concentrated on basic curriculum, not on Chinese Studies. . . . Concerns other than busing were never dealt with to the satisfaction of the Chinatown community: quality education, affirmative action in the hiring and promotion of school personnel, linguistic and cultural needs, and safety in the schools.[89]

Most Freedom School supporters were new immigrants living in Chinatown. Given the broad range of problems confronting their children, it was surprising that they were sensitive to so many of them. The recency of their arrival helps explain the value many placed on Chinese language and other cultural aspects of their children's education.

Conservative ideologues in the Freedom School movement emphasized the ills of busing as central to desegregation. Public opinion polls showed the success of this argument among Whites and Asians in San Francisco. When asked whether or not they approved of busing, the following percentages replied in the negative:[90]

	1971	1975
Blacks	47	23
Whites	62	90
Orientals	64	73

Yet, busing came to be viewed by Asians more as an unnecessary evil than as an all-consuming bar to effective education. As the Freedom Schools faded away, Chinese American activists were already engaged in another campaign for improved education with which desegregation was not inconsistent.

In March 1970, they had filed a lawsuit against the San Francisco school board, *Lau v. Nichols.* The plaintiffs contended, essentially, that some 2,500 immigrant Chinese schoolchildren did "not receive a meaningful education when they are taught in a language they do not understand."[91] During the next 4 years, litigation proceeded until, in January 1974, the U.S. Supreme Court decided in favor of the plaintiffs. The high court accepted the core argument that a meaningful equal education required the use of an understandable instructional language. (Native-born students, of course, already exercised a right to such an instructional language.)

Wang wrote that:

> The *Lau* decision is important and necessary to Asians, Chicanos, Native Americans and others precisely because it is addressed directly to the problem of equal educational rights for non-English speakers, an issue otherwise ignored in the *Brown* decision and all its court-ordered school integration. . . . *Brown* and *Lau* are [not] mutually exclusive. . . . The mandates of both could be carried out with no difficulty. . . . There are different needs, and the quest for equality requires sensitivity, tolerance, and cooperation. Failing to do that, the results could be divisive and counter-producive.[92]

Wang also reported that early school board efforts to implement the ruling were exceedingly defective. Nevertheless, the Chinese community in San Francisco had succeeded in defining language as an urgent area for educational action. Not only had the board of education persistently refused to acknowledge the importance of language, but a federal court of appeals had once turned away the Chinese American parents with the argument that the children's problems were "not the result of law enacted by the state . . . but the result of deficiency created by (the children) themselves in failing to learn the English language."[93] Both the school board and the appeals court must have viewed a bilingual program as supererogatory or even frivolous.

ELSEWHERE IN CALIFORNIA

Most Chinese Americans in the state lived outside San Francisco. Here they were subjected, in varying degrees, to discrimination. White neighbors felt free to ignore state laws when these required school opportunities for Chinese children. Thus, as was previously shown, in 1884 a court had struck down the total exclusion of Chinese American children from public schools; the next year, the legislature amended the school law to accord with the decision. But a number of communities took their time about admitting the excluded children.

Stockton acted only in 1899.[94] It took until 1893 in Sacramento. In Fresno, four high schools existed. Edison Technical High School was the one attended by most Asian students. Not until 1933, however, was Edison placed on the list of accredited high schools.[95] A study found in 1938 that 36 Chinese American high school graduates from Fresno had attended college at the following institutions:[96]

15	Fresno State College
8	Junior College
3	University of California
10	Others (one each)

It should be noted that the University of California charged no tuition or tuition substitute at this time, and still few graduates could go there.

Community harassment of Chinese went on apace over the years. In 1887, the school board of Riverside contracted with a group of Chinese bricklayers to build Grant Elementary School. A White union (the Knights of Labor) protested because a state law forbade building schools with bricks made by Chinese. (Chinese were employed by most brick-making firms.) Nevertheless, Chinese bricklayers finally built the school anyway.[97]

During the 1920s and 1930s, the Ku Klux Klan was highly active in Southern California. It organized a Riverside branch in 1925 and was still attacking Chinese in the 1930s.[98] In Los Angeles during 1923, Louis Oaks, the chief of police, was found to be a Klan member, as were the sheriff and the United States Attorney.[99] Asians and other minorities were prime targets of the Klan.

In many parts of the state, including large cities, one could find an isolated individual Chinese American student attending a White school. This was true even during 1871 through 1885, when Chinese children were omitted from the state school code. Almost always, this crack in the door depended on a sympathetic principal and acquiescence of White parents. At various times, the law provided for levying monetary penalties on schools that looked the other way.

HAWAII

During the period of Hawaiian independence that ended in 1898, Chinese immigrants were not subjected to racism resembling that of California. Native Hawaiians accepted them as just another kind of foreigner.[100] Circumstances for educating their young, however, were not favorable. As Hwang stated, "nearly seven out of every ten Chinese people lived in rural areas and the children among them had little access to either public or private education."[101] These plantation children were located very far from high schools. It was only around the turn of the century that significant numbers of Chinese women emigrated to Hawaii, and family formation quickened. Yet, during the 1890s, some two thirds of working Chinese were unskilled laborers, many of whom still thought of returning someday to China.

As population expanded and Chinese Americans moved off the plantations to cities, more schooling opportunities materialized. American-born Chinese turned to the schools and colleges in increasing numbers. Wealthier merchants still continued to send their eldest sons to China to acquire a traditional education but the Chinese Revolution of 1911 and economic opportunities in Hawaii turned the attention of native-born Chinese Americans to openings closer at hand.

By 1930, Hawaiian Chinese were overrepresented in 8 of the 15 professions listed in the census of that year.[102] At the same time, Chinese, who constituted fewer than 10% of the population, numbered one fifth of all teachers in the Territory.[103] As Glick pointed out, "a disproportionately large number of the

[im]migrants who established families in the Islands were in business and able to get preference for their sons in managerial, proprietary, clerical and sales occupations."[104]

Underlying Chinese success in Hawaii, according to Chang, was their policy of avoiding direct clashes with the White economic and political elite. Chinese entrepreneurs avoided competition with the *haole* (White) business leaders. Nor did they generate any consistent criticism of Hawaiian society: "During the 1930s the Chinese produced not one single labor leader, radical intellectual or left-wing politician."[105] It was quite different with the Japanese Americans who not only were prominent in organizing farm workers into unions but also were represented along a broad range of political positions during the same years, as well as later. The *haole* elite repaid the Chinese community leadership with encouragement and aid.

Nothing like this happened in California or elsewhere on the mainland. On the mainland, Chinese were kept out of significant parts of the large-scale economy. Both in California and Hawaii, higher education became the foundation for Chinese representation in the professions. The upper reaches of the professions, however, were largely closed to aspirants in California as they were in corporate businesses. The substance of Chinese success in Hawaii was not mythical but real. Its only mythical element was the contention that the success depended on some ill-defined Chinese cultural characteristics that could be acquired as well by other ethnic groups.[106]

NEW YORK CITY

In 1898, some 4,000 Chinese lived in New York City's Chinatown but fewer than 80 were children.[107] In the metropolitan area, a total of about 13,000 resided. Little about their schooling ever appeared in published English-language sources.

Even as recently as 1977, a leading researcher, Betty Lee Sung, found that no studies of immigrant Chinese children had been conducted. A full decade later, the situation was essentially unchanged. In a single research setting, however, directed by Sung, three interrelated reports were completed during the years 1977 to 1987.[108] Two schools were involved: The first, an elementary school in Chinatown, and the second, a K through 5 school in Jackson Heights—Elmhurst, Queens. The former was 75% Chinese, the latter 10% Chinese.

Rose Chao, a field researcher, visited schools, homes, and workplaces of employed mothers. She interviewed many children while walking with them through the neighborhood. Garment shops in Chinatown, in which mothers worked, were located right across the street from the schools. Mothers dropped their children off at school in the morning and after school, many children went directly to the shops where some played, napped, or received a shopping list. The immigrant children had been in this country for less than 2 years. Their living conditions were not untypical for Chinatown. Chao reported, "I saw tiny rooms over-crowded with bunk beds, or in other cases, wall-to-wall mattresses. . . . I asked the children in the various classes that I observed whether anyone slept in a room by themselves. Not a one."[109]

At school, language was the central problem. Yet, few special provisions were made. At the seven schools in Chinatown, ESL classes were held, but only one bilingual teacher was assigned to each school. About one third—or 2,000—of the children in Chinatown schools had language difficulties. For purposes of language instruction, however, classes were divided into three subgroups, thereby severely reducing teacher time spent with students. Both teachers and parents were divided on the issue of bilingual education. Many families of elementary students searched for ways to move out of Chinatown, partly to locate more adequate schools. Sung observed that bilingual education for Chinese students was regarded by the schools "as a frill to be dispensed with as soon as federal and state funds cease."[110]

A science teacher told Sung:

> I teach science, but I don't give them a mark in science. I was told that at this point it is not that important for them to keep up with the science class. They are here mostly to learn Englsh, so they just get a grade from the ESL teacher.[111]

Parents favoring bilingual classes did so in part because they were pleased to see their children keeping pace with course subject matter as well as with English.[112]

According to Peter Kwong:

> A 1984 Board of Education report showed that all the schools in Chinatown were rated far below citywide standards. Among the four local elementary schools, only 28.4 percent of the students reached the standard English reading level; the city-wide average was 55 percent. At Seward Park High School on the Lower East Side 97 percent of the Chinese students were above the normal age for their grade level. . . . Of the 600 students in P.S. 1 (an elementary school), there are 200 immigrants. According to the principal there is insufficient funding to provide the bilingual instruction they need.[113]

In 1985, three high schools enrolling many Chinese Americans were ranked among the 72 worst of the city's 600 schools. "Not only did students at these schools have poor reading and writing," added Kwong, "they also had exceedingly high dropout and truancy rates."[114] He also attributed some of the problems to the sizable influx of mainland Chinese immigrants, many of whom came from villages where schooling was not strong. (Certain health problems, too, were more prevalent among these students.)[115] Even as early as 1973 and 1974, before large numbers came from the mainland, reading scores of a Chinatown junior high school "were 1½ to 2½ grades below average and the math scores were only slightly below grade level."[116]

It will be recalled that the Sung studies also reviewed a school in Elmhurst, a comparatively new area of Chinese residence. In the area's high school during

1976, Asians—mostly Chinese—constituted only 10% of the enrollment. School-wide reading and math scores were slightly higher than city-wide averages. Two years earlier, however, math scores were a bit lower than average.

Unfortunately, city-wide test results were reported only for entire populations. Thus, in 1994, the New York City school board announced the following percentages of student ethnic groups had equalled or surpassed grade-level scores on reading tests:[117]

Non-Hispanic Whites	70.4
Asian and Pacific Islanders	64.7
Blacks	42.7
Hispanics	36.7

Math scores were comparable but Asian children were highest and African-American children were lowest. The global averages were scarcely beneficial to children scoring at lower-than-average levels. These children were mistaken for their group averages, thereby relieving schools of a responsibility to provide needed instruction.

One consequence of inadequate language programs in Chinatown schools is the overrepresentation of Chinese graduates from these schools in scientific and technical fields. In 1985, more than half of the nearly 5,000 Chinese enrolled in the City University of New York (CUNY) were enrolled in these fields. Kwong contended that most Chinese American students attending Ivy League institutions are children of Uptown Chinese rather than of Chinatown residents.[118] Few of the latter are beneficiaries of affirmative-action programs at the Ivy League colleges and universities. When Sung conducted a survey of Chinese American students in City College of New York—a CUNY institution—"many of those interviewed mentioned their lack of social graces and contacts as a huge barrier to career advancement."[119]

MISSISSIPPI

Soon after the end of the Civil War in 1865, Southern planters began recruiting Chinese workers from China and Cuba. After completion of the transcontinental railroad in 1869, many other Chinese laborers beame available. Demand was strongest in Mississippi and Louisiana.[120] In fact, however, almost none of the Chinese remained for long as laborers or sharecroppers. Instead, a number became operators of small grocery stores located in the midst of Black neighborhoods and settlements in towns and villages. They formed the centers of scattered Chinese communities.

Many of these grocers headed families based on common-law or formalized marriages with African-American women. Family stability depended largely on the presence of children. The dominant White community regarded the grocers as neither White nor African-American and thus they were in a socially ambiguous position. The Census of 1870 classified them as a separate category although before that date, they were counted as White.[121]

Chinese families throughout the state of Mississippi were forbidden by law to send their children to White schools. In small towns, however, where only a few lived, they attended such schools until or unless Whites objected.[122] Meanwhile, Chinese parents refused to use the Black schools for their children because they were so inferior to the White ones. When recourse was had to the courts, they were turned down. In the *Bond* case, the state supreme court defended the practice of exclusion.[123] In 1927, the U.S. Supreme Court accepted the segregation reasoning in another Mississippi case, *Gong Lum*. This was the first time the high tribunal had ruled on the school rights of Chinese American children.

At about this time, in a number of different larger towns, separate public schools for Chinese children were authorized along with White and Black schools. Thus, the Chinese were relieved of having to attend Black schools but were compelled to accept the principle of racial separation. Loewen wrote:

> Delta Chinese sent their children to live with relatives in other states so that they could obtain an education, and other families employed private tutors at home. In general, however, the children who came of age in the Delta before 1956 received little formal schooling of any kind. In a few cases, they did attend the parochial grade school and high school for Negroes in Greenville.[124]

By the early 1950s, the bars to Chinese entry into White schools were lowered. In part, this coincided with the rise of African-American pressure to disestablish the entire structure of segregated schools: The harder the African-Americans pressed, the more Whites opened their schools to Chinese Americans. Many young African-American activists resented this rapprochement and began targeting Chinese stores for retaliation.[125]

College-aged Chinese Americans attended one of the state universities: the University of Mississippi in Oxford, Mississippi State University in Starkville, and Delta State University in Cleveland. At all three institutions, they tended to be excluded from sororities and fraternities (as African-Americans were). There they stayed out of campus politics and did not try to obtain scholarships.[126] A male student complained:

> In high school I saw myself at first as Delta Chinese, but my friends and everyone else treated us as a White American. Then, when I went to college, I tried to be in with the Whites, and they told me I was Chinese and sort of shunned me. I feel it, and it hurts.[127]

A twist on this view, however, was placed by a young Chinese American woman student who said, "Just 'cause I'm not White in the Delta doesn't mean I can't be White somewhere else."[128] Sam Sue, who had grown up in Clarksdale, Mississippi, wrote:

I went to . . . Oberlin. This was my first big experience outside of a fifty-mile radius of Clarksdale. . . . So I show up and meet these rich professors' kids, and you feel inferior towards them and you resent all the privileges they've had, so there was a class thing, too.[129]

Now a lawyer in his mid-30s, Sue recalled that as a young person, "I was basically ashamed of being Chinese."[130]

The first numerous Chinese emigrants left for the United States around the mid-19th century. In Kwangtung province, whence most originated, only rudimentary common schools existed that were available to very few children and then only for 2 to 4 years of instruction. Because families from gentry and wealthy merchant backgrounds did not typically emigrate, exceedingly few immigrants had a classical education. Further, the relative absence of children relieved pressure for creating schools. By the 1920s, a sizable generation of native-born children came into existence and began to crowd the schools.

From the viewpoint of numbers alone, the new trend permitted Chinese Americans to outdistance their contemporary peers in China. Apparently, American-born Chinese girls were far more likely to attend school here than was the case in China. In part, this was because "the vast majority of the second generation Chinese Americans were children of merchants who grew up in family settings with a petit bourgeois orientation."[131] Girls in such families were more likely to receive some education. A generation later, during the 1950s, two developments stood out: Near-parity between girls and boys in school was attained, and Chinese Americans as a group were rising rapidly in educational attainment.

Before World War II, a number of visiting students from China gained their higher education in the United States. Children of the gentry class, they were self-supporting or financed by the Chinese government.[132] Very few ever remained in the United States after completing their studies. It may have been via this kind of cultural connection that in 1907, a group of Chinese students in Tokyo staged a play, *The Black Slaves' Cry to Heaven*, that was based on an earlier Chinese translation of *Uncle Tom's Cabin*.[133] During the 1930s and 1940s, Chinese who received their university training in the United States tended to remain there and practice the profession they had prepared to enter. It was during these latter years that China was enveloped in a war with Japan and a civil war. The great majority of these Chinese were, along with their predecessors, from the upper ranks of China's society.[134] After the culmination of the revolution in 1949, they remained in the United States and formed a major source of the Chinese American middle class.

Chinese populations in the United States were subjected to exclusion beginning with the Chinese Exclusion Act of 1882. As the laborers aged and died, few left descendants as did most European immigrants. Another distinctiveness of the Chinese Americans was that they were one of the few ethnic minorities that developed a sizable, educated, middle class. The early generations of Native Americans, African-Americans, and Mexican Americans lacked such a sizable class. This was one of the reasons that Chinese were mistakenly regarded as especially gifted in the field of education. Ethnic factors were confused with class factors, indigenous development with that stemming from immigration.

CONCLUDING REMARKS

Chinese who emigrated to the United States during the past generation encountered many conditions with which they were well acquainted. Chief among these was a tightening class structure that increasingly governed the allocation of life necessities, including education. In China, upper-class status led to enrollment in elite educational institutions, culminating in the most selective universities. In the United States, a parallel hierarchical structure awaited the children of the most privileged Chinese immigrants who settled in urban and suburban areas accessible to high level and expensive schools and colleges. Class privilege was truly international.

But so also was class disadvantage. The great majority of Chinese could look forward only to meager educational fare. Among the peasantry and urban working class, the upper reaches of education were unattainable. Except for a historical moment, unequal schooling was the everyday experience. During the century after exclusion, few Chinese peasants immigrated into the United States. But when they did, particularly during the past generation, they confronted a familiar deprivation as their children attended large urban schools that were invariably crowded, unstaffed, and underfinanced. Most of all, they were impervious to the need for special language instruction to accommodate equal educational achievement.

A third group of Chinese immigrants was frequently misclassified with the second group. These were persons who came from a highly educated background and who had held professional–managerial jobs in China. Now, however, they could be found working at the most menial occupations in the United States. Former college teachers, engineers, factory managers, and lawyers stressed to their children the centrality of higher education, thus supplying indispensable academic motivation. Outsiders might view the resulting upward mobility as a stirring of ambition in the lower ranks of society. More so, it was a continuation of a trend within the upper reaches of Chinese society. (The same was also true of other Asian-American groups.) This is not to say, however, that past education was a guarantee of similar accomplishment by one's children or that high academic attainment from a modest social background was rare.

Historically, wealth and power had served effectively as material rewards of education. During the life of the classical Chinese Examination System, it escaped few ordinary Chinese that wealth and power followed the trajectory of academic success. Whereas the scholar was admired for his scholarship, popular admiration was based on far more than acclaim for assiduous study. On a different institutional basis, in the United States, similar goals were widely accepted.

Nevertheless, in the United States and elsewhere, a far-ranging debate arose over the sources of Chinese American academic attainment. Peculiarly, only one aspect of the issue was considered: It was supposed by some that Chinese Americans were, across the board, high achievers. Discussion among educators and others simply omitted mention of Chinese Americans who were low achievers. Having thus narrowed the span of concern, high academic achievement was then equated with being Chinese or Chinese American. (Presumably, those with low achievement were less Chinese or even un-Chinese.)

Contemporary American educational and general commentary seems to regard Chinese of low achievement as an oxymoron, a self-contradiction in terms that is outside the pale of academic discussion. Yet, in China itself—the most Chinese of all locations—school authorities readily attest to pupil failure and slowness in learning. As we saw previously, similar trends among Chinese Americans are paid little heed in favor of sciolistic assertions about the distinctive attractions of learning among Chinese. Kwong courageously declared: "There is no truth to the belief that the Chinese have a greater respect for knowledge than other groups. . . . The claim linking Chinese achievement in education to Confucianism is a myth."[135] This assertion is highly consistent with the historical record and is discussed further in other chapters.

NOTES

[1] John King Fairbank, *China. A New History* (Harvard University Press, 1992), p. 106.

[2] Wolfram Eberhard, *Social Mobility in Traditional China* (E. J. Brill, 1962), p. 26.

[3] Thomas H. C. Lee, *Government Education and Examinations in Sung China* (Chinese University Press, 1985), p. 21.

[4] Ibid., p. 157.

[5] Denis Twitchett and John K. Fairbank, eds., *The Cambridge History of China*, vol. 10 (Cambridge University Press, 1978), p. 155. See also Edgar Kiser and Xiaoxi Tong, "Determinants of the Amount and Type of Corruption in State Fiscal Bureaucracies," *Comparative Political Studies*, 25 (October 1992) pp. 300–331.

[6] Lee, *Government*, p. 140.

[7] Ibid., p. 224.

[8] A partial, if abortive, effort to reverse this inattention during the Ming Dynasty is reported in William S. Atwell, "From Education to Politics: The Fu She," pp. 333–367 in William Theodore De Bary, ed., *The Unfolding of Neo-Confucianism.* (Columbia University Press, 1975).

[9] David Johnson, Andrew J. Nathan, and Evelyn S. Rawski, eds., *Popular Culture in Late Imperial China* (University of California Press, 1985), p. 58.

[10] Evelyn S. Rawski, "Economic and Social Foundations of Late Imperial Culture," in ibid., p. 7.

[11] Evelyn S. Rawski, *Education and Popular Literacy in Ch'ing China* (University of Michigan Press, 1979), p. 23.

[12] Gail Hershatter, *The Workers of Tianjin, 1900–1949* (Stanford University Press, 1986), p. 80.

[13] Sally Borthwick, *Education and Social Change in China. The Beginnings of the Modern Era* (Hoover Institution Press, 1983), p. 118.

[14] Ping Wen Kuo, *The Chinese System of Public Education* (Teachers College, Columbia University, 1915), p. 149. The title of this puzzling work seems not to support the contents.

[15] Helen R. Chauncey, *Schoolhouse Politicians. Locality and State During the Chinese Republic* (University of Hawaii Press, 1992), pp. 92–93. The author notes that "female students with bound feet were a common sight in local schools north of the Yangzi" (p. 93).

[16] Ibid., p. 119. See also Thomas D. Curran, *Education and Society in Republican China* (Doctoral dissertation, Columbia University, 1986), p. 188.

[17] Curran, *Education and Society in Republican China*, pp. 436–437.

[18] Wen-Hsin Yeh, *The Alienated Academy. Culture and Politics in Republican China, 1919–1937* (Council on East Asian Studies, Harvard University, 1990), p. xi. See also Jeffrey Wasserstrom and Liu Xinyong, "Student Protest and Student Life: Shanghai, 1919–49," *Social History,* 14 (January 1989), p. 1–29.

[19] Lin Chun, "China Today: 'Money Dissolves the Commune'," *New Left Review,* No. 201 (September–October 1993), p. 39.

[20] Maureen Woodhall, *Student Loans in Higher Education: 2 Asia* (UNESCO, 1991), p. 4.

[21] Fairbank, *China. A New History,* p. 392.

[22] Twitchett and Fairbank, eds., *The Cambridge History of China* (Cambridge University Press, 1991), vol. 15, p. 569.

[23] Ibid., p. 579.

[24] Ibid., p. 580.

[25] Ibid., p. 582. See also Stanley Rosen, "The People's Republic of China: Education during the World Recession: The Paradox of Expansion," pp. 105–22 in Frederick M. Wirt and Grant Harman, eds., *Education during the World Recession and The World Village: A Comparative Political Economy of Education* (Falmer, 1986).

[26] Martin Schoenhals, *The Paradox of Power in a People's Republic of China Middle School* (Sharpe, 1993), p. 7.

[27] Ibid., p. 7.

[28] Ibid., p. 8.

[29] Ibid., p. 205.

[30] William Hinton, *The Great Reversal. The Privitization of China, 1978–1989* (Monthly Review Press, 1990), p. 79.

[31] Rone Tempest, "Officials in China Ordered to Stop Withholding Teachers' Wages," *Los Angeles Times,* January 13, 1994.

[32] Ibid.

[33] Dave Lindorff, "China's Great Leap Downward," *In These Times,* January 24, 1994.

[34] Lin Chun, "China Today," p. 43. See also Patrick E. Tyler, "China's Country Schools Are Failing," *New York Times,* December 31, 1995.

[35] Norman A. Fernandes, *The San Francisco Board of Education and the Chinese Community: Segregation-Desegregation, 1850–1975* (Doctoral dissertation, University of Denver, 1976), p. 55.

[36] Ibid., p. 74.

[37] Victor Low, *The Chinese in the San Francisco Public School System: An Historical Study of One Minority Group's Response to Educational Discrimination, 1859–1959* (Doctoral dissertation, University of San Francisco, 1981), pp. 68, 105.

[38] Letter dated April 8, 1885, reprinted in *Daily Alta California,* April 16, 1885, page 1, column 3, quoted in ibid., p. 401.

[39] Ibid., pp. 174–175.

[40] Ibid., p. 258.

[41] Fernandes, *San Francisco Board of Education,* pp. 106, 110.

[42] Low, *The Chinese,* p. 181.

[43] Ibid., p. 58.

[44] Christopher Chow and Russell Leong, "A Pioneer Chinatown Teacher: An Interview with Alice Fong Yu, "*Amerasia Journal*, 5 (1978), pp. 76–86.

[45] Charles Caldwell Dobie, *San Francisco's Chinatown* (D. Appleton-Century, 1936), p. 270.

[46] Wallace M. Taylor, "Problems of a Chinatown School," *California Journal of Secondary Education*, 18 (October 1943), p. 351.

[47] Mary Bo-Tze Lee, *Problems of the Segregated School for Asiatics in San Francisco* (Master's thesis, University of California, Berkeley, 1921), p. 30.

[48] Low, *The Chinese*, p. 361.

[49] Ibid., p. 192; Lee, *Problems of the Segregated School*, p. 6; and John Hood Laughlin, "Chinese Children in American Schools," *Overland Monthly*, 57 (May 1911), p. 503.

[50] See Fernandes, *San Francisco Board of Education*, p. 64 and Low, *The Chinese*, p. 84.

[51] Low, *The Chinese*, p. 188.

[52] Lee, *Problems of the Segregated School*, p. 13.

[53] David G. Herman, *Neighbors on the Golden Mountain: The Americanization of Immigrants in California. Public Instruction As an Agency of Ethnic Assimilation, 1850 to 1933* 2 volumes (Doctoral dissertation, University of California, Berkeley, 1981), pp. 186–187.

[54] Ibid., p. 190.

[55] Ibid., p. 266.

[56] Low, *The Chinese*, p. 39.

[57] Ibid., p. 150.

[58] Ibid., pp. 262–263.

[59] Ibid., p. 364.

[60] Ibid., pp. 112–113.

[61] Dobie, *San Francisco's Chinatown*, p. 325.

[62] Arthur G. Butzbach, *The Segregation of Orientals in the San Francisco Schools* (Master's thesis, Stanford University, 1928), p. 81.

[63] Francis Yung Chang, *A Study of the Movement to Segregate Chinese Pupils in the San Francisco Public Schools Up to 1885* (Doctoral dissertation, Stanford University, 1936), p. 279.

[64] Linda Pomerantz, "The Chinese Bourgeoisie and the Anti-Chinese Movement in the United States, 1850–1905," *Amerasia Journal*, 11 (Spring–Summer 1984), pp. 1–34.

[65] Michael S. H. Chang, *From Marginality to Bimodality: Immigration, Education, and Occupational Change of Chinese Americans, 1940–1980* (Doctoral dissertation, Stanford University, 1988), p. 4.

[66] Ibid., p. 53. The former included service workers, laborers, and household workers; the latter, professionals and technicians.

[67] Ibid., pp. 102–103.

[68] Larry Neal and Paul Uselding, "Immigration, a Neglected Source of American Economic Growth: 1790–1912," *Oxford Economic Papers*, 24 (March 1972), pp. 68–88. See also Sucheng Chan, *This Bittersweet Soil. The Chinese in California Agriculture, 1860–1910* (University of California Press, 1986), p. 330.

[69] Dudley L. Poston, Jr. and Mei-Yu Yu, "The Distribution of the Overseas Chinese in the Contemporary World," *International Migration Review*, 24 (Fall 1990), pp. 494–495.

[70] Chang, *From Marginality to Bimodality*, pp. 99–100.

[71] Beulah Ong Kwoh, *Occupational Status of the American-born Chinese College Graduates* (Master's thesis, University of Chicago, 1947), p. 114.

[72] Chang, *From Marginality to Bimodality*, p. 53. See also note 66.

[73] Wen-hui Tsai, "The Chinese American Poor," p. 108 in Yuan-li Wu, ed., *The Economic Condition of Chinese Americans* (Pacific/Asian American Mental Health Research Center, 1980).

[74] L. Ling-Chi Wang, "The Chinese Community in San Francisco," p. 13 in Meyer Weinberg, ed., *Chinese Americans: School and Community Problems* (Integrated Education Associates, 1972).

[75] L. Ling-Chi Wang, "The Chinese-American Student in San Francisco," p. 54 in ibid.

[76] Ibid., p. 55.

[77] Lonnie Chin, "Chinese and Public School Teaching," p. 59 in ibid.

[78] Low, *The Chinese*, p. 313.

[79] Wang, "The Chinese-American Student in San Francisco," p. 55.

[80] Low, *The Chinese*, p. 4.

[81] *East—West*, April 1, 1967, quoted in Mely Giok-lan Tan, *The Chinese in the United States. Social Mobility and Assimilation* (Orient Cultural Service, 1971), p. 197.

[82] Robert S. Perlzweig, "California's Chinese," *Patterns of Prejudice*, 6 (March–April 1972), p. 11.

[83] Min S. Yee, "Busing Comes to Chinatown," *Race Relations Reporter*, 3 (1972), p. 18.

[84] Philip A. Lum, "The Creation and Demise of San Francisco Chinatown Freedom Schools: One Response to Desegregation," *Amerasia Journal*, 5 (1978), p. 62.

[85] See for example, Yee, "Busing Comes to Chinatown," p. 20, Fernandes, *San Francisco Board of Education*, p. 178, and Lum, "The Creation and Demise," p. 63.

[86] This estimate is given by Benjamin Tom, "On Politics and Education in San Francisco: Commentary by the President, Board of Education," *Amerasia Journal*, 5 (1978), p. 92.

[87] Yee, "Busing Comes to Chinatown," p. 19.

[88] Lum, "The Creation and Demise," pp. 60–61.

[89] Ibid., pp. 69–70.

[90] Fernandes, *San Francisco Board of Education*, p. 142.

[91] Stephen D. Sugarman and Ellen G. Widess, "Equal Protection for Non-English-speaking School Children: *Lau* v. *Nichols*," *California Law Review*, 62 (1974), p. 158.

[92] L. Ling-chi Wang, "*Lau* v. *Nichols*: The Right of Limited-English-speaking Students," *Amerasia Journal*, 2 (1974), p. 38.

[93] L. Ling-chi Wang, "*Lau* v. *Nichols*: History of a Struggle for Equal and Quality Education," p. 185 in Russell Endo, Stanley Sue, and Nathaniel N. Wager, eds., *Asian Americans. Social and Psychological Perspectives*, II (Science and Behavior Books, 1980).

[94] Irving G. Hendrick, *The Education of Non-Whites in California, 1849–1970* (R & E Research Associates, 1977), p. 36

[95] Neil Clifford Perry, *An Investigation of Certain Aspects of the Social, Economic and Educational Status of Second-Generation Chinese and Japanese Graduates of the High Schools of Fresno California* (Master's thesis, University of Southern California, 1938), p. 21.

[96] Ibid., p. 129.

[97] The Great Basin Foundation, *Wong Ho Leun. An American Chinatown* (Great Basin Foundation, 1987), pp. 86–87.

[98] Ibid., p. 129.

[99] Judith Rosenberg Raftery, *Land of Fair Promise. Politics and Reform in Los Angeles Schools, 1885–1941* (Stanford University Press, 1992), p. 103, p. 139, footnote 91.

[100] Clarence E. Glick, *Sojourners and Settlers. Chinese Migrants in Hawaii* (University Press of Hawaii, 1980), p. 328.

[101] Xu Hwang, *The Schooling of the Children of Early Chinese Immigrants in Hawaii* (Master's thesis, University of Hawaii, 1989), p. 79.

[102] Glick, *Sojourners and Settlers*, p. 115.

[103] Hwang, *The Schooling*, p. 87.

[104] Glick, *Sojourners and Settlers*, p. 112.

[105] William Bun Chin Chang, "The Myth of Chinese Success in Hawaii," p. 43 in Meyer Weinberg, ed., *Chinese Americans: School and Community Problems* (Integrated Education Associates, 1972).

[106] See ibid., pp. 37, 48.

[107] Louis J. Beck, *New York's Chinatown* (Bohemia Publishing Co., 1898), pp. 12, 38–39.

[108] See Rose Chao, *Chinese Immigrant Children*. Edited by Betty Lee Sung (Department of Asian Studies, The City College, CUNY, 1977); Betty Lee Sung, *Transplanted Chinese Children* (Depart-

ment of Asian Studies, CUNY, 1977); and Betty Lee Sung, *The Adjustment Experience of Chinese Immigrant Children in New York City* (Center for Migration Studies, 1987).

[109] Chao, *Chinese Immigrant Children*, pp. 20, 21.

[110] Sung, *The Adjustment Experience*, p. 101.

[111] Sung, *Transplanted Chinese Children*, p. 74.

[112] Chao, *Chinese Immigrant Children*, p. 13.

[113] Peter Kwong, *The New Chinatown* (Hill and Wang, 1987), p. 74. See Randi Glatzer, "Downward Mobility," *Village Voice Education Supplement*, April 16, 1996, p. 9 for comment on P.S. 1 in Chinatown.

[114] Ibid., pp. 74–75.

[115] Minh Ly Griffin, *Health and Health Care Profile of New York City's New School Admissions, 1990–1991* (Community Service Society, 1993), p. xvi: "The rates for dental problems reported were highest for new entrants from China (13.4 percent). . . ."

[116] Sung, *The Adjustment Experience*, p. 72.

[117] Charisse Jones, "Test Scores Show Gaps By Ethnicity," *New York Times*, July 8, 1994.

[118] Kwong, *The New Chinatown*, p. 74.

[119] Sung, *Transplanted Chinese Children*, p. 18.

[120] Lucy M. Cohen, "Entry of Chinese to the Lower South from 1865 to 1870: Policy Dilemmas," *Southern Studies*, 17 (Spring 1978), pp. 5–38.

[121] Lucy M. Cohen, *Chinese in the Post-Civil War South. A People Without a History* (Louisiana State University Press, 1984), p. 167.

[122] Robert Seto Quan with Julian B. Roebuck, *Lotus Among the Magnolias. The Mississippi Chinese* (University Press of Mississippi, 1982), pp. 45–46. See also James W. Loewen, *The Mississippi Chinese. Between Black and White* (Harvard University Press, 1971), p. 66.

[123] *Bond, State Superintendent of Education* v. *Tij Fung et al.*, 114 So. 332, cited in *Notre Dame Lawyer*, 3 (January 1928), pp. 150–51.

[124] Loewen, *The Mississippi Chinese*, p. 68.

[125] Ibid., pp. 176–77.

[126] Quan, *Lotus Among the Magnolias*, pp. 117, 123.

[127] Ibid., p. 126.

[128] Ibid., p. 150.

[129] Joann Faung Jean Lee, *Asian American Experiences in the United States* (McFarland and Co., 1991), p. 125.

[130] Ibid., p. 3.

[131] Sucheng Chan, "The Exclusion of Chinese Women, 1870–1943," p. 139 in Chan, ed., *Entry Denied. Exclusion and the Chinese Community in America, 1882–1943* (Temple University Press, 1991).

[132] Weili Ye, *Crossing the Cultures: The Experience of Chinese Students in the U.S.A. 1900–1925* (Doctoral dissertation, Yale University, 1989), p. 145.

[133] Ibid., p. 444.

[134] Edwin Clausen, "Chinese Intellectuals in the U.S.: Success in the Post World War II Era," *Annals of the Chinese Historical Society of the Pacific Northwest* (1983), p. 136.

[135] Kwong, *The New Chinatown*, p. 72.

Japan

Barely a century ago, Japan instituted a public school system. The action followed a thousand years of desultory provision of education for the country's elite. By 1920, the Japanese school system was the most extensive in the world. Nevertheless, inequality characterized the schools at numerous points in their history.

As early as A.D. 701, sons of government officials and local elites could attend the Grand School. Examinations for purposes of qualifying for government employment were given, but children of officials were exempt from taking them. They occupied official positions as a matter of right. During the following 5 centuries, aristocratic families organized their own schools that were thought to be a more effective avenue to officialdom. By the 13th century, five such schools existed. Not accidentally, the dominant great families of the country also numbered five.

Meanwhile, the aristocracy had been largely shunted aside by the warrior class, the *samurai*. Largely illiterate, the warriors exercised extensive power in society. As Kobayashi wrote, after the 17th century, "the military class transferred themselves to the military–bureaucratic class and literary abilities were required to carry out this new function."[1] Special schools, some directly financed by the central government, were established for *samurai*. Distinctions among the *samurai* were respected and upper and lower *samurai* attended separate schools. The sons of wealthy commoners might also attend the same schools but were not permitted to share classrooms. The nearest thing to universal schooling between the 13th and 17th centuries were schools conducted in Buddhist temples. They were designed to educate priests as well as teach writing to a broad social span of children.

During the Tokugawa period (1603–1868), military rule was preeminent. In the closing years, *samurai* were all but completely literate. "The education of a *samurai* boy was to include the military arts and training to read and write both Chinese and Japanese and to extend as well to other accomplishments expected as a gentleman."[2] At schools located on feudal domains (the fief schools), many *samurai* children were taught this regimen. Private academies were operated and charged tuition. Most of the teachers were *samurai*.[3] The poorest peasants could not afford to attend.

Education designed for commoners was conducted in some 15,500 one-room schools that enrolled both girls and boys. (It should be recalled that commoners were not equivalent to the poorest people. They included a very broad range of persons who were ranked under aristocrats and *samurai*.) These writing schools, as they were known, were voluntary institutions, and were not subject to government regulation. Fees were charged in most *terakoya* although private contributions were also given.[4] The existence of a variety of schools should not be confused with an equal system. As Keenleyside and Thomas observed, "Here was no democratic system opening opportunities of education and an official career to all men of talent regardless of birth and social status. . . . Candidacies for all important posts [were confined to] the sons of approved families."[5] Another historian points out that when, in 1792, the national government established a new system of annual examinations, "the odds were . . . stacked against candidates of humble status, no matter how able."[6]

Popular culture was another evidence of growing literacy in the 18th and 19th centuries. In the villages, texts on farming and other subjects were the object of a growing commercial industry.[7] Popular literature including stories, plays, and novels attested to expanding literacy.[8] Kobayashi cautioned:

> The consumers [of imaginative literature] were mostly townspeople who had the time and money to afford such leisure pursuits. In the villages the ordinary peasants had neither the time nor the money, and only the upper-class farmers could enjoy it.[9]

There was a great variation in literacy within the average village in 1868, a time when 87% of the total population lived in villages:[10]

Village notables	Almost 100%
Village middle layers	50 to 60%
Lower peasant levels	30 to 40%
Peasants in more isolated areas	20%

It may be imagined that relatively few of the country's 600 publishers and booksellers in 1710 were located in the countryside.[11]

Tokugawa society was severely stratified but upward social mobility was narrowly possible with the aid of specialized education. Occasionally, an upper commoner might ascend to *samurai* status. Scholars, priests, and physicians could also be recruited from commoners.[12] The higher reaches of military and civil power, however, were all but exempt from such incursions from below.

The sanctity of the social order was constantly preached in the schools. When central authorities feared the *terakoya* were not effective enough in this regard, new institutions were created. The *gogaku*, for example, were village schools designed to teach commoners the right way of life and counter social unrest. Emphasis was also placed on "moral indoctrination for . . . obedient industrious workers."[13] Textbooks loyally embodied such preachments. Dore accurately summarized the situation during Tokugawa: "Schools tended always and everywhere to encourage submissive acceptance of the existing order."[14]

The Meiji period (1868–1911) was a landmark in Japanese history. For the first time, mass education started to take shape. It was not, however, the result of widespread demands. Instead, the system was imposed on a puzzled and partly resistant people. Some of the elements of it were familiar from Tokugawa: Rising popular literacy and schooling had already recorded some triumphs; scattered initiatives by the central government benefited upper commoners; by period's end, the *samurai* were being pressed toward the outer margins of power. In Meiji, the emperor gained a new prominence as the source of new national goals, including mass education. The *samurai* were pensioned off as individual members of a class that had outlived its historic uses. If anything, the top layers of the military establishment gained in significance as advisers and officials of the new imperial government. In early Meiji years, numerous *samurai* held positions in lower and middle government ranks.

The new regime's economic program singled out farmers as a principal source of tax revenues. A heavy land tax was levied that produced over half of all national government revenues until 1900.[15] This laid an extraordinary financial burden on farmers who could ill afford it. Unprecedented was the requirement that the tax be paid in cash. Because the majority of farmers consumed most of what they grew, they were forced to enter the market at a time when all others were doing the same. Prices fell sharply at harvest time, forcing many farmers to sell some, at least, of their land to raise the needed money to pay taxes. The result was that "between 1883 and 1890 over 367,000 landholding farmers were dispossessed because of their inability to pay land taxes."[16]

The establishment of public schools added to the economic woes of poorer farmers as local taxes were imposed to build and operate the schools. In addition, tuition fees were charged. The national government contributed little more than exhortation.[17] Many of these economically pressed farmers rioted in protest and burned a number of the new schools.[18] (In part, these violent demonstrations were also aimed at the newly enacted conscription law and the formal granting of some rights to an oppressed minority, the *burakumin*.)

The Education Code of 1872 created a 4-year compulsory-education elementary program that was to be financed locally. Tuition was set at a very high level.[19] Although the compulsory feature was stated without equivocation, in fact compulsory attendance was only enforced spottily. Prefectural governors were empowered to close down elementary schools altogether in certain circumstances.[20] Nevertheless, the government reported large attendance figures. In 1877, just under 40% of school-age children attended school, although variations by prefecture ran from 22.6 to 67.1%. The great majority of those in attendance were in early grades:

> In 1875, children enrolled in the first semester of the lower division of the elementary school constituted roughly 65% of the total school enrollment. Second semester pupils accounted for about 17%. . . . [1877] enrollment in the upper division of the elementary school was 0.8% of total enrollment.[21]

During a depression decade, 1883 to 1892, the proportion of children attending elementary school failed to increase.[22] On the other hand, in an overlapping decade, the relevant figures for girls and boys separately were as follows:[23]

	1890	1900
Boys	65.1	90.6
Girls	31.1	71.7

The sharp general increase was directly due to the abolition of tuition fees and the rise in attendance by girls was helped greatly by government encouragement.

Expanded schooling occurred within a fixed design of tracking. By 1900, the great majority of children concluded their education after 4 years. In 1907, the term was extended to 6 years. But even as late as 1920, "between one-half to three quarters of young Japanese got no formal education beyond the compulsory elementary level, by then . . . six years."[24] In Okayama Prefecture, landless tenants in the early 1920s made up nearly three fourths of persons lacking any education.[25]

The education of girls was gaining ground during the last three decades of the 19th century. Although much of the schooling was aimed at cultivating the traditional roles of wife and mother, "for the first time in modern history Japanese women began to be interested in the possibility of obtaining an education equivalent to that of the men."[26] In secondary and higher education, however, sex discrimination ran rampant. During the 1870s, "most ordinary people believed . . . modern education for girls was not only a waste of time but potentially harmful."[27] By the mid-1890s, girls' high schools were organized, but these were a lesser sort than the high schools—or middle schools—that some boys attended. Education Minister Kabayama Sukenori stipulated that the girls' institutions must "furnish the knowledge of arts and crafts necessary for middle to upper class life."[28]

The education of working-class women, however, was of small concern to education authorities. Most factory workers in the last decade of the 19th century were women. Exceedingly few of these could be classed as fully literate. As Taira wrote, in 1910, "only 40.6% of males and 22.6% of females in the employable age brackets are estimated to have completed compulsory elementary education."[29] Taira continued: "The development of factory production during Meiji was largely based on illiterate and semi-literate workers."[30] This is consistent with another observation: After 1905 and thereabouts, "the city jobs available to those with only a basic education were menial and poorly paid."[31] Women workers bore the major part of this burden.

Immigration and Education

During the years 1885 to 1924, some 200,000 Japanese emigrated to Hawaii, as follows:[32]

1885 to 1894	29,069
1894 to 1908	125,000
1908 to 1924	48,000
	202,069

As early as 1894, nearly two thirds of sugar plantation workers there were Japanese. Wage levels back home were only one tenth to one fifth of those in the new land.[33] No wonder that 28,000 applied for the 600 vacancies on the first ship headed for Hawaii.[34] Also, that year—1885—was a famine year in Japan.

What was the educational heritage of the immigrants? They came from an educational system which offered 3, 4, or at the end of the period, 6 years of schooling. Nearly all, however, originated from rural areas where schooling opportunities were least available. The Japanese government controlled the quality of the immigrants. They had to pass strict health examinations. Educational qualifications were prescribed. All in all, they were a highly select group. Although practically none were illiterate, a number had more schooling than the average. Tamura wrote:

> *Issei* [members of the early immigrant generation] men, the bulk of whom came to Hawaii between 1885 and 1907, had an average of about four to six years of schooling; *issei* women, most of whom came from 1900 to 1924, had completed between two or five years of schooling. Thus most of the *issei* were at least functionally literate.[35]

Between 1885 and 1906, the compulsory term of attendance was 3 or 4 years; only in 1907 was it made 6 years. Very few of the men could have qualified for the new requirement. Tamura's figure for women seems a bit low. To be sure, government inspectors could easily have put a gloss on the affair by selecting candidates carefully, and they seem to have done this. As a result, a myth arose among some descendants of the *issei* that the compulsory term of schooling had been 8 years long before World War I. This was a considerable exaggeration. Many Japanese were schooled beyond the compulsory span of years, but it was primarily because their families could afford to pay the additional tuition fees and not because people generally could do the same.

The central motive behind Japanese immigration was to put laborers to work on the sugar plantations of Hawaii. At the outset, nearly all the newcomers were farmers or farm workers. In time, as the Japanese community grew, immigrants from other classes were attracted: "Represented . . . were all classes of Japanese society, socially and economically—from the upper classes, which included members of the nobility, political refugees, priests, scholars, doctors, and businessmen, to the lower classes, which included even criminals and prostitutes."[36]

On the mainland, there was a much less urgent need or desire to attract Japanese laborers. Neither the United States nor Japan was eager to facilitate this traffic. In an exchange of notes on the subject, Foreign Minister Tadasu "revealed that the Japanese government shared the American prejudice against *imin* [migrant] laborers as less than equal members of society and had no qualms about unequivocally eliminating their travel."[37] Japanese of a professional or business background, according to Foreign Affairs vice-minister Sutemi, "had to have . . . at least eleven years of education or appropriate technical training, employment prospects as clerks or technicians in commercial houses, and fluency in English."[38]

Schooling in Hawaii

Japan and Hawaii had agreed initially that 30%—later 25%—of immigrants be women.[39] This assured a supply of children to be schooled. Seven years later, only 60 Japanese students were attending public schools in all Hawaii.[40] The great majority of Japanese were plantation workers, and schools were scarce in plantation areas. Also, many of the earliest workers did not intend to remain for long in Hawaii and so did not plan to build a family. In addition, the great bulk of workers were in their 20s and had not yet completed building their families. Finally, because many viewed themselves as only temporarily absent from the homeland, they felt no need for their children to become thoroughly acclimated to the new country and its language. Indeed, this was one reason for opening Japanese-language schools on the Islands.[41]

Plantation managers regarded public schooling as a needless luxury. If unavoidable, they pressed school officials to schedule hours of attendance to accommodate the requirements of the children's jobs. These included plantation work as "blacksmiths' helpers, camp cleaners, cane cutters, carriers, loaders, store clerks, field hands, hospital servants, and mill laborers."[42] Workers kept after managers to provide schooling opportunities. During a 1909 strike by Japanese workers, the strikers wrote to the manager of Waipahu Plantation, "Children to educate."[43] Parents were aware of the relative lack of enforcement of a school law passed in 1896 that established compulsory attendance.[44] In 1910, 39% of the population of Hawaii was comprised of Japanese, many of whom had decided to remain there. Only one fourth of the public school children were Japanese. By 1910, it had reached one half.

Much energy was spent in combating the expansion of educational opportunity in Hawaii. Leading these efforts were the Islands' economic and political elite, the territorial board of education, and top officials of the public school and higher education systems. Major targets of the campaign were members of the Japanese American community who were both ethnic minorities and working-class persons.

"To the planters of Hawaii," wrote Fuchs, "the labor problem was clear-cut: to get enough workers, to get them cheaply, and to keep them on the plantations."[45] We may add a further point: to ensure their docility. Plantation managers on the whole viewed the schools as an interference with solving the labor problem. Especially galling to the managers was the strong tendency of plantation laborers' children to seek work off the plantation. They charged the schools with miseducating the children by failing to prepare them for lives of hard labor. Most elites thought likewise.

In 1931, University of Hawaii president Arthur L. Dean declared that "our school system is drifting into the communist theory that it is the business of the public to take care of everyone."[46] Six years earlier, John Hind, president of the Hawaii Sugar Producers Association (HSPA), was upset at the sight of students walking about town as they carried books, and asked, "Why try to mislead them with the idea that more education works for progress?"[47]

A plantation manager, James C. Camps, warned, "Public education beyond the fourth grade is not only a waste, it is a menace. We spend to educate them and they will destroy us."[48]

Between 1924 and 1960, the board of education installed a set of English Standard Schools for the major benefit of White students. Admission was by oral English proficiency. Whites, who constituted only 8% of Hawaii residents in 1924, comprised from 50 to 70% of the special schools. In non-Standard schools, on the other hand, they made up only 2.5% of students. Anything but standard, the schools received considerably more money than others did, thus allowing better structures, more highly trained teachers, and other advantages. Most were located in highly urbanized places. Parents of children in the non-Standard schools complained at the discrimination. In 1937, testimony at a hearing on statehood for Hawaii included an assertion that "during . . . recent years there has been almost no objection nor complaint that unfair discrimination exists [on the subject of Standard Schools]."[49] This was far from the case.

Shortly after the initial English Standard Schools were created and became majority–White institutions, the school board also started English Standard sections as parts of non-Standard Schools. The school board hoped thereby to dull the edge of minority criticism of English Standard Schools by allowing a number of non-Whites in the sections. They continued to be excluded from the Standard Schools. Criticism of the entire Standard system went on after World War II. Parental and other pressure was successfully brought to bear on the territorial legislature to outlaw the arrangement. In 1948, the legislature adopted a plan of gradual abolition: The English Standard Schools were to end in 1960 after another cycle of students had gone through first through twelfth grades. In fact, the ethnic composition of the schools had been undergoing a basic change since World War II when many White parents left Hawaii for the safety of the mainland. White students in the Standard Schools numbered 4,024 in 1941 but only 1,261 in 1942.[50] To prop up enrollment, many Asians—primarily Japanese—were allowed to enter the Standard Schools. By 1947, Asians (Orientals) made up 41% and Whites 29% of students in English Standard Schools.[51] It took another 13 years until the entire project was ended. Initiated at the instance of middling White families who could not afford the tuition of the Territory's expensive private schools, the English Standard Schools served as publicly financed substitutes.[52]

An entire generation of Hawaii's children had experienced the realities of unequal and separate education without benefit of legislative or judicial enactment. They learned less as they languished in the substandard schools. In sixth grade, students scored nearly a full year less in non-Standard schools; by twelfth grade, the gap had grown to 2 years.[53]

Trying further to head off the Japanese and other workers' children from the upper grades of the schools, the elite missed few openings. For example:

in 1920 . . . the Chamber of Commerce Committee on Public Schools and Vocational Education passed a resolution urging that tuition be charged to all high school students who were not American citizens or who were citizens but had not given satisfactory proof that their sole allegiance was to the United States.[54]

The policy was implemented between 1933 and 1937, the depth of the worldwide depression. All public high school students had to pay $10 a year.[55]

Still another technique used by educators was to directly restrict the number of enrollees in high schools. This was accomplished in 1928 when the Department of Public Instruction ruled that the bottom fifth of all junior-high-school graduates would not be permitted to enroll in high schools beginning in 1930. This maneuver, it appears, did not succeed in its aim. Instead of resulting in less high school enrollment and greater employment on the plantation, it simply enlarged attendance in private high schools, thus sorely disappointing the plantation managers.[56] During the 1930s and after, a complex system of school fees was installed. During the early 1920s, students had also been required to pay annual fees to the Territory. If the fees were not collected, teachers and school board members could be subjected to civil and criminal proceedings.[57]

The 1920s was the decade of the Nisei in two senses. First, this first large-scale indigenous Japanese American generation signified the presence of a new group of American citizens with undoubted rights of entry into voting and universities. Nisei citizenship rights rested upon the 14th Amendment of the U.S. Constitution that provided that persons born in the United States were citizens. Second, their arrival stimulated the Islands' elite to begin confronting the undoubted challenges the rising Nisei constituted to the historic social order of Hawaii. These ranged from the place of Nisei in the plantation economy to their role in the governing of Hawaii. We have seen how resistant the elite was to the idea of education beyond a few years of elementary schooling, and how numerous obstacles were placed in the path of upwardly mobile children of immigrant workers.

At the behest of Hawaii Governor Farrington, in 1922 the U.S. Department of Labor formed the Hawaiian Labor Commission, which issued a report early the next year. It reflected the strong influence of plantation interests by referring to the Japanese menace in the Islands' political life and advocating the cancellation of Nisei citizenship. The public advocacy of these measures by a federally initiated body would have drawn protests from the government of Japan, which the U.S. government wanted to avoid at that time, and so the report was never published. In 1924, on the other hand, Congress passed an Immigration Act that forbade the further immigration of persons who were ineligible for citizenship. Nisei remained citizens but the future supply of potential Nisei was drastically reduced.

It was around this time that a new elite tactic was instituted. In 1927, the first New Americans Conference, an annual event, occurred. From that year until 1941, over 900 Nisei delegates attended. "Throughout the . . . conferences," wrote Nomura, "the Nisei were counseled by the haole elite to accept the existing status quo in Hawaii which limited their occupational opportunities and condemned them to unskilled work."[58] Elite speakers ignored the fact that many delegates were living rejections of the advice. Eighty percent were high school graduates and more than 30% had graduated from universities or normal schools.[59]

At the Sixth Conference, delegate Sayama said, "That while he was a 1937 graduate of the University of Hawaii in sugar technology . . . haole [white] university classmates who were students in training . . . got double his wages. He had . . . left plantation work to engage in business in Honolulu."[60] Another delegate, Clifton H. Yamamoto, who represented Honolulu at the First Conference, declared:

> That a chief barrier that sealed the doorway to "reasonable opportunities" for Nisei was that "many of the large employers . . . fail to look upon the thousands of young men of Japanese ancestry here as genuine Americans" and that these employers "place the youths of Japanese ancestry last in their employment list."[61]

Neither delegates nor elite speakers were unfamiliar with the plight of educated

Nisei. Even when employed in line with their advanced training, Nisei specialists were denigrated at the workplace. For example, "sometimes Asians were
promoted but not permitted to move into the kind of housing normally assigned
to employees in their position."[62] The editor of a Japanese-language newspaper
"criticized racial discrimination that banned Nisei chemists and civil engineers
from participating in the social life of the plantation elites."[63]

Thus, Japanese Americans were not treated as persons of equal human
worth. Many Whites rejected them out of a sense of personal racism and Japanese Americans also suffered from institutional exclusion. The elite was quite
aware of its command of all the institutional resources needed to implement its
economic goals. Fuchs stated, "During the last decades of the nineteenth century and into the second decade of this century, the elite generally agreed that
the Oriental was inferior to the white man and should be kept in a subordinate
status."[64] In 1920, Royal M. Mead, speaking for the HSPA before a Congressional hearing, asserted openly, "I do not think that there is any contest as to
who shall dominate: the white people, the Americans in Hawaii are going to
dominate and will continue to dominate—there is no question about it."[65] This
was not an assertion of personal hate but of institutional power.

Part of the power of the plantation depended on the managers' ability to deny
workers the advantage of unified action. Managers set one ethnic group against
another. The records of various companies provide ample evidence of such a
tactic. In 1895, the manager of McKee Sugar Company wrote, "Keep a variety
of laborers . . . and thus prevent any concerted action in case of strikes, for there
are few, if any, cases of Japs, Chinese, and Portuguese entering into a strike as a
unity."[66] Liu observed that by 1895, "planters were united in their desire to split
the labor force along racial lines."[67] "Diversity," according to Takaki, "was deliberately designed to break strikes and repress unions."[68] Despite this sweeping
policy, however, occasionally workers of two or more ethnic backgrounds successfully engaged in strikes.

Just as the elite reserved for themselves the best housing, jobs, and health facilities, so, too, did they make the best schools a special preserve for their children. The private schools were chosen for this distinction. Before 1920, most
White children attended such schools; between 1925 and 1947, the figure fell to
some 40%.[69] To be sure, most Whites were not members of the elite. Whites of
more modest economic circumstances, as we have seen, were given the privilege
of entering the English Standard high schools in disproportionately high numbers. A token quota of Japanese American and Chinese American students was
permitted to enroll in the most exclusive private schools. A few private schools
before World War II were fairly open to Asian children. This was especially so
for Roman Catholic parochial schools; up to half of the Japanese Americans in
private schools were enrolled in these schools. Here they constituted 7 to 13% of
total attendance.[70] Expenditures per student in the private schools may have
been double those in the public schools. Clearly, one feature of the former was
the higher technical quality of teaching and learning. Another was the often-re-

peated description of a high-ranking private school as exclusive, thus stressing the socially excluding feature of the institution.

Higher education was the capstone of Hawaii's hierarchical educational system. The deliberate failure to build more public high schools automatically narrowed the stream leading to the University of Hawaii. Tamura emphasized that "before 1929 fewer than 20 percent of all *Nisei* who attended school reached the twelfth grade, a proportion that increased to only 28 percent by 1935."[71] The next decade or so saw more progress. "While less than 28 percent of the *Nisei* children in the second grade in 1925 were in the twelfth grade in 1935, 58 percent of those in the second grade in 1933 were in the twelfth grade in 1943."[72] By 1941, the number of Japanese American boys and girls in high school reached parity; in 1918, girls in high school had constituted less than one sixth the number of boys. When these relatively few finally reached the university, they almost never met a *Nisei* faculty member, as these and other non-Whites were virtually excluded from teaching positions.[73] (Among the common schools, underrepresentation rather than exclusion was the experience of Japanese Americans applying for teaching posts.) University of Hawaii *Nisei* students were customarily barred from joining campus fraternities and sororities. Even the original chapter of the national honor society in sociology, Alpha Kappa Delta, tarried for some years before admitting its first non-White sociologist.[74]

On the Mainland

Japanese arrived in numbers during a comparatively short period, 1890 through 1924. The great majority worked for wages but in a decade or so, many had become owners of their farms.[75] By using family and kin as laborers, they were able to dominate labor-intensive crops. Raising strawberries became a specialty in the Moneta-Gardena area of Southern California. On this economic basis, family life was far more vigorous than elsewhere. In 1906, for example, the ratio of Issei men to women was only 3.6 to 1 in the area while it was more than double that in Los Angeles city; in Los Angeles county and Santa Barbara, the figures were 55.2 to 1 and 176 to 1.[76] By 1920, one fifth of all students in Gardena High School were Japanese Americans.[77]

"In some respects," wrote Cox, "race relations on the [West] Coast are internationality relations. . . ."[78] Japan's government played a considerably more active role in defending their emigrants than any other Asian country. As Chan observed: "The federal government treated Japanese immigrants in a far more gingerly way than it did Chinese, Koreans, Indians, and Filipinos."[79] Underlying this relationship between the United States and Japan was a confluence of interest in world politics, especially in the Far East. In resource-rich Manchuria, the northeastern section of China, both Great Powers were united in countering efforts by Czarist Russia to extend its economic and military interests. The two Powers were also mutually accommodating in counteracting each other's territorial expansion in the larger Pacific area. Thus, when the United States annexed the Philippine Islands in 1898, the Japanese did not make an issue of it. In 1910, when Japan annexed Korea, the same forbearance was demonstrated on the part of the United States.[80] When Japan and Russia went to war in 1904 and 1905 the United States offered to mediate at a point at which the exhaustion of Japan's military power was increasingly apparent. The offer was accepted and brought peace as well as a Nobel peace prize for President Theodore Roosevelt.

In 1893, when the San Francisco board of education declared that Japanese students must attend the Chinese school, the Japanese consul protested. Soon the school board retracted its policy.[81] When, however, in 1905, the board of education adopted a similar resolution, it stood fast in the face of objections by the Japanese consul as well as pressure from the federal government. The principal difference in school-board response was a matter of timing. In 1893, an anti-Japanese movement had not yet developed beyond a narrow circle of people. By 1905, it had become a plaything of political parties in the city and beyond.[82] In a compromise whose architect was the Roosevelt administration, the few Japanese (and Korean) students in attendance were permitted to transfer out of the Oriental School and return to nonsegregated schools elsewhere in the city.[83] Just 2 years after this settlement, in 1909, the state assembly passed a bill to segregate Japanese children but on pressure by the federal government, the measure was reconsidered and defeated.[84]

In the years 1909 through 1920, relations between Japan and the United States continued to be mutually supportive on the world scale despite a growing anti-Japanese movement here. It proved politically impossible for the federal government to stop the passage of anti-Japanese measures in state legislatures, especially when the state action was the product of the national administration's own party. In California, the Land Laws of 1913 and 1920 were designed specifically to limit the freedom of Japanese Americans to own or lease farm land. Although Japan protested in each case, and the federal government attempted to alter the decisions, the measures remained on the books. After the conflict in 1905 through 1907 over segregation in San Francisco schools, the issue never again became a matter of national involvement. Land replaced schools as a concern of the anti-Japanese movement in California.[85] This was an indirect evidence that there was nothing inherent in the school issue other than political advantage.

The direct involvement of the Japanese government in Japanese American affairs meant that Japanese Americans were almost the sole immigrant group that could count on the aid of a foreign government, even if the assistance often proved not very helpful. (From time to time, the Mexican government also intervened in matters concerning Mexican Americans being forced to attend segregated schools. At no time, however, was there any special world–political issue at stake between Mexico and the United States. As a result, the intervention bore little fruit.)

Japanese Americans were housed in scattered fashion in towns and cities. In rural areas, where many lived and worked, their dwellings were as isolated as those of anyone else. As Daniels wrote, "Their number in any school was generally so small that the classrooms they attended were truly integrated. Therefore, they participated from early childhood in at least part of the larger society." [86] In Sacramento County, only four elementary schools in small rural towns had sizable Japanese American enrollments. They were Bates Union (Courtland), Florin, Isleton, and Walnut Grove. Florin was the only school in the United States where Japanese Americans made up a majority of the students. Of the 225 students, 172 were listed as Orientals. [87]

Anti-Japanese circles repeatedly pointed to Florin as the wave of the future. Instead of conceding its rarity, they referred to it as the first of many more that threatened to develop. An observer who visited the school around 1915, however, reported a most benevolent scene. Children were playing without friction. To meet the problem of inadequate English among Japanese American first graders, plans were being made for a kindergarten to help them in English instruction. In the community, however, the Japanese Americans were split over school issues. In 1919, a number of their children had failed in school because of inadequate English. Some of the elders voted to stop teaching Japanese in classes sponsored by a Christian church in town. Nearly all of the Christian Japanese supported the move. (A writer in a national magazine described them as principally landowners "who want their children to grow up as American citizens." [88]) Dissenters, organized as a Buddhist party, built a large temple and resumed teaching Japanese. Many Christian children left their Sunday School to study Japanese at the temple. Meanwhile, in 1923, the town's dominant political group, headed by Whites, decided to build two schools, one for the Japanese and one for the Whites. [89] Something like this had happened long before when White Methodists refused to permit Japanese Americans to worship at their church whereon the latter organized one for themselves. [90]

In nearby Livingston where a number of Japanese farm families lived, the economics of the situation were quite different. "Whereas Florin has eight Japanese stores and one American store, the Japanese in Livingston have from the beginning stuck to farming, with the result that the storekeepers became and have remained their friends." [91] Millis reported that most Livingstonian Japanese were Christians who worshipped at the same churches with their White neighbors. Millis added that, "there is no discrimination against them in the school or elsewhere." [92]

In rural sections of Los Angeles County around 1920, agitation for the segregation of Japanese American students centered in Gardena and Moneta school districts. At Gardena High School, Japanese students were prominent among the membership of the California Scholastic Federation (CSF). This was an honor society that was chartered only at schools certified as having high academic standards. In 1920 and 1921, a time when one fifth of all students at Gardena were Japanese Americans, only four Japanese were members of CSF. By 1924 and 1925, the number had risen to 20, and by 1932 and 1933 to 48.[93]

While Japanese Americans were rarely reelected as student leaders, they did participate in various extracurricular affairs. Ethnic factors sometimes led to complications. As Freeman observed, "Racial differences present obvious difficulties for the Japanese in dramatic and musical productions of an occidental nature. However, these people are extraordinarily skillful in the art of make up and are leading members of the make-up crew.[94] They "more than hold their own" in sports, Freeman added, while in the Spanish Club, 57% of the Japanese American members had earned an *A* in Spanish. Socially, four out of five Japanese American fathers and nearly as many White American fathers were artisans, small businessmen, or skilled laborers. Practically none of either group of Gardena parents were professionals, upper executives, or owners of large business.[95] In short, the two groups were very nearly alike, a feature that facilitated integration in the school. (Over a half-century later, Gardena had become an upper middle-class suburb in which Asian-Americans—85% of them Japanese Americans—constituted one third of the town's population. The average educational level of Japanese Americans who had recently moved to the town was a Bachelor's degree.)[96]

In Los Angeles, Japanese Americans were segregated but almost never completely so. Little Tokyo had a White majority of residents. Other minorities were considerably more likely than Whites to live alongside Japanese Americans. As Modell pointed out, "in 1940 roughly half of all city Japanese lived in houses defined as substandard—twice the proportion as among Negroes, although somewhat below the proportion of Mexicans so housed."[97] The neighborhood schools that Japanese American children attended were neither ethnically homogeneous nor academically selective. Teachers warmly welcomed them for their obedience, dependability, and regular attendance. At the same time, during the late 1920s and early 1930s, "starting in junior high, Japanese grades declined toward the average received by all students, until by graduation Japanese grades were slightly below average."[98] (An anonymous publisher's reader suggested: "A possible explanation for relative lowering of Japanese American class rank is that the pressure to stay in school on Japanese children was stronger than on others so that the dropout rate was lower and thus those continuing were less self-selective.") A slightly sour taste was glimpsed in a 1930s "survey of 400 Los Angeles teachers [who] revealed that they believed that the Nisei were not exceptionally bright students; rather, their will to please and achieve was responsible for their academic success."[99]

In Sacramento, Japanese Americans found living space in Japan Town near Lincoln Elementary and Sacramento high schools. In 1910, 64 Japanese children attended one or the other. Aside from this fleeting contact, the children otherwise lived a segregated existence.[100] "They went to Japanese Language School. . . . They participated in all-Japanese Little League . . . went to all-Japanese dances, all-Japanese churches, all-Japanese picnics. . . ." In 1935, a visiting European scholar found that the supposed language handicaps of Japanese American students was used as a pretext in order to separate them from other students. "In a number of elementary schools throughout the state, there are rooms with none but Oriental pupils, or there are separate classes in the lower grades for Orientals." [101] The number of immigrant Japanese children must have been exceedingly small in 1935 when that was written. Since 1924, it had been illegal for persons ineligible for citizenship to immigrate into this country. Very likely, many of the native-born American children thus segregated spoke English as clearly as did their tormentors.

Sometimes, embarrassment led White Americans to advocate the segregation of Japanese American children. In Florin, for example, not only did Japanese engage in the bothersome practice of operating their own stores, their children knew how to play baseball better than some White children. One complaint put it this way:

> The principal was letting Japs crowd our boys off the grammar-school team just because they could play better baseball. The towns around us began to razz our kids because of that, and that created antagonism toward the Japs. You know we have a low grade of Jap here. Even in their own country they are looked down on as a class. They haven't got much ability. Well, we couldn't stand for it any longer, so we segregated our schools. [102]

Reference to "a low grade of Japs here" may have meant to designate the outcaste Burakumin, who in the previous decade had been said to number 10% of the entire Japanese American community. [103]

Sometimes, student services were withheld from Japanese American students, presumably for their own benefit. In Seattle, at the Washington State Vocational School, Monica Sone sought secretarial training. She was told by a counselor, Miss Thompson, that because the school was unable to obtain jobs for Nisei graduates in downtown offices—that is, a color line existed—Nisei could be accepted as students in the school only if they were promised a job by their own people. Miss Sone "knew that the Nisei girls competed fiercely among themselves for white-collar jobs in the Mitsui and Mitsubishi branch firms downtown, local newspaper establishments, Japanese banks, shipping offices and small export and import firms." [104]

There was no shortage of Nisei high-school graduates eligible to attend colleges and universities in California. Proportionately, they were more numerous than White graduates. Nor were Japanese Americans saddled with quotas or other exclusory devices. They were not barred from any academic field. Instead, White employers drew a hard-and-fast color line that simply declared Japanese American college graduates as racially unfit to perform jobs for which they had just completed 4-year courses of study. They now had to seek employment inside the Japanese American community, which had no jobs that required a university preparation. Modell reported that "in 1940 only about 5 percent of Los Angeles City Nisei were working for Caucasian employers, and then very often in 'Japanese' occupations, especially produce."[105] On the sidewalk in front of many Los Angeles supermarkets could be found fruit stands that were attended by recent Nisei graduates of nearby universities and colleges. The picture was the same elsewhere in the state. "Nisei returned home to Sacramento, degrees in hand, only to be denied the jobs for which they were qualified because of racist discrimination against them. . . ."[106] As late as the 1940 through 1941 school year, not a single Japanese American teacher was employed in the Los Angeles public schools. (In 1935, 414 Nisei were public school teachers in Hawaii.[107]) Up and down the West Coast, a similar situation obtained.

During the 1930s, many college-aged Nisei based their college program on the perspective engendered by their father's employment. Because the Nisei were typically small businessmen, their sons tended to specialize in business curricula. At UCLA in 1940, the principal subjects were chosen from business and, less so, economics.[108] These paths led to few opportunities in the larger society and were too expansive for small-scale undertakings such as fruit stands. No wonder that Imazeki, editor of a Japanese-language newspaper, *Hokubei*, recalled in later years that, "a story about the appointment of a Nisei engineer would have been featured on the front page in 1939."[109] This was, after all, the era of a graduate engineer educated at Harvard but now employed as an elevator boy in an apartment house in Los Angeles.[110] Nor was it unknown for Nisei graduates of recognized law schools at the University of Southern California or Gonzaga University to be "prevented from taking the state bar examination, [who then] utilized their training to serve their fellow countrymen simply as 'legal advisers'; none could hang out his shingle or take cases to court."[111]

On the eve of World War II, extremely few Nisei women had graduated from college. Their vocational opportunities were more scarce than those of Nisei men, with or without a degree. A number of Issei and Nisei women were compelled by circumstance to accept positions as domestic workers, low in status and poorly paid. Facility with English seemed irrelevant: In the country as a whole, in 1940, Nisei women were two and one half times more likely to be domestics than Issei women. Nisei predominance held also in San Francisco, Oakland, Los Angeles, and Seattle, but by a much smaller margin.[112] One of the few alternative employments was an office job in Japan-owned businesses. As Glenn reported:

> Because they were barred from jobs in white firms, the pool of qualified Japanese vying for the few white-collar jobs was large. Thus Japanese-owned enterprises could exploit their employees, demanding longer hours and offering lower wages than white employers.[113]

(Japanese companies' discrimination against Nisei women office employees was not unknown in Hawaii, either.[114])

The distribution of Japanese Americans in the labor market was affected by three major factors: (a) employment trends arising out of the changing nature of the economy, (b) the initial economic status of immigrants reflecting the wealth and income of their families back home, and (c) the intensity and breadth of discrimination in their new American home.

During the years of Japanese immigration, the American West was undergoing a process of commercialization and industrialization. The region was being integrated into the larger capitalist economy. This required great amounts of labor, supplied by migrants and immigrants who were plentiful. From their ranks were also recruited small businessmen to service the community needs of laborers. Neither immigrants nor migrants provided any of the large-scale capital projects—such as railroads and mechanized mining equipment—that were financed by East Coast and foreign investors. In 1912, there were 58,555 Japanese in California and around 70% of them were engaged on farms—mostly as laborers.[115] They produced fruit and vegetables for local and national markets. Many moved to towns and cities, out of agriculture altogether, and others became farm owners and commercial tenants. By 1920, wrote Iwata, "the Japanese had been written off as an appreciable source of farm labor."[116] Instead of constituting around 70% of the Japanese population as in 1910, only 37% were now involved in agriculture.[117] It was at this point that farm capitalists rapidly stepped up their hiring of Mexican migrant laborers. Japanese farm owners followed suit. Twenty years later, shortly before World War II, the figure rose to 42%.

"Background characteristics in Japan," according to Woodrum and associates, "are systematically associated with modes of economic adaptation within the United States."[118] Thus, in the United States, Issei who came from large land-holding families in Japan tended to "become self-employed, either as farmers or nonfarm proprietors, or to become elevated managerial or official employees."[119] This suggested that economic ascent in this country was aided by an initial accumulation of capital or advanced education or both. Christian Issei were especially successful in attaining high occupational status.[120] Another avenue for old-country influence was the selective character of Japanese immigrants after 1908 as a consequence of the so-called Gentlemen's Agreement between Japan and the United States. This pact excluded further immigration of Japanese laborers who, of course, were poorer and less educated than other Japanese. Thereafter, the children of these wealthier immigrants made up another middle-class element to the Japanese American community. In 1924, this source was closed off when the Immigration Act of that year ended immigration of persons who were not eligible for U.S. citizenship.

Daniels wrote, "By the eve of World War II most Issei were mildly prosperous members of the lower middle class. By that time Issei families owned farms and businesses to a much greater degree than did the general population."[121] The success of the Issei aroused more envy than admiration. They seemed able to resist the worst effects of restrictive legislation aimed at them. The land law passed by the California state legislature in 1913 was designed to restrict Issei access to farm land, but it failed of its purpose. During the next 7 years, "their lands under lease [rose] from 155,488 to 192,150 acres and their lands under ownership from 26,707 to 74,769 acres."[122] A new, more effective land law was enacted in 1920. Leased land dropped to 76,397 acres and owned land to 41,898 acres.[123] Even then, cooperative Whites helped numerous Issei avoid or evade the law. In addition, Nisei, as citizens, were permitted by law to be registered as owners of their father's farm.

Discrimination against Japanese Americans was effected in several ways: (a) exclusion, either by preventing initial entry or through deportation once here; (b) denial of naturalization, by refusing an initial grant or annulment of a past grant; (c) economic discrimination, such as the land laws; and education discrimination, such as measures requiring segregation. Chan counted 95 cases involving Japanese Americans that were litigated in federal courts; she suggested there were many more.[124]

As of 1939, there was not a single federal law or administrative regulation forbidding racial discrimination in employment. Nor had there ever been. The federal Constitution was not thought to cover such matters. Asian-Americans, along with other minorities, were subjected to job bias without any legal recourse. Politicians on all levels of government were free to indulge their racial dislikes in selecting candidates, formulating employment and other policies, and constructing programs for legislative action. Private employers manipulated racial factors at will. Japanese Americans thus joined a long line of citizens and noncitizens alike who lacked a remedy for some of the gravest injuries they suffered.

Before World War II, wrote Yoo:

> Virtually all Nisei journalists used the term "American" to refer to white Americans and used racial qualifiers to denote other groups including themselves. Despite the fact that the many Nisei saw themselves as "Americans," they rarely referred to themselves as such.[125]

American was a term reserved for persons who exercised the freedoms so volubly present in speech, sermon, and song, if not otherwise in daily life.

The wartime years 1942 through 1945 were the most sorrowful in the history of Japanese Americans. In the past, the connection with Japan had served as a shield from some of the most painful deprivations. Now, it became a mark of disgrace. Activated by the highest levels of the United States government, approved by President Roosevelt and the Supreme Court, the federal Constitution was laid aside in the name of military necessity and justified by a racist theory. Persons of Japanese ancestry living in the Western Military District, whether citizens or not, were declared to be a danger to the country and ordered to be imprisoned in 1 of 10 concentration camps.[126] Japanese Americans living in the midwest or east were not affected. No charges were lodged against individuals for having committed specific acts, nor were any trials held before or after some 110,000 Japanese Americans were confined. In the camps, Okamura noted, "the written orders were enforced with barbed wire fences, guard towers, search lights, and machine guns."[127]

In Hawaii, mass arrests of Japanese Americans did not occur. Businessmen and others argued successfully that imprisoning a third or more of the Island's labor force would only paralyze the local economy, including the war effort. Nevertheless, some Japanese Americans were incarcerated. Somewhat fewer than 1,500 were placed in concentration camps built in Hawaii. Another 1,100 or more became inmates in mainland camps.[128] As Okihiro reported:

> The Japanese [in Hawaii] were generally excluded from higher-paying defense work and were concentrated in lower-paying agricultural and service jobs, were harassed and intimidated in union activities, were impressed into labor battalions that donated their weekends to "voluntary" work, and were sentenced to hard labor for petty offenses.[129]

The 100th Infantry Battalion of the U.S. Army consisted solely of Hawaiian Nisei, giving rise among its members to a bitter self-characterization of "Jap Crow."[130]

In the mainland camps, some 30,000 students attended school. They were doubly isolated. Physically, the camps were located in virtually uninhabited areas and thus there were extremely few neighboring regular schools. Even where there were such schools, nearly all rejected overtures from the concentration camp institutions. In addition, the children of the camps were isolated in another sense: Almost no national or regional educators' organization publicly defended or advocated the cause of camp schools. This included the Los Angeles and Berkeley campuses of the University of California and the National Education Association. An exception was the American Federation of Teachers, which "stressed that discrimination against loyal Americans and aliens was contrary to American principles and beliefs."[131] On a more mundane level, when the PTA at the Manzanar, California, concentration camp was turned away from the regional organization of PTAs in surrounding districts, the Manzanar group affiliated directly with the National Congress of Parent–Teacher Associations in Chicago, nearly 2,000 miles away.[132]

Physical facilities were singularly inadequate. At Manzanar, for example, "there were no seats, desks, books or other school equipment for a considerable time after school opened, a condition which prompted many students to drop out, believing the program would be of little value."[133] Maintenance work was minimal. "The Engineering section gave the construction of hog pens in the fall of 1943 precedence over making schoolroom doors tight against the winter weather."[134] At the camp in Minidoka, Idaho, "inside a typical building that was closed as tightly as it could be without alterations, the dust covered a typewritten page so thickly that it could no longer be read after a fifteen minute interval had elapsed."[135] At the Tule Lake, California concentration camp, "there were no blackboards, textbooks, or teaching materials when school opened [in September 1941]." [136] Referring to the camp schools as a whole, Wollenberg wrote that "the facilities, equipment [and] materials . . . were second-rate at best." [137]

Nevertheless, the quality of education offered at the concentration camps was validated, in part at least, by other institutions. For example, senior students at Hunt High School at Minedoka camp sent a transcript of their grades to their old high school so that they could receive a diploma from it. The one-time principal at Hunt observes that he knew "of no instance in which a school refused to do so upon the request of the pupil." [138]

Another form of validation was based on the number of camp high-school graduates who were accepted by colleges during the war. Generally, such students were assisted by camp authorities only if they ranked in the top 10% of their graduating class. [139] This suggested that many seniors could not realistically expect much encouragement to go on to college. Indeed, it was not unknown for some teachers actively to discourage entry into college. James, having studied the results of standardized tests given young inmates, found that, "previously average students with a good number of high achievers in their schools before the war, Japanese Americans had fallen more than a year behind their grade in basic subjects." [140]

The concentration-camp schools were marked by a central contradiction: They were expected to educate people who were being unjustly deprived of their freedom every day. Students were quite aware of this and frequently voiced their objections to it. James recorded some examples: A Nisei girl wrote:

> This action will cause the history of the United States to have another black mark: first the Indians, next the Negroes, and now the Japanese. . . . And then deportation? . . . [A girl screams in class.] Why did they do this to us? . . . . Why were we treated like animals? . . . . If we are citizens, why are we in concentration camps?

A student speaker at a junior high school graduation declared, "We stand for tolerance for we know the injustice and bitterness that can arise where there is bigotry and intolerance." [141]

To be sure, as one teacher put it, "It was extremely difficult to teach the ideas and ideals of democratic society . . . when constant reminders confronted boys and girls with evidence of prejudice and undemocratic procedures." [142] A number of teachers, acting on their own, urged students to examine the problematic aspects of this situation. At Minidoka camp, a committee of seven students wrote a 40-page report on minorities in the United States. It carried this dedication: "Our committee . . . dedicates this booklet to the colored people all over the world, knowing what it means to be discriminated against and disliked." [143] The official goals of the concentration-camp schools, on the other hand, did not embrace any such value.

Early on, inmate students feared that teachers would wish to justify the concentration camps. Few apparently did. Shimano noted the result in one instance:

> In a high school civics class . . . the instructor following the textbook, attempted to

teach that the United States government is a democratic institution based on the principle "that all men are created equal." The pupils, uprooted from their homes without due process of law, guilty of no crime except being born of Japanese parents, American citizens with no right of appeal, penned in by barbed wire fences, laughed uproariously. The class had to be dismissed.[144]

It must be kept in mind that in each of the 10 concentration camps, parents were imprisoned along with their children. The oppression was stark, immediate, and sweeping, leaving no room for idle theorizing.

By 1945, the number of camp inmates had fallen to some 80,000 from 110,000 2 years before.[145] Enrollment in the schools declined correspondingly. A small part of the reduction represented young men who had volunteered for the armed services. Others had successfully applied to attend colleges or universities in areas far removed from the camps. Still others had moved as entire families to Chicago and other cities. Many of the remaining inmates were hesitant about returning to their homes on the West Coast out of fear for the reception they might experience.[146]

Decades after the last concentration camp closed, the whole episode was being described as unique and unprecedented. In fact, it was neither. Forerunners of various parts of the experience could be found throughout United States and world history.

Concentration camps seem to have arisen in the late 19th century within a context of colonialism. In the 1890s, Spain introduced them to help suppress the Cuban revolutionary movement for independence; later in the same decade, Great Britain used the camps in South Africa to put down the Boers. An essential element in this technique was a readiness to erase the long-existing line between military and civilian forces. Concentration-camp inmates were not camp followers who had freely chosen to accompany an armed force. They were unarmed civilians whose incarceration had been designated as a military objective. Nearly always, the military authorities charged that secret ties linked the civilians and enemy armed forces.[147]

During the early stages of World War I, on the Russo–German front, Russian government sources suddenly declared that many Russian Jews living in that area were pro-German spies. Up and down the line, entire communities of Jews were moved hundreds of miles into the interior. They lost their homes, most possessions, and were subjected to extreme personal indignities. Further to the south, in Turkey at about the same time, thousands of Armenians were treated far more horrendously. They were torn out of far-flung regions and marched for hundreds of miles. Children and the aged died in large numbers. Although the usual charges of treason were hurled at the innocent, executions were the order of the day. Their farms and other properties were confiscated. These events were some of the first genocides of the 20th century.[148]

In U.S. history, Native Americans were subjected to enslavement and genocide as well as concentration camps in the form of reservations. In the 1830s,

Southern Indians were compelled to participate in long forced marches in which many died, especially the very young and the aged. There were many similar experiences among Native Americans. During the Great Depression of the 1930s, Mexican Americans, including many who were American citizens, were deported to Mexico. This event was called *repatriation* by the Americans even though many of the deported had been born in the United States. An unsuccessful effort was also made to deport large numbers of Filipinos.[149]

Government violations of the personal security of citizens and immigrants were widespread in the three decades preceding World War I. Many of these actions originated in class conflicts between employers and workers involved in unionization. In the Southwest, strike leaders and participants were arrested by sheriffs and shipped away from the scene of the conflict. They were packed onto trains and transported like iron bars. Rifles, machine guns, and later, tear gas, were utilized by employers in these battles as they greatly outgunned unionists. Japanese farm workers—as well as their predecessors, the Chinese—were swooped up by White workers and others and shipped away. In 1934, the governor of Georgia called out the National Guard to suppress the textile workers' strike in that state. The Guard set up a detention camp where strikers—arrested on vague charges—were placed. A statement by the American Civil Liberties Union denounced the establishment of concentration camps for workers. Within days, Nazi newspapers in Hitler Germany hailed the U.S. camp as meriting for Roosevelt the title of Nazi Fuehrer of America.[150]

Military historians had undoubtedly analyzed the use of concentration camps in the Cuban Revolution and the Boer War. It was not surprising that a former Assistant Secretary of the Navy-turned-U.S. President—Franklin D. Roosevelt—should have been familiar with the device. Even the Hitler regime's use of concentration camps did not deter Roosevelt from suggesting in 1936 that the United States might also use these in the event of a war with Japan. He also employed the term positively in September, 1942, when 110,000 Japanese Americans were already in the camps.[151]

A historian of the Nazi concentration camps defined them as "camps in which persons are imprisoned without regard to the accepted norms of arrest and detention."[152] The absence of specific charges and no opportunity to defend themselves in any adversarial proceeding directly violated U.S. norms of due process of law. In addition, as historian Pingel noted of the Nazi camps, "the regime imprisoned in such camps political adversaries and persons considered socially or racially undesirable."[153] In the U.S. military orders decreeing imprisonment in concentration camps, persons were singled out for no other reason than that they were of Japanese ancestry. Pingel correspondingly pointed out that during the latter half of 1938, German "Jews were interned in the camps solely because they were Jews."[154] Extermination camps such as Auschwitz were far worse than concentration camps and had no counterpart in the United States. Nevertheless, older people in the U.S. camps expected the worst. A teacher in Minidoka concentration camp recalled, "They believed, I was told, that they were to be thrown out of the train to die in an inhospitable desert, the habitat of deadly rattlesnakes."[155]

Although not a single Japanese American was found guilty of a disloyal act, all were denied the government protection due to citizens. Citizen or not, all were subjected to the daily humiliation of degrading treatment that was designed to suppress feelings of self-worth. Virtual impoverishment followed the few days of advance notice all had received before boarding the trains. Outright confiscation would not have been a much more effective blow for most. Life savings vanished. People who had prided themselves for generations on their capacity to withstand adversity were left helpless in the face of a man-made calamity.

Japanese Americans were stunned by the camp experience. Living in a free republic did not protect them from tyranny. Their rights as human beings, let alone as citizens, had proven impermanent and fragile. They were as unprepared, however, to remedy its effects as they had been to experience the event in the first place. In the end, a relative handful migrated to Japan, but by far, most remained and struggled for their dignity. Japanese Americans were now less autonomous culturally; as the Issei died, traditional Japanese culture became more distant. But they also became more self-reliant politically and socially; their fate was less in the hands of others.

In an extremely laggard response to a Japanese American community movement for redress for the concentration-camp experience, in 1948 and 1988 Congress passed the Japanese American Claims Act and the Civil Liberties Act that awarded each survivor a cash grant; a blanket apology was also included.

Recovery from the calamity was aided by large-scale changes in the U.S. economy that extended until the mid-1970s. By then, a new basis had been created for the Japanese American community.

Takahashi wrote that "the occupational shifts for each of the historical generations within the community parallel structural shifts in the larger economy."[156] In the post-World War II years, Japanese American students were shifting to engineering and the physical sciences and more were studying law and education. Takahashi explained:

> This type of clustering suggests that Japanese American educational strategies were largely conditioned by the shifts in a postwar political economy that placed greater emphasis on technological and science-oriented occupations, as well as jobs at all levels of the state bureaucracies.[157]

During the late 1950s and early 1960s, at the University of California, Berkeley, Japanese American students were still concentrated in "business administration, optometry, engineering, or some middle-level profession. . . . For them, education was obviously a means of acquiring a salable skill that could be used either in the general commercial world or, if that remained closed, in a small personal enterprise."[158] The few well-trained Japanese American technical and scientific researchers at this time "could not find good jobs and advance very far in California."[159]

In Hawaii, the 1950s saw a political change that was especially consequential for Japanese Americans. In 1954, the Democratic Party swept the elections and 5 years later, Hawaii attained statehood. Japanese Americans had been highly active in both developments and were able to expand and consolidate their employment position as a result. This included electoral candidates as well as civil service and other administrative positions.

By 1980, Japanese Americans constituted 24.9% of the state's population and 32% of the labor force. At or about the same time, they filled the following slots:[160]

1970	61.5% of dentists
1970	21.4% of architects
1970	24.7 of attorneys
1978	59.8% of teachers, librarians, and registrars
1978	65.6% of principals and state and district school officers
1980	33.1% of professionals
1985	47.0% of state department heads
1985	62.5% of state legislators

Japanese Americans were also well-represented in small and medium-sized businesses. They proved less able to breach the walls of large business that continued to be almost an exclusive precinct of the White elite.

Higher education played a critical role in producing an increasingly professionalized Japanese American labor force, both in Hawaii and California. Unlike the Chinese Americans, however, Japanese American professionalization proceeded apart from any significant aid from rising immigration after 1965. The Japanese American social structure was home-grown, not imported. It was able to develop on the basis of earlier achievements. The first Japanese American is said to have received a bachelor's degree in 1914. By the early 1930s, and perhaps before that, a University of California Japanese Alumni Association already existed.[161] In the many chapters of the book of anti-Japanese discrimination in the United States, higher education remained open to Japanese Americans. (At one time or another, African-Americans, Jews, and Catholics were subjected to exclusion and/or quotas.) When civil rights measures struck down many of the remaining discriminations in the field of employment, Japanese Americans were well-positioned to take advantage of the new opportunities.

CONCLUDING REMARKS

In the mid-1960s, at the height of the Civil Rights movement, a new stereotype arose in the United States. It was the Japanese American as a model for other minorities. They were described as being among the most patriotic of Americans. Despite their years of discrimination, topped by the concentration-camp experience, Japanese Americans were said to be uncomplaining and successful. Conservatives who were upset by the demonstrative and critical ways of African- and Hispanic Americans urged adoption of the quiet and well-behaved model instead. Greatly disturbed by the cynical doubts cast by civil rights participants on the supposed principles of equality, conservatives needed nothing so much as living proof that racism was merely an evil memory.

The new stereotype served this need well. As embodied in newspaper and magazine articles, Japanese Americans were characterized as self-reliant, not dependent on charity, industrious and achievement-oriented, and not eternally dwelling on their grievances.[162] Conservatives insisted that if African-Americans could not match this record, it was their fault, not American society's. As Ogawa pointed out:

> The tragedy for white America in the 1960s was that its precarious value system came under bombardment by dissident forces that exposed the existence of racism (in fact) and equality (in fantasy) within the same structure. Many Anglo Americans found themselves in crisis, torn between what they feared to be true—their racism—and what they knew to be right—their equalitarianism.[163]

A somewhat similar analysis presented by Ueda contended that making "the Japanese American the ethnic superstar . . . satisfies the popular need to believe in the mythology of America as the land of opportunity and equality."[164] The makers of the new stereotype also believed their own mythology.

The greatest myth of both old and new stereotypes held that Japanese Americans abstracted themselves from collective action aimed at changing community conditions. In fact, however, this was not true. Much of what appeared as political quietism among Issei immigrants was a result of their noncitizen status. Nothing in Japanese politics had prepared them for party conflicts in this country. On the other hand, the Issei generation recorded many collective accomplishments in the public arena. In Hawaii, the Issei sugar plantation workers organized unions, conducted strikes, and from time to time won some. They did not have any experience in Japan that helped in this regard, as strikes were severely suppressed in the homeland. Lobbying was conducted in Hawaii and California against bills requiring racial segregation in schools, delegations appeared before local school boards and municipal commissions, and community collections of funds were often conducted to file lawsuits on significant issues related to immigration and citizenship matters. Often, the Issei used contacts at the Japanese consulates to pursue community interests.

In the 1930s, the Nisei were beginning to replace the Issei in community leadership. Takahashi reported of a group of Nisei progressives late in the decade, "They worked with their Chinese American counterparts to secure more government jobs. Circulating a petition in 1939, they sought support for bills aimed at guaranteeing equal rights for racial minorities in the areas of employment, housing, and civil liberties."[165] Such cooperation with Chinese Americans was not typical. After the full-scale Japanese invasion of China in 1937, relations between the two groups in the United States became deeply embittered. Thirty years later, many of the Sansei were following the lead of a latter-day model minority, African-Americans who organized and led the U.S. Civil Rights movement. These Japanese Americans did not advocate blending into the African-American movement as much as learning from that movement how to combine the sometimes clashing features of liberation and group identity.[166] Out of this involvement came the Asian-American Studies Movement, although it had other sources as well.[167] It will be recalled that the seven young Nisei students at the Minidoka concentration camp school declared their solidarity with African-Americans out of a profound identification of the Japanese Americans, African-Americans, and Native Americans.

NOTES

[1] Tetsuya Kobayashi, *Society, Schools, and Progress in Japan* (Pergamon Press, 1976), p. 8.

[2] John Whitney Hall, ed., *The Cambridge History of Japan*, Vol. 4: *Early Modern Japan* (Cambridge University Press, 1991), p. 717.

[3] Richard Rubinger, *Private Academies of Tokugawa Japan* (Princeton University Press, 1982), pp. 9–10.

[4] Kobayashi, p. 19.

[5] Hugh L. Keenleyside and A. F. Thomas, *History of Japanese Education and Present Educational System* (Hokuseido Press, 1937), p. 36.

[6] Hall, p. 469.

[7] Marius B. Jensen, ed., *The Cambridge History of Japan*, Vol. 5: *The Nineteenth Century* (Cambridge University Press, 1989), p. 3.

[8] E. Sydney Crawcour, "The Tokugawa Heritage," p. 35 in William W. Lockwood, ed., *The State and Economic Enterprise in Japan* (Princeton University Press, 1965).

[9] Kobayashi, p. 19.

[10] Herbert Passin, *Society and Education in Japan* (Teachers College, Columbia University, 1965), p. 57.

[11] See R. P. Dore, *Education in Tokugawa Japan* (University of California Press, 1965), p. 20.

[12] Kobayashi, pp. 12, 20.

[13] Ibid., p. 19.

[14] Dore, p. 299.

[15] Alan Takeo Moriyama, "The Causes of Emigration: The Background of Japanese Emigration to Hawaii, 1885 to 1894," p. 250 in Lucie Cheng and Edna Bonacich, eds., *Labor Immigration under Capitalism* (University of California Press, 1984).

[16] Ibid., p. 251.

[17] Peter Duus, ed., *The Cambridge History of Japan*, vol. 6: *The Twentieth Century* (Cambridge University Press, 1988), p. 402.

[18] See Kobayashi, p. 27; Passin, p. 80; Lockwood, p. 378; Jensen, p. 371; Isao Horinouchi, *Educational Values and Preadaptation in the Acculturation of Japanese Americans* (Sacramento Anthropological Society, Sacramento State College, 1967), p. 7, and Edward K. Strong, Jr., *The Second-Generation Japanese-Problem* (Stanford University Press, 1934), pp. 186–187.

[19]Research and Statistics Division, Minister's Secretariat, Ministry of Education, Science and Culture, ed., *Japan's Modern Educational System. A History of the First Hundred Years* (Printing Bureau, Ministry of Finance, 1980), p. 42. Curiously, Keenleyside and Thomas write that fees were low or nonexistent, p. 90.

[20]Ibid., p. 100.

[21]Ibid., p. 51.

[22]R. P. Dore, "Education in Japan's Growth," *Pacific Affairs*, 37 (Spring 1964), p. 70.

[23]Ibid., p. 69.

[24]Duus, *The Twentieth Century*, p. 402.

[25]Ibid., p. 562.

[26]Keenleyside and Thomas, p. 107.

[27]*Japan's Modern Educational System*, pp. 50–51.

[28]Ibid., p. 119.

[29]Koji Taira, "Education and Literacy in Meiji Japan: An Interpretation," *Explorations in Economic History*, 8 (Summer 1971), p. 375.

[30]Ibid., p. 387. Taira explained his nomenclature: "One would equate education shorter than 4 years to 'semi-literacy,' 4 or 5 years to 'literacy', and 6 years or more to functional literacy," p. 377.

[31]Duus, p. 590.

[32]Alan Takeo Moriyama, *Imingaisha. Japanese Emigration Companies and Hawaii 1894–1908* (University of Hawaii Press, 1985), p. xviii.

[33]Yasuo Wakatsuki, "Japanese Emigration to the United States, 1866–1924: A Monograph," *Perspectives in American History*, 12 (1979), p. 410.

[34]Moriyama, *Imingaisha*, p. 22.

[35]Eileen H. Tamura, *The Americanization Campaign and Assimilation of the Nisei in Hawaii, 1920 to 1940* (Doctoral dissertation, University of Hawaii, 1990) p. 50. See also Harry A. Millis, *The Japanese Problem in the United States* (Macmillan, 1915), p. 230; and Masakazu Iwata, *Planted in Good Soil. The History of the Issei in United States Agriculture*, vol. 1 (Peter Lang, 1991), pp. 94, 166.

[36]Wakatsuki, p. 515.

[37]Mitziko Sawada, "Culprits and Gentlemen: Meiji Japan's Restrictions of Emigrants to the United States, 1891–1909," *Pacific Historical Review*, 60 (1991), p. 352.

[38]Ibid., pp. 349–350. The document is dated July 1904.

[39]John M. Liu, "Race, Ethnicity, and the Sugar Plantation System: Asian Labor in Hawaii, 1850 to 1900," p. 195 in Lucie Cheng and Edna Bonacich, eds., *Labor Immigration Under Capitalism* (University of California Press, 1984).

[40]Lawrence H. Fuchs, *Hawaii Pono: A Social History* (Harcourt, Brace and World, 1961), p. 38.

[41]See Takie Okumura, *Seventy Years of Divine Blessings* (N.p., 1940, pp. 37–40.

[42]Ronald Takaki, *Pau Hana. Plantation Life and Labor in Hawaii 1835–1920* (University of Hawaii Press, 1983), p. 80.

[43]Ibid., p. 158.

[44]Fuchs, *Hawaii Pono*, p. 33.

[45]Ibid., p. 206.

[46]Tamura, *The Americanization Campaign*, p. 162.

[47]Ibid., p. 162.

[48]Gary Y. Okihiro, *Cane Fires, The Anti-Japanese Movement in Hawaii, 1865–1945* (Temple University Press, 1991), p. 140.

[49]Amy Agbayani and David Takeuchi, "English Standard Schools: A Policy Analysis," p. 38 in Nobuya Tsuchida, ed., *Issues in Asian and Pacific American Education* (National Association for Asian and Pacific American Education, 1986). A rather weak defense against charges of school discrimination can be found in Bernhard L. Hormann, "Integration in Hawaii's Schools," *Social Process in Hawaii*, 21 (1957), p. 7.

[50]Michael Haas, *Institutional Racism*, p. 169.

[51] Hormann, "Integration in Hawaii's Schools," p. 6.

[52] Ralph K. Steuber, "Twentieth-Century Educational Reform in Hawaii," *Educational Perspectives*, 20 (Winter 1981), pp. 12, 16.

[53] Okihiro, *Cane Fires*, p. 140.

[54] Tamura, *The Americanization Campaign*, p. 161.

[55] Connor B. Stroupe, *Significant Factors in the Influx to Private Schools on Oahu Since 1900* (Master's thesis, University of Hawaii, 1955), p. 40.

[56] Fuchs, *Hawaii Pono*, p. 291.

[57] Tamura, *The Americanization Campaign*, p. 256. See also Fuchs, *Hawaii Pono*, p. 29 and James H. Okahata, ed., *A History of Japanese in Hawaii* (United Japanese Society of Hawaii, 1971), p. 247.

[58] Gail M. Nomura, "The Debate Over the Role of Nisei in Prewar Hawaii: The New Americans Conference, 1927–41," *Journal of Ethnic Studies*, 15 (Spring 1987), p. 103.

[59] Ibid., p. 103.

[60] Ibid., p. 106.

[61] Ibid., p. 107.

[62] Tamura, *The Americanization Campaign*, pp. 173–174.

[63] Ibid., p. 178.

[64] Fuchs, *Hawaii Pono*, p. 50.

[65] Ibid., p. 153.

[66] Ibid., p. 210.

[67] Liu, "Race, Ethnicity, and the Sugar Plantation System," p. 203.

[68] Ronald Takaki, *Strangers from a Different Shore. A History of Asian Americans* (Penguin, 1989), pp. 25–26.

[69] Fuchs, *Hawaii Pono*, p. 61 and Tamura, *The Americanization Campaign*, p. 231.

[70] Tamura, *The Americanization Campaign*, p. 234.

[71] Ibid., p. 210.

[72] Ibid., p. 220.

[73] Ibid., p. 395.

[74] William Carlson Smith, *Americans in Process. A Study of Our Citizens of Oriental Ancestry* (Arno Press, 1970, orig. 1937), p. 193.

[75] Masakazu Iwata, *Planted in Good Soil. The History of the Issei in United States Agriculture*, 2 vols. (Peter Lang, 1992), vol. 1, p. 400. See also Eric Woodrum and others, "Japanese American Economic Behavior: Its Types, Determinants, and Consequences," *Social Forces*, 58 (June 1980), p. 1237 who write about this change having transpired over a period of 25 years.

[76] Lane Ryo Hirabayashi and George Tanaka, "The Issei Community in Moneta and the Gardena Valley, 1900–1920," *Southern California Quarterly*, 70 (Summer, 1988), p. 139.

[77] George H. Freeman, *A Comparative Investigation of the School Achievement and Socio-economic Background of the Japanese-American Students and the White-American Students of Gardena High School* (Master's thesis, University of Southern California, 1938), p. 2.

[78] Oliver C. Cox, "The Nature of the Anti-Asiatic Movement on the Pacific Coast," *Journal of Negro Education*, 15 (October 1946), p. 613.

[79] Sucheng Chan, "European and Asian Immigration into the United States in Comparative Perspective, 1820s to 1920s," p. 62 in Virginia Yans-McLaughlin, ed., *Immigration Reconsidered* (Oxford University Press, 1990). See also Roger Daniels, "The Japanese," p. 41 in John Higham, ed., *Ethnic Leadership in America* (Johns Hopkins University Press, 1978).

[80] See Chan, "European and Asian," p. 63 and James K. Eyre, Jr., "Japan and the American Annexation of the Philippines," *Pacific Historical Review*, 11 (1942), pp. 55–72.

[81] Roger Daniels, *Asian America. Chinese and Japanese in the United States Since 1850* (University of Washington Press, 1988), pp. 111–112.

[82] See James Boswell Herndon, *The "Japanese School Incident." An Anecdote for Racial Hostility* (Master's thesis, San Francisco State College, 1967); David Brudnoy, "Race and the San Francisco

School Board Incident: Contemporary Evaluations," *California Historical Quarterly*, (September 1971), pp. 295–312; and Roger Daniels, *The Politics of Prejudice. The Anti-Japanese Movement in California and the Struggle for Japanese Exclusion* (University of California Press, 1977).

[83] Frank F. Chuman, *The Bamboo People: The Law and Japanese-Americans* (Publisher's, Inc., 1976), p. 31.

[84] Daniels, *The Politics of Prejudice*, p. 47.

[85] Ibid., p. 48.

[86] Daniels, "The Japanese," p. 47.

[87] Reginald Bell, *A Study of the Educational Effects of Segregation Upon Japanese Children in American Schools* (Doctoral dissertation, Stanford University, 1932), pp. 22–23, footnote 26.

[88] Millis, *The Japanese Problem in the United States*, p. 168.

[89] Winifred Raushenbush, "Their Place in the Sun. Japanese Farmers Nine Years after the Land Laws," *Survey Graphic*, 56 (May 1, 1926), p. 143.

[90] Millis, *The Japanese Problem in the United States*, p. 169.

[91] Raushenbush, "Their Place in the Sun," p. 144.

[92] Millis, *The Japanese Problem in the United States*, p. 195.

[93] Freeman, *A Comparative Investigation*, pp. 25, 27.

[94] Ibid., p. 50.

[95] Ibid., p. 71.

[96] Philip Motoo Okamoto, *Evolution of a Japanese American Enclave: Gardena, California. A Case Study of Ethnic Community Change and Continuity* (Master's thesis, University of California, Los Angeles, 1991), pp. 41, 53.

[97] John Modell, *The Economics and Politics of Racial Accommodation. The Japanese of Los Angeles, 1900–1942* (University of Illinois Press, 1977), pp. 71–72.

[97] Ibid., pp. 157–158. Modell is here reporting findings of a 1935 study by Reginald Bell.

[98] Ibid., p. 159.

[100] Cheryl L. Cole, *A History of the Japanese Community in Sacramento, 1883–1972: Organizations, Businesses, and Generational Response to Majority Domination and Stereotypes* (R and E Research Associates, 1974), p. 34.

[101] B. Schrieke, *Alien Americans. A Study of Race Relations* (Viking Press, 1936), p. 45.

[102] Ibid., p. 45.

[103] Raushenbush, "Their Place in the Sun," p. 143.

[104] Monica Sone, *Nisei Daughter* (Little, Brown, 1953), p. 133.

[105] Modell, *The Economics and Politics of Racial Accommodation*, p. 132.

[106] Cole, *A History of the Japanese Community in Sacramento*, p. 34.

[107] Okahata, *A History of Japanese in Hawaii*, p. 249.

[108] Modell, *The Economics and Politics of Racial Accommodation*, p. 128.

[109] Dorothy Anne Stroup, *The Role of the Japanese Press in Its Community* (Master's thesis, University of California, Berkeley, 1960), p. 99.

[110] *Orientals and Their Cultural Adjustment* (Social Science Institute, Fisk University, 1946), pp. 81–82.

[111] Iwata, *Planted in Good Soil*, I, p. 9.

[112] Evelyn Nakano Glenn, "Occupational Ghettoization: Japanese American Women and Domestic Service, 1905–1970," *Ethnicity*, 8 (1981), pp. 363–364.

[113] Ibid., p. 367.

[114] Nomura, "The Debate Over the Role of Nisei in Prewar Hawaii," p. 107.

[115] Kaizo Naka, *Social and Economic Conditions Among Japanese Farmers in California* (Master's thesis, University of California, Berkeley, 1913), p. 15; and Robert M. Jiobu, "Ethnic Hegemony and the Japanese of California," *American Sociological Review*, 53 (June 1988), p. 360

[116] Masakuzu Iwata, "The Japanese Immigrants in California Agriculture," *Agricultural History*, 36 (January 1962), p. 29.

[117]Robert M. Jiobu, "Ethnic Hegemony and the Japanese of California," *American Sociological Review*, 53 (June 1988), p. 360.

[118]Woodrum and Associates, "Japanese American Economic Behavior," p. 1253.

[119]Ibid., p. 1243.

[120]See Sucheng Chan, *Asian Americans. An Interpretive History* (Twayne, 1991), p. 73.

[121]Roger Daniels, "Japanese Immigrants on a Western Frontier: The Issei in California, 1890–1940," p. 86 in F. Hilary Conroy and T. Scott Miyakawa, eds., *East Across the Pacific. Historical and Sociological Studies of Japanese Immigration and Assimilation* (Clio Press, 1972). A more glowing picture of Issei prosperity can be found in Robert Higgs, "Landless by Law: Japanese Immigrants in California Agriculture to 1941," *Journal of Economic History*, 38 (March 1978), p. 223.

[122]Takaki, *Strangers from a Different Shore*, p. 205.

[123]Ibid., p. 206.

[124]See Sucheng Chan, *Asian Americans*, pp. 90–94, p. 209, footnote 11.

[125]David Yoo, "'Read All About It': Race, Generation and the Japanese American Press, 1925–41," *Amerasia Journal*, 19 (1993), p. 74.

[126]See Raymond Y. Okamura, "The American Concentration Camps: A Cover-Up through Euphemistic Terminology," *Journal of Ethnic Studies*, 10 (Fall 1982), pp. 95–108. See also Harry P. Howard, "Americans in Concentration Camps," *Crisis*, 49 (1942), pp. 282–284, 301–302. This magazine was published by the NAACP.

[127]Okamura, "Concentration Camps," p. 100.

[128]Okihiro, *Cane Fires*, p. 267.

[129]Ibid., p. 271.

[130]Roger Daniels, *Concentration Camps: North America Japanese in the United States and Canada During World War II* (Krieger, 1989), p. 151.

[131]William D. Zeller, *An Educational Drama. The Educational Program Provided the Japanese Americans During the Relocation Period, 1942–1945* (American Press, 1969), p. 174.

[132]Ibid., pp. 139–140.

[133]Rollin Clay Fox, *The Secondary School Program at the Manzanar War Relocation Center* (Doctoral dissertation, UCLA, 1946), p. 39.

[134]Ibid., p. 76.

[135]Jerome T. Light, *The Development of a Junior-Senior High School Program in a Relocation Center for People of Japanese Ancestry during the War with Japan*, 4 volumes (Doctoral dissertation, Stanford University, 1947), vol. 1, p. 126.

[136]Donald O. Johnson, *The War Relocation Authority Schools of Tule Lake, California* (Master's thesis, Stanford University, 1947), p. 41.

[137]Charles Wollenberg, *All Deliberate Speed. Segregation and Exclusion in California Schools, 1855–1975* (University of California Press, 1976), p. 80.

[138]Light, *The Development of a Junior-Senior High School Program*, vol 2, pp. 448–449. See the relevant remark in Frances E. Haglund, "Behind Barbed Wire," *Integrateducation*, 16 (March–April 1978), p. 6.

[139]Michi N. Weglyn, *Years of Infamy. The Untold Story of America's Concentration Camps* (Morrow Quill Paperbacks, 1976), p. 107.

[140]Thomas James, *Exile Within. The Schooling of Japanese Americans 1942–1945* (Harvard University Press, 1987), p. 74.

[141]Ibid., pp. 62–63, 76.

[142]Ibid., p. 135.

[143]Light, *The Development of a Junior-Senior High School Program*, vol. 2, p. 456.

[144]Eddie Shimano, "Blueprint for a Slum," *Common Ground*, 3 (Summer 1943), p. 80.

[145]James, *Exile Within*, p. 128.

[146]For accounts of the actual reception accorded returnees, see Kevin A. Leonard, "'Is This What We Fought For?' Japanese Americans and Racism in California, The Impact of World War

II," *Western Historical Quarterly*, 21 (November 1990), pp. 463–482; Sandra C. Taylor, "Leaving the Concentration Camps: Japanese American Resettlement in Utah and the Intermountain West," *Pacific Historical Review*, 60 (1991), pp. 169–194; and Tetsuden Kashima, "Japanese American Internees Return, 1945 to 1955: Readjustment and Social Amnesia," *Phylon*, 41 (Summer 1980), pp. 107–115. The temper in some quarters of the United States is apparent in a late 1944 Gallup Poll in which 13% of respondents "suggested that after the war all Japanese remaining alive should be exterminated," Christopher Thorne, "RacialAspects of the Far Eastern War of 1941–1945," *Proceedings of the British Academy*, 66 (1980), p. 352.

[147] See Louis A. Perez, Jr., *Cuba Between Empires 1878–1902* (University of Pittsburgh Press, 1983), pp. 55–56; and Sheila Patterson, *The Last Trek. A Study of the Boer People and the Africaner Nation* (Routledge & Kegan Paul, 1957), pp. 32, 34. There were 200,000 people in the South African concentration camps at the end of the war in 1901.

[148] See Hans Rogger, "The Beilis Case: Antisemitism and Politics in the Reign of Nicholas II," *Slavic Review*, 25 (December 1966), p. 629; and Alexis Goldenweiser, "Legal Status of Jews in Russia," p. 113 in Jacob Frumkin, Gregor Aronson, and Alexis Goldenweiser, eds., *Russian Jewry (1860–1917)*, trans. Mirra Ginsburg (Thomas Yoseloff, 1966). On Turkey, see Stephan Astourian, "The Armenian Genocide: An Interpretation," *The History Teacher*, 23 (February 1990), pp. 111–160.

[149] See Grant Foreman, *Indian Removal. The Emigration of the Five Civilized Tribes of Indians* (University of Oklahoma Press, 1972); and Abraham Hoffman, *Unwanted Mexican Americans in the Great Depression. Repatriation Pressures 1929–1939* (University of Arizona Press, 1974).

[150] See James W. Byrkit, *Forging the Copper Collar. Arizona's Labor-Management War of 1901–1921.* (University of Arizona Press, 1982); and Jerry M. Cooper, *The Army and Civil Disorder. Federal Military Intervention in Labor Disputes, 1877–1900* (Greenwood Press, 1980). On treatment of Japanese farm laborers, see Charles N. Reynolds, *Oriental-White Race Relations in Santa Clara County, California* (Doctoral dissertation, Stanford University, 1927), pp. 349–351; and on Chinese workers, see Michele Shover, "Chico Women. Nemesis of a Rural Town's Anti-Chinese Campaigns 1876–1888," *California History*, 67 (December 1988), p. 243. On the 1934 events in Georgia, see Carl Weinberg, "The National Guard and the General Textile Strike of 1934 in Georgia and North Carolina," unpublished paper written for course "America Between the Wars," Yale University, December 16, 1987.

[151] Peter Irons, *Justice At War* (Oxford University Press, 1993).

[152] Falk Pingel, "Concentration Camps," p. 308 in Israel Gutman, ed., *Encyclopedia of the Holocaust*, I (Macmillan, 1990).

[153] Ibid., p. 308.

[154] Ibid., p. 311.

[155] Haglund, "Behind Barbed Wire," p. 3.

[156] Jerrold Haruo Takahashi, *Changing Responses to Racial Subordination: An Exploratory Study of Japanese American Political Styles* (Doctoral dissertation, University of California, Berkeley, 1980), p. 240.

[157] Ibid., pp. 240–242.

[158] William Petersen, *Japanese Americans. Oppression and Success* (Random House, 1971), pp. 115–116.

[159] Sheridan M. Tatsuno, "High Technology Policies," p. 257 in Paul Ong, ed., *The State of Asian Pacific America: Economic Diversity, Issues and Policies* (LEAP Asian Pacific American Public Policy Institute and UCLA Asian American Studies Center, 1994).

[160] Roland Kotani, *The Japanese in Hawaii: A Century of Struggle* (Hawaii Hochi, Ltd., 1985), p. 170.

[161] Edward K. Strong, *Japanese in California* (Stanford University Press, 1933), p. 163, footnote 10.

[162] Dennis M. Ogawa, *From Japs to Japanese: An Evolution of Japanese-American Stereotypes* (Mc-

Cutchan Publishing Corp., 1971), p. 31. An influential conservative voice on this issue was that of demographer William Petersen in an article that was later expanded into a book. See "Success Story: Japanese American Style," *New York Times Magazine,* January 9, 1966, pp. vi–20; and *Japanese Americans: Oppression and Success* (Random House, 1971).

[163] Ogawa, *From Japs to Japanese,* p. 53.

[164] Reed Ueda, "The Americanization and Education of Japanese-Americans," p. 74 in Edgar G. Epps, ed., *Cultural Pluralism* (McCutchan Publishing Corp., 1974).

[165] Jere Takahashi, "Japanese American Responses to Race Relations: The Formation of Nisei Perspectives," *Amerasia Journal,* 9 (1982), p. 43.

[166] Don T. Nakanishi, "Seeking Convergence in Race Relations Research. Japanese Americans and the Resurrection of the Internment," p. 168 in Phyllis A. Katz and Dalmas A. Taylor, eds., *Eliminating Racism. Profiles in Controversy* (Plenum Press, 1988).

[167] This movement can be conveniently studied in the pages of *Amerasia Journal,* published by the Asian-American Studies Center at UCLA.

CHAPTER FOUR

Korea

Traditional Korea was highly stratified, topped by an imperial court and an aristocracy. During the Yi dynasty (1392–1910), political rights were reserved to the Yangban class, an aristocratic elite. All other, lower classes were considered incapable of handling political decisions. "Such strata had no wisdom, and only wisdom, as demonstrated by a combination of high lineage and high educational attainments, could qualify one to participate in political matters."[1]

An examination system based on the Chinese model largely reserved top official positions to sons of Yangban origin. At times, the law expressly excluded all others from taking examinations, an extreme that was unknown in China. At the base of Korean society was a large slave contingent comprising at times about one third of the population—comparable to the United States during the early 19th century.[2] Slaves possessed certain minimal rights such as marriage and property holding but were excluded from political activity. Nevertheless, slave revolts were not unknown. Peasants were free persons but depended on sporadic insurrections for occasional expansion of their rights. A scant education was offered in village schools where the lower orders were drilled principally in obedience rather than cognitive knowledge. Women were excluded from political activity; they were barred from the examination system as well as from attendance at any educational institution.[3] The gentry, owning land and being more educated than other classes, were dominant powers in many localities. Some even moved into Yangban circles where they could participate in, although not dominate, national decisions as they did local issues.

From time to time, commoners attended schools and, rarely, even some very poor folk did the same. These temporary openings resulted either as a by-product of a large-scale political upheaval or a short-lived reform from higher up. During the late 1860s and early 1870s, for example, the ruler, Yi Ha-ung, struck a blow at the Yangban by closing down around 550 Confucian academies, leaving only 47 others open. Because the academies prepared Yangban sons to take the imperial examinations for official positions, the closures struck hard at the privileged classes. The closures also ended the practice of permitting academy ownership of large farming estates as well as slaves.[4] Firm boundaries separating the classes of Korea were shaken in the 1890s as a result of the peasant insurrection known as the Tonghak uprisings.[5] Slavery was abolished. The folk alphabet (*han'gul*) was used by the government and in the new, modern schools, Korean history was taught. But the essential institutions of the regime lay untouched. Corruption in the buying and selling of official positions continued apace, making a mockery of the examination system.[6]

The dynamic of change in political and educational life dwelled outside the country, in the realm of foreign affairs. Japan was seeking to incorporate Korea into its empire. To ward off this blow, Korea concluded a treaty in 1882 with the United States, providing that the United States would come to the aid of Korea if attacked by a third power. For centuries, China had constituted a major political and cultural force in Korea. By the end of the 19th century, this leadership role had been displaced by the resurgence of Japan. Russia, which had pressed for economic and political advantage in Korea, also gave way before Japanese power. In 1894 and 1895, Japan defeated China and forced China to acknowledge the special interest Japan had in Korea. In 1905, Korea became a Japanese protectorate. Five years later, Japan annexed Korea, which became a Japanese colony for the next 35 years. When in 1905 Korea tried to activate its 1882 treaty with the United States, President Theodore Roosevelt, who was strongly pro-Japanese, refused to make even a formal protest about the protectorate. (Japan, in 1898, had not objected to U.S. annexation of the Philippines.)

In the Protectorate Treaty of 1905, Japan absorbed the Korean education ministry and began converting the colony's schools into instruments of Japanese foreign policy. Within 3 years, Japanese constituted one third of the teaching force. Textbooks were censored; any material conducive to fostering Korean national pride was banned.[7]

Once annexation was under way, education and every other institutional order in Korea was integrated into the structure of Japanese rule. Efforts were made to gain the collaboration of the Korean governing elite. Titles of nobility and cash payments were distributed to 3,645 Koreans. "Altogether six marquises, three counts, twenty-two viscounts and forty-five barons were created and each of them received a [financial] grant."[8] Members of the former Korean ruling family were pensioned off, married into Japanese families, and schooled in Japan. About their only remaining tie to Korea was an annual payment received from the Government-General of Korea.[9]

Japan developed Korea economically to serve the needs of the Japanese empire. "Unlike most colonial powers, Japan located heavy industry in its colonies, bringing the means of production to the labor and raw materials. . . . By 1945 Korea proportionally had more railroad miles than any other Asian country save Japan. . . ."[10] The large corporations that were formed to organize such production were staffed by Japanese, especially at upper levels. Small and medium-size enterprises tended to be owned or managed by Koreans who were strictly subordinated to the Japanese.

Over the entire colonial period, 1910 to 1945, the standard of living of most people in Korea suffered. Real wages of farm workers fell and mass consumption of staple foods, including calorie intake, followed suit. Housing may have also deteriorated. The extension of education was a clear gain although, as pointed out later, Koreans were given a separate and unequal school system. A declining mortality rate was also a gain.[11] In the eyes of Koreans, none of the bad news was unexpected and none of the good news was sizable enough to counterbalance the oppression that accompanied colonization.

In the field of educational policy, Japan saw in Korea an opportunity to use Korean resources to educate Japanese children, all the while devoting proportionately less to educate Korean children. During the years 1912–1942, for example, the inequalities were quite sizable:[12]

Expenditure per Korean students as percent of expenditure on Japanese students:

1912	55.5	1930	40.4
1915	67.2	1935	39.6
1920	58.3	1937	45.1
1925	54.4	1940	19.3
		1942	27.6

The number of students per teacher was increasingly unequal as time went on:[13]

	Korean Schools	Japanese Schools
1912	27.9	31.7
1913	31.5	30.2
1940	73.2	35.3
1942	73.1	35.9

After nearly 20 years of colonialism, virtually all Japanese children in Korea attended school whereas only one sixth of Korean children were permitted to do so.[14]

Thus, even if per-student expenditures had been the same, the unequal attendance proportions insured gross discrimination against Korean children. After another decade, Korea still lacked a compulsory education law, but Japan itself had one. A wish to attend school was not deficient among Koreans, so the absence of such a law proved to be a lesser burden. Nevertheless, by 1928, "there was one public elementary school for every 974 Japanese in Korea, while there was [only] one school for every 13,075 Korean children."[15] In the last colonial year, 1945, over half of the Korean children were not receiving any formal education. Restricted almost wholly to primary education, only 5% of all the children ever went on to middle schools.[16] The census of a year earlier revealed that 45.5% of the population was illiterate.[17]

Soon after annexation, Korean representatives requested the building of a university for their children, but the Japanese refused. In 1924, however, the Keijo Imperial University was begun under government auspices. Admission depended on one's secondary-school record, but secondary schools were exceedingly rare in Korea, especially for Korean students. For the latter, secondary school curricula had a strongly vocational emphasis, thus discouraging thoughts of preparing for advanced academic studies. Indeed, as early as 1906, high school for Koreans had been reduced by the Japanese from 4 to 3 years, thereby making further education even less likely. As few as 0.2% of Korean boys of relevant age groups actually became secondary-school students.[18]

At Keijo Imperial University, Japanese students outnumbered Koreans by a ratio of three to one. Quotas governed enrollment of Koreans: 12% in natural sciences and 37% in humanities and social science fields.[19] Japanese students were not subjected to quotas. Just over half of the Koreans in higher education attended not Keijo Imperial but three private colleges operated by various Christian missions. Between 1920 and 1940, chances for Koreans to enter higher education declined sharply as expansion of secondary education continued to lag far behind primary education:

> In 1920 one out of about six Korean students in primary schools, that is, common schools, had a chance of secondary education within Korea but . . . twenty years later only one of 30 primary school students in Korea could obtain a secondary education in Korea.[20]

Bright students of well-to-do families who collaborated with colonial authorities not infrequently gained permission to study in Japanese universities. Altogether, in 1941, the number of Koreans in all kinds of higher education made up less than 1% of college-aged youth.[21]

Inside the Japanese-run schools of Korea, unremitting war was waged on traditional Korean national culture. Fronts in this encounter included language, history, employment, and curriculum.

By law, only Japanese could be school principals. The success in employing Japanese was clear from the composition of school personnel in 1945, the last year of colonialism. "Close to one-third of the elementary school teachers, two-thirds of the high school teachers, and the majority of college and university professors" were Japanese.[22] Korean educators were paid less than Japanese, sometimes only half as much. In the numerous public primary schools, Japanese constituted the following percentages of teachers:[23]

1922	29.6
1930	27.8
1935	32.3
1940	47.8
1942	42.2

As representatives of the colonial governing power, Japanese teachers were obliged to wear a sword in the classroom, a constant reminder of the superior force awaiting objectors to Japanese rule.

A prime goal of the Japanese was to replace Korean as the language of instruction in the common schools. Textbooks were published in Japanese even for the first three primary grades. Between 1920 and 1930, the percent of the population who could speak Japanese rose from over 2 to over 8.[24] Until 1938, some Korean-language texts continued to be prepared, but in that year all such texts were outlawed. Students were forbidden to speak Korean in class or on the playground; teachers were directed to report any violators observed speaking Korean even off school grounds. Besides being listed in the school's official records, "individuals caught conversing in their mother tongue were severely pinched on the neck and arms, or forced to hold a chair in both hands, high above their heads for thirty minutes."[25] Authorities also kept tab on Korean teachers, one of whom recounted, "being warned by one of his high school students in 1941 not to speak Korean in school, because detectives had been asking whether he in fact spoke Japanese in class."[26]

During the years 1937 to 1939, the colonial regime forbade the use of Korean in government affairs, schooling, and newspapers.[27] Koreans sought out ways of evading regulations. Proscribed books were bought secretly and underground classes in Korean history and culture were conducted. Police arrested students who were found to possess notes on lectures in these classes.[28] Proficiency in Japanese nevertheless expanded as more and more daily necessities required: "Out of a total of eleven different types of schools in the colonial educational system, eight required almost total Japanese language comprehension."[29] One motive for adults learning Japanese was to enable them to help their children in school. Most parents did not learn, however.[30] The Korean Language Society (KLS) led a campaign to conserve and develop the native language. Leading members of the KLS "were arrested and put on trial during World War II essentially for the heinous crime of compiling a dictionary."[31] When, in 1939, Koreans were ordered to adopt a Japanese name in addition to their Korean one, nearly 85% did so.[32] School and job applications required both names to be given.

Henderson summed up the language situation in the society as a whole:

Knowledge of Japanese rose from 0.6 percent of fifteen million in 1913 to over 15 percent of twenty-five million Koreans in 1945, or from ninety thousand to some three and a half million speakers. Every intellectual knew Japanese, and many schooled in the last decade of the regime [1936–1945] came to read, if not speak, it better than they did Korean.[33]

Success in learning how to speak and read Japanese came to depend on attendance in the public schools, especially during the final years of the colonial regime. Thus, in 1942, Japanese military officials found that, "among some 210,000 Korean youths of military ages, about 110,000 (52.4 percent) did not graduate from even common (elementary) schools and did not speak the Japanese language."[34] On the other hand, in some of the largest cities, by 1943 over half the population could speak Japanese.[35]

By the early 1930s in Japan itself, the military had become the leading political force in the national legislature. In Korea since 1910, however, the military headed the colonial government; in 1920, a law required that the Governor-General must be either a general or an admiral. The military intended to use armed might to establish law and order—by which they meant obedience. Koreans, however, resisted these efforts and conducted a series of guerrilla actions. Between 1907 and 1920, 135,711 insurgents were involved in 2,672 separate clashes.[36] In the following 3 years, the numbers fell to 2,185 and 193; during 1913 and 1914, the count was only 25 and 3. Koreans were stripped of their arms; they were forbidden to own firearms or swords.[37]

An explosion of resistance sounded again on March 1, 1919, when thousands of Koreans the country over demonstrated for independence. The movement was peaceful and marked by actions of civil disobedience. Businesses closed, parades were held, and public speeches given. Japanese authorities were thunderstruck, having imagined that their earlier suppression of Korean armed resistance would end agitation for independence. Their response was savage: 7,000 demonstrators were killed and 52,000 were imprisoned.[38] Otherwise, the colonial government was conciliatory. Promises were made of improved and increasingly equal schools as well as greater freedom of association for organizations representing labor, youth, and educational groups. In fact, however, the new reality was more complex. "The Japanese would use a policy of divide and rule, conciliation for non-threatening activities and a more skillful repression of dangerous nationalist and social revolutionary elements."[39] Budget appropriations for police were greatly increased. About half were Koreans. "The colonial thought police also employed a vast network of native informers."[40]

The 1920s saw a series of strikes at high schools designed to resolve many historic grievances. These included demands for appointment of Korean school principals, compulsory education, Korean language to be used in textbooks, building of more colleges and universities, and approval of student meetings in high schools.[41] National independence was the unspoken undergirding of the demands.

Many Korean nationalists were Christians and adherents of the United States. The two were interrelated. As Lee explained:[42]

> The peculiar fact that Korea had become the colony of a non-Western power dif-
> ferentiates Korean nationalism from any other colonial nationalism. Whereas most
> of the colonial nationalists around the world looked upon the Western powers, or
> the white race as a whole, with at best suspicion and at worst hatred, the Korean
> nationalists looked upon the Western world as the pioneer of liberalism and a new
> civilization. Liberalism in the West preached equality of mankind and liberty and
> welfare of individuals.[42]

Chan noted, too, that for roughly similar reasons, "Koreans did not equate Christianity with Western imperialism."[43] Once faced with the daily realities of American racism, however, these beliefs would be sorely tested.

The military defeat of Japan in 1945 ended the colonial regime in Korea.[44] From 1945 to 1948, U.S. military forces governed in the latter; in 1948, the Republic of Korea was organized under U.S. sponsorship. Under Soviet sponsorship, the People's Republic of Korea was formed. Two years later began a war involving both Koreas, the United States, China, and other countries and lasted until 1953. A year before the war started, China became a Communist country. That same year, the Soviet Union exploded its first atomic bomb. The Cold War was well underway by 1949 and proved to be a fundamental factor in Korea's history for the next four decades. A neighbor of both Communist China and the Soviet Union, Korea became a highly desirable partner for U.S. military power. The United States in turn paid a high price to implement that promise.

"Between 1946 and 1976 the U.S. supplied a total of $12.6 billion in economic and military assistance to South Korea. . . ."[45] Until 1964, the great bulk of the aid was delivered as nonrepayable grants. At one point in the late 1950s, "about 70 percent of the government's total revenue came from foreign aid."[46] Meanwhile, the regime controlled an economy that the Japanese had left after their defeat. Many of the new owners, designated by an extremely repressive regime sponsored by the United States, were Koreans who had collaborated closely with the Japanese during colonial times. A new elite arose on the basis of a government that was eager to cooperate. As Eckert pointed out, these elites "have historically been the recipients of a cornucopia of special privileges and favors from the state."[47] A prime example is government aid to the *chaebols,* giant conglomerate industrial corporations. Since 1972, "the government has generally continued to provide special emergency loans to chaebols threatened by bankruptcy."[48] In competition with the chaebols, public education ranked very low on the ladder of public funds.

At liberation in 1945, about half of Korea's school-age children were not attending school. Among older children and youth, only a tiny minority were in secondary and higher institutions. For many Koreans, independence called for a great expansion in education. As the following index numbers show, this indeed happened. Taking 1945 enrollment as 100, 42 years later, the enrollment figures had grown enormously.[49]

	1945	*1987*
Elementary school	100	349
Middle school	100	3288
High school	100	5556
Higher education	100	18767

The national government, however, refused to pay the full bill for the expansion. Instead, two alternative avenues were pursued: Tuition was charged in the public institutions and private schools and universities were encouraged. Both shifted the financial burden onto the shoulders of parents, regardless of their ability to pay. Thus, a basic inequality was built into the educational structure of the country.

Not until the 1970s did elementary schooling become entirely free. In 1989, middle schools followed suit. Public high schools and colleges and universities, however, remained subject to tuition. Because high schools and colleges and universities are so few in number, competition to enter these is intense and many applicants are rejected. Private tutoring is very extensive in order to improve one's chances in the struggle for entrance. In 1980, McGinn wrote about higher education:

> The son of a professional, technical, or managerial worker is 3.5 times as likely to be enrolled as the son of a farmer and 2.6 times as likely as the son of a laborer. For daughters, these ratios are even higher, 7.4 and 4.2 to 1.0, respectively.[50]

Growing income inequalities during the 1980s likely aggravated such trends.[51]

Private education continued to grow. By the opening of the 1990s, schools on various levels were private:[52]

Elementary	1.2 percent
Middle	29.0 percent
High schools	50.4 percent
Junior colleges	86.3 percent
Universities	78.0 percent

Around this time, over 90% of Korean parents looked forward to their children attending college or university. Yet there was room only for slightly over one third of the applicants.[53]

By 1990, virtually four out of five college students attended private institutions. Some of these colleges and universities were of questionable quality, being organized primarily to earn a profit for their founders:

> Taking advantage of the strong, educational demand of the Korean people, entre-preneurial and opportunistic individuals opened many private schools, some of

which flagrantly violated the qualifications set forth by the government. . . . Education was an investment which often brought the investors profit and nearly always brought them status and honor. . . . The system gave room for unfairness and corruption in the process of student selection by some private universities with profit-making orientations.[54]

Kwan Lee, himself the president of the University of Ulsan, in Korea, wrote of the higher education institutions established after World War II, "Most . . . were founded without referring to a set of qualitative standards."[55] In 1981 and 1982, the national government began subsidizing private colleges and universities with construction funds as well as financing costs. In addition, some government payments also covered pension and health-insurance obligations of private institutions.[56]

In 1980, McGinn declared that, "if the enrollment ratio structure remains as it was in 1975, more than 90 percent of the pupils now enrolled in primary school will fail to gain admittance to college."[57] By the early 1990s, it appeared that McGinn's possibility was approaching fruition: Out of a highly select population—that is, graduates of academic high schools—only 35% passed the college examination and entered higher education.[58] Part of the reason for this is the expansion of nonacademic secondary schooling that tends to direct its graduates away from higher education. As long ago as 1980, proportionately more than twice the number of academic high school graduates than vocational high schools entered a college or university.[59]

Differential utilization of tutoring and related private services is an important force for inequality. Among the 3,288 students who entered Seoul National University—the country's best—in 1980, 61% had been tutored.[60] Sorensen pointed to "the affluent, educated middle-class areas south of the Han River in Seoul, where educational competition is generally conceded to be most intense and where larger proportions of the population attend cram schools than in other parts of Korea."[61] Tutoring stood the test of time even in the face of government opposition. In 1980, all tutoring was barred except for music and the arts.[62] One reason for the action was to end the practice of regular classroom teachers tutoring some or all of their own students. In 1989, however, the prohibition was narrowed to permit college students to tutor.

Gender bias was the single greatest source of inequality in Korean education at the time of liberation. In 1975, however, sex parity in primary-school enrollment was reached; 15 years later, male and female students attended high schools in equal numbers.[63] Higher education continued to lag: Between the 1960s and the early 1990s, the proportion of women students rose from less than 20% to somewhat over 30%; very recently the percentage started to drop.[64] Women student-protestors against the rule of the military dictatorship were treated with the same brutality as were men students:

A number of women students who protested against . . . repression were arrested by the KCIA [Korean Central Intelligence Agency], tortured, and repeatedly raped, as in the case of several Ewha University students in late 1973. . . . Savageries at the hands of torturers turned hundreds of articulate and conscientious Koreans who were involved in the democratic movement into the living dead, suffering from both physical damage and psychological trauma.[65]

It was not until 15 years or so later that the Korean regime began to reduce its resort to state violence in encounters with popular protest.

After 1953, the end of the Korean War, many Korean youth wished to go overseas for their collegiate education. So popular was the movement that government authorities intervened to slow it down. One method chosen was to require stiff exams to select candidates. From 1961 to 1980, about 6,000 Koreans a year were permitted to attend U.S. colleges or universities. In 1981, when government policy was eased, the annual number climbed to 15,000.[66] Nevertheless, this large exodus did little to reduce the overall pressure on Korean higher education. Many of the traveling students remained in the United States after the conclusion of their schooling.

This was especially true in the fields of mathematics, computer science, and engineering. Jobs in these fields were scarce in Korea whereas they were plentiful in the United States during the 1960s and 1970s. However, the Korean government undertook to change the situation. In 1966, the Korean Institute of Science and Technology was organized by the government to serve the growing needs of high technology. Special aid was granted to Korean universities with schools of engineering. To attract Korean scientists and engineers working and living in other countries, during the 1970s and 1980s, associations of such personnel were organized in the United States, Europe, Japan, and Canada. Repatriation programs were successful, especially as the Cold War waned and released thousands of scientists and engineers to seek work elsewhere. By 1991, the Korean government no longer offered permanent repatriation programs.[67] The brain drain had ceased.

Although qualitative progress across the entire range of Korean education was considerable, many basic weaknesses of the country's schooling process persisted.

The failure to solve problems of physical space was one of the foremost. Thus, in 1990, after elementary schooling had become universal, 13.3% of all elementary school classes were on double shift.[68] This meant that more than one eighth of total enrollment was receiving only part-time instruction.

Quality differences between individual schools, especially on the secondary level, are another enduring problem. After many complaints by parents, school authorities began the High School Equalization Policy (HSEP) in 1973. Its purpose was to "remove inequities among academic high schools in terms of school facilities, finances, and teacher quality."[69] After 1980, school authorities applied the policy only to existing schools, thereby reserving the right to build new schools that were especially staffed or equipped. In fact, however, "Even in the high schools in the urban areas which continued implementation of the policy, quality gaps in school facilities and teachers have remained among the high schools. Moreover, new, prestigious academic high schools have emerged."[70] A frequent parental maneuver against poor schools in rural areas was to send children to live in Seoul with their relatives, and thus be able to attend better schools in the capital city.[71] In 1979, this procedure was declared illegal.

Still another structural arrangement during the 1970s was said to be intended to equalize educational opportunities, but it failed in this respect. As McGinn explained:

> Each residential district is supposed to contain an equal balance of schools of high and low prestige, but the common district contains only prestige schools. Students whose scores are not high enough to get them into the common district are randomly assigned to a school in a residential district.[72]

Middle-class children are virtually guaranteed privileged attendance if only because of the strong connection between high test scores and socioeconomic position.

It took years to recover from the damage of the Korean War. Meanwhile, the universities expanded moderately. Between 1958 and 1969, however, the number of graduates grew rapidly. So did the graduates' employment prospects. At Seoul National University:

> While 60 percent of university graduates in 1958 found occupations that were highly comparable with their majors, only 15 percent were able to do so in 1969. [In the natural, physical, and applied sciences] while 83 percent of 1958 graduates found compatible employment, only 70 percent were able to do so in 1969.[73]

During the 1980s, unemployment among university graduates grew greatly.[74] "To obtain a desirable job," wrote Henderson, "the winner might have to compete in up to 34 written examinations against more than 100 other applicants."[75] As a rule, government jobs are available only to graduates of Seoul National or a few other universities.[76] Writing in the late 1960s, Henderson contended that, "the limited job opportunities genuinely offered in the open market can probably be filled with the graduates of the top half-dozen universities, or 7 percent of existing colleges and universities."[77]

Women graduates fared even worse. Many Korean firms refuse to employ women. Indeed, educated women seem to gain little job advantage from their education.[78] Although these unfavorable job prospects have not in general dampened women's strivings for higher education, as was pointed out previously, very recently the percentage of women in colleges and university has dropped.[79]

The unyielding employment situation, settled atop highly restricted universities and colleges, set the scene for desperate resorts by parents. One such recourse was outright bribery of teachers. "Large gifts of money given to teachers by students' parents are not uncommon in Korea but are officially illegal."[80] In 1993, over 50 national education officials were disciplined for "leaking answers to state-administered national exams."[81] Envelopes containing cash passed during a single year might equal a teacher's annual salary. A national teachers' group that called for an end to the practice was criticized as challenging the authority of the military government.

The cultural heritage of Japan and the United States constitutes another continuing problem in Korean education. Soon after liberation, steps were taken to extirpate all Japanese influence from the schools. "[There] was a violent repudiation of everything Japanese. Nearly all traces of Japanese language and literature were eliminated from the schools. Japanese books and works of art were burned or otherwise destroyed."[82] In fact, however, in the longer run, for "South Korea's elite, largely educated in the Japanese language, Japanese newspapers, magazines, and books continued to be a source of the latest information on everything from fashion to economic trends and industrial technology."[83] By 1971, Japan's investments in South Korea were nearly twice as large as those of the United States. The military and economic dominance of the United States, especially in the first 25 years after liberation, moved many critics to charge that Korea had simply exchanged masters.[84]

IMMIGRATION

Before World War II, fewer than 8,000 Koreans emigrated to the United States, both in Hawaii and California. The great majority of these—from 7,000 to 7,500—arrived in Hawaii during a short period, January 1903 to July 1905.[85] Most were poor laborers from cities, who had had few opportunities for schooling. Hawaiian sugar planters, seeking potential strikebreakers to be used against Japanese sugar workers, had arranged the migration for this reason. Both in 1904 and 1905, Koreans broke such strikes.[86] Most of the Koreans, however, did not relish such activity and between 1905 and 1910, nearly two thirds of them left the plantations for jobs elsewhere.[87]

After the end of World War II and liberation from Japan, emigration was strongly discouraged until 1962, when an office for emigration was established.[88] Three years later, a new U.S. immigration law passed that resulted in vast increases in Asian emigration to the United States. Most of the Koreans were highly educated, both by Korean and U.S. standards, and they came from upper socioeconomic levels.[89] One out of four had been self-employed before emigrating.[90] By 1972, some 30,000 Koreans arrived in the United States; in each of the succeeding 15 years, the same threshold was equalled or exceeded. Compared with the pre-1945 figures, the numbers were astronomical.

The Korean government was more reluctant to lose American dollars than see their citizens move to the United States. Accordingly, a maximum was established to regulate the amount of money emigrants could bring with them. By 1986, the permitted maximum was $100,000 per family.[91] These sums were derived from selling their homes in Korean cities. In addition, the regulations were easy to evade, as money was often sent abroad a year or longer in advance of the move overseas. Money could also be distributed among relatives and friends to be returned after removal. As Park wrote, "Sending money abroad is a sensitive topic in Korea."[92] In general, however, the affluence of incoming Koreans was exaggerated. As Barringer and Cho put it, "For every immigrant's daughter at Harvard, there is at least one Korean woman in a low-paying service job. And for every Korean physician, there are several industrial helpers."[93] Income figures of immigrant Koreans by economic class are virtually nonexistent.

IN AMERICA

After 1898, when Hawaii formally became part of the United States, Koreans and others on the Islands found it much easier to move to the mainland. Wherever they were, Korean Americans devoted themselves to the nationalist struggle for independence from Japan. Although most were quite poor, they found the means to make modest financial contributions. A very high percentage of early Korean immigrants were Christians. Another group became Christians after arriving.

Education was of prime interest to them. Reportedly, "Koreans acquired English very rapidly."[94] Public schooling was far more available than in independent or colonized Korea. By 1920, Koreans were second to the Chinese in the percentage of school-aged children attending school.[95] Both in 1910 and 1920, fewer Koreans in Hawaii were illiterate than the Chinese and Japanese.[96] The same ranking was obtained on the mainland where highly literate workers sometimes put on informal poetry parties.[97] Korean Christians were almost uniformly literate in Korean.[98] In the United States, they continued the tradition in church-built schools. As early as 1906, the Korean Methodist mission established the Korean Boarding School in Honolulu. The institution prepared boys aged 7 to 12 to enter American senior high schools.[99] They also studied the Korean language. Until 1940, six Korean language schools operated within California.

In the public schools, Korean children were not segregated but neither were they welcomed by their classmates, who sometimes attacked them.[100] Throughout the community Koreans and others were confronted by Whites Only signs. "We could not go to restrooms, theaters, swimming pools, [and] barber shops. . . ."[101] Outright discrimination was the rule in Riverside. "It was a common practice to give the nonwhite students lower grades than the whites."[102] Although many of the exclusory signs were removed in the 1950s from public buildings, less blatant techniques replaced them. "But although there were not signs on barber shops, theaters, and churches, Orientals were told at the door that they were not welcome."[103]

On the eve of World War II, only about 650 Koreans lived in Los Angeles

County, half of whom were immigrants. Fifteen years earlier, all persons ineligible for citizenship through naturalization—and this included all Asians— were barred from immigration into the United States. In 1939, only about 170 Koreans attended elementary and secondary schools in the country; another 38 were college students.[104] Nevertheless, professional jobs on the mainland were off limits even to college-trained Korean Americans, who had to go to Hawaii in search of work. As of 1939, "No Koreans in Los Angeles County are engaged in . . . law, engineering, dentistry, education, or social work. Two Koreans are engaged in the practice of medicine."[105] Many young women also headed for Hawaii in search of appropriate work, with the result of creating a shortage of marriageable women in California-Korean circles.

The end of World War II opened a new chapter in Korean American history. The receding of restrictive legislation benefited Asian-Americans, including Koreans. A U.S. Supreme Court decision invalidated the use of state courts to enforce residential segregation through restrictive covenants. The California Land Law was struck down as well. The McCarran-Walter Act of 1952 removed the bar on the naturalization of non-Whites; it had few immediate consequences because only a tiny immigration quota was then assigned to Asian countries. In 1964, the Civil Rights Act was passed in Congress. It forbade discrimination against minorities in schools, employment, and other areas of daily life. The next year, a sweeping immigration law abolished the quota system that had discriminated for four decades against Asian, African, and Eastern and Southern European countries, and in favor of Western European countries.

Before World War II, the small-scale Korean immigration was almost completely composed of working-class persons. After 1965, the great majority consisted of college-educated, middle-class persons. A survey in Los Angeles in 1978, however, found that:

> Fifty-three percent of the working household heads, experienced downward mobility in occupation after emigrating. This is especially true of those who held professional occupations in Korea, among which only 35 percent entered professional occupations while the rest took jobs below their rank. . . . Downward occupational mobility was severest among Korean working wives.[106]

Some three fifths of the numerous Korean operators of small retail businesses were college graduates who had completed their education before emigrating. Although downward mobility was a troubling reality to many of these, nevertheless it should not be thought that a large number of them would have qualified in Korea for prime positions in government or industry.

Increasing numbers of Korean Americans reside in middle-class suburbs populated in part by other Asian Americans. Thus, wrote Lee, "school peer groups for Korean students . . . tend to be comprised of Asian American and other middle-class students, who generally have high educational standards."[107] In the vicinity of Rochester and Buffalo, New York, this pattern held true of numerous dispersed groups of Koreans.[108] During the mid-1970s, Koreans in San Francisco were scattered throughout the city. One Korean child, Meewha, who was the only Korean student in a city elementary school, recalled seeing other Asian students and following them around to hear their language: "I couldn't understand them. . . . They were Filipinos, Chinese, and Japanese."[109] In Chicago, several years later, a number of Korean families lived close together and school enrollment reflected the fact. Poorer Koreans resided in inner-city areas and their children attended school with African-American and Hispanic students.

Both in Los Angeles and Chicago, researchers found that teachers in such schools frequently expressed highly favorable attitudes about the Korean children. Kim, one of the researchers, saw this as potentially troublesome:

> [Teachers] often viewed the Korean-American children in a favorable light because they did *not* exhibit the learning and behavioral problems common to the other minority children in the schools. . . . The Korean-American children may come to look down on other minorities . . . and acquire a false sense of their own capabilities and of the ease with which they are accepted by the majority culture. They may be in for a severe shock when they later attempt to compete on equal terms with the majority culture, either at college or in the business and professional world.[110]

Despite the favorable reception accorded children by teachers, Kim reported that nearly half the children reported they did not always readily understand what the teachers had said in class. Kim also wrote that, "about 30% of both parents and children reported that the child had encountered discrimination at school in the form of harassment or name-calling."[111]

Korean parents and children often perceived school in similar terms. Teachers, however, just as often perceived the situation quite differently. In the metropolitan Denver, Colorado area, for example, the following percentages of each group responded affirmatively when asked whether "most teachers are sympathetic in their efforts to help Korean students":[112]

Parents   72
Students   74
Teachers   92

As to the seemingly more factual question whether "career guidance for Korean students is available in the schools," affirmative responses were as follows, in percentages:[113]

Parents   42
Students   32
Teachers   90

With respect to a query whether "school personnel are cooperative in working with Korean parents when parents need to be more involved in school problems," affirmative responses varied in the following percentages:[114]

> Parents   58
> Students   44
> Teachers   68

Affirmative responses varied as follows when asked whether "Korean language, history, morals, and customs should be taught to Korean students":[115]

> Parents   50
> Students   70
> Teachers   26

Whether the schools were providing the same students with sufficient information regarding college preparation and requirements brought a parallel disjunction in responses, with teachers reporting a much higher affirmative response.[116]

In Philadelphia, Stacey Lee studied the roles of Asian-American students in Central High School, an elite institution that drew students from the entire city. Admission to Central required, "all As and Bs with the one C allowed in the 7th and 8th grades, and standardized test scores . . . at or above the 85th percentile."[117] For the class of 1993, Asians were accepted at a rate of 40% whereas the rate was 37.3% for all students. Students who did not maintain prescribed academic standards were deselected. "Students who fail three academic subjects are recommended for transfer, and students who fail two academic subjects for a second year are automatically deselected."[118]

Korean American students at Central were solidly middle-class and tended to keep apart from the other Asian-Americans (i.e., Cambodians, Chinese, and Vietnamese). They preferred to be identified as Korean rather than Asian-American. Whites were the insiders of Central and had been so for decades. They occupied most of the top positions of honor in the school, including high places in the tracking system. According to Lee, "Korean students explained that their parents instructed them to socialize only with Koreans and [white] Americans."[119] Many of the Korean students "wore preppy-style clothes associated with elite private schools attended by wealthy whites."[120] Nevertheless, few friendships were struck up by Whites and Korean Americans.

At a graduation exercise, "With the letter 'C' came the first large group of Asian students. At this point the audience suddenly grew silent and a small group of white adults sitting near the front of the hall began to hiss."[121] African-Americans, who are not plentiful in high-tracking placements, seem much more resentful of the relative academic success of Asian-Americans than they are of the high-ranking Whites. A class factor is at work in the entire ethnic-ranking system because poorer Italian-American students from South Philadelphia are regarded by wealthier Whites as marginal members of the White student body. In their turn, the successful Whites do not fear the Asian-Americans' success because the latter are a small group. Nor are the more numerous African-Americans —35% of enrollment—seen as a threat because they occupy so few positions of success in the school.

Employment of Koreans as faculty members of institutions of higher education increased over the years, as follows:

1976	208
1986	359
1996	414

These figures represent counts of persons bearing the surname *Kim*.[122] Clearly, other Korean surnames also appear in standard listings, but they are not all recognizable to the present writer.

In 1993, it was reported that 26,500 Asian-Americans, or 5% of the total, served as faculty in the country as a whole. Unfortunately, it is not possible to break down this figure into various national groupings, but there is little doubt that most are of Chinese and Japanese background. Frequently, Asian-Americans are the largest minority group among college and university faculty.[123] On the negative side, Asian-Americans generally have the lowest tenure rate and are rarely found among the administrators.[124]

Because Korean Americans are an overwhelmingly recent immigrant group, their occupational success or failure is related far more to educational preparation in Korea than in the United States. Choy declared that Korean-educated medical professionals who failed their licensing examinations in the United States as well as Korea-educated teachers and professors and skilled workers have been unable to practice their specialties in this country.[125] They have had to settle for a lesser occupation. Encouragement of their children's further education in the United States, however, has been based on middle-class socialization. When a former professor settles for a grocery clerk's position, he continues to influence his children along the academic lines of his past employment and social milieu.

Medical specialists who succeed in obtaining licensure after immigration still operate at a disadvantage. The most financially rewarding employments are not made available to them. Graduates of foreign medical schools:

> constituted about 30 percent of all interns and residents in the United States in 1977, and in New York State they made up, in 1977, 52 percent of the total, with the heaviest concentration being in state, city, and municipal hospitals.[126]

Kim stated clearly that, "it is the Korean, Philippine, Indian, and Pakistani immigrants who have filled the shortage of medical workers in inner cities of the United States."[127] He continued that "the majority of Korean medical professionals work for second- or third-rate public hospitals such as city, state, or federal hospitals that have recruited 'cheap' foreign medical workers."[128] Of the some 3,000 Korean physicians who practiced in the United States in 1975, three fourths had graduated from what Kim called "the five most eminent medical schools in Seoul."[129]

During the 1960s and 1970s, the Korean economy was becoming industrialized but on a low-tech, cheap-wage basis. Young Koreans who wished to obtain credentials for professional jobs in high-tech industries frequently attended U.S. universities, where they earned doctorates in science, engineering, and computer studies. Most immediately received positions in American industries at far higher salaries than they could earn in Korea. During the 1980s, however, significant changes occurred. The Korean government initiated the development of high-tech industry and research. Also, with the ending of the Cold War, U.S. defense officials—the principal source of support for much scientific research—cut expenditures sharply. During the 1980s, two thirds of Korean scientists and engineers who received doctorates at U.S. universities went back to Korea within 3 years of receiving their degrees.[130] This return movement did not make a noticeable dent in the overall flow of Koreans to the United States. It was quite important, however, within the restricted circle of highly specialized personnel and underscored the great mobility of such labor in the contemporary world economy.

CONCLUDING REMARKS

"To many Korean immigrants," wrote Chang, "'prejudice' or 'discrimination' does not really mean much, although they have a vague understanding of these terms."[131] Because most Americans are sorely unacquainted with Korean history, few are ready to test Chang's statement against the historical experience of Korean immigrants. But both prejudice and discrimination are central elements of the Korean experience. This can be seen in the history of slavery in Korea, the period of Japanese colonialism, and, on a smaller scale, the status of persons indigenous to Cholla province.

Slavery existed in Korea for some 3,000 years. At times, the number of slaves mounted to one third of the total population, among the largest on world record. The slaves were Koreans, as were their enslavers, who took care to incorporate the institution within the legal structure of the country. Expressions of prejudice against the slaves were common whereas social and other discrimination against them was fundamental and enduring. Only in the period 1886 to 1895 were slavery and other forms of forced labor legally abolished.[132] Nevertheless, as Eckert wrote in 1993, "even today one can find Koreans of landlord background who speak of having had slaves (*nobi*) in their household as late as the Korean War [1950–1953]."[133]

As we saw earlier, during the years of Japanese annexation (1910–1945), prejudice and discrimination were the hallmarks of the colonial system. There were no efforts to disguise the Japanese-designed dual school system as anything other than what it plainly was. Education, employment, and the administration of justice were all purveyed in a discriminatory manner. The hurt of it was only magnified by the contempt with which the Japanese inflicted it.

For centuries, the Cholla province has been what Choi called "Korea's most exploited and marginalized region."[134] Buruma characterized Cholla as "a region that is full of resentment over job discrimination and economic deprivation" and described Cholla people as having "a reputation for being sly, quarrelsome, untrustworthy; the big corporations are still loath to hire people from Cholla, and most parents from Kyongsang won't let their sons and daughters marry Cholla people."[135] Choi added that the Cholla dialect has long been a stigma that signified a speaker's debased status.[136]

It would seem that acquaintance with these historical experiences would readily afford Korean immigrants a sound and definite basis for understanding the American dimensions of prejudice and discrimination.

NOTES

[1] William Shaw, ed., *Human Rights in Korea. Historical and Policy Perspectives* (Council on East Asian Studies, Harvard University, 1991), p. 32.

[2] Carter J. Eckert and others, *Korea Old and New. A History* (Ilchokak, 1990), p. 121. See also Hyong In Kim, *Rural Slavery in Antebellum South Carolina and Early Choson Korea* (Doctoral dissertation, University of New Mexico, 1990).

[3] See Choi Kum-suk, "Rise in the Legal Rights of Korean Women," *Koreana*, 4, No. 2 (1989), pp. 13–23; Soon Man Rhin, "The Status of Women in Traditional Korean Society," pp. 11–37 in Harold Hakwon Sunoo and Dong Soo Kim, eds., *Korean Women in a Struggle for Humanization* (Korean Christian Scholars, Association of Korean Christian Scholars in North America, Spring, 1978); and Park Sun-young, "Confucianism Molds Core of the System," *Koreana*, 5, No. 2 (1991), p. 21.

[4] Eckert, *Korea Old and New*, p. 193.

[5] Ibid., p. 227.

[6] Ibid., pp. 214, 225.

[7] Lee Won-ho, "Modern [Educational] System Came Hard Way to Korea," *Koreana*, 5, No. 2 (1991), p. 28.

[8] Andrew J. Grajdanzev, *Modern Korea* (Institute of Pacific Relations, 1944), p. 45.

[9] Ibid., p. 281.

[10] Bruce Cumings, *The Two Koreas* (Foreign Policy Association, May–June 1984), p. 24.

[11] Mitsuhiko Kimura, "Standards of Living in Colonial Korea: Did the Masses Become Worse Off or Better Off Under Japanese Rule?" *Journal of Economic History*, 53 (September 1993), pp. 629–652.

[12] Wanmo Dong, *Japanese Colonial Policy and Practices in Korea, 1905–1945: A Study in Assimilation* (Doctoral dissertation, Georgetown University, 1965), p. 385.

[13] Ibid., p. 385.

[14] David Brudnoy, "Japan's Experiment in Korea," *Monumenta Nipponica*, 25 (1970), p. 187.

[15]Hung Kyu Bang, *Japan's Colonial Educational Policy in Korea, 1905–1930* (Doctoral dissertation, University of Arizona, 1972), p. 203.

[16]Gregory Henderson, *Korea. The Politics of the Vortex* (Harvard University Press, 1968), p. 89.

[17]Ibid., p. 89.

[18]Bang, *Japan's Colonial Educational Policy in Korea*, p. 134.

[19]Russell A. Vacante, *Japanese Colonial Education in Korea, 1910–1945: An Oral History* (Doctoral dissertation, State University of New York at Buffalo, 1987), p. 76.

[20]Dong, *Japanese Colonial Policy and Practice in Korea*, pp. 425–426.

[21]Henderson, *Korea. The Politics of the Vortex*, p. 89.

[22]Sung-hwa Lee, *The Social and Political Factors Affecting Korean Education, 1885–1950* (Doctoral dissertation, University of Pittsburgh, 1958), p. 152.

[23]Dong, *Japanese Colonial Policy and Practice in Korea*, pp. 423–424, footnote 65.

[24]Ibid., p. 354.

[25]Vacante, *Japanese Colonial Education*, p. 319.

[26]Ronald Toby, "Education in Korea under the Japanese: Attitudes and Manifestations," *Occasional Papers on Korea*, No. 1 (1974), p. 61.

[27]Michael E. Robinson, *Cultural Nationalism in Colonial Korea, 1920–1925* (University of Washington Press, 1988), p. 92.

[28]Vacante, *Japanese Colonial Education*, pp. 300–301.

[29]Ibid., p. 106.

[30]Seung-Hak Cho, "Elementary Education in Korea," *School and Society*, 49 (1939), p. 58.

[31]Eckert, *Korea Old and New*, p. 294.

[32]Ibid., p. 318.

[33]Henderson, *Korea. The Politics of the Vortex*, p. 90.

[34]Dong, *Japanese Colonial Policy and Practice in Korea*, p. 388.

[35]Ibid., p. 483.

[36]Ibid., p. 190.

[37]Brudnoy, "Japan's Experiment in Korea," p. 168.

[38]Vacante, *Japanese Colonial Education*, p. 47.

[39]Eckert, *Korea Old and New*, 285.

[40]Ibid., p. 259.

[41]Bang, *Japan's Colonial Educational Policy in Korea*, p. 205.

[42]Chong-Sik Lee, *The Politics of Korean Nationalism* (University of California Press, 1963), pp. 277–278.

[43]Sucheng Chan in Mary Paik Lee, *Quiet Odyssey: A Pioneer Korean Woman in America* (University of Washington Press, 1990), p. xxxii.

[44]Henceforth, South Korea will be dealt with because information is sufficient only to deal with that country.

[45]Eckert, *Korea Old and New*, p. 396. The author noted that this sum represented, "more dollars per capita of aid than to any other foreign country except South Vietnam and Israel."

[46]Jang Jip Choi, "Political Cleavages in South Korea," p. 22 in Hagen Koo, ed., *State and Society in Contemporary Korea* (Cornell University Press, 1993).

[47]Carter J. Eckert, "The South Korean Bourgeoisie: A Class in Search of Hegemony," p. 126 in Hagen Koo, ed., *State and Society in Contemporary Korea* (Cornell University Press, 1993).

[48]Ibid., p. 104.

[49]Shin-Bok Lim, "Educational Policy Changes in Korea: Ideology and Praxis," p. 388 in Gill-Chin Lim and Wook Chang, eds, *Dynamic Transformation: Korea, NICS and Beyond* (Consortium on Development Studies, 1990).

[50]Noel F. McGinn and others, *Education and Development in Korea* (Council on East Asian Studies, Harvard University, 1980), p. 159.

[51] See the relevant comments in Don Adams and Esther E. Gottlieb, *Education and Social Change in Korea* (Garland, 1993), pp. 30, 175, 223.

[52] Moon Yong-lin, "Facts About Education Present No Shangri-La," *Koreana*, 5 (1991), p. 35.

[53] Ibid., p. 39.

[54] Adams and Gottlieb, *Education and Social Change in Korea*, pp. 19, 158; and Lim, "Educational Policy Changes in Korea," p. 386.

[55] Kwan Lee, "Past, Present and Future Trends in the Public and Private Sectors of Korean Higher Education," p. 67 in *Public and Private Sectors in Asian Higher Education Systems* (Research Institute for Higher Education, Hiroshima University, 1987). ERIC ED 291 329.

[56] Ibid., p. 78.

[57] McGinn, *Education and Development in Korea*, pp. 152–154.

[58] Douglas C. Smith, *Elementary Teacher Education in Korea* (Phi Delta Kappa Educational Foundation, 1994), p. 28.

[59] McGinn, *Education and Development in Korea*, p. 168.

[60] Clark W. Sorensen, "Success and Education in South Korea," *Comparative Education Review*, 38 (February 1994), p. 31.

[61] Ibid., p. 19, footnote 33.

[62] Lim, "Educational Policy Changes in Korea," p. 399.

[63] Adams and Gottlieb, *Education and Social Change in Korea*, p. 171.

[64] Bae Chong-keun, "Education Top Reason Behind Rapid Growth," *Koreana*, 5 (1991), p. 57; and Adams and Gottlieb, *Education and Social Change in Korea*, p. 171.

[65] Jerome Alan Cohen and Edward J. Baker in Shaw, *Human Rights in Korea*, p. 180. Ewha University, the first women's university in Korea, was established in 1886 as a lower school for girls.

[66] Hong Sah-myung, "All About Koreans Studying Overseas," *Koreana*, 5 (1991), p. 81.

[67] Bang-Soon L. Yoon, "Reverse Brain Drain in South Korea: State-led Model," *Studies in Comparative International Development*, 27 (Spring 1992), p. 7.

[68] Adams and Gottlieb, *Education and Social Change in Korea*, p. 46.

[69] Ibid., p. 171.

[70] Ibid., p. 174.

[71] Sorensen, "Success and Education in South Korea," p. 21.

[72] McGinn, *Education and Development in Korea*, p. 6.

[73] Ibid., pp. 204–206.

[74] Kim Yoon-tai, "Businesses Demand High-skilled Grads," *Koreana*, 5 (1991), p. 71.

[75] Henderson, *Korea. The Politics of the Vortex*, p. 170.

[76] Ibid., p. 221.

[77] Ibid., p. 222.

[78] McGinn, *Education and Development in Korea*, p. 175. See Bun Song Lee, "Sex Discrimination in Korea's Job Market" in Sung Yeung Kwock, ed., *The Korean Economy at a Crossroad* (Quorum Books, 1994). See also Cho Kyung Won, "Overcoming Confucian Barriers: Changing Educational Opportunities for Women in Korea," pp. 206–222 in Joyce Gelb and Marian Lief Palley, eds., *Women of Japan and Korea* (Temple University Press, 1994).

[79] See Adams and Gottlieb, *Education and Social Change in Korea*, p. 176; Mi-Na Lee, *Education Effects on Earnings in the Korean Labor Market: Education As a Policy Device for Mobility of the Disadvantaged* (Doctoral dissertation, Harvard University, 1986), p. 137; and Roh Mihye, "Women Workers in a Changing Korean Society," pp. 240–256 in Joyce Gelb and Marian Lief Palley, eds., *Women of Japan and Korea* (Temple University Press, 1994).

[80] Smith, *Elementary Teacher Education in Korea*, p. 39.

[81] Teresa Watanabe, "Bribes Buy Trouble in New Korea," *Los Angeles Times*, June 23, 1993.

[82] Don Adams, "Problems of Reconstruction in Korean Education," *Comparative Education Review*, 3 (1959–1960), p. 27.

[83] Eckert, *Korea Old and New*, p. 392.

[84]See Gil San Lee, *Ideological Context of American Educational Policy in Occupied Korea, 1945–1948* (Doctoral dissertation, University of Illinois, 1989), p. 12; and Chungmoo Choi, "The Discourse of Decolonization and Popular Memory: South Korea," *Positions,* 1 (Spring 1993), pp. 82–83.

[85]Wayne K. Patterson, *The Korean Frontier in America: Immigration to Hawaii, 1896–1910,* volume II (Doctoral dissertation, University of Pennsylvania, 1977), p. 410.

[86]Ibid., p. 486.

[87]Hyung June Moon, *The Korean Immigrants in America: The Quest for Identity in the Formative Years, 1903–1918* (Doctoral dissertation, University of Nevada, Reno, 1976), p. 89.

[88]Luciano Mangiafico, *Contemporary American Immigrants* (Praeger, 1988), p. 95.

[89]Insook Han Park and others, *Korean Immigrants and U.S. Immigration Policy: A Predeparture Perspective* (East–West Population Institute, March 1990), pp. 32, 55.

[90]Ibid., p. 45.

[91]Ibid., pp. 64–65

[92]Park, *Korean Immigrants and U. S. Immigration Policy,* p. 63.

[93]Herbert R. Barringer and Sung-nam Cho, *Koreans in the United States. A Fact Book* (Center for Korean Studies, University of Hawaii, 1989), p. 116.

[94]Hyung June Moon, *The Korean Immigrants in America,* p. 165.

[95]Ibid., p. 258.

[96]Ibid., p. 267.

[97]Ibid., p. 279.

[98]Kingsley K Lyu, "Korean Nationalist Activities in Hawaii and the Continental United States, 1900–1945. Part I: 1900–1919," *Amerasia Journal,* 4 (1977), p. 30.

[99]Lee Houchins and Chang-su Houchins, "The Korean Experience in America, 1903–1924," *Pacific Historical Review,* 43 (November 1974), p. 565.

[100]Lee, *Quiet Odyssey,* p. 16.

[101]Ibid., p. 49.

[102]Ibid., p. 56.

[103]Ibid., p. 105.

[104]Helen Lewis Givens, *The Korean Community in Los Angeles County* (Master's thesis, University of Southern California, 1939), p. 30.

[105]Ibid., p. 35. See also Eui-Young Yu and others, eds., *Koreans in Los Angeles. Prospects and Promises* (Koryo Research Institute, California State University, Los Angeles, 1982), p. 16.

[106]Eui-Young Yu, "Korean Communities in America: Past, Present, and Future," *Amerasia Journal,* 10 (1983), p. 34.

[107]Yongsook Lee, "Koreans in Japan and the United States," in Margaret A. Gibson and John U. Ogbu, eds., *Minority Status and Schooling. A Comparative Study of Immigrant and Involuntary Minorities* (Garland, 1991), pp. 156–157.

[108]Chang Hyun Shin Geer, *Korean Americans and Ethnic Heritage Education: A Case Study in Western New York* (Doctoral dissertation, State University of New York at Buffalo, 1981), p. 43.

[109]Melanie Hahn and Frederick Dobb, "Lost in the System," *Integrateducation,* 13 (July–August 1975), p. 14.

[110]Bok-Lim C. Kim, *The Korean-American Child at School and at Home* (The Author, 1980), p. 100.

[111]Ibid., p. 36.

[112]Michael G. Fowler, *An Analysis of the Problem of Korean Students in American Secondary Schools As Perceived by Korean Students and Parents and the Teachers in Public Schools* (Doctoral dissertation, University of Northern Colorado, 1978), p. 23.

[113]Ibid., p. 34.

[114]Ibid., p. 35.

[115]Ibid., p. 37.

[116] Ibid., p. 60.

[117] Stacey J. Lee, *Ethnic Identification and Social Interaction: A Study of Asian-American Students at a Philadelphia High School* (Doctoral dissertation, University of Pennsylvania, 1991), p. 32.

[118] Ibid., p. 34.

[119] Ibid., p. 97.

[120] Ibid., p. 98.

[121] Ibid., p. 62.

[122] See issues of *The National Faculty Directory* for the years 1977, 1987, and 1997.

[123] See Yvonne M. Lau, "Asian Americans on College Campuses: Profiles and Trends," p. 144 in Illinois Advisory Committee to the United States Commission on Civil Rights, *Civil Rights Issues Facing Asian Americans in Metropolitan Chicago* (The Commission, May 1995).

[124] Diane Reis, "Minorities on Slow Tenure Track at Chicago Universities," *Chicago Reporter*, 16, No. 5 (1987), pp. 3–5.

[125] Bong-youn Choy, *Koreans in America* (Nelson-Hall, 1979), p. 121.

[126] Ilsoo Kim, *New Urban Immigrants. The Korean Community in New York* (Princeton University Press, 1981), p. 153.

[127] Ibid., p. 154.

[128] Ibid., p. 157.

[129] Ibid., pp. 163–164; and Eun-Young Kim, "Assimilation Patterns of Koreans in the United States," p. 147 in Scott M. Morgan and Elizabeth Colson, eds., *People in Upheaval* (Center for Migration Studies, 1987).

[130] Ha-Joong Song, *Who Stays? Who Returns? The Choice of Korean Scientists and Engineers* (Doctoral dissertation, Harvard University, May 1991), p. 1.

[131] Edward Tea Chang, *New Urban Crisis: Korean-Black Conflicts in Los Angeles* (Doctoral dissertation, University of California, Berkeley, 1990), pp. 40–41.

[132] See Hyong-In Kim, *Rural Slavery in Antebellum South Carolina and Early Chosen Korea* (Doctoral dissertation, University of New Mexico, 1990), chapter 1, "Development of Slavery."

[133] Eckert, "The South Korean Bourgeoisie," p. 114, footnote 41.

[134] Chungmoo Choi, "The Discourse of Decolonization and Popular Memory," p. 97.

[135] Ian Buruma, "Will the Wall Come Tumbling Down?" *New York Review of Books*, November 3, 1994, p. 27.

[136] Choi, "The Discourse of Decolonization and Popular Memory," p. 97.

CHAPTER FIVE

Philippines

When the Spanish invaded the Philippines in 1565, they found that "the inhabitants, men and women alike, knew how to read and write and that they preserved their laws, stories, and proverbs on pieces of tree bark, bamboo, or palm leaves on which they incised characters that looked more or less like Greek or Arabic, by using a stylus."[1] After a century or so of Spanish settlement, the native system of writing had disappeared, as did the archives of written native culture. The spiritual custodians of the conquerors, the Roman Catholic clergy, had destroyed the latter while they effectively forbade further teaching of the native script. The people of the Philippines spoke many dialects, but the writing system was apparently uniform for all of them. The alphabet had contained 12 consonants and three vowels. Schumacher contended that "the use of the syllabary seems to have been confined to such practical and ephemeral uses as letters and the noting down of debts."[2] Other sources, such as Bernabe—quoted earlier—held that "laws, stories, and proverbs" were also recorded.[3]

The natives' "long tradition of literacy"[4] was abruptly cut off by the conquerors. Despite repeated orders from Madrid, the friars refused to teach Spanish to the natives. Enough of the regional dialect was taught to enable the memorization of translated prayers. This practice also helped perpetuate division among the peasant masses, which served the Spaniards' political purpose.

The religious missionaries, who actually ruled from day to day, sought out collaborators from among the native chiefs whose children received a more advanced education. "The children proved enthusiastic and effective auxiliaries of the religious in winning over the parents to the new religion, reporting clandestine pagan rituals, and in catechizing the older generation."[5] The Spanish transformed the indigenous elite into "a native nobility" that supplied local officials in the Spanish-designed municipal government[6] as well as in lower church positions. The religious orders owned very large tracts of arable land that came to be worked by Chinese and indigenous Filipino laborers. Local political power was monopolized by a small group of native elite landowners.

The Spanish, including the clergy, regarded the *indios*, the large indigenous class of laborers, as inferior human beings, incapable of worthy accomplishments. "In nearly every situation of Spanish and native interaction the derogation of native character was pursued relentlessly—in school, in church, in the work place."[7] Aquino Oades observed that "the Dominican newspaper of Manila not infrequently referred to the people as 'monkeys.'"[8] This view of the indio, however, was more ideological than factual. The Spanish had elsewhere in their empire tried out a policy of wider educational opportunity for native people. It had proved far more successful than anticipated, much to the chagrin of the conquerors.

In 1536, for example, Spanish authorities in Mexico opened the Colegio de Santa Cruz de Tlaltelolco to indios. Soon, indios became professors and teachers of Spanish students. The Spanish retreated and announced the institution would have to close because of lack of funds.[9] Similarly, in 1595 the Jesuits in the Philippines opened the Colegio de Manila. The next year, an adjunct institution, known as the Colegio de Niños, was begun to serve indios who were sons of native elite families. Their curriculum included religion, the three Rs, music, and handicrafts. Two years afterward, Jesuit vice-provincial Father Prado wrote in his annual report that "the Tagalog boys have their own teacher from whom they learn reading, writing and arithmetic, in all of which they give promise."[10] In 1601, the college closed because of lack of funds. This was at a time when native people in the general area still practiced their own literate tradition, as observed by Father Chirino between 1590 and 1602:

> All these islanders are much given to reading and writing. . . . There is hardly a man, and much less a woman, who does not read and write in the characters used in Manila, which are entirely different from those of China, Japan and India.[11]

Chirino had visited Luzon and the Visayas.

Historians and contemporary observers were agreed that only up to 10% of the Filipinos could understand Spanish by the close of the Spanish period in 1898. Costa wrote that "hardly two percent . . . could barely understand . . . conversational Spanish."[12] Abella accepted this figure.[13] Aquino Oades, however, questions the variety of Spanish involved. "Less than two percent of the indigenous population could speak a brand of Spanish that was not pidgin or *chabacano* at the close of the Spanish regime."[14] According to Phelan, fewer than 10% could speak Spanish[15] and Rafael held that, "only about 10 percent of the population could actually understand" the language.[16] A curious explanation for the situation was offered by Fox, who contended, "One very strong reason why Filipinos did not achieve wide literacy in Spanish prior to 1863 was because they did not wish it. They preferred their own regional tongues."[17] Because, however, indio students were not customarily offered a choice of instructional language, it is not clear how they did not wish Spanish. Other historians note that in Cebu during the mid-19th century, it was up to different teachers whether to use Spanish or Visayan.[18]

The tiny contingent of children who attended school before 1863 were a highly select group. Aquino Oades wrote that, "before 1863 public schools were hardly known in the Philippines."[19] The only government support for education of the indio was in the form of occasional help to missionary schools. Children of Spaniards received schooling more or less equal to what they would have received in Spain. Private schools were organized for those who could afford it. The Royal College of San Felipe, organized by the Spaniards for their own children, had severe admission requirements: "The collegiates must be of pure race and have no mixture of Moorish or Jewish blood to the fourth degree, and shall have no negro or Benegal blood, or that of any similar nation in their veins, or a fourth part of Filipino blood."[20] A certain number of elementary schools were supported by contributions of wealthy persons and did not charge tuition.[21] There were no such institutions in secondary or higher education.

A major turning point in Filipino education occurred in 1863 when, for the first time, a national system of education was installed. Initiated by the Spanish government, the change was aimed in part at overcoming the padres' tight hold over schooling in the Philippines. Padre Joaquin Fonseca, a member of the royal education commission that prepared the new system, argued against the change. "He maintained that it was impossible for the Philippines to follow the plan of Cuba as they had been asked to do, because of 'the natural apathy of the aborigines who populate this extensive archipelago' compared 'with the intellectual superiority of the white race' of the Cuban Antilles."[22]

The 19th century was a time of great political change in Spanish politics, centering in part on liberal objections to the power of the Catholic church:

> In the century running from 1767 to 1868 Spain banished the Jesuits five times. In 1835–1836 a Spanish liberal government confiscated and sold large amounts of church property after having closed 2,000 religious houses. . . . Between 1812 and 1876 . . . Spain had five constitutions. The civil war lasted from 1833 to 1839.[23]

A revolution broke out in 1868. The religious establishment in the Philippines feared these political currents and sought to prevent them from infecting the Filipinos. One way was to forestall indios from learning Spanish that would otherwise open their world to critical thought and disobedience.

The educational decree of 1863 established a public school system in the Philippines. Each town was to have at least one primary school. Attendance was compulsory and poor children could attend without charge. Spanish was made the language of instruction. The curriculum was to include the four Rs (including religion), Spanish language and grammar, the history of Spain (but not of the Philippines), geography, music, courtesy, and agriculture. Most significant perhaps, the parish priest was appointed school inspector in each locality.[24] Corpuz wrote that, "in the average village school in the provinces instruction remained hardly changed in quality from the pre-1863 period. . . ."[25]

Placing parish priests in charge of determining whether schools were properly implementing the new law was one way to ensure a minimum of implementation. For example, priests still opposed using Spanish in the primary schools. As a result, between 1867 and 1889, 14 decrees concerning the use and teaching of Spanish were issued.[26] They had little effect.

Nevertheless, elementary education became more available under the 1863 law. In 1870, for example, Luzon's 1,114 public and private schools enrolled 195,425 children.[27] This area, of course, was the most urbanized in the Philippines and comparatively well-supplied with schools even before the 1863 law was enacted. National school-attendance figures varied greatly during the years 1870 through 1897. In the first year, the total was 385,907 and in the last year, 360,000. However, in 1877 it was only 177,113.[28] Attendance at secondary schools was sharply less. In 1870 it was only 1,883.[29] By 1895, their numbers had risen to 6,026.[30] One notable aspect of this lesser number was that three quarters of enrollment were indios or mestizos. In earlier years, Spanish children had constituted almost the entirety of secondary school students. Still, the number was exceedingly small and undoubtedly socially selective. In the 1890s, over 3,000 students attended higher education, but this was a minuscule percentage of a total population of 6 million.[31]

Until late in the 19th century, wrote Abella, the priesthood was "the top academic career of the period."[32] Attending a university for purposes of a liberal education was almost unknown. Only in the last century or so of the Spanish occupation were Filipinos eligible to share higher educational opportunities on a roughly equal basis. In earlier years, Spanish authorities in higher education took special pains to exclude indios from their ranks. In time, they admitted some but minimized their number. At the Dominican University of Santo Tomas, for nearly 3 centuries the keystone of higher education in the Philippines, indios were scarce until later years. By that time, native-born clergy were dissatisfied with their subordinate position in the churches where they served as assistants to Spanish churchmen. As Schumacher observed, "Practically all the priests executed or exiled in 1872 for their activity in defense or Filipino rights, were alumni of the University [of Santo Tomas]."[33] At the same time, however, the universities continued to serve as a training ground for Spanish culture. In addition, "all higher education, because of its cost, had been inaccessible to the great majority of the people."[34]

Enrollment statistics in higher education must be read with care. Thus, in 1886 to 1887, 1,981 students were said to be enrolled at the University of Manila.

But more than two thirds of these were receiving secondary-school instruction. Following is an illuminating ethnic breakdown of the enrollment:[35]

	Total	Secondary	Percent Secondary
Spanish Europeans	123	45	36.6
Insular Spaniards	93	37	39.8
Spanish mestizos	180	95	52.8
Natives	1,367	1,074	78.6
Chinese mestizos	219	82	37.4
Total	1,981	1,333	67.3

Indios made up 80.6% of secondary students but only 45.2% of collegiate students. How many completed their course of study is unknown.

A revolution for independence from Spain broke out in 1896. Under the leadership of Andres Bonifacio, the Katipunan—a revolutionary organization—grew rapidly until it reached a peak of 400,000 members. Its membership was mainly Tagalog, in the general Luzon area. Aquino Oades declared that many upper-class Filipinos first "flocked to the Spanish authorities to make protestations of loyalty to Spain" but as the uprising spread, more began to support the revolutionary forces.[36] Spain had rejected many earlier demands of reformers before hostilities began. These included representation in the Cortes (national legislature), positions in government, and the opening of a secular university as well as abolition of censorship, lessening of friars' political power, and ending of inequality of Filipinos. (In 1896, the Spanish were especially unlikely to yield on any of these demands because in that year their remaining colony in Latin America—Cuba—also erupted in a revolution for independence.)

In June 1898, Emilio Aguinaldo, the ranking military head of the revolution, declared independence, and in January 1899, the first Philippine Republic was proclaimed. Meanwhile, however, U.S. military authorities received orders to occupy all of the Philippines. In 2 weeks, U.S. forces attacked the guerrilla armies of the Filipinos, until recently their allies against Spain. By the end of 1899, some 55,000 U.S. troops were in the field. Two years later, the number had grown to 126,000 and a bloody war was underway.

Once Filipinos had declared independence, they wrote a constitution and began to legislate. One of their first laws established a public university, solely under secular, not church, control. Primary education was declared to be free and compulsory. A Filipino author was directed to write what was perhaps to be the first school textbook of Philippine history.[37] Religion was no longer to be part of the curriculum in higher education. Some of this legislating occurred as United States and Filipino armed forces fought each other.

The war itself, which lasted until 1902, was greatly one-sided in favor of the United States, whose soldiers committed a number of atrocities against Filipinos.[38] "White enlisted men, almost without exception, saw the Filipino as 'nigger'."[39] Gates reported "nigger" was also "used in the English-language newspapers published in Manila."[40] In 1899, the first full year of the U.S.–Filipino war, the U.S. commanding officer, Major-General Arthur MacArthur, proposed the United States use schooling for Filipinos as a pacification measure. "This appropriation is recommended primarily and exclusively as an adjunct to military operations calculated to pacify the people and to procure the restoration of tranquility throughout the archipelago."[41] Individual soldiers were assigned as teachers, often with no training or supplies. Examining this experience in the province of Batangas, May wrotes:

> It would be difficult to argue that the U.S. Army's educational efforts in Batangas did any harm, but it would be equally difficult to argue that they did much good, or that they won many friends for the Americans in the province.[42]

It is not clear what role, if any, was played in this educational episode by the racial stereotypes held by American troops.

With the end of the war in 1902, Americans authorized the creation of a public school system that superseded the schools operated by the revolutionaries. Hayden, who later referred to "our Filipino wards," acknowledged that, "the revolutionary governments and the Philippine Republic of 1898–1900 exhibited remarkable concern for education. . . . They made every effort to keep the existing schools alive. . . ."[43] All this was set aside when, in January 1901, the Philippine Commission—the American-appointed executive and legislative body—adopted Act No. 74 to create a public primary-school system that provided free education.[44] The next year, a secondary-school system was added. English was declared to be the language of instruction throughout the public schools. In 1908, legislative Bill No. 148 established the regional languages as instructional languages, but the Philippine Commission vetoed the action.[45] Even though the legislative body that had passed 148 was filled with adherents of the U.S. colonial regime, nevertheless opposition to the sole use of English was deeply felt.

The old native elite whose power under the Spanish had rested on control of the land and local governments lost few of their prerogatives under the Americans. If anything, these expanded. Thus, once the American authorities felt certain the elite supported the new colonial order, elites were permitted to occupy positions in the government bureaucracy. Between 1901 and 1913, 35,829 Filipinos took civil service examinations in the English language; 8,834, or 24.6%, passed; and 72% of those passing were appointed, primarily to lower-level jobs.[46] By 1921, over 90% of all career civil servants were Filipinos, including a number on the middle and higher levels. Practically all came from upper ranks of Filipino society. When Filipinos were chosen to attend universities on the U.S. mainland, candidates from elite layers of society were given special consideration.[47]

The U.S. government did not promote education in the Philippines other than by exhortation. For example, on the mainland, every state had received federal lands to help finance public schools. Between 1803 and 1864, the average land grant to a state was 890,439 acres.[48] The aid was critical. In neither newly acquired colony—Puerto Rico or the Philippines—were land grants donated for schools. Nevertheless, despite American niggardliness, the colonial school system was an improvement over that of the Spanish. Low and stagnant incomes were inadequate to finance schools and privileged groups were eager to avoid taxation for this purpose. In the 1903 national elections in the Philippines, only 3% of the population was deemed eligible to vote.[49] It was such groups that laid weak foundations for public education. Funds were collected by insular, provincial, and municipal taxes. Insular revenues were derived principally from taxes on exports. Voluntary contributions were solicited, especially to build schools. In 1905, the large sum of 232,988 pesos were contributed, mainly by poor Filipinos.[50] In addition, some of the latter also contributed their labor; others gave materials. Although some funds were given by various federal bodies from time to time, U.S. funds were contributed more as charity than as a matter of entitlement.

Primary schools were established on a basis of a 4-year program whereas intermediate schools were expected to extend for 3 more years. Yet, the formal goal called only for a total of 3 years of instruction to be gained between 6 and 15 years of age.[51] Wholesale dropouts became the rule from the outset. In 1909, 95% of all children in the public schools were enrolled in the first four grades, which indicated a large dropout rate.[52] Barrows, an American who in 1903 became Director of Education, visited existing schools 2 years earlier and described them as follows:[53]

> You go into almost any town, or you go into a barrio, way off, it may be miles from the center of the town, and you will find little schools, and an old woman or an old man will have a small class of children to whom he or she is teaching the syllabary of their language (the local language)—the alphabet and the syllables and the church catechism, fitting them for participation in the parish church. That degree of education . . . the great majority of Filipinos possess.

This picture did not change greatly in the first 20 or so years. At times, it grew worse.

In 1903 and 1904, the elementary course was cut from 4 to 3 years. Although a teacher-training school had been authorized in 1901, 8 years later, "almost half [the teachers] were unable to teach beyond the second grade."[54] Between 1910 to 1911 and 1912 to 1913, enrollment in the colony's public schools fell from 610,493 to 440,050. In the latter years, "as before, pupils generally received no more than two years of schooling."[55] The spirit of Filipino schooling—directed by U.S. officials until 1935—was summarized by May. "Believing from the outset that Filipinos were backward and inferior, they applied programs they deemed appropriate for backward and inferior people."[56] Little was done to remedy enormous dropout rates. For example, "during the school year 1907–08, 63,178 pupils moved from Grade One to Grade Two, 31,101 from Grade Two to Grade Three and only 13,849 from Grade Three to Grade Four."[57]

An assessment of the school system was conducted by the Philippine Educational Survey Commission in 1925. Counts, a member of the staff, summarized some highlights. A total of 1,100,000 were in the public schools:

> More than four-fifths of these pupils are found in the first four years of the system, the primary school, while but fifty thousand are in the secondary school and three or four thousand in the University of the Philippines. . . . 50 percent of the children of school age are not in school. . . . The achievements fall far below the American standards. The inferiority of achievement . . . varies directly as the function measured is dependent on the mastery of the English language. In arithmetic . . . Filipino children do as well as American children. . . . Fifth-grade pupils, though older by several years than their American brothers and sisters, read no better than second-grade children in the United States. First-year high-school pupils read only as well as fourth-grade American children, and during the four years of secondary education they gain but a single American grade in reading power.[58]

Counts specified three highly significant problems: the English requirement, relatively untrained teachers, and a curriculum unrelated to Philippine life. As Counts explained: "The six or more years of [English] language training which the American child brings to the work of formal education the Filipino boy or girl lacks when he [sic] enters school."[59]

Counts' attention to language reflected far more than his personal preference. As he explained, the ordinary student, "is endeavoring to acquire strange ideas through a language that he does not understand. The outcome in functional knowledge must be very meager."[60] Outside the classroom, students had no need for English. Nor were many of their teachers fluent in the language, for more or less the same reason. For the latter, the issue embraced considerably more than language: "The overwhelming majority of the twenty-seven thousand teachers . . . are without even the most meager professional preparation."[61] Implicitly criticizing the U.S.-oriented school system of the Philippines, Counts concluded that, "the great object of education should be that of inducting young people into membership in their own society and into the use of the instrumentalities of their own culture."[62] This could be contrasted with a recollection about colonial school days in the Philippines: "I knew the Gettysburg Address by heart in fourth grade."[63]

In 1934, the U.S. Congress passed the Tydings-McDuffie Act that created the Philippine Commonwealth, a transition of indefinite duration to independence. A year later, the Commonwealth came into formal existence and lasted until 1946. Under the Commonwealth, it was widely expected that the Philippines would begin to adopt public policies more consistent with its own interests. Yet the Commonwealth remained the colony in all but name. This was especially true in education, where the economic elite continued to reap by far the greatest benefits.

In 1935, only somewhat over one third of the school-age population between 7 and 17 attended school.[64] During the 1931 to 1932 school year, school enrollments had begun to drop. Around the same time, 57 towns started to charge tuition at their public schools, which further reduced attendance. In large-city schools, during 1933, double sessions became standard for the first two grades; in village (*barrio*) schools, all grades were placed on half time.[65] Douglas noted at the mid-1930s, "nearly half the children enrolling in first grade during the Commonwealth did not stay in school long enough to complete fourth grade."[66] A further regression occurred in 1940 when the Commonwealth abolished the seventh grade in all public schools. As the world depression deepened, certain existing trends were aggravated. Such, for example, was the long-term tendency for high schools to de-emphasize the academic curriculum. In 1910, over 81% of secondary-school students had been in such curricula; in 1932, the figure had fallen under two thirds (65.42%). Reflecting the bitter economic situation at the time, Douglas commented: "Every bit as demoralizing as having academic graduates wandering around the country looking for jobs would be the prospect of vocationally trained individuals following them."[67]

Dropout rates continued high into the later 1930s. As Hayden reported about the year 1936:

> Of the third of a million children who were entering the first grade each year about 77 percent survived and enrolled in grade two, while 23 percent were eliminated; 62 percent reached grade three and 38 percent did not; and 48 percent enrolled in the fourth grade, while 52 percent of those who had entered grade one had been eliminated before completing the [four] primary grades."[68]

In the 1939 census, illiterates over 10 years of age—who made up close to half the entire population—outnumbered public school students by more than a two-to-one margin. Many of the illiterates were dropouts and others had never had much of a chance to learn. In 1938, overall literacy was reported at 48.8% of persons aged 10 years or older; although somewhat difficult to accept, literacy was defined as ability to read or write in any language. Manila, the most literate city, was 80.7% literate.[69]

Until 1938, elementary schools were financed by municipalities who could draw on various sources including a land tax. Secondary schools depended on provincial funds, although tuition was also charged. The insular government supported special schools. The only financial contribution by the U.S. government was for the salaries of high-ranking Filipino teachers and administrators, as well as all Americans employed in the school systems. During the 1939 to 1940 school year, the Commonwealth government (no longer the insular government) began supporting the 4-year primary schools while the municipalities took responsibility for the 3-year intermediate elementary schools.[70] In any case, the financing fell far short of filling the need. In the 1937 to 1938 school year, over one third of all elementary classes met in temporary buildings.[71] As indicated previously, 2 years later, the national government took responsibility for primary school but at the same time abolished the seventh grade.

Nearly 95% of all school children attended public schools in 1940; the remainder were in private schools that were a mixed bag. Only some of the latter were recognized by the government; more were not. As Swendiman noted, "there was no law to prevent a person disqualified by greed, ignorance, or even immoral character from opening a school."[72] Yet, the public and private schools together in 1940 only provided enough facilities to house fewer than half of all school-age children. This was true despite the extremely high dropout rate and the use of double sessions in many schools.

Shortly after the bombing of Pearl Harbor in December 1941, Japanese forces occupied the Philippines. They directed that the schools continue to operate under Japanese protection. Filipino guerrilla groups organized their own schools, however, and wherever they could, they disrupted the other schools. In Leyte, for example, guerrilla forces warned teachers in the latter schools to stop teaching there. The guerrilla schools did not attempt to enroll all the eligible children inasmuch as structures and supplies were minimal. To the extent possible, lessons were based on the prewar curriculum, reflecting in part the prominent role played by public-school teachers who organized the guerrilla schools. Only the first four grades were offered.[73] Among the many guerrilla organizations active during the war, Mahajani named the Hukbalahap as mounting "the most effective and widespread resistance to Japanese occupation."[74]

Japan's cultural policy in the occupied Philippines was far broader than control of the schools. Its fundamental goal was to replace American influence, beginning with the English language. Although Japanese was required to be taught in the schools, it did not become the sole language nor even the instructional language, as in Korea. Instead, Japanese authorities employed Tagalog, one of the five principal indigenous languages of the Philippines, in an effort to utilize nationalism as an instrument of war. Military Ordinance No. 13 proclaimed Tagalog and Japanese as official languages while Spanish was banned and English temporarily retained as a minor languge.[75] In government affairs, English gave way to Tagalog. After October 13, 1943, when the Japan-sponsored Philippine Republic was proclaimed, "an executive order [was issued] to change American names of streets, towns, and buildings to Japanese and Filipino names so as to remove all traces of Anglo-Saxon influence."[76]

Other steps were taken to broaden the new cultural directions. In the 14th Army, Japanese formed the Propaganda Corps to survey the larger cultural scene. Its members noted that there were many more beauty parlors than bookstores to be seen. In Manila, nearly 40 bookstores and some 85 other stores sold books among other products. Among the books for sale, the Corps found the following distribution by language, in percentages:[77]

70	English
10	Spanish
12	Chinese
5	Tagalog

Popular leaflets were printed in various languages, including Ilocano and Visayan.[78] Religion also became a weapon:

> On 4 December [1942], the Blessed Virgin of the Immaculate Conception was proclaimed patroness and protector of the Philippines by a papal bull. This signified that the Vatican officially and openly recognized the Japanese occupation of the Philippines.[79]

Little is known of the practical effects of this step.

Agoncillo pointed out that the prewar literary intelligentsia scoffed at the indigenous languages:

> In pre-war years, the writers had nothing but scorn for things indigenous, for having imbibed the Western concepts and ideals of truth and beauty, they looked upon the literary and artistic manifestations of their *confreres* in the Philippine languages with indifference, if not indeed with contempt. Oriental in feeling and sentiment, their one-sided education had made them strangers in their own country.[80]

To help reverse this attitude, Japanese began publishing *Filipina*, a monthly bilingual magazine. Fees to authors writing in Tagalog were set high and honors were conferred on them.[81] Dramatic Philippines, another Japanese-sponsored group, staged Tagalog plays and plays translated into Tagalog. These productions were viewed by broader circles than university audiences. Subject matter was relatively open as "the Japanese . . . allowed any kind of writing except those critical of the 'new order'."[82] Members of the traditional sort initially, at least, found it difficult since most Filipino writers "did not know, nor could they write a correct sentence in [Tagalog]. . . . There were, in their sentences, English overtones or sentence construction that appeared awkward in Tagalog."[83] Agoncillo concluded that "the Japanese succeeded in projecting Tagalog to the consciousness of the Filipinos as a language to be desired and developed."[84]

Not for a moment, however, did Japanese stratagems about replacing English negate the broad popular distaste for the Japanese occupation. Guerrilla action was suppressed with the utmost force as were any direct challenges to Japanese rule: "The Japanese military launched a series of bloody 'punitive expeditions' that led to the slaughter of 12,000 civilians on one island and countless atrocities across the archipelago."[85]

In 1946, one year after the end of World War II, the Philippines became independent. During the ensuing 4 or more decades, a succession of governments created educational structures that served best the middle and upper classes of the new republic. The great, poor majority experienced little progress. At times, their fortunes turned downward.

Dropout rates continued high. As the following table shows, in the 1950s by sixth grade, nearly two thirds of the students were no longer attending school. Even by second grade, over one sixth of the original first graders had dropped out. This should be evaluated from the viewpoint of Gerardo Flores's 1951 statement that "with the present system of elementary education, about seven years are necessary to make a learner functionally literate for useful citizenship."[87]

TABLE 5.1

Retention and Dropout Rates of Pupils in Public and Private Schools
Enrolled in the First Grade in 1949–1950 to the 4th Year in 1958–1959[86]

School Year	Grade Level	Enrollment	Retention rate (%)	Cumulative Dropout Rate (%)
1949–1950	I	969,693	100.0	0.0
1950–1951	II	802,749	82.8	17.2
1951–1952	III	722,035	74.5	25.5
1952–1953	IV	597,887	61.6	38.4
1953–1954	V	433,538	44.7	55.3
1954–1955	VI	330,988	34.1	65.9
1955–1956	1	187,080	19.3	80.7
1956–1957	2	148,666	15.3	84.7
1957–1958	3	129,458	13.3	86.7
1958–1959	4	112,430	11.6	88.4

In 1960, a national survey of the Philippine schools was conducted by a team directed by University of California educator J. Chester Swanson. He reported that, "out of every 100 pupils who enrolled in Grade I in 1952–53: 80 reached Grade II; 73 reached Grade III; 64 reached Grade IV; 50 reached Grade V; and 39 reached Grade VI."[88] These figures closely corresponded to those cited previously. Over the previous decade, Swanson wrote, some 300,000 school-age children had not attended any elementary school at all.

The Survey Operations Team found a retrogression in academic achievement since 1925 and 1947:

> In general, sixth graders in these schools were around one grade below the 1925 group on the reading tests, more than one grade below on arithmetic computation and language, and over two grades below on arithmetic reasoning. In comparison with the 1947 pupils, they were about two grades below in reading and arithmetic, and about one grade below in language and dictation.[89]

Many high schools were found to have been organized since the end of the war but the quality of a number was doubtful. Little effective government regulation existed. "About all that could be attempted was enforcement of minimum standards and frequently this was difficult."[90] The library holdings of 161 high schools were examined and found to be sorely deficient; about one seventh had less than one book per student. One third to one half of elementary and high school teachers had failed or did not yet take a qualifying examination offered by the Civil Service Commission. In 1955 and 1956, only around one third of the teachers who actually took the exam passed it.[91]

The Swanson Report spoke out frankly on a then-current problem of secondary and higher education:

> The blunt fact is . . . that most of the private schools are profit-making. It is possible for such a school to offer a good education; some do. But the temptation to 'cut

corners', to make more money, is very great—so great that only high-minded, conscientious people can resist it. When schools are operated for profit they have to make decisions as to whether some available fund shall be used, on the one hand, to expand library resources or provide additional science equipment, or on the other hand to return dividends to the owners or stock holders. The decision may not always be in favor of the students who are paying tuition, presumably for the best education possible.[92]

In the late 1930s, a little over one third of all high-school students attended private high schools. By 1957 to 1958, more than three fifths did so.

The Swanson group also examined the situation as regards split session or half-time classes. Students then in primary school, up to a sixth had been on split session since 1953 to 1954. It was factors such as these that led a 1961 study by a U.S. government agency to conclude of Philippine education that "the quality of elementary and secondary schooling has deteriorated."[93]

By 1960, the seventh grade had been eliminated for 20 years. This factor alone helped to explain part of the deterioration of Philippine schooling. Two years before, out of 553 primary schools, about 25 had restored the grade. Most of these, however, were schools connected with colleges and universities. Typically, such schools usually enrolled children of higher education faculty and served as experimental institutions for colleges of education. Some Catholic schools also added the grade. Restoration of the grade in public schools was authorized by Republic Act No. 896, but no funds were ever voted to implement the step.[94] Into the present, this remains the case. The result is that pre-collegiate Philippine schools extend over 10 years rather than 12 years as in most modern countries. If elementary and secondary schools were exceptionally strong, the 10-year program might not be a handicap. There is, however, no evidence to suggest this is the case.

Much of Philippine schooling is neither free nor compulsory; where it is compulsory, enforcement of attendance is virtually nonexistent; and where it is free, parents nevertheless often pay considerable sums of money. The primary schools were declared compulsory in 1953. As the Swanson group explained, the system can more accurately be described as semicompulsory: "Children are required to remain in school only until they finish Grade IV if they enroll in Grade I; and little or no enforcement of this requirement exists."[95] Because hundreds of thousands of school-age children have never begun primary school, they are outside the circle of enforcement. This is especially true in rural areas where 70% of the population lives today. During the late 1960s, schooling in Central Luzon, where schools were most plentiful, was sharply differentiated as between rural and urban areas. Bennett wrote, "An average urban dweller has over three times as much chance of achieving a high school diploma or more than his rural counterpart; his chance of having gone as far as grade 6 are almost twice as good and finally, his chances of having attended school at all are 61 percent better than his rural cousin."[96] Carroll and Keane, writing around the same time, stated that "there are millions of children living in the more remote barrios who have neither the opportunity nor the incentive to continue their formal schooling beyond the first few grades."[97]

The health status of poor children was not conducive to educational advancement. According to a 1982 UNESCO report, nearly half (47.3%) of children 6 years of age and younger "are suffering from first degree malnutrition."[96] Further, despite often-cited figures about positive economic growth during the 1970s, "on the average only 22 percent of the children of the age group 0–6 have normal nutritional status. The remainder suffer from malnutrition of various degrees."[99] A 1982 survey by the Food and Nutrition Research Institute reported that 69% of the country's preschool children were found to be underweight; one in six were less than 75% of the weight-for-age standard."[100]

This bleak state of affairs occurred in a confusing context. During the 1960s and 1970s, the Philippine economy grew rapidly, as did the share of upper incomes. The poor, however, grew poorer. Between 1965 and 1985, beneath-poverty-line families increased from 41 to 59% of the total.[101] Real wages fell catastrophically. Farm real wages declined from $2.00 to $1.40 a day between 1962 and 1986. During the same period, urban workers did even worse: Unskilled workers went from $4.37 to $1.12 a day and skilled workers slid from $6.18 to $1.72.[102] In the 1970s and 1980s, Boyce wrote, wage workers in metropolitan Manila suffered an economic collapse "with few precedents in modern economic history."[103] Workers who protested against such trends frequently met with violence from police and the military. In 1972, President Marcos proclaimed a dictatorship that did not, however, succeed in ending further protests. Instead, a guerrilla army grew under the dictatorship, but it failed to overthrow Marcos.

Meanwhile, little attention was paid to educational issues by the government. In 1970, before the dictatorship, nearly one fourth of the national budget was spent on education. In 1980, it fell to 9.0%; the next year, it was only 7.6%. Only after Marcos was ejected from office in 1986 did the expenditures rise; by 1989, it rose to 20.15%, falling the following year to 17.26%.[104] Very few upper- and middle-class families used the public schools, so they were little affected.

It so happened that 2 years after Marcos left office, that is, in 1988, the Linguistic Society of the Philippines published a volume containing, among other things, an evaluation of certain aspects of the common school system.

Many deficiencies among teachers emerged. Among science teachers, for example, grade 10 teachers scored lower in science proficiency than grade 6 teachers. Even grade 4 teachers edged grade 10 teachers.[105] A general weakness of secondary school teachers in subject-matter knowledge was observed. Student achievement was very weak. As the evaluators observed, "There is a real failure in achievement, an indication of real problems in the system."[106] One consistent predictor of high achievement scores of secondary students was attendance at an excellent elementary school. In most cases, this was simply another expression of upper- or middle-class background. Critical attention was paid to low standards of achievement in primary grades:

> The fifty percent level of understanding subject matter in the elementary schools is not enough preparation for the understanding of higher level subject matter. . . . The place for improving secondary schools does not start in the high schools themselves but in the elementary schools where the groundwork . . . for secondary schooling is laid.[107]

Low achievement scores at the end of grade 10 were called cause for alarm.

No issue has been more critical in Philippine education than the suitable language of instruction. Before the advent of the Spanish, the local vernaculars became the instructional language in learning indigenous reading and writing. Under the Spanish, the local vernaculars were used in mission schools. Only in secondary and higher education schools was Spanish used. This involved exceedingly few Filipinos. Under American rule, at first primary schools also tended to use vernaculars. During the 1920s, however, English became the language of instruction in all schools. In the first two or three grades of primary school, local vernaculars were permitted but not encouraged or prescribed. After Independence, in 1946, English continued to be utilized through the later primary grades, as well as in secondary and higher education. During the Commonwealth period, a conception of a national language took more definite shape. Based closely on Tagalog, the native language of Central Luzon—including the Manila region—it was known as Pilipino until 1987 and since then as Filipino.

The prominence of English was not basically pedagogic as much as political and economic. As the language of the conquering power, English replaced Spanish as the language of government and Congressional enactments. U.S. industry and commerce also required English proficiency. Middle-class Filipinos, eager for themselves and their children to fill jobs in both these spheres, sought facility in English through the schools. In the rural by-ways of the colony, far from the daily realities of U.S. rule, the issue of English seemed abstract and distant. American authorities saw English predominance as a cultural guarantee of their own rule and a mark of colonial loyalty. English usage also tied the knot of common interest between the Philippine elite and the American occupiers, both before and after independence.

Under the American flag, students were forbidden to use their native language in school. If they did so, suspension ensued or their grades were marked down. In the Ilocos provinces, teachers appointed students to report any of their peers who used Ilokano on school premises.[108] After Independence, the indigenous languages were neither welcomed nor excluded. By the early 1970s, however, they languished in the shadows of a new ideal: an indigenous language that would perform as a common language for the entire Philippines. Because all the native languages were related in origin, it was expected that the learning of Tagalog—the language chosen to be the core of Pilipino—would be readily achieved.[109]

When, however, the entire language issue was placed within a context of Pilipino–English bilingualism, the indigenous languages lost any educational relevance in the schools. Whereas children reared in Tagalog had a great advantage in learning Pilipino, persons whose native language was one of the others suffered a real disadvantage. In addition, the bilingual system afforded no substitutes. The average poor Cebuano or Ilocano who attended school for only 4 or 5 years could not master English and Pilipino, let alone learn to do more than speak their native tongue.[110]

In terms of facilitating a national conversation, however, Pilipino became the *lingua franca*. By the late 1980s, a Philippine language succeeded where English had failed; some three fourths of the people now spoke Pilipino. In the schools, the bilingual program was somewhat less successful, as Gonzalez and Sibayan found in their evaluation.

According to a 1974 directive (DEC Order No. 25), the English domain of the bilingual-education program would embrace English communication arts, mathematics, and science; all other subjects would be taught in Pilipino. The evaluators found that Pilipino was widely used, even in classes theoretically to be taught entirely in English.[111] Attitudes toward the Bilingual Education Program (BEP) were as follows:

> The Pilipino and English faculty, the school principals, and the students' parents taken together, were found to be at best 'non-commital.' Generally, their attitudes (except for the Pilipino faculty and principals of public schools) were negative towards BEP; the negative attitude of the English faculty was true for both public and private schools. The Pilipino faculty had a positive attitude towards BEP, more favorable than the non-committal principals or even negative English faculty and parents. The principals of excellent private schools—most likely because of their bias for English—had a negative attitude towards BEP; the parents in general, except for those who were parents in excellent public schools, were reported to be negative towards BEP.[112]

For the most part, parents viewed BEP as extraneous to their children's vocational success as mediated through English proficiency.

Gonzalez and Sibayan also confronted several widespread criticisms of BEP. Perhaps the leading one attributed a deterioration of student achievement in the educational system to BEP. They could not find justification for such a charge.[113] Instead, they pointed to structural deficiencies of "the poor educational system as a whole, due to lack of competent teachers, lack of materials and lack of financial support."[114] Also specified was an urgent need for what they called the intellectualization of Pilipino; that is, to include preparation of new printed instructional materials that would permit a broader range of subject matter to be treated in Pilipino classes. Gonzalez and Sibayan also stressed a deeper problem:

> Both teachers and students still conceptualize in English, then translate into Pilipino especially in the upper grades (in other words, the better the student is in English, the better he also is in Pilipino, but not the other way around). This is understandable because most . . . Pilipino texts are borrowed from English.[115]

The deepening of this problem may also be occurring because of the scarcity of indigenous languages other than Pilipino in the schools.

Secular higher education had no place in the Spanish Philippines. Its earliest beginnings occurred in 1909 with the founding of the University of the Philippines. Ever since, UP and higher education in general have been reserved for upper and middle classes. In 1987, UP attracted "students from the wealthiest and most educated families. More than half of these students have fathers who ... completed a college degree and more than three quarters of these fathers are professionals or administrators."[116] The Ateneo de Manila, an old private college, was accurately described as the preeminent educator "of the sons of the social and economic elite."[117] A sample of women university students "indicated that 43 percent had fathers of professional or managerial status. Only 2½ percent came from families of laborers skilled or unskilled."[118] Extremely few loans or scholarships have been available to poor students. On the other hand, at UP during 1989 to 1990, "only about one third of the undergraduate students who came from the highest income levels paid full tuition and fees."[119] As a former vice-president for academic affairs of the institution declared, "The government should not spend its money on students who will not profit from exposure to higher education."[120] The state colleges enroll students from a broader span of socioeconomic backgrounds.

Some 85% of Filipino college and university students attend private institutions that charge tuition and fees. Most of these institutions were organized to earn a private profit for their founders and successors. In 1906, under American rule, Act No. 1459 directed all private schools to become either stock or non-stock corporations. The former were to be allowed to earn a return on their investments, the latter had to devote any surplus to educational improvement. Foundations, another form of organization, were tax-exempt and devoted their surplus to educational activities.[121] Between 1941 and 1969, the number of private universities and colleges rose from 8 and 84 to 36 and 558. Of the 558 private colleges, 293 or 49.3% were for-profit stock corporations. By 1977, the total number of private colleges and universities had risen to 694, or by one sixth.

Most of these new private institutions were known as diploma mills. They had low academic standards, inadequately trained and overworked faculty, crowded classes, and high tuition. Little heed was paid government regulations. Organizers of these mills sought to minimize costs and maximize profits. One way to accomplish this was to specialize in teacher training and business curricula, as these could be offered with a minimum of specialized equipment and little more than chalk and blackboard. Because the need for elementary teachers was so strong in the years after World War II, few school boards challenged the academic preparation their new teachers received.

Some limits were placed on the avidity with which pecuniary gain was pursued. P.D. No. 451, a tuition law, "allocates 60% of the tuition fee to teachers and employees, 28% to the improvement of campus and facilities, and 12% to return of investment." [122] Nevertheless, some of these shares were listed on the Manila Stock Exchange, where their principal owners were also often the proprietors of large landholdings and factories. In 1977 and 1978, the Philippine Securities and Exchange Commission listed three universities among the 1,000 top corporations, arranged by sales, net income, and total assets. One of these universities earned a net income of $6,321,000 on sales of $17,926,000. [123] The sales were a consequence of nearly all the for-profit colleges throwing open their doors to all comers with no real selection process. [124] An account written in 1971 reported that 13 of 25 universities had earned a net profit. [125] Another account written at the same time stated, "I would go so far as to argue that any school that shows a profit must be doing something wrong." [126]

In 1982, a law changed the situation somewhat: All new schools had to incorporate as nonstock, nonprofit organizations. [127] Existing diploma mills that had eluded any legal sanction could remain in business. So long as they paid their taxes, they were not disturbed. Although the mills had filled a social need, they did so in a destructive manner, helping create a tradition of educational inferiority. When Americans in 1906 had enacted the measure that legitimized what became diploma mills, they were not legislating out of a U.S. or Philippine heritage. Neither American school law nor Spanish colonial law provided for corporate schools operated for profit. During the 19th century, many medical schools in the United States were proprietary enterprises. By 1906, however, these had all but disappeared. Unfortunately, in the Philippines, the same spirit infected not merely higher education but the common schools as well where proprietary organization has continued until the present day. In a country where half or more of the population lived in poverty, a chance to learn depended in large part on capacity to pay for schooling.

IMMIGRATION

Within 5 years of the U.S. suppression of the Philippine revolution, emigration to the United States began. Initially, the greatest number went to Hawaii where the HSPA arranged for their distribution on sugar plantations. Between 1906 and 1946, more than 125,000 Filipinos followed this route. [128] Leaders of the HSPA hoped to use the newcomers to weaken the bargaining power of the Japanese plantation workers. From time to time, Filipino workers complained about their employers and wrote Philippine officials at the Bureau of Labor in Manila. This office, however, simply passed the letters on to the HSPA office in Manila. In 1923, a Filipino resident labor commissioner was installed in Hawaii, where he remained for the next 10 years. He turned out to be a veritable tool of the HSPA. [129]

During the 1920s and 1930s, the greatest number of immigrant laborers came from the Ilocos region of the Philippines, where farm workers were among the poorest paid and uninvolved in movements of peasant unrest. After 1924, when a new law made Japanese immigration less likely, importation of Filipino workers rose rapidly. After a few years, Filipino workers organized unions and went on strike; even when they were imported as scabs, to replace striking Japanese, they joined the strikers instead.

In 1934, Congress passed a law declaring a U.S. intention to grant independence to the Philippines in 10 years. Meanwhile, the Philippines were transformed into a Commonwealth. At the same time, the United States instituted a program to repatriate the Filipinos. Transportation costs would be paid by the United States and once returned, they could not come back to the United States. Very few chose to accept the offer.[130] On the other hand, many were pressured to leave. Haas wrote that, "from 1933, aliens on relief [i.e., welfare] could be deported from hospitals."[131] (Parallel treatment was accorded Mexicans in the United States, including a large number of children who were American citizens.)

Filipinos arrived in the United States in three waves. In the words of Pena:

> The first one started in 1920 to 1935. Those early immigrant Filipinos were mostly laborers with sprinklings of high school graduates and a few with college educational backgrounds. They became . . . menial workers. . . . The second wave started during the end of World War II. . . . [These] were affluent student sons and daughters of the wealthy Filipinos . . . [who] stayed temporarily in the country. . . . Many found employment by . . . marrying American citizens. . . . Others just worked and challenged the officials to find them.[132]

The third wave began in 1965 on the occasion of the U.S. immigration act of that year. Most prominent among Filipino immigrants were professionals. A critical difference between the third and earlier waves is evident from comparing educational characteristics of immigrants over the age of 20 who arrived before 1959 and were still in the United States in 1980 with those who arrived between 1965 and 1969 and were still in the United States in 1980.[133]

	Pre-1959	1965–1969
Not completed 5th grade	18.4%	3.1%
High-school graduates	42.5%	84.3%
Completed college	14.6%	49.3%

These very large differences did not reflect improvements in educational attainment inside the Philippines; the period between the two sets of years was too short for that. Instead, the U.S. immigration law of 1965 favored persons with a professional education.[134] By the early 1980s, however, the flow of professionals had slowed down considerably.[135] In another decade, most Filipino professionals—immigrants qualified for entry on the basis of family reunification—rather than on educational–occupational grounds.[136]

By the 1990s, Filipino Americans constituted the second-largest Asian-American group in the United States. This was the result of more than the sum of individual strivings for a new life. The Philippine government built a complex superstructure of laws, regulations, agencies, and institutions to encourage and profit, both financially and politically, from this new wave of emigration. As part of the Marcos dictatorship, presidential decrees required overseas workers to remit most of their wages to their families via Philippine banks. This gave Marcos a huge reserve of American dollars, a considerable part of which ended up in the private accounts of Marcos and his cronies in foreign banks. (Philippine government loans from overseas also helped swell these private accounts.[137]) Special taxes were levied on emigrating workers who also had to pay the government a considerable amount of money for obtaining a job overseas. Around 1990, the figure ranged from $370 to $740.[138] Poor or unemployed workers could not afford such sums of money and did not ordinarily emigrate. It was more often experienced, skilled workers who made the trip.

The prospect of employment in the United States directly affected educational developments in the Philippines. Students whose employment aspirations pointed overseas tended to avoid, where possible, a bilingual program, preferring to learn English only.[139] A 1989 study by the Philippine Nurses Association found that "of the 150,000 registered Philippine nurses some 93,000 or 61.2 percent of the nation's total number had gone abroad."[140] Two years later, a new law required nurses to work in the Philippines for at least 1 year after graduation from public colleges and universities.[141] Alegado wrote about medical education:

> The proliferation of medical schools, many of which are below standard, has also produced an increasingly large group of poor quality graduates. There were 28 medical schools in the country in 1985, producing 1,500 physicians annually. Only five of these schools, says [Amelita] King, provide quality education.[142]

Similar problems of quality do not necessarily exist in other highly technical fields that are also subject to high rates of emigration.

Between 1966 and 1976, 12,382 scientists and engineers emigrated to the United States. "That number included . . . 136 . . . [geophysicists], 172 geologists, 159 mathematicians, 10 physicists, 50 aeronautical engineers, 2,907 mechanical engineers, 1,950 chemical engineers, and 486 badly-needed agricultural engineers."[143] This marked a serious depletion in the ranks of Filipino science and technology. It was also an ironic absorption of the costs of training personnel for American academe and industry by a Third World country. Filipino scientists and engineers in the United States during the 1980s and 1990s apparently did not begin returning to their home country as did Korean scientists in the United States. One reason for this difference was the failure to develop high-technology industries or widespread advanced technical education in the Philippines. Another reason was the severity of the Marcos dictatorship until 1986 and the continued social and political irresolution after Marcos's overthrow.[144]

HAWAII

Sugar planters saw in Filipinos not only labor but docile workers. A chief indicator of docility was illiteracy. Hawaiian labor agents in the Philippines were scrupulous in rejecting anyone who might be literate. "Pens in a shirt pocket were enough to disqualify a prospective laborer."[145] Recruitment of laborers from rural *barrios* with few schools had the same effect.[146] Once the laborers were located on a Hawaiian plantation, sugar planters did not lessen their vigilance against literacy. "Social workers who tried to provide instruction in English were summarily evicted from the camps by the plantation owners."[147] To attract and retain plantation laborers, however, schools on the plantation were provided for children of the workers.[148]

For years, Filipino youngsters had few chances to attend high schools that were most often located in or near cities. It was not until 1924 that the first Filipino graduated from high school, at the age of 24.[149] Because in the Philippines, children did not begin primary school until age 7 but age 6 in Hawaii, Filipino students arrived in Hawaii one year behind. To make matters worse, they were then placed in grades according to age, which aggravated the deficiency in learning.[150] Filipino children—along with native Hawaiians—tended to be enrolled in relatively poorly equipped schools.[151] During the 1992 to 1993 school year, per-pupil spending in the schools ranged between $3,839 and $9,706. Because less than 60% of these expenditures were devoted to classroom instruction, a number of schools were left with exceedingly slim pickings.[152]

Few Filipinos in Hawaii succeeded in rising on the social ladder. Between 1930 and 1980, Filipinos in administrative, professional, and managerial jobs increased from 4 to 9%.[153] A severe system of tracking in the schools helped channel them into lower-paying positions. The same trend emerged in completion of high schools. "Only about half of the Hawaii Filipinos were high school graduates in the 1980s, in contrast with . . . 77 percent of non-Filipinos. . . ."[154] Nevertheless, this was an improvement over 1970, when only 39.4% of Filipinos had completed high school.[155] In public schools, counselors "were discouraging Filipinos from applying to four year colleges, insisting that their future lay in community colleges. . . ."[156] Once in community college, neither Filipinos nor Hawaiians received adequate information about transferring to the University of Hawaii. At the latter institution, the average graduation rate is 49%; for Filipino students, the rate is 40%.[157] Haas noted that the greater Filipino dropout rate reflected financial rather than academic difficulties.

In Hawaiian society as a whole, the Filipino people contended with many violations of their civil rights, including education. Relatively few Filipinos work in government or school jobs and they have mounted campaigns for affirmative action to be implemented. "Hawaii State Government refused to institute affirmative action plans for Filipinos and other underrepresented groups until 1979, when the U.S. Office of Revenue Sharing indicated that they would stop sending revenue-sharing funds to Hawaii until affirmative action became a reality in the Aloha State."[158] Hawaii public schools refused to provide special language instruction to Filipino students who could not readily handle English reading. Charges of language discrimination were leveled by Federal authorities in 1977, 1979, 1980, 1981, 1982, and 1990.[159] Haas pointed out that, "the only times when Hawaii agencies have listened to Filipino complaints, it appears, have followed Federal investigations, with the threat of termination of Federal funding as an impetus to the abandonment of discriminatory policies."[160]

Few Filipinos could be found in teaching or administrative positions. At the end of the 1970s, Filipinos made up 18.7% of enrollment but only 2.6% of the teaching force.[161] A single high school offered Tagalog as one language option.[162] At the University of Hawaii since the 1960s, a broad program of Tagalog language and literature had been offered. It took a number of years until such a perspective began to affect the lower schools. As Ilokanos came to predominate among Filipino immigrants, pressure mounted to offer some instruction in their language. During the mid-1970s, nine Honolulu schools offered an Ilokano–English bilingual program in K through 3rd grades.[163]

U.S. MAINLAND

The abrupt ending of Japanese immigration in 1924 opened the doors to an increased flow of Filipinos to the United States. Between 1922 and 1929, 5,513 Filipinos entered through the Port of Los Angeles; over 95% were men, most under 25 years of age.[164] Many attended high schools after or before work; fewer were college students. During the 1920s and 1930s they worked as busboys, cooks, dishwashers, domestic help, and gardeners.[165] By 1940, Filipino men and women aged 25 and over averaged 7.4 years of schooling. Half of the employed males were farm workers, 6.7% worked as domestic servants, and 1.2% were professionals.[166] Between 1940 and 1950, the proportion of college educated rose from 7.7 % to 10.8%.[167] Nevertheless, by 1960, a California Department of Industrial Relations survey found that most Filipinos were still working as unskilled laborers.[168]

The preceding 4 decades of immigration had been accompanied by sweeping discrimination against Filipinos. In the area of family life, Filipinos in California and other states were forbidden to marry persons of another race. Couples who wished to contract an interracial marriage had to search out a state where this was legal.[169] In 1920, not a single Filipino belonged to a labor union in Los Angeles.[170] Noncitizens were excluded from most public employment. Filipinos, however, fell under a separate exclusion: They were neither citizens nor noncitizens (that is, aliens). Instead, California ruled they were U.S. nationals and as such excluded along with noncitizens.[171]

Bulosan, a leading Filipino writer in the United States, wrote to a friend in 1937, "The terrible truth in America shatters the Filipinos' dreams of fraternity."[172] In the fields of education, many a dream was shattered. One immigrant who arrived in 1956 recalled, "The only job I could get at that time was as a janitor initially and later as a restaurant waiter."[173] This became a familiar fate for Filipinos. At the University of Southern California around 1930, Filipino and other Oriental students were not permitted to live in campus dormitories. Chinese, Korean, and Filipinos were allowed to room at the campus International House, and the Japanese Club House was also available. A group of Protestant church people founded the Filipino–American Fellowship and leased dwelling places that were then rented to Filipino students.[174]

In an unnamed western city, "Filipinos who wished to attend high schools in the more desirable portions of the city (usually because they have jobs as part-time houseboys there) have been discouraged by the school principals and are forced to travel long distances to be enrolled in less exclusive neighborhoods."[175] This practice reflected a more general community policy throughout large cities that coordinated school and residential segregation.

A short-term modification of discriminatory policies could be introduced to prepare Filipinos and other Asians to work in another country. Thus, Marcos Pera Barbano

> was ordained and accepted into the membership of the Oregon Annual Conference of the Methodist Episcopal Church, with the understanding that he should not expect nor demand an appointment; and that it would entitle him to preach the Gospel only when asked to supply any pulpits, or in any opportune times to preach to groups of Filipinos; and to give him the right and standing as a preacher to get an appointment when he gets back to the Philippines, not here.[176]

Pera Barbano stressed that the crucial element in the exclusion decision was whether or not the fully educated minority person was likely to exercise leadership over White Americans. This could not be permitted.

Outside the field of education, discrimination against noncitizen Filipinos was the rule. They were not allowed to take Bar examinations so as to exclude them from the practice of law, regardless of their education.[177] In the Alaska canneries, where many Filipinos worked after World War II:

> Filipino workers were still segregated from white workers; they had to live in separate quarters. They slept in bunk beds, and they were not furnished bedding, so they had to bring their own blankets. Food for white workers was different from what the Filipino workers got. . . . Not only did the Filipino workers bear the brunt of discrimination in living quarters, but they also had lower wages than Caucasian workers. Filipino workers were given different foods, mainly rice and fish heads.[178]

Filipino physicians were recruited to work at assignments usually rejected by White American physicians. These included work at large municipal hospitals, state mental hospitals, and Veterans Administration hospitals. Filipino nurses and physicians were disproportionately assigned to work with AIDS patients, according to community advocates.[179]

From time to time, employers explained their hesitancy to employ Filipinos at professional levels by contending that their educational preparation in the Philippines was substandard. In 1973, for example, the California Board of Accountancy announced "that the training of Filipino accountants was ten to fifteen years behind that in the United States."[180] In 1990, an official of the Manila-based Commission on Filipinos Overseas observed that graduates of Philippine institutions often have difficulty in obtaining jobs consistent with their training. She wrote:

> This may be attributed to differences in the educational systems and curriculum adopted by the Philippines and the host countries. An emigrant who has completed a four-year course in a local [Philippine] institution would normally need to pursue additional training and studies to compensate for the two years of education lacking in our educational system.[181]

Between 1950 and 1970, the proportion of Filipino Americans who had completed college rose from 10.8% to 43.2%.[182] In the following decade, the ratio of Filipino American earnings in relation to those of Whites rose measurably; those for men increased from 60 to 68% and for women from 42 to 51%.[183] Yet, these leaps forward in standards were only statistical artifacts, not living actualities. During the years 1950 to 1980, primarily as a consequence of changes in U.S. immigration law in 1965, a vast increase in Filipino immigration occurred. As we saw earlier, an unusual feature of this immigration was the large component of educated middle-class persons. The seeming rise in Filipino American living standards by and large did not in fact occur. It simply reflected the movement of better-off-people into a community that had been considerably poorer and less educated.

By the 1980s, when the immigration of middle-class persons slowed and was beginning to be replaced by less well-off persons, signs of poverty and its attendant phenomena rose. These included unemployment, school dropouts, and juvenile delinquency.[184] There is little if any evidence to suggest that the poorest Filipinos were better off in the 1980s than they had been 40 years earlier. By 1990, Filipinos were nearly the largest Asian-American group, 70% of them were immigrants, and the group as a whole was riven by major socioeconomic differences. When, however, the University of California, Berkeley in 1986 removed Filipinos from affirmative-action admissions eligibility, this strengthened the misimpression that Filipinos as a whole were no longer disadvantaged. In fact, few public universities in California had taken any cognizance of Filipino issues in their curriculum. In the late 1980s, only 4 of the 20 units of the California State University system had even a rudimentary Philippine American Studies program; the same was true for three of the nine University of California campuses.[185] At the same time, no Filipino American in the latter institutions occupied a tenured faculty position.[186]

CONCLUDING REMARKS

A common statement by both American and Filipino writers is that the United States established a public educational system in the Philippines patterned after its own. Embedded in this assertion is a judgment of generosity by Americans, abetted by a rugged belief in universal education. Little evidence, other than rising numbers of children enrolled in the schools, exists. Nor can one readily support the implication that the United States believed in, let alone practiced, education for all children.

When American rule in the Philippines began, its own public educational system was a dual one. Divided by race, in 1900 53.6% of White children but only 31.1% of African-American children were enrolled in school.[187] African-American schools were unrelievedly inferior, as they were meant to be. As late as 1946, W.E.B. Du Bois wrote that "the majority of Negro children in the United States from 6 to 18, do not have the opportunity to learn to read and write."[188] In Texas and California, Mexican American children suffered a similar fate in segregated schools. These were not the children American educators in the Phillipines meant when they spoke of universal education.

As we saw earlier, American authorities refused to finance Philippine schools as they did in the United States. No federal grants, for example, were extended to encourage the building of schools and colleges. For many years, most funds appropriated by Congress to finance educational legislation were denied to the Philippines. Many requests for money to build schools or extend instruction were turned aside with an explanation that U.S. taxpayers would object to paying for schooling so many thousands of miles away. At the same time, the Philippine economic and political elite easily managed to finance the education of their own children in private institutions. These families supplied almost all the members of various legislative and administrative bodies and did not see the urgency of mass education. Until 1935, an American was the chief educational officer of the Philippines and financing the extension of education during these years was a mere topic of conversation.

Some Filipinos congratulated themselves with the thought that the United States had a greater involvement in schooling than in fact it did. Although in the earliest years, a number of American teachers worked in the schools, at all times, native-born teachers predominated. This was especially true by the 1920s or even earlier. The poor diction in English of many Filipino children resulted from trying to educate them in a foreign language of instruction. It would have taken an army of English-speaking American teachers to make a dent in this.

NOTES

[1] Emma J. Fonacier Bernabe, *Language Policy Formulation, Programming, Implementation and Evaluation in Philippino Education (1565–1974)* (Linguistic Society of the Philippines, 1987), p. 9. See also Juan R. Francisco, *Philippine Palaeography* (Linguistic Society of the Philippines, 1973).

[2] John N. Schumacher, *The Making of a Nation. Essays on Nineteenth-Century Filipino Nationalism* (Ateno de Manila University Press, 1991), p. 102.

[3] Fonacier Bernabe, *Language Policy Formulation*, p. 9.

[4] John L. Phelan, *The Hispanization of the Philippines, Spanish Aims and Filipino Responses 1565–1700* (University of Wisconsin Press, 1959), p. 58.

[5] Ibid., p. 55.

[6] Ibid., p. 121.

[7] Josefina G. Nepomuceno, *A Theory of Development of Filipino Colonized Consciousness* (Doctoral dissertation, University of Michigan, 1981), pp. 171–172.

[8] Rizalino Aquino Oades, *The Social and Economic Background of Philippine Nationalism, 1830–1892*, 2 vols. (Doctoral dissertation, University of Hawaii, 1974), pp. 371–372.

[9] Domingo Abella, "State of Higher Education in the Philippines to 1863—A Historical Reappraisal," *Philippine Historical Review*, 1 (1965), pp. 8–9

[10] Ibid., p. 10.

[11] Ibid., p. 25.

[12] H. de la Costa, "A Brief Introduction to the Study of Western Cultural Penetration in the Philippines," *East Asian Cultural Studies*, 6 (March 1967), p. 181.

[13] Abella, "State of Higher Education," p. 1.

[14] Aquino Oades, *Social and Economic Background*, p. 260, footnote 27.

[15] Phelan, *Hispanization of the Philippines*, p. 131.

[16] Vicente L. Rafael, *Contracting Colonialism. Translation and Christian Conversion in Tagalog Society Under Spanish Rule* (Cornell University Press, 1988), p. 56.

[17] Henry F. Fox, "Primary Education in the Philippines, 1565–1863," *Philippine Studies*, 13 (April 1965), p. 229, footnote 65.

[18] Frederick Fox and Juan Mercader, "Some Notes on Education in Cebu Province, 1820–1898," *Philippine Studies*, 2 (March 1954), p. 37.

[19] Aquino Oades, *Social and Economic Background*, p. 246. See also O. D. Corpuz, a former Minister of Education, "Education and Socio-Economic Change in the Philippines, 1870–1960s," *Philippine Social Science and Humanities Review*, 32 (June 1967), p. 200: "Before 1863, there was hardly a school of primary instruction . . . which merited the name."

[20] Quoted in Karl Schwartz, "Filipino Education and Spanish Colonialism: Toward an Autonomous Perspective," *Comparative Education Review*, 15 (June 1971), p. 208.

[21] Evergisto Bazaco, *History of Education in the Philippines. Spanish Period 1565–1898*, 2nd revised edition (University of Santo Tomas Press, 1953), p. 250.

[22] Renate Simpson, "Higher Education in the Philippines under the Spanish," *Journal of Asian History*, 14 (1980), p. 20.

[23] Henry F. Fox, "Primary Education in the Philippines," p. 120, footnote 7, and p. 211, footnote 8.

[24] Aquino Oades, *Social and Economic Background*, pp. 247–248.

[25] Corpuz, "Education and Socio-Economic Change," p. 205.

[26] Fonacier Bernabe, *Language Policy Formulation*, p. 17.

[27] Aquino Oades, *Social and Economic Background*, p. 248, footnote 6.

[28] Ibid., pp. 535–536.

[29] Ibid., pp. 260–261.

[30] Bazaco, *History of Education in the Philippines*, p. 323.

[31] Aquino Oades, *Social and Economic Background*, p. 284.

[32] Abella, "State of Higher Education," p. 4.

[33] Schumacher, *The Making of a Nation*, p. 38.

[34] Aquino Oades, *Social and Economic Background*, p. 276.

[35] Tomas G. Del Rosario, [Education] *Census of the Philippines, 1903*, p, 612.

[36] Aquino Oades, *Social and Economic Background*, p. 508.

[37] Nepomuceno, *A Theory of Development*, p. 398.

[38] See Richard E. Welch, Jr., "American Atrocities in the Philippines: The Indictment and the Response," *Pacific Historical Review*, 43 (1974), pp. 233–253.

[39] Ibid., p. 242.

[40] John M. Gates, *Schoolbooks and Krags. The United States Army in the Philippines, 1898–1902* (Greenwood, 1973), p. 105. See also Warwick Anderson, *Colonial Pathologies: American Medicine in the Philippines, 1898–1921* (Doctoral dissertation, University of Pennsylvania, 1992), p. 181 for material on medical and social stereotypes about African-American soldiers in the Philippines.

[41] Quoted in Dorothy D. Swendiman, *The Development of Education in the Philippine Islands Since 1898* (Master's thesis, Duke University, 1942), p. 3.

[42] Glenn A. May, *Battle for Batangas. A Philippine Province at War* (Yale University Press, 1991), p. 160. See also Gates, *Schoolbooks and Krags*, p. 137.

[43] Joseph R. Hayden, *The Philippines. A Study in National Development* (Macmillan, 1942), p. 465.

[44] Renato Constantino with Letizia R. Constantino, *The Philippines: A Past Revisited* (Tala Publishing Services, 1975), p. 309.

[45] Ibid., p. 311.

[46] Corpuz, "Education and Socio-Economic Change," pp. 215–216.

[47] Constantino and Constantino, *The Philippines*, p. 310.

[48] Meyer Weinberg, *A Chance to Learn*, 2nd edition (The University Press, California State University, Long Beach, 1995), pp. 32–33. See also Fletcher Harper Swift, *Federal and State Policies in Public School Finance in the United States* (Ginn, 1931), pp. 67–68; and *A History of Public Permanent Common-School Funds in the United States, 1795–1905* (Holt, 1911).

[49] Corpuz, "Education and Socio-Economic Change in the Philippines," p. 214.

[50] Swendiman, *The Development of Education*, p. 33.

[51] Ibid., p. 38.

[52] Ibid., pp. 58–59.

[53] Quoted from the Barrows Papers in Mary Bonzo Suzuki, *American Education in the Philippines, the Early Years: American Pioneer Teachers and the Filipino Response, 1900–1935* (Doctoral dissertation, University of California, Berkeley, 1991), p. 115.

[54] Glenn A. May, *Social Engineering in the Philippines. The Aims, Execution and Impact of American Colonial Policy, 1900–1913* (Greenwood, 1980), p. 107.

[55] Ibid., p. 122.

[56] Ibid., p. 179.

[57] Chester L. Hunt, "Education and Economic Development in the Early American Period in the Philippines," *Philippine Studies*, 36 (1988), p. 356.

[58] George S. Counts, "Education in the Philippines," *Elementary School Journal*, 26 (October 1925), pp. 98–99.

[59] Ibid., p. 100.

[60] Ibid., p. 102.

[61] Ibid., p. 103.

[62] Ibid., p. 106.

[63] Leny Mendoza Strobel, "A Personal Story: Becoming a Split Filipina Subject," *Amerasia Journal*, 19 (1993), p. 121,

[64] Donald E. Douglas, *American Education in the Creation of an Independent Philippines: The Commonwealth Period 1935–1941* (Doctoral dissertation, University of Michigan, 1979), pp. 63–64.

[65] Ibid., pp. 149–150.

[66] Ibid., p. 157.

[67] Ibid., p. 195.

[68] Hayden, *The Philippines*, p. 472–473.

[69] Ibid., pp. 604–605.

[70] Swendiman, *Development of Education*, p. 88.

[71] Ibid., p. 41.

[72] Ibid., p. 143.

[73] See Elmer N. Lear, "Education in Guerrilla Territory Under a Regime of Enemy Occupation," *History of Education Quarterly*, 7 (Fall 1967), pp. 312–328.

[74] Usha Mahajani, *Philippine Nationalism, External Challenge and Filipino Response, 1565–1946* (University of Queensland Press, 1971) p. 459.

[75] Ibid., p. 449.

[76] Ibid., p. 450.

[77] Grant K. Goodman, ed., *Japanese Cultural Policies in Southeast Asia During World War 2* (Macmillan, 1991), p. 188.

[78] Ibid., p. 189.

[79] Ibid., p. 196.

[80] Teodoro A. Agoncillo, "The Cultural Aspect of the Japanese Occupation," *Philippine Social Science and Humanities Review*, 28(1963), p. 361. See also Lope K. Santos, "Educational Problems in the New Regime," *Philippine Review*, 2 (October–November 1944), p. 52.

[81] Ibid., pp. 366–367.

[82] Ibid., p. 380.

[83] Ibid., p. 385.

[84] Ibid., pp. 392–393.

[85] Alfred W. McCoy, "The Philippines: Independence without Decolonization," p. 56 in Robin Jeffrey, ed., *Asia—the Winning of Independence* (St. Martin's Press, 1981).

[86] John J. Carroll and John T. Keane, "Education in the Philippines," *Solidarity*, 3 (July 1968), p. 19.

[87] Gerardo Flores, "A Study on Functional Literacy for Citizenship in the Philippines," *Fundamental and Adult Education*, 2 (July 1951), p. 27.

[88] *A Survey of the Public Schools of the Philippines—1960*. U.S. Operations Mission to the Philippines (Carmelo and Bauermann, 1960), p. 32.

[89] Ibid., p. 117.

[90] Ibid., p. 289.

[91] Ibid., p. 299.

[92] Ibid., p. 533.

[93] Arthur L. Carson, *Higher Education in the Philippines* (U.S. Department of Health, Education, and Welfare, 1961), p. 194.

[94] Gregoria C. Borlaza, "Education in the Philippines," p. 238 in A.S. Lardizabal and F. Tensuan-Leogardo, eds., *Readings on Philippine Culture and Social Life* (Rex Book Store, 1970).

[95] *A Survey of the Public Schools*, p. 31.

[96] D. C. Bennett, "Aspects of Literacy and Educational Attainment in the Philippines," *Philippine Studies*, 17 (1969), p. 603.

[97] Carroll and Keane, "Education in the Philippines," p. 14.

[98] Bikas C. Sanyal, Waldo S. Perfect, and Adriano A. Arcelo, *Higher Education and the Labour Market in the Philippines* (UNESCO, 1981), p. 65.

[99] Ibid., p. 24.

[100] James K. Boyce, *The Philippines. The Political Economy of Growth and Impoverishment in the Marcos Era* (University of Hawaii Press, 1993), p. 114.

[101] Ibid., p. 47.

[102] Ibid., p. 27.

[103] Ibid., p. 29.

[104] M. C. Sutaria, "Philippines: System of Education," p. 4437 in Torsten Husen and T. Neville Postlethwaite, eds., *The International Encyclopedia of Education*, 2nd ed., Vol. 8 (Pergamon, 1994).

[105] Andrew B. Gonzalez and Bonifacio P. Sibayan, eds., *Evaluating Bilingual Education in the Philippines (1974–1985)* (Linguistic Society of the Philippines, 1988), p. 30.

[106] Ibid., p. 42.

[107] Ibid., p. 58.

[108] See J. J. Smolicz, "National Language Policy in the Philippines: A Comparative Study of the Education Status of Colonial and Indigenous Languages with Special Reference to Minority Tongues," *Southeast Asian Journal of Social Science*, 12 (1984), p. 53; and James P. Young, "Intimate Allies in Migration: Education and Propaganda in a Philippine Village," *Comparative Education Review*, 26 (June 1982), p. 224.

[109] See Virgilio G. Enriquez and Elizabeth Protacio-Marcelino, *Neo-Colonial Politics and Language Struggle in the Philippines. National Consciousness and Language in Philippine Psychology (1971–1983)*. (Akademya Ng Sikolohiyang Pilipino, 1984), p. 6; and Pascual Capiz, "Politics and the English Language in the Philippines," *Diliman Review*, 8 (1960), p. 313.

[110] See Smolicz, "National Language Policy," pp. 56, 58–59, and 63; Gonzalez and Sibayan, *Evaluating Bilingual Education*, pp. 56–57, and James W. Tollefson, *Planning Language, Planning Inequality. Language Policy in the Community* (Longman, 1991), pp. 150, 156.

[111] Gonzalez and Sibayan, *Evaluating Bilingual Education*, p. 27.

[112] Ibid., pp. 27–28.

[113] Ibid., p. 143.

[114] Ibid., p. 144.

[115] Ibid., p. 148.

[116] E. Nelson Swinerton, *Philippine Higher Education. Toward the Twenty-First Century* (Praeger, 1991), p. 36.

[117] Carl H. Lande, "The Philippines," p. 328 in James S. Coleman, ed., *Education and Political Development* (Princeton University Press, 1965).

[118] Arthur L. Carson, *Higher Education in the Philippines* (U.S. Department of Health, Education, and Welfare, 1961), pp. 83–84.

[119] Swinerton, *Philippine Higher Education*, p. 42.

[120] Antonio Isidro, *Trends and Issues in Philippine Education* (Alemar-Phoenix Publishing House, 1972), p. 194.

[121] Sanyal, *Higher Education*, pp. 93–94.

[122] Vivencio R. Jose, "Contemporary Education and Culture: Basic Problems and Perspectives," *Philippine Social Sciences and Humanities Review*, 44 (January–December 1980), p. 39.

[123] Ibid., p. 41.

[124] Borlaza, "Education in the Philippines," p. 244.

[125] Epifania R. Castro Resposo, *The Role of Universities in the Developing Philippines* (Asia Publishing House, 1971), p. 106.

[126] Robert O. Tilman, "The Impact of American Education on the Philippines," *Asia*, 21 (Spring 1971), pp. 76–77.

[127] Andrew B. Gonzalez in *Public and Private Sectors in Asian Higher Education Systems. Issues and Prospects*. Research Institute for Higher Education, Hiroshima University, 1987, p. 60. ERIC ED 291 329.

[128] Gonzalo A. Velez, *A Study of the Historical Development of the Congress of Filipino American Citizens* (Doctoral dissertation, Rutgers University, 1983), p. 104.

[129] Ruben R. Alcantara, *Sakada: Filipino Adaptation in Hawaii* (University Press of America, 1981), pp. 29–30.

[130] See Casiano Pagdilao Coloma, *A Study of the Filipino Repatriation Movement* (Master's thesis,

University of Southern California, 1939). The present writer was unable to obtain a copy of this work.

[131]Michael Haas, *Institutional Racism. The Case of Hawaii* (Praeger, 1992), pp. 220–221.

[132]George Pena, *Philippines Mail,* July 1969, reprinted in Hyung-chan Kim and Cynthia C. Mejia, eds., *The Filipinos in America, 1898–1974* (Oceana Publications, 1976), pp. 117–118.

[133]Luciano Mangiafico, *Contemporary American Immigrants. Patterns of Filipino, Korean, and Chinese Settlement in the United States* (Praeger, 1988), pp. 56–57.

[134]Antonio J.A. Pido, *The Pilipinos in America* (Center for Migration Studies, 1986), p. 32.

[135]Belen T. G. Medina, "The New Wave: Latest Findings on Filipino Immigration to the United States," *Philippine Sociological Review,* 32 (1984), pp. 136–137.

[136]Benjamin V. Carino and others, *The New Filipino Immigrants to the United States: Increasing Diversity and Change,* Papers of the East-West Population Center, No. 115 (East–West Center, May 1990), p. 53.

[137]See Boyce, *The Philippines,* pp. 319, 348.

[138]Ibid., p. 305.

[139]Gonzalez and Sibayan, *Evaluating Bilingual Education,* p. 45.

[140]Dean T. Alegado, *The Political Economy of International Labor Migration from the Philippines* (Doctoral dissertation, University of Hawaii, 1992), p. 82.

[141]Ibid., p. 84.

[142]Ibid., p. 291. Reference is to Amelita King's remarks in Y. Atal and L. Dall'Oglio, eds., *Migration of Talent: Causes and Consequences of Brain Drain (Three Studies from Asia)* (Bangkok: UNESCO, 1987), pp. 15–118.

[143]Ibid., p. 166.

[144]See Benedict Anderson, "Cacique Democracy in the Philippines: Origins and Dreams," *New Left Review,* 169 (May–June 1988), p. 26.

[145]Miriam Sharma, "Labor Migration and Class Formation Among the Filipinos in Hawaii, 1906–1946," p. 585 in Lucie Cheng and Edna Bonacich, eds., *Labor Immigration Under Capitalism* (University of California Press, 1984). See also Alcantara, *Sakada,* p. 35.

[146]Alcantara, *Sakada,* p. 35.

[147]Michael Haas, "Filipinos in Hawaii and Institutional Racism," *Philippine Sociological Review,* 32 (January–December 1984), p. 44.

[148]Roman R. Cariaga, *The Filipinos in Hawaii. A Survey of Their Economic and Social Conditions* (R and E Research Associates, 1974 reprint), p. 103.

[149]Juan C. Dionisio and others, *The Filipinos in Hawaii. The First 75 Years. 1906–1981* (Hawaii Filipino News Specialty, 1982), p. 86.

[150]Virgie Chattergy and Belen C. Ongteco, "Educational Needs of Filipino Immigrant Students," *Social Process in Hawaii,* 33 (1991), p. 143.

[151]Haas, *Institutional Racism,* p. 208.

[152]See account of study by Bruce S. Cooper in Lonnie Harp, "Spending Disparities Found in Single District," *Education Week,* September 21, 1994.

[153]Michael Haas, "Filipinos in Hawaii," p. 45.

[154]Joyce Chapman Lebra, *Women's Voices in Hawaii* (University Press of Colorado, 1991), p. 246.

[155]Luis V. Teodoro, Jr., ed., *Out of This Struggle. The Filipinos in Hawaii* (University of Hawaii Press, 1981), p. 31.

[156]Haas, *Institutional Racism,* p. 210.

[157]Ibid., p. 203.

[158]Haas, "Filipinos in Hawaii," p. 47.

[159]Haas, *Institutional Racism,* p. 182. See also p. 199.

[160]Haas, "Filipinos in Hawaii," p. 50.

[161]Dionisio, *The Filipinos in Hawaii,* p. 87.

[162] Teodoro, *Out of This Struggle*, p. 47.

[163] Ibid., p. 47.

[164] Marcos Pera Berbano, *The Social Status of the Filipinos in Los Angeles County* (Master's thesis, University of Southern California, 1930), p. 4.

[165] H. Brett Melendy, "Filipinos in the United States," *Pacific Historical Review*, 43 (1974), p. 530.

[166] Peter C. Smith, "The Social Demography of Filipino Migrations Abroad," *International Migration Review*, 10 (1976), p. 324.

[167] Ibid., p. 326.

[168] Melendy, "Filipinos in the United States," p. 531.

[169] A digest of state laws forbidding intermarriage of Filipinos and Whites can be found in Iris B. Buaken, "You Can't Marry a Filipino. Not If You Live in California," *Commonweal*, 41 (March 16, 1945), p. 536.

[170] Pera Barbano, *The Social Status of Filipinos*, p. 95.

[171] Ibid., p. 64.

[172] Carlos Bulosan to Dorothy Babb, December 12, 1937, in Carlos Bulosan, *Sound of Falling Light. Letters in Exile*, edited by Dolores S. Feria (Quezon City, 1960), p. 3

[173] Lemuel F. Ignacio, *Asian Americans and Pacific Islanders (Is There Such an Ethnic Group?)* (Pilipino Development Associates, Inc., 1976), p. 9.

[174] Pera Berbano, *The Social Status of the Filipinos*, pp. 96–97.

[175] Bruno Lasker, *Filipino Immigration to Continental United States and to Hawaii* (University of Chicago Press, 1931), pp. 137–138.

[176] Pera Berbano, *The Social Status of the Filipinos*, p. 23.

[177] Roberto V. Vallangca, ed., *Pinoy: The First Wave (1898–1941)* (Strawberry Hill Press, 1977), p. 28.

[178] Caridad Concepcion Vallangca, *The Second Wave: Pinay and Pinoy (1945–1960)*, edited by Jody B. Larson (Strawberry Hill Press, 1987), p. 187.

[179] Susumu Awanohara, "High Growth, Low Profile," 151 *Far Eastern Economic Review*, February 7, 1991, p. 40. See also C. C. Vallangca, *The Second Wave*, p. 236.

[180] C. C. Vallangca, *The Second Wave*, p. 154.

[181] Catherine P. Paredes, "The Truth and Myth About Filipino Migration," *Asian Migrant*, 3 (October–December 1990), pp. 123–124.

[182] Smith, "The Social Demography of Filipino Migration Abroad," p. 326.

[183] Amado Cabezas, Larry Shinagawa, and Gary Kawaguchi, "New Inquiries into the Socioeconomic Status of Pilipino Americans in California," *Amerasia Journal*, 13 (1986–87), p. 5.

[184] Bruce Occena, "The Filipino Nationality in the U.S.: An Overview," *Line of March*, (1985), pp. 40–41. See also Jo Ann Agcaoili, "The Pilipino Youth of Central City and the San Francisco Educational System," p. 79 in Jovina Navarro, ed., *Diwang Pilipino. Pilipino Consciousness* (Asian American Studies, University of California, Davis, 1974). Two articles by Barbara M. Posadas and Roland L. Guyotte touch on the modest amount of upward social mobility among earlier Filipino nationals in the United States: "Unintentional Immigrants: Chicago's Filipino Foreign Students Become Settlers, 1900–1941," *Journal of American Ethnic History*, 9 (1990), pp. 26–48; and "Occupational and Educational Choice among Filipino Migrants to Chicago, 1900–1935," *Illinois Historical Journal*, 85 (Summer 1992), pp. 89–104.

[185] Edwin B. Almirol, "The Filipino Experience in the American University System," *Asian Profile*, 16 (1988) p. 287.

[186] Ibid., p., 289.

[187] Weinberg, *A Chance to Learn*, p. 44.

[188] Ibid., p. 82.

CHAPTER SIX

Vietnam

Between 221 B.C. and A.D. 939, Vietnam was ruled by China. In independent Vietnam, however, Chinese language and literature remained for the next 1,000 years as the core of education. After the first century or so of independence, the Vietnamese monarchy established an Examination System, closely patterned after that of China, to train potential officials serving the king. Between 1075 and 1918, when the system was closed down, examinations were held, on the average, every 4½ years. In that long period, 2,991 candidates attained the doctorate. This was a success rate of about 1%.[1]

In 1076, King Ly Nhan Tong established the Quoc Tu Giam (Institute for Children of the State) as the country's first university to train administrators. Children of aristocrats and high officials (mandarins) were the sole students. The state did not create any schools for the common people. This task was left to the Buddhist monks, who established pagoda schools attached to village temples. There, children of commoners learned to read and write and studied Buddhism and Chinese literature and thought. The instructional language was classical Chinese; although in everyday life, Vietnamese continued to be used despite its interdiction by the state.[2] Between the 12th and 15th centuries, both streams of national education developed successfully.

After a time, outstanding students from the village schools began to be admitted to an enlarged Quoc Tu Giam that could now house scholarship students. In 1397, educational mandarins were appointed in each province and district. They presided over the creation of local schools patterned after Quoc Tu Giam. Children of commoners profited from these measures by gaining entrance to higher education. As in China, women in Vietnam were forbidden to participate in the Examination System, as they were ineligible to serve as officials. At the same time, some did organize and operate village schools.[3]

Teachers in these local schools did not receive set salaries from the state, nor even tuition from students' families. They worked on farms after school and received gifts at traditional festivals. Teachers who were gravely in need could depend on support from the entire community. Buddhist monks were being replaced in village schools by graduates of the Quoc Tu Giam by late in the 12th century.

For most years, the Examination System worked to broaden the social composition of the highly educated in Vietnam. "The sons of the mandarins, and even the Princes, were subject to the same process of selection as the sons of ordinary peasants if they wanted to hold high governmental positions."[4] By around 1737, however, royal offices could be purchased with cash.[5] A Vietnamese historian wrote that, "in the 18th century, competitive examinations degenerated into a traffic in diplomas. . . ."[6] Demoralization set in and "by the end of the nineteenth century . . . the quality of higher learning was hardly comparable to that in the period before the fifteenth century."[7]

The *literati*, the learned products of the Examination System, retained the integrity of their office in at least one respect: They upheld the traditional political element of their role. In ancient Viet Nam, the literati "in a number of cases . . . overthrew a degraded and incapable King to replace him with a more qualified one."[8] Since achieving independence, Viet Nam had frequently found excellent military leaders among the literati who led successful campaigns against Chinese efforts to regain control of a former colony.[9] In the latter half of the 19th century, once again an armed protest movement led by the literati arose against a new invader: France. The "scholars' insurrection"[10] materialized in 1858 when the king of Cochinchina (South Vietnam) bent before the French. In 1884 and after, both in Tonkin (North Vietnam) and Annam (Central Vietnam), scholars and retired mandarins led armed revolts against the French. The teachers recruited soldiers from the village schools.[11] By the 1890s, the revolts petered out in the face of "the ability of French forces to secure collaboration from local [Vietnamese] elites and ethnic groups, as well as from Chinese border officials who restricted China as a refuge for resistance bands."[12]

Despite the defeats, the traditional village schools continued operating effectively under French occupation. Vietnamese parents viewed the institutions as a political reproach to their new masters. On the eve of the French conquest, about 80% of the Vietnamese were literate, according to Buttinger.[13] Hồng wrote, "There were few illiterates in the strict sense of the word, since most people could read and write a certain number of essential characters in common use."[14] A Vietnamese researcher who reported a higher literacy rate in rural than in urban areas is cited by Long.[15]

During the first generation or so of French rule, traditional schooling continued as usual. Changes introduced by the French resulted in fewer children being educated.[16] The number of schools was severely reduced. Before French planners began their work, there were some 20,000 indigenous schools in Tonkin and Annam. In just one year, 1924, more than 1,800 were closed.[17] By that time, the structure of indigenous schooling had been fatally weakened. Its replacements were far fewer in number and could accommodate only a minority of the country's children. Not least, the new French-sponsored schools contradicted Counts' principle, "The great object of education should be that of inducting young people into membership in their own society and into the use of the instrumentalities of their own culture."[18]

Thus, the Franco-Vietnamese schools that were organized in 1917 and 1918 taught the inferiority of Vietnamese society. Many point-to-point comparisons were made between Vietnamese and French societies, always ending in proclamations of superiority for the latter. Vietnamese society was portrayed as corrupt, backward, and insecure. French rule, on the other hand, was depicted as a successful effort to rescue the Vietnamese people from their own worst tendencies. The official schools "did not teach French culture at all; rather, they taught French interpretations of Vietnamese culture and society."[19] Vietnamese society was viewed through French lenses.

The French were deeply aware of divisions within Vietnamese society and were experienced in adapting them to their own purposes. The royal elite, from the monarch down, was accorded privileges in every major sector of society, including education. Least of all did France attempt to compel them to educate the mass of the people willy-nilly. Neither the French nor the indigenous royal elite preached or practiced mass education. The village schools were the nearest to the reality of mass education, and they receded as long as French rule endured. Special educational privileges were awarded to the children of the commoner elite—professionals, industrialists, traders, and great landlords, lower and middle bureaucrats. But French authorities had to be cautious not to seem to be offering these wealthy Vietnamese the prospect of actual power. If they did so, resident Frenchmen in Vietnam would be aroused to protest against competition to themselves and their offspring.

> European parents complained bitterly that Vietnamese were usurping their rights to elite status by crowding the benches of French schools. They maintained that . . . Vietnamese who received French education . . . would demand equality in access to government jobs, in how the government treated them, and, in the long run, in making political decisions.[20]

In fact, in the 1930s, the principal French official in Tonkin (North Vietnam) advocated closing the schools there because educated Vietnamese were demanding government jobs.[21]

Children of peasants and industrial workers stood barely any chance of developing ultimately any quantum of real power. Schooling was arranged to prevent any such outcome. Compulsory attendance was never adopted in Tonkin and only after 1927 in Cochinchina (South Vietnam).[22] Urban poor and rural folk received only 2 or 3 years of rudimentary education whose medium of instruction was *quoc ngu*, the common everyday language. In the North Vietnamese town of Son-Duong, "access to modern education beyond third grade was limited mainly to the children of upper indigenous social stratum because of the considerable direct and indirect expenses of an education beyond this level."[23]

Although the gross numbers of Vietnamese children attending French-organized schools were impressive, they concealed more than they revealed. Exceedingly few of the children progressed very far beyond third grade. A cardinal reason for this was the discontinuity in instructional languages between the earliest and the most advanced grades; the former was usually Vietnamese, the latter French. Because only French or wealthy Vietnamese had access to French from the beginning of their schooling, they monopolized the higher reaches of academic affairs. Ninety percent of the Vietnamese enrollment was in the first three grades.[24] "In any given year," wrote Kelly, "between 70 and 90 percent of students applying for succeeding levels of schooling were eliminated by examinations."[25]

Post-primary schools for children aged 14 through 18 were attended by a tiny minority whose size grew slowly, if at all. Thus, in 1920, such enrollments made up 1.9% of the entire student population; 18 years later, the figure had fallen to 1.8%.[26] Scholarships to these institutions were available only to persons of French background.[27] During the school year 1929 to 1930, only 397 students in all of Vietnam and Cambodia attended higher primary schools.[28]

The University of Hanoi, the country's only institution of higher education under the French, was founded in 1906. It was, according to Kelly, only "a sort of higher vocational school with many faculties [i.e., subject-matter specializations] unheard of in French institutions bearing the same name."[29] A strong motive behind its organization was to deflect affluent Vietnamese from attending universities in France.[30] During the Japanese occupation of Vietnam from 1939 to 1945, both the University of Hanoi and the lower schools modified the French policy of restricted enrollment of Vietnamese. Enrollment in the latter rose from 450,000 to 700,000, an increase of 55%.[31] In all the years between 1918 and 1944, only about 3,000 students attended the University of Hanoi, with rising numbers in more recent years.[32] Degrees from the University of Hanoi were devalued. As a Vietnamese physician recalled, "[With a medical degree from the University of Hanoi] I could practice in Vietnam only under the supervision of a French doctor. So I went to France to get a more reputable degree."[33] This remained the case until the end of the French era.

A revolution for independence from the French was well underway by the World War II years. Vietnamese resentment at the exploitative policies of the French was fundamental in this movement. Most of the expenses incurred by

French colonial authorities were covered by income from three government monopolies: opium, alcohol, and salt. "Although the possession of opium was a criminal offense in France, the French administration purchased raw opium in India and Yunnan [a southern province in China], brought it to Saigon [in South Vietnam] for processing, and then sold it at official outlets at a profit of 400 percent." [34] (The French also monopolized the sale of opium in Laos, discussed in chapter 8.) Vietnamese were compelled to buy alcohol:

> Quota systems were established whereby a province was obliged to purchase a certain amount of whiskey each month, based on "normal usage." Then within each province every village had to buy a certain amount of whiskey or face harsh punishment on the charge that illicit distilling was being condoned. [35]

The monopoly over salt yielded high profits as well. "A salt worker had to sell to the colonial government every last grain of salt he produced and then repurchase the salt required for his household use at six to eight times the price he had just received for it." [36] Vietnamese were also subjected to forced labor without pay (the *corvée*), supposedly for the good of the community. Europeans were exempted from the corvée as well as the alcohol and salt requirements. Norlund noted that "from 1913 to 1922 the monopoly on opium was the main source of government revenue." [37]

During the years 1888 through 1928, about half of the French investments in Vietnam were in industry and mining, while another quarter were in trade and agriculture. Until 1942, 284 French companies were formed to exploit the resources of Vietnam. In fact, however, a very narrow range of ownership was involved:

> Almost 90 percent of the capital investment in Vietnam in 1939 belonged to companies controlled by only three financial syndicates. These syndicates, two banks, and a few dozen business firms, all with interlocking management at the very highest levels, controlled the economy of Vietnam as if it were an exclusive club. . . . A mere handful of men exerted near total influence over the entire financial and economic structure of Vietnam. [38]

This structure was modified only slightly before 1954 to allow a handful of selected Vietnamese businessmen to participate in the profits.

One of the most valuable Vietnamese products was natural rubber, which grew abundantly in the country. With the advent of mass production of automobiles in Western countries during the 1920s, the demand for rubber tires grew rapidly. Huge tracts of land were given by the French government to French companies. Workers were drafted in corvées to build roads to the rubber plantations. To house wage workers, military barracks were built, surrounded by barbed wire. Private police kept the barracks under surveillance. Workers who quit were dubbed deserters and tried for committing a crime. Some were kept in private prisons with the aid of "handcuffs, iron collars and chains." [39]

In 1940, the Nazis defeated France, and the collaborationist Vichy government was less able to rule over the colonies in the accustomed manner. Economic opportunities widened as some Vietnamese businessmen were allowed to participate in deals involving French syndicates. The civil service was opened to more Vietnamese. Some inequalities were abolished between French and Vietnamese. As indicated earlier, the schools and the university were open to more Vietnamese.

In September 1945, the Democratic Republic of Viet Nam (DRVN) was proclaimed. For the next 9 years, France fought a losing war with the revolutionaries. In 1954, the French armies at Dien Bien Phu surrendered. Although a united Vietnam was proclaimed by the victorious armies, two Vietnams emerged. South Vietnam was urged on by United States financial and military support. Meanwhile, the DRVN launched a literacy and schooling program designed to erase nearly a century of planned educational retardation by the French.

DRVN leader Ho Chi Minh set off a "war campaign" against illiteracy in 1945.[40] It took another 5 years before a formal national school system was designed.[41] Some 2.5 million persons acquired literacy in less than 1½ years after the war was waged by nearly 96,000 volunteer instructors.[42] In 1945, Ho had indicted the French: "They have built more prisons than schools."[43] The Viet Minh changed the priorities. Between 1946 and 1950, 10 million more Vietnamese joined the ranks of the literate while also helping fight a war against the French. As Woodside commented: "This feat was unprecedented in Southeast Asian history."[44] The school population also grew rapidly. From 700,000 in 1944, it reached some 1.125 million in 1954 and 4 million in 1961.[45]

The same pace of development could be glimpsed in individual villages. Such, for example, was the case with the North Vietnam village of Son-Duong. During the 1930s, only children from elite families could go beyond third grade. Within a year of Ho Chi Minh's call to "destroy illiteracy as an enemy":

> The movement expanded from a single class in the communal meeting hall to fifty classes with a total of 1,250 students, including women and the elderly. . . . By the end of 1946, 70 percent of illiterate villagers had been certified to pass the literacy tests.[46]

Freed from the restrictions of French rule, villagers proceeded to reorganize the school system:

> The village school . . . [began] offering junior high school classes as early as 1958–1959. . . . [By the 1980s] the equal access to education for boys and girls stood in sharp contrast to the almost all-male enrollment of 35 students in the three-grade village school on the eve of the August 1945 uprising.[47]

The presence of numerous teachers in the revolutionary ranks added to the prominence of school changes in the local political agenda.

Between 1954 and 1975, the Republic of Vietnam (South Vietnam) also engaged in a significant educational expansion. School growth rather than nonformal literacy instruction was stressed. A participant summed up the trend by saying, "We built classrooms and trained teachers and printed textbooks that permitted the number of students attending school in the Republic of Vietnam to double between 1955 and 1960 and then double again by 1969."[48] Unlike in the North, however, certain social inequalities continued to infuse schooling in South Vietnam:

> The rich had better educational opportunities than the poor, and people who lived in towns found it much easier to continue their educations beyond a certain point than those who lived in remote villages. So too did boys receive more encouragement than girls to continue their education.... Wherever a family lived and whatever their socioeconomic status, young males tended to have the most education and older women the least.[49]

School shortages were most striking in Saigon, the largest city in South Vietnam.

Shortened school shifts were widespread in Saigon. In 1972, an observer found some schools with as many as four shifts a day. Even two shifts meant only a 2½-hour school day.[50] Seven years later, the situation had worsened at the same school. The most selective government high schools turned away the greatest number of students.

> Children who do not gain admittance to government secondary schools attend private schools which greatly outnumber government schools. Most of these are business undertakings employing untrained or semi-trained staff. There are often more than a hundred pupils per class and many university students take part-time jobs as teachers in these schools. This situation is tolerated by the authorities since it is felt that some instruction is better than none.[51]

In such a context, it was idle to speak of standards. In 1975, when the Vietnam War ended and the country was unified, in the South, "access to health care and education [for the poorest of the poor was] greatly increased."[52]

Although warfare swept the entire country during three decades after 1945, substantial educational progress was nevertheless recorded. At the same time, however, Vietnam paid a heavy price for its victories over France and the United States. Soldiers killed in action numbered nearly 1 million in the ranks of North Vietnam and its supporters, 254,257 from South Vietnam, and over 47,000 from U.S. military forces.[53] Harrison wrote that "Vietnam . . . suffered more bombardment than all others put together, in all previous wars."[54] "Most of the bombs (about 4 million tons) and virtually all of the defoliants were dropped on . . . South Vietnam . . . [in which] over half of the forests and 9,000 of 15,000 hamlets were heavily damaged."[55] During 1978 and 1979, Vietnam invaded Cambodia (Kampuchea) and China attacked Vietnam. Only during the 1980s was Vietnam not involved in a major military encounter.

Literacy in Vietnam, according to the 1989 census, was close to 90%.[56] For men and women, the rates were 93 and 84%.[57] Schooling differences were slight. Considering the population over 10 years of age, "80 percent of the men and 74 percent of the women had only primary education, while 12 percent of the men had secondary or higher education compared to 9 percent of the women."[58] Between 1984 and 1988, real expenditures on education fell but seem to have recovered substantially in 1989.[59] Ravaged by war and denied extensive international economic aid, Vietnam's living standards suffered grievously during the 1980s. In 1986, the government adopted reforms that permitted the growth of a market economy. Many of the country's achievements in education were threatened as new criteria for individual profit began to replace social well-being.[60] Rising primary-school dropout rates were one indication of this. Day-care expenses are less likely to be covered by cooperatives and must be paid by parents. Jagan reported:

> Whereas in 1980 about 96 percent of children attended primary school, by 1985 only 86 percent did so. The proportion now [i.e., 1992] is probably closer to two-thirds and an increasing number of children are leaving without completing their primary schooling.[61]

Since 1989, only 3 years rather than the first 12 years of schooling are free.[62] Teachers are permitted to offer private classes. Double and triple shifting has been reported. Enrollments in secondary schools are declining. Dropout rates are 25 to 30% in lower-secondary schools and 15 to 19% in upper-secondary schools.[63]

Ethnic minorities have traditionally not received equal education in Vietnam. Because the language of instruction is Kinh (i.e., the language spoken by the great majority of Vietnamese), many minorities are unfamiliar with it and suffer in their schoolwork. Although the primary curriculum extends for 160 weeks for most students, it lasts for 120 weeks for ethnic minorities, and only 100 weeks for schools in remote areas.[64] As Jagan pointed out, "while the government talks about preserving the language and culture of minorities, there is actually much more emphasis on protecting 'the community of the Vietnamese nation'."[65] In Sa Pa, a heavily-Hmong area near the Chinese border, most of the people are illiterate, "school attendance is poor, and is unlikely to improve while only 10 of the district's 200 teachers are from ethnic minorities."[66] In Son La province, near the Laos border, "a typical school attendance chart for a single village . . . showed that 44 percent of the village's eligible Tai children were in school, 25 percent of the eligible Khmer children, but only 6 percent of the eligible Hmong children."[67]

CHINESE IN VIETNAM

From the earliest days of French dominance in Cochinchina (South Vietnam) during the last third of the 19th century, the invaders used the Chinese (Hoa) as collaborators in economic and governmental affairs. Chinese businessmen gained sole rights over importation of goods and represented the French in sales

of opium. They also controlled the sale and taxation of salt. The Chinese became the principal tax collectors. In rural areas, they monopolized transportation and were the dominant money lenders.[68] By the 1940s, the Hoa constituted
about 2½% of the total population; 85% of them lived in the South, mostly in
Cholon, a neighbor city adjacent to Saigon. Stern referred to the Vietnamese
"popular and historical animosity toward the minority Hoa."[69] Although the
large majority of Chinese were working-class persons, before World War II the
Vietnamese Communist Party did not search them out for concentrated recruitment and involvement. During the French occupation, 1941 through 1945,
Communists through the Viet Minh called upon all minorities, including the
Chinese, to fight against the Japanese.

Soon after the war ended, in 1945 and 1946, "the Viet Minh . . . guaranteed
ethnic minorities . . . the right to study their own languages in primary schools
and use their native languages in courts of law."[70] For many years preceding
this decision, Hoa schools existed in the Saigon area. They were taught in the
Chinese language and followed a classical curriculum. In the early 1900s, private
schools were organized; they were financed by tuition and private contributions
as well as by gifts by the government of China. Until 1949, the year of Communist triumph in China, graduates of the Hoa schools in Vietnam could attend
universities in China. In Vietnam itself, many Hoa attended French schools after completing their secondary education.

With the defeat of the French in 1954, the Communist administration set out
to change the Chinese schools, among others. Efforts were made to adapt the
curriculum to more modern themes, to reduce the amount of time devoted to
instruction in Chinese, and to give priority to study of the Vietnamese language. These changes applied only to North Vietnam, where the Communist
government held sway. In South Vietnam, a separate government was in power,
dedicated to the elimination of the government of the North. It was strongly
supported by the United States. Headed by Ngo Dinh Diem, the southern government adopted severely anti-Chinese policies. In 1956, Hoa were explicitly
banned from 11 trades where they were the majority of workers.[71] By executive
decree, all Hoa in the South were forced to become citizens of that country.[72]
The next year, a region-wide registration of Hoa was conducted. Various obstacles were placed on the operation of traditional Hoa schools. Seeking to assert
their superiority over the South, "the Vietnamese Communists articulated a
minimal commitment to freeing the Chinese from the 'racist' policies of the . . .
[South], abolishing discriminatory laws, and allowing the preservation of cultural practices and languages."[73] In fact, however, the very opposite of this
happened.

The government of the North, in Hanoi, viewed Hoa economic power as a
threat to the budding socialist system. Sweeping efforts were made to scatter
Chinese businesses and communities throughout the North, although schools
were returned to urban centers in 1970. Many small Chinese businesses and fac-

tories were compelled to become cooperatives. Large firms were simply nation-
alized. In 1969 and 1970, textbooks for the Hoa schools were revised to maximize Vietnamese. Once again, time spent on Chinese was to be reduced, and
teaching methods and teacher quality in the Hoa schools were to be evaluated.

Nineteen-seventy-five brought an end to the Vietnam War. For the first time,
the Hoa of the South came under the direct rule of Hanoi. A full-scale anti-
Chinese program emerged over the following 4 years. Hoa schools were given
Vietnamese names and in provincial schools Chinese-language instruction was
stopped.[74] In February 1977:

> Chinese who failed to . . . register themselves as Vietnamese citizens were . . . sim-
> ply sacked from their jobs with their residence registrations cancelled and their
> food rations stopped. They were further prohibited from entering the civil service
> or working for public enterprises, engaging in the retail trades or farming, or
> moving from one place to another.[75]

In September 1976, Chinese-language schools and newspapers were closed
down.

In Fall 1977, "Chinese throughout the country were placed under surveillance and subjected to various forms of physical harassment, and thousands
were reportedly discharged from their jobs without just cause."[76] The following
spring, Vietnamese armed forces encircled Cholon, adjacent to Ho Chi Minh
City—formerly Saigon—and took possession of some 50,000 retail shops.
"Those who were stripped of their properties and businesses were ordered to
move within one month or so to one of the 'new economic zones' set up in remote border provinces to reclaim virgin land and become agricultural producers."[77] Chinese victims of the armed raids and resulting orders protested and
conducted demonstrations. The government was not deterred whereby "the entire middle and lower-middle class population of the country was stripped
overnight of the only cash assets they had still been able to hold on to."[78]

Meantime, a border dispute between China and Vietnam heated up and in
October 1977, Chinese living in Vietnamese provinces bordering on China were
ordered to move. A number of wealthier Chinese businessmen in the South had
fled the country in 1975, just after the Communist victory. During the winter of
1977 and 1978, however, thousands of Hoa from the North began an exodus to
China via an overland route. By July 1978, some 160,000 had crossed the border.[79] In December, 1978, Vietnam invaded Cambodia on its southern border,
and in February 1979, China invaded Vietnam on the latter's northern frontier.
At war on two fronts simultaneously, Vietnam sought to prevent any internal
threat from the Hoa. The Chinese "were not able to find jobs, [and] ethnic Vietnamese were not allowed to associate with them."[80] Remaining Hoa schools
were closed in March 1979.

With war in the North, it was no longer possible for Hoa to escape to China
by land. Arrangements were made to escape by water. The Vietnamese govern-

ment charged the boat people—most of whom were ethnic Vietnamese—from U.S. $500 to $3,000 per person for permission to leave the country. Chinese living in various parts of the world helped supply these funds:

> According to sources in Hong Kong's banking circles, in the month of April 1979 alone, a total of U.S. $242 million was remitted through Hong Kong to Ho Chi Minh City by overseas Chinese in order to help their relatives or friends in Vietnam buy their way out of the country. This amount was already equivalent to half the total value of Vietnam's exports in 1978.[81]

After the war ended and the emigration stopped, nearly 100,000 Chinese still remained in Cholon. Almost none lived in Hanoi and a relative handful in the once-thriving port city of Haiphong.[82] By the late 1980s, Vietnamese authorities had greatly moderated their policies toward the Hoa. In the largest school in Cholon, Chinese was taught as a foreign language; it offered 22 classes in Chinese but 38 in English. There were, however, no longer any schools in which Chinese was the language of instruction.[83]

IMMIGRATION

The end of the Vietnam War in 1975 initiated a large-scale movement of Vietnamese to the United States. By 1990, 614,547 lived in this country. They came not as immigrants but as refugees. Immigrants have time to plan their move, to accumulate the means to make the trip, and to arrange the trip to suit their circumstances. Refugees, on the other hand, have little choice in the matter. At the same time, the United States felt constrained to facilitate the movement of its one-time allies and supporters. Its motive was not so much a moral commitment to former friends as the need to demonstrate to present and future allies and supporters elsewhere in the world that support for U.S. policy would be rewarded in emergencies. As a result of congressional legislation and executive policies, Vietnamese refugees traveled to camps in third countries where they awaited permission to enter the United States. Such countries were Thailand, the Philippines, and, for a time, Indonesia.

Prominent among the first refugees in 1975 were "South Vietnamese soldiers, government officials, business owners, employees of the U.S. government and U.S. companies—professionals, middle-and upper-class leaders of the defeated South."[84] A rudimentary educational program was drawn up; the U.S. State Department provided the funds for the program. According to Tollefson, a number of assumptions underlay the educational effort including: learn to work hard, become self-sufficient, learn democracy and do not go on welfare, do not break U.S. laws, do not discriminate against Americans, adopt a subservient position in American life, give up your cultural traditions, you have no skills to contribute to American society, while working in the United States you can pick up English, if you work hard you will be rewarded rapidly by upward mobility, you will enjoy social and economic equality, the hard workers get the best jobs, and Americans accept a body of values that you must adopt.[85]

Among the first wave of Vietnamese who arrived in 1975 were a considerable number who came from highly select social circles. In one sample population:

> About 45 percent . . . were part of the small Vietnamese ruling class. . . . About 82 percent . . . over age 18 had secondary or better education (in Vietnam, less than 64 percent of the school-age population entered primary school). Over 20 percent of the immigrants were university educated (2.5 percent in Vietnam received higher education).[86]

Half or more were Catholics, and only 10% in South Vietnam were the same. From the viewpoint of social origins, the refugees also included many ordinary Vietnamese who had only a modest education.

Children of the former ruling class could count on good schools for further education. Often they lived in affluent suburbs where the public schools were among the best. Sufficient capital was available to invest in various businesses. Parents with a French education were quite familiar with the requirements of a precollegiate program, as well as professional training. The greater number of Vietnamese refugees, however, lived a more bleak existence. Residing frequently in central cities with inadequate schools, they encountered educational programs that had few means for meeting special needs of immigrant students.[87] Children whose education had been interrupted by war and civil disturbance were placed in schools and programs inappropriate to their circumstances. Widespread dropouts and gangs among Vietnamese children were frequent in such schools.

Vietnamese—as well as other Asian-Americans—were subjected to another obstacle: the myth that they were not limited by poor schools or low socioeconomic conditions. Numerous educators cooperated with the mass media in contending that children of these backgrounds easily overcame conditions that could have interfered with their learning. Pointing to Vietnamese children of a janitor's family who had won academic honors, it was implied that other minorities could just as readily do the same, if they wished to do so. (It was not explained why most Vietnamese or other Asian-American classmates had failed to win similar honors.[88])

Another aspect of this issue relates to the educational and economic characteristics of Asian-American fathers who are themselves immigrants. It is well known that many college graduates among these individuals work far underneath their qualifications; downward social mobility is widespread. The census of 1990 showed "that 43 percent of Asian immigrants with a graduate or professional degree do not work in a managerial or professional category."[89] Quite likely, some of the children of these underemployed degree holders are the valedictorians hailed in the press for their scholarship and the humble employments of their fathers and/or mothers. Doubtless, few of the downwardly mobile parents neglected to instruct their children in the avenues to high academic success. In these cases, it is more accurate to speak of the operation of middle-class educational standards, regardless of the immediate economic circumstances of the parents.

The same could have been said of Vietnamese refugees even before they left for the United States. Jamieson analyzed the social scene in South Vietnam during the decade ending in 1975. Vietnamese who sold goods and services primarily to Americans in their "businesses, shops, bars, hotels, or fleets of taxis grew rich beyond their wildest dreams."[90] At the same time, "those who served their own people but not the Americans . . . tended to suffer a severe loss of relative well-being and hence in social status and influence."[91] Among these downwardly mobile persons were "doctors, nurses, schoolteachers, accountants, civil servants, journalists, scholars, army officers, writers, poets, lawyers, dentists, scientists, laboratory technicians, pharmacists."[92] "Education, position, wealth, and social influence," according to Jamieson, "no longer went together."[93] A severe inflation made matters worse as persons with relatively fixed incomes suffered deterioration of their living standards. It was from such a complex situation that the first wave of Vietnamese refugees came. Those who had experienced the greatest declines in status and wealth back home now sought to recoup their fortunes in the United States. Education of their children was a prime avenue that appeared far more available than it had been in South Vietnam.

As in Vietnam, so, too, in the United States did social class continue to divide the people. Sometimes, the feelings were voiced openly. Two observers reported:

> Status-conscious Vietnamese are reluctant to participate in programs designed to include compatriots from a lower social class. . . . They feel that their children's education may be hampered by a homogeneous school program which does not take into consideration the differences in socioeconomic and academic background.[94]

Directors of the Southeast Asian Refugee Youth Study, the largest-scale such inquiry, found that with respect to the four groups of refugees (Vietnamese, Hoa, Cambodians, and Hmong), their ranking "exactly parallels that of their parents' education."[95] Because so many refugees—and immigrants, as well—found themselves moving downward on the social scale, "adjusting to American culture was essentially adjusting to a change in class position."[96]

The younger generation was also enveloped by this new reality. In Vietnam, many could depend on their family's financial support to attend private schools if they were unable to compete their way into the best public schools.[97] The extra crutch of family assistance was far less available in the United States. The contrast was vivid in the remembrance of a Vietnamese American who had arrived as a child: "Where once we had been lively, upper-middle-class families in that tropical country so far away, here we were mousy, impoverished miserable exiles living in a deep, dark hole."[98]

Problems of class pervaded the large, West Coast communities of Vietnamese but they were not blunted even in much smaller places. In Toledo, Ohio, for example, 258 Vietnamese lived in some 70 households. Social-class membership was distributed as follows:[99]

	WHILE IN VIETNAM		WHILE IN TOLEDO	
	Number	Percent	Number	Percent
Upper class	1	1.4	0	0
Middle class	22	31.4	21	30.0
Lower	39	55.7	34	48.5
Urban poor	7	10.0	15	21.4
Peasant	1	1.4	0	0
	70	99.9	70	99.9

The urban poor live on welfare or Social Security. They are "very much looked down upon by the community and are seen as people without shame."[100] The numbers in the middle class are somewhat more prospective than actual inasmuch as some students simply anticipated future status as engineers, doctors, and computer scientists.[101] In the households as a whole, 88.9% of children over age 18 attended college. This included 60% of children of that age in the urban poor class. Undoubtedly, this greatly outnumbered those in the White community in college. Léons and Nguyen reported nevertheless that, "many in the Lower and Urban Poor classes are embittered and angry resenting the successes of others while some remembering their past status now feel profoundly affected by their inability to cope in their new country."[102]

In Orange County, California, containing the country's largest Vietnamese population, "virtually none of the unemployed refugees receives unemployment benefits."[103] Yet, "68 percent of ... [the] refugees live in households supplemented by some form of government aid."[104] This latter figure refers to the early 1980s. In California as a whole during 1992, 89% of Vietnamese were on welfare.[105] Their educational level, however, was somewhat inconsistent with their welfare status. In 1984, the Orange County Vietnamese reported the following:[106]

16 percent   Less than high school
37 percent   High school graduate
41 percent   Some college
6 percent   College graduate/post graduate

Six years later, one fourth of all Vietnamese households in the country were at under-poverty levels.[107] Many Vietnamese who reported such low incomes were full or part-time workers engaged in extremely low-paid jobs. The same was also true of many non-refugee workers.

Vietnamese Americans readily moved long distances to find better-paying work. In Garden City, Kansas, for example, Erickson interviewed many Vietnamese who had jobs in meat-packing plants with entry-level positions that paid $6.75 or more an hour.[108] Southwest Kansas, the cattle-feeding capital of the country, is also the locale of a number of meat-packing plants. In Spring, 1986, 640 Southeast Asians worked in the Garden City plant operated by IBP Corporation, an industry leader. Almost all of the Asians were Vietnamese, along with a few Cambodians and Laotians. In 1984, a total of over 2,000 Asian people lived in Garden City, 90% of whom were Vietnamese.[109] The IBP plant was organized by a national union so that a number of Vietnamese were union members. Employee turnover in these plants was extremely high, reaching in some years 100% or more.[110] Most Vietnamese worked on the second shift to earn night shift premium pay and because the supervision was relatively light on that shift.

Although most Vietnamese Americans live in central cities, they are not especially attracted to mainly Asian areas.[111] At the same time, they have tended to avoid public housing. In Denver, for example:

> threats and physical violence directed at Vietnamese living in a public housing complex . . . seem to have been connected to feelings among Chicano residents that the material possessions of Vietnamese in the community indicated that they did not need access to public facilities and therefore had been given preferential treatment by city housing officials.[112]

In Philadelphia, the same kind of hostile reception was met by Vietnamese who were moved into public housing traditionally utilized by African-Americans: "Seventy-five percent of the Black respondents gave . . . [affirmative] responses when asked if they objected to refugees living in public housing projects they occupied."[113] While Southeast Asian occupance in African-American neighborhoods has frequently led to victimization by Blacks, Thayer pointed out that where they "live among lower income whites, the same kinds of problems exist."[114] In any case, for Asian-Americans as a whole, isolation in housing was an increasing reality. Between 1970 and 1990, the proportion of Asian-Americans in Los Angeles living in predominantly non-Asian neighborhoods fell from two thirds to one third.[115]

Vietnamese refugee children from highly literate middle- and upper middle-class homes encountered few obstacles in the way of further education in the United States. Indeed, for many the pace seemed quite slow compared with the frenzy of gateway examinations that had been routine in Vietnam. To children whose schooling had been interrupted by years of warfare, the very opportunity to attend school as a matter of right was invaluable. Few failed to take advantage of it. Historically, children who had been prevented by law or violence from going to school developed a yearning for learning.[116] This turn toward education was strengthened as long as the tie between schooling and career held fast. The yearning faded when class and other factors began to restrict opportunities.

Standardized tests were utilized in two large-scale sample investigations of academic achievement among Southeast Asian refugees. The first was directed by Ima and Rumbaut and related exclusively to San Diego County, California. Smaller samples were studied by Caplan and associates in five locations: Boston; Chicago; Houston; Orange County, CA; and Seattle. Both studies included Vietnamese, Hoa, and Laotian refugee children, but only the Ima-Rumbaut study also covered Hmong and Cambodian children. Unfortunately, neither study took into account socioeconomic changes that occurred in the home countries during wartime. Upward and downward social mobility changes were analyzed only when these occurred in the United States. This makes it difficult to compare the role social-class factors played in education-related changes between home country and the United States.

Another factor to keep in mind are the great differences between the refugee and the home populations. In Vietnam, for example, some 70% of the people were farmers, but only 3% of Vietnamese refugees described themselves as farmers.[117] "The refugees as a whole . . . are much more urban, more highly educated, and more skilled in jobs related to the urban environment than the majority in the societies they left behind."[118] This was especially true of the Vietnamese who arrived in the United States between 1975 and 1978, but less so of Cambodians and Hmong, even during the 1980s. Religious affiliation is also unrepresentative. Whereas only 10% of Vietnamese are Roman Catholic, the figure is twice as large in the United States.[119]

In terms of education attained in Vietnam, "36 percent of . . . adults had not gone beyond elementary school, almost two-thirds . . . had attended high school, [and] 14 percent . . . had gone to college."[120] Vietnamese parents now in the United States averaged more than 9 years of school in Vietnam whereas Hoa parents had reached nearly 7 years.[121] Parents did not send their children willy-nilly to the United States without selective criteria in mind: "Some Vietnamese parents . . . did not send mentally retarded or less capable children . . . because they reasoned that the high risks and costs of escape would not be worth the low probability that these children would succeed in America."[122] It would seem that parents who themselves had experienced much education were in a better position to draw such judgments.

Rumbaut summarizes some leading aspects of standardized tests results and grade-point averages (GPAs):

> Less than half of the Vietnamese and . . . [Hoa] are classified by the [San Diego] school district as Limited-English-Proficient (LEP); the majority are classified as Fluent-English-Proficient (FEP). Although their reading scores are below the national average, reflecting their limitations with the English language as recently arrived newcomers, their GPAs are well above those for white Anglos (U.S.-born English-monolingual, white majority students of European ancestry) in the district (and for that matter, all other native-born students) and their math achievement scores place them in the top quartile of the nation—a striking and remarkable level of performance.[123]

According to Ima and Rumbaut, Vietnamese math scores place them in the highest quartile of all test-takers and indicate that they are "a highly selected group."[124]

In attempting to predict GPA, the math component of the Comprehensive Tests of Basic Skills (CTBS) is more important than the reading component. As Ima and Rumbaut found, "CTBS mathematics scores alone account for nearly half of the variance in GPAs among Southeast Asian students, whereas reading scores are not significant predictors of GPA."[125] At the same time, however, reading scores improve readily along with duration of residence in the United States. As was pointed out earlier, the relative educational positions of the Vietnamese, Hoa, Cambodian, and Hmong refugee children "exactly parallels that of their parents' education."[126] It is also true, however, that the individual child's educational status does not invariably reflect that of the parent. Another aspect that bears importantly on the children's academic achievement is the degree of maintenance of traditional culture that occurs in the family. Especially important is the development of "a sense of ethnic resilience and solidarity among parents who intend to stay [in the U.S.] . . . and to do so while affirming their ethnic culture and social networks."[127]

In the longer run, however, Rumbaut and his associates predicted a dimmer future for the academic attainment of younger refugees:

> We predict that this effect will soon plateau and then begin to diminish if and when the younger family members become more inculcated with values prevailing among American youth which (according to national poll data) emphasize self-fulfillment and gratification over self-sacrifice and hard work—a process of "becoming American" that may ironically prove counterproductive for educational attainment in competitive school settings.[128]

A similar prediction was made in 1962 about Japanese Americans by sociologist Kitano.[129] Recently a study on immigrant students in Los Angeles noted that they had a better attendance record than American-born students. But, lamented some teachers, "immigrant students Americanize all too soon."[130]

The work by Caplan and associates tends to overstate the achievements of refugee parents. For example, they wrote that "Indochinese parents have found employment and climbed out of economic dependency and poverty with dispatch."[131] Yet, in 1992, the same year in which this statement was published, 89% of Vietnamese living in California were receiving some form of government assistance.[132] Two years earlier, one fourth of all Vietnamese households were at or below poverty levels.[133] Elsewhere, the Caplan researchers wrote that, "not every refugee climbed out of poverty in rapid fashion and not every refugee child was doing well in school."[134] This statement is so indefinite that it may as well apply to 5 as to 95%. In fact, neither of the two books written by the Caplan group contains even one case study of a child who did not do well in school. Additionally, the authors have an unaccountably elevated conception of the educative capacity of schools in low-income areas of American cities that are attended by Southeast Asian refugee children. "Our schools do well in teaching children from backgrounds that are disadvantaged in many ways."[135] More realistic is the observation of the RAND researchers:

> The quality of schooling that immigrant students receive largely depends on the capacity of the local communities in which they reside. Yet most of these districts and schools lack the human and fiscal resources to educate students well, whether they are immigrant or native-born.[136]

It should be noted that even in very poor schools there are some students who manage to gain an acceptable education, usually with the enthusiastic cooperation of selected teachers. This does not lessen the degree of educational failure in the same schools for most students.

Educationally problematic developments in schools attended by Southeast Asian refugee children remain largely unmentioned. In part, this is accomplished by omission of the groups with the greatest educational problems. Whereas, for example, one of the Caplan books mentions Cambodians and Hmong several times in the introductory chapter, neither of the books discusses anything regarding the educational experience of the two groups. No explanation is given for the omission of these two Southeast Asian groups of children. At the time of the Caplan study, thousands of Cambodians resided in the United States and many Hmong had arrived.

Mastering English is the gravest academic difficulty facing Vietnamese students:

> English reading vocabulary and comprehension scores remain low even for Southeast Asian students who are in mainstream classes. . . . In spite of their higher GPA, Southeast Asian LEP students have lower reading scores than those of Hispanic LEP students. . . . Their reading vocabulary subtest scores place them in the bottom quartile nationally.[137]

Researchers report other serious signs. With reference to a Kansas high school, "all ESL teachers realized that their students often graduated with English reading and writing skills at or below a third-grade level."[138] In higher education, too, difficulties abound. Studying Vietnamese students at the University of Massachusetts, Boston, Kiang reported on their difficulties. (Most Asian students there are Vietnamese.) "Asians . . . comprise 24% of the students who never pass a Writing Proficiency Exam graduation requirement, compared to only 7% who are White. Those students are forced to withdraw from the University.[139] Kiang spoke of their "severe risk of dropping out."[140]

Bilingual programs are inadequate, even when many years have transpired. As Table 6.1 indicates, the number of Vietnamese children in California who were classified as Limited English Proficiency students increased by one half between 1985 and 1992. During the same years, however, the number of bilingual teachers—both credentialed and in training—actually *fell* by 64.6%. The number of bilingual aides rose marginally.

ESL classes were far more widespread than bilingual instruction. Their num-

TABLE 6.1

Vietnamese Bilingual Education in California, 1983–1992

	Number of LEP Students (1)	Number of Bilingual Teachers (2)	LEP Students per Bilingual Teacher (3)	Number of Bilingual Aides (4)	LEP Students per Bilingual Aide (5)
1983	29,033	NA	NA	NA	NA
1984	29,535	NA	NA	NA	NA
1985	29,990	322	93.1	627	47.8
1986	30,592	336	91.0	610	50.1
1987	30,906	306	101.0	629	49.1
1988	32,055	249	128.7	578	55.4
1989	32,454	215	150.9	615	52.7
1990	34,934	124	281.7	620	56.3
1991	40,477	99	408.8	667	60.6
1992	45,155	117	385.9	685	65.9

Note. LEP = Limited English Proficiency

Data for columns 1, 2, and 4 are taken from California Department of Education, "Trends in Number of Limited English Proficient Students in California Public Schools, by Language, 1985 through 1992," July 27, 1992; "Number of Bilingual Teachers and Percent Change from 1985 to 1992 by Language," July 27, 1992; and "Number of Bilingual Aides and Percent Change from 1985 to 1992 by Language," July 27, 1992. "Bilingual Teachers" includes all teachers, credentialed or in training.

bers, however, were insufficient to meet the need or demand. In addition, such programs, usually installed in ongoing mainstream-school buildings, had lower-priority ranking in terms of budget and personnel. Also, the traditional faculty frequently resented any special features of the ESL programs, such as smaller class size. Because ESL programs were less formalized in terms of objectives and student evaluation, it was easy to raise questions about their substance and educational value. In one high school, "the vague state of affairs surrounding the ESL program . . . not only left LEP immigrant students feeling left out of the school—but it had contributed to their (and their teachers') lower status among mainstream teachers and students." [141]

In Philadelphia, Southeast Asian high-school students complained to interviewers that ESL English was "not connected with their other classes, so that outside their . . . [ESL] classes, they are not able to comprehend their science, math, and social studies classes." [142] Another object of student complaint was the supposed haste with which ESL students were placed in mainstream classes. "Too many of the older students . . . describe feelings of helplessness when they sit in classes they do not understand. They complain that they are bored and frustrated by being placed into regular classes before they are ready. [143] In California, the Long Beach City College, a community college, enrolled some 4,800 Southeast Asian adults in two ESL programs. A waiting list contained 2,800 additional names in 1982. Although managers of the programs maintained that the teacher-student ratio was around 1:25 to 1:30, an independent analysis placed it closer to 1:86.[144] At California State University, Long Beach, an ESL-based American Language Program turned out to have enough space to enroll only 40% of registrants. The director of the program was the only full-time faculty member.[145]

Although numerous debates revolved around questions of bilingual education versus ESL, the more relevant issue turned out to be the lack of either offering.

Vietnamese students reported numerous acts of discrimination against them in San Diego high schools: "Students . . . felt that teachers often (6%) or sometimes (62%) discriminated against them, whereas counselors discriminated less (9% and 37%) in the same categories."[146] Davis and McDaid reported that although Vietnamese American youth aspire to higher education, "the reality . . . often is that limited English proficiency, minimal or nonexistent finances, insufficient credits towards graduation, and lack of understanding of post-high school options and requirements are barriers to fulfilling their expectations."[147]

In three Western Michigan schools, "when asked what they wished their teachers understood about them, the majority theme [of Vietnamese students] was, 'I wish my teachers understood more about my homeland and culture and the experience I've been through'."[148] Summarizing the views of these students, Dillinger wrote about mainstream teachers:

> A few display elements of prejudice. A majority lack understanding and make no allowances for the cultural-linguistic barrier, expecting the same work from these students as the others in the class. A few display genuine caring, concern and make the extra effort to help these students succeed. . . . This mainstream teacher helped to make the way a little easier for these [Vietnamese] students by sensitizing the mainstream students. Unfortunately such situations are very rare.[149]

In Philadelphia schools that he visited, reported Du Bois, "successful Southeast Asian students were constantly paraded forth in front of other students in the schools . . . used as living examples that the American Dream was alive and well and that hard work and ingenuity would always be rewarded."[150] This approach left unsuccessful Vietnamese students in an especially difficult position, implying as it did that a personal shortcoming was at issue.

In a Kansas high school, teachers vocally preferred Southeast Asian students over those of a Latino background. "Teachers and administrators openly admire these students' 'work ethics' and many state that they would take 'a room full of them anytime' over *any* other group of students."[151] At the same time, however, Vietnamese students complained about the exclusivity of White students in the lunchroom. They "don't sit with us because we have lower class . . . lower status."[152] Each group had its day in the sun, however fleeting. Thus, the school soccer team consisted mainly of immigrants. School authorities, however, were displeased by the prominence of the team's games and in 1988 the team was dismantled. Mark Grey observed that "open hostility is virtually nonexistent" in the school.[153] Rather, the nonimmigrant students enforce their distance from immigrants with the aid of stereotypes concerning immigrants.

In Orange County, California, can be found Little Saigon, the U.S. concentration point of Vietnamese. Young adults who arrived from Vietnam around 1978, the second wave:

> Find playing "catch up" in the American high schools virtually impossible, with the result that many eventually have dropped out from school. . . . Mr. My Ta, a Vietnamese aide in an Orange County high school, reported that many of the high-school dropouts spend their time sipping French coffee and listening to Vietnamese rock music at the malls in Little Saigon by day and congregating at the local pool halls by night. Without English, the only work available to them is in Little Saigon.[154]

One career open to them is to become an auto mechanic. A study by the Immigrant and Refugee Planning Center found that 70% of refugees were jobless and two thirds (68%) lived partly on government assistance. "The number one concern of the refugees in Orange County is unemployment, followed by language barrier, racial prejudice, housing costs, and the well-being of their families [still living] in Southeast Asia."[155]

Many Vietnamese youth found their U.S. schools inhospitable or noncaring. In Philadelphia, for example, when these students had problems with others, especially African-American students, they appealed to their teachers in vain. "If they feel that they cannot get fair treatment from the teachers or the principal, to whom can they turn for help?"[156] The school system struck Vietnamese and other Asian parents as so unresponsive to their children's educational needs that the parents filed a lawsuit against the system.[157] Thayer went further into some problems of Southeast Asian students in the city's schools:

> Southeast Asian students in the public schools speak almost universally of the abuse—both verbal and physical—that they encounter there and of the poor responses of school authorities to the problem. Several people interviewed for this report, including former students, school staff, and human relations professionals, went so far as to say that harrassment and violence . . . [against] Asians in the schools is severe enough that it is a factor in the high dropout rate for Southeast Asian youth. The city's public schools—particularly the high schools—are consistently the scenes of incidents of racial harrassment and violence.[158]

Asian Americans United, a Philadelphia advocacy group, reported in 1990 that "an Asian person in Philadelphia is 50 times more likely than a white to be the victim of a racially-motivated incident of harassment or violence."[159] Reviewing the national scene, the U.S. Commission on Civil Rights came to parallel conclusions.[160]

It was only in the 1980s that large numbers of Vietnamese American youth reached college age. Kiang's extended study, completed in 1991, is one of the few dealing with Southeast Asians at a single institution of higher education. At the University of Massachusetts, Boston, in Fall 1990, 194 Vietnamese, 26 Cambodians, and 3 Lao were enrolled.[161] During the years 1981 through 1987, Asians recorded a retention rate of 69.4% as contrasted to one of 56.1% for White students. During the eighth semester, however, the respective retention rates were 24.1 and 33.8%. Over a 5-year period, of the Asian students who entered in 1981 and 1982, only 13.8% graduated. Clearly, these first Southeast Asian enrollees experienced considerable dropout rates. As Kiang pointed out, they continued to do so:

> These stories of discouragement and dropping out are typical of the Southeast Asian experience at UMass/Boston, and contrast sharply with the whiz-kid, model minority image of super-achieving Asian-American students who have no problems in school.[162]

Having overcome successfully enormous life-size obstacles in Vietnam, they were left to grapple alone with a complex university career.

Kiang explained:

> Southeast Asian students experience serious isolation at UMass/Boston. In the academic domain, students have minimal relationships to faculty or staff, and they receive little help with either course difficulties or on-going advising and mentoring. . . . The social networks provide very limited guidance, however, especially within the academic domain.[163]

He adds that the nonresidential, urban character of the institution heightens the risk of academic failure. In addition, the myth of the super-achiever serves to condone institutional inattention to problems of study and learning. "Many, at first, simply choose the 'easy way' of majoring in scientific and technical fields in order to minimize the 'hard times' associated with reading, writing, and speaking English in their courses."[164] Kiang raised a serious question: "What are the social consequences if this generation of Southeast Asian students concentrates overwhelmingly in business, science, and engineering when the communities, in fact, desperately need bilingual lawyers, health care providers, policy makers, writers, filmmakers, teachers, and organizers?"[165]

The experience of separateness and isolation in the academic realm harmonized with discordant treatment they encountered elsewhere. Southeast Asian students shared with Kiang "numerous discrimination stories and a high level of awareness about racism in U.S. society, particularly from their work experience in both the local service economy and within the university."[166] Race has a further meaning to the students to whom having an American friend means having a White friend. As Kiang explained:

> Blacks, Latinos, or American-born Asians, though also "Americans," are often not recognized as such by Asian immigrants and refugees. The definition of "Ameri-

can" being white is a deeply rooted and on-going social and epistemological issue confronting the peoples of the United States.[167]

(The same issue was noted in chapter 3, on Japanese Americans.)

CONCLUDING REMARKS

Colonialism was one of the heaviest burdens borne by the Vietnamese people. During the century or so of French rule, one sector of Vietnam's society after another was subordinated to French self-interest. As in economic life, so, too, in education were policies established that converted Vietnamese resources to the primary benefit of French residents. As we saw earlier, a dual school system was largely financed out of Vietnamese tax revenues and the education was greatly disparate. French children received an education closely parallel to that received in France itself. School funds, however, were so managed that Vietnamese children received only a barely recognizable version of the same.

The school curriculum treated Vietnam as a suburb of France in which the Vietnamese were hardly more than tourists. They were urged to admire the wonders worked by French civilization and ingenuity. At the same time, Vietnamese history was ignored or treated as a time of backwardness and disorder. Indeed, students were subjected to lessons in racism with the aim of portraying Vietnamese as inferior beings altogether. Yet, a little space in the throne room was reserved for exceptional Vietnamese whose characteristic was a willingness to cooperate wholeheartedly with the French conqueror, whether in lucrative business enterprises or classrooms that normally excluded all but French citizens.

French colonialism did not differ greatly from others. As we saw earlier, the Japanese in Korea and the Americans in the Philippines ruled in similar ways. The French did not seek altogether to replace indigenous languages whereas the Japanese aimed at just such an eventuality. A middle position was adopted by the Americans. None of the three conquerors sought to institute truly universal education in the colonies. In the United States itself, African-American, Mexican American, and Native American children were totally or in part excluded from educational opportunities, as were children from another of its colonies, Puerto Rico.

Everywhere, the end of colonialism brought a great expansion of education. Although the economic consequences of national independence were not so immediate, the proliferation of schooling was instant evidence of significant change. Nowhere was the transition so sweeping as in Vietnam. Among rural Third World countries, it occupied the forefront in schooling, despite a punishing war and consequent poverty that endured for decades.

NOTES

[1] Nguyen Trong Hoang, "Traditional Education in Viet Nam," *Vietnamese Studies,* 30 (1971), p. 143. Reference is made to Cao Xuan Duc's *Index of Examination through the Dynasties.*

[2] Ibid., pp. 129–130.

[3] Ibid., p. 141.

[4] Doan Viet Hoat, *The Development of Modern Higher Education in Viet Nam: A Focus on Cultural and Socio-political Forces* (Doctoral dissertation, Florida State University, 1971), p. 17.

[5] R. B. Smith, "The Cycle of Confucianization in Vietnam," p. 19 in Walter F. Vella, ed., *Aspects of Vietnamese History* (University Press of Hawaii, 1973).

[6] Quoted in Hoang, "Traditional Education," p. 143.

[7] Hoat, *The Development of Modern Higher Education,* p. 25. Compare, however, Neil L. Jamieson, *Understanding Vietnam* (University of California Press, 1993), p. 52: "The examination system was still thriving in the 1890s, especially in the north."

[8] Ibid., p. 6.

[9] Ibid., p. 20.

[10] Hoang, "Traditional Education," p. 144.

[11] See Gail P. Kelly, "Colonial Schools in Vietnam: Policy and Practice," p. 96 in Philip G. Altbach and Gail P. Kelly, eds., *Education and Colonialism* (Longman, 1978) and Kelly, *Franco-Vietnamese Schools, 1918–1938: Regional Development and Implications for National Integration* (Center for Southeast Asian Studies, University of Wisconsin, April 1982), p. 5.

[12] J. Kim Munholland, "'Collaboration Strategy' and the French Pacification of Tonkin, 1885–1897," *Historical Journal,* 24 (1981), p. 649.

[13] Joseph Buttinger, *Vietnam: A Dragon Embattled.* 2 vols. (Praeger, 1967), p. 46, quoted in Nhu Duc Duong, *Education in Vietnam under the French Domination, 1862–1945* (Doctoral dissertation, Southern Illinois University, 1978), p. 35.

[14] Lê Quang Hông, "Compulsory Education in Viet-Nam," p. 115, in Charles Bilodeaux and others, *Compulsory Education in Cambodia, Laos and Viet-Nam* (UNESCO, 1955).

[15] Ngo Vinh Long, *Before the Revolution: The Vietnamese Peasants Under the French* (MIT Press, 1973), p. 73.

[16] See Kelly, *Franco-Vietnamese Schools,* p. 32 and "Schooling and National Integration: The Case of Interwar Vietnam," *Comparative Education,* 18 (1982), p. 186.

[17] Ngo Vinh Long, *Before the Revolution,* p. 73 and Kelly, *Franco-Vietnamese Schools,* p. 32.

[18] George S. Counts, "Education in the Philippines," *Elementary School Journal,* 26 (October 1925), p. 106.

[19] Kelly, *Franco-Vietnamese Schools,* p. 377.

[20] Kelly, "Colonial Schools in Vietnam," p. 99.

[21] Kelly, *Franco-Vietnamese Schools,* p. 43.

[22] Hông, "Compulsory Education in Vietnam," pp. 117, 119.

[23] Hy V. Luong and Nguyen Doc Bang, *Revolution in the Village. Tradition and Transformation in North Vietnam, 1925–1988* (University of Hawaii Press, 1992), p. 47.

[24] Kelly, "Colonial Schools in Vietnam," p. 104.

[25] Kelly, *Franco-Vietnamese Schools, 1918 to 1938* (Doctoral dissertation, University of Wisconsin, 1975), p. 93.

[26] Kelly, *Franco-Vietnamese Schools,* p. 16.

[27] Duong, *Education in Vietnam,* p. 27.

[28] Ibid., p. 30, footnote 1.

[29] Kelly, *Franco-Vietnamese Schools, 1918 to 1938,* p. 71.

[30] Gail P. Kelly, "The Myth of Educational Planning: The Case of the Indochinese University,

1906–38," p. 99 in Irving J. Spitzberg, Jr., ed., *Universities and the International Distribution of Knowledge* (Praeger, 1980).

[31] Truong Buu Lam, "Japan and the Disruption of the Vietnamese Nationalist Movement," p. 248 in Walter F. Vella, ed., *Aspects of Vietnamese History* (University Press of Hawaii, 1973).

[32] Ken Post, *Revolution, Socialism and Nationalism in Viet Nam*, Vol. 1 (Wadsworth, 1989), p. 39.

[33] Gisele Bousquet, "The Colonial Era: Vietnamese Migration to France," p. 80 in Robert R. Reed, ed., *Patterns of Migration in Southeast Asia* (Centers for South and Southeast Asia Studies, University of California, Berkeley, 1990).

[34] Jamieson, *Understanding Vietnam*, p. 62.

[35] Ibid., p. 63.

[36] Ibid., p. 63.

[37] Irene Norlund, "The French Empire, the Colonial State in Vietnam and Economic Policy: 1885–1940," *Australian Economic History Review*, 31 (March 1991), p. 82.

[38] Jamieson, *Understanding Vietnam*, p. 91.

[39] Martin J. Murray, " 'White Gold' or 'White Blood'? The Rubber Plantations of Colonial Indochina, 1910–40," *Journal of Peasant Studies*, 19 (April–July 1991), pp. 47–55.

[40] Alexander Woodside, "The Triumphs and Failures of Mass Education in Vietnam," *Pacific Affairs*, 56 (Fall 1983), p. 404.

[41] Ibid., p. 405.

[42] David Marr, "Vietnam: Harnessing the Whirlwind," p. 202 in Robin Jeffrey, ed., *Asia—The Winning of Independence* (St. Martin's Press, 1981).

[43] Luong and Bang, *Revolution in the Village*, p. 130.

[44] Woodside, "The Triumphs and Failures of Mass Education," p. 401.

[45] Jamieson, *Understanding Vietnam*, p. 277.

[46] Luong and Bang, *Revolution in the Village*, p. 145.

[47] Ibid., pp. 145, 173.

[48] Jamieson, *Understanding Vietnam*, p. 292.

[49] Ibid., p. 303.

[50] B. G. Brent, "Writing Brush and Inkstand," *Education News* (Canberra City), 13 (1971–72), p. 6.

[51] Ibid., p. 7.

[52] Jamieson, *Understanding Vietnam*, p. 367.

[53] Malcolm W. Browne, "Vietnamese Also Extending the Search for Their MIAs," *New York Times*, May 20, 1994.

[54] James P. Harrison, "History's Heaviest Bombing," p. 130 in Jayne S. Werner and Luu Doan Huynh, eds., *The Vietnam War* (Sharpe, 1993).

[55] Ibid., p. 131.

[56] Börje Ljunggren, ed., *The Challenge of Reform in Indochina* (Harvard Institute for International Development, Harvard University, 1993), p. 169.

[57] Ibid., p. 236.

[58] Ibid., p. 237, footnote 2.

[59] Ibid., p. 245.

[60] See ibid., p. 364. See also Philip Shenon, "In the Free Market Vietnam's Poor Pay a Price," *New York Times*, November 2, 1994.

[61] Larry Jagan, *Vietnam. The Price of Peace* (Oxfam, 1992), p. 23.

[62] Ibid., p. 37. Compare, however, D. C. Bernard and Le Thai Can, "Vietnam: System of Education," p. 6612 in Torsten Husén and T. Neville Postlethwaite, eds., *The International Encyclopedia of Education*, 2nd ed. (Pergamon, 1994).

[63] Bernard and Can, "Vietnam," p. 6610.

[64] Ibid., p. 6612.

[65] Jagan, *Vietnam*, p. 51.

[66] Ibid., p. 51.

[67] Woodside, "Triumph and Failures of Mass Education in Vietnam," p. 421.

[68] Lewis M. Stern, *Vietnamese Communist Policy Toward the Overseas Chinese, 1920–82* (Doctoral dissertation, University of Pittsburgh, 1982), p. 40.

[69] Ibid., p. 1.

[70] Ibid., p. 97.

[71] Pao-min Chang, "The Sino-Vietnamese Dispute over the Ethnic Chinese," *China Quarterly*, 90 (June 1982), p. 198.

[72] Stern, *Vietnamese Communist Policy*, p. 178.

[73] Ibid., p. 218.

[74] E. S. Ungar, "The Struggle Over the Chinese Community in Vietnam, 1946–1986," *Pacific Affairs*, 60 (Winter 1987–1988), p. 605.

[75] Chang, "The Sino-Vietnamese Dispute," p. 203.

[76] Ibid., p. 204.

[77] Ibid., p. 206.

[78] Ibid., p. 207.

[79] Stern, *Vietnamese Communist Policy*, p. 295.

[80] Ibid., p. 308.

[81] Chang, "The Sino-Vietnamese Dispute," p. 228.

[82] Ungar, "The Struggle Over the Chinese Community," p. 610–611.

[83] Ibid., p. 611–612, 613.

[84] James W. Tollefson, *Alien Winds. The Reeducation of America's Indochinese Refugees* (Praeger, 1989), p. 24.

[85] Ibid., pp. 70–82.

[86] Gail P. Kelly, "Schooling, Gender and the Reshaping of Occupational and Social Expectations: The Case of Vietnamese Immigrants to the United States," *International Journal of Women's Studies*, 1 (1978), p. 326. This distribution apparently referred to Vietnamese refugees housed at Fort Indian Town Gap, PA, in 1975.

[87] See, for example, Lorraine M. McDonnell and Paul T. Hill, *Newcomers in American Schools. Meeting the Educational Needs of Immigrant Youth* (RAND, 1993).

[88] This question is raised by Bill Ong Hing, *Making and Remaking Asian America Through Immigration Policy* (Stanford University Press, 1993).

[89] Paul Ong and Tania Azores, "Asian Immigrants in Los Angeles: Diversity and Divisions," p. 111 in Paul Ong E. Benacich, and L. Cheng, eds., *The New Asian Immigration in Los Angeles and Global Restructuring* (Temple University Press, 1994). See also Hyunjung Park, *Interpreting the High Educational Achievement and Socioeconomic Status of Asian-Americans* (Doctoral dissertation, Harvard University, 1990), pp. 241, 252–253, and 255.

[90] Jamieson, *Understanding Vietnam*, p. 294.

[91] Ibid., p. 294.

[92] Ibid., p. 294.

[93] Ibid., p. 294.

[94] Lynell Burmark and Hyung-chan Kim, "The Challenge of Educating Vietnamese Children in American Schools," *Integrateducation*, 16 (January-February 1978), p. 3.

[95] Ruben G. Rumbaut, "The Agony of Exile: A Study of the Migration and Adaptation of Indochinese Refugee Adults and Children," p. 82 in Frederick L. Ahearn, Jr. and Jean L. Athey, eds., *Refugee Children. Theory, Research and Services* (Johns Hopkins University Press, 1991).

[96] Gail P. Kelly, *From Vietnam to America* (Westview, 1977), p. 199.

[97] See Nazli Kibria, *Family Tightrope. The Changing Lives of Vietnamese Americans* (Princeton University Press, 1993), pp. 62–63.

[98] Andrew Lam, "Love, Money, Prison, Sin, Revenge," *Los Angeles Times*, March 13, 1994.

[99] William M. Léons and Kim-Anh Nguyen, "Class Relations in the Viet Community of Toledo, Ohio," *Viet Nam Generation* 4 (Spring 1992), pp. 65, 68.

[100] Ibid., p. 168.

[101] Ibid., p. 168.

[102] Ibid., p. 169.

[103] C. Beth Baldwin, *Patterns of Adjustment: A Second Look at Indochinese Resettlement in Orange County* (Immigrant and Refugee Planning Center, n.d.), p. 32.

[104] Ibid., p. 61.

[105] Paul Ong and Evelyn Blumenberg, "Welfare and Work among Southeast Asians," p. 124 in Ong, ed., *The State of Asian Pacific America: Economic Diversity, Issues and Policies* (LEAP Asian Pacific American Public Policy Institute and UCLA Asian American Studies Center, 1994).

[106] Baldwin, *Patterns of Adjustment*, pp. 59–60.

[107] Paul Ong and Suzanne J. Hee, "Economic Diversity," p. 36 in Ong, ed., *The State of Asian Pacific America: Economic Diversity, Issues and Policies* (LEAP Asian Pacific American Public Policy Institute and UCLA Asian American Studies Center, 1994).

[108] Ken C. Erickson, *Household Composition and Scores on the Vietnamese Depression Scale: Vietnamese Refugee Youth in Garden City, Kansas* (Master's thesis, University of Wyoming, 1986), p. 8.

[109] Ken C. Erickson, "Vietnamese Household Organization in Garden City, Kansas: Southeast Asians in a Packing House Town," *Plains Anthropologist*, 33 (1988), p. 28.

[110] Ibid., p. 31.

[111] Robert P. Thayer, *Who Killed Heng Lim? The Southeast Asian Experience of Racial Harassment and Violence in Philadelphia* (Asian Americans United, 1990), p. 11.

[112] Kenneth A. Skinner, "Vietnamese in America: Diversity in Adaptation," *California Sociologist*, 3 (1980), p. 114.

[113] Letha A. (Lee) See, "International Migration and Refugee Problems: Conflict between Black Americans and Southeast Asian Refugees," *Journal of Intergroup Relations*, 14 (Winter 1986–1987), p. 41.

[114] Thayer, *Who Killed Heng Lim?*, p. 49.

[115] Ong and Azores, "Asian Immigrants in Los Angeles," p. 118.

[116] See Meyer Weinberg, "A Yearning for Learning: Blacks and Jews Through History," *Integrated Education*, 7 (May–June 1969), pp. 20–29.

[117] Nathan Caplan, Marcella H. Choy, and John K. Whitmore, *Children of the Boat People. A Study of Educational Success* (University of Michigan Press, 1991), p. 48.

[118] Ibid., p. 48.

[119] Nathan Caplan, John K. Whitmore, and Marcella H. Choy, *The Boat People and Achievement in America. A Study of Family Life, Hard Work, and Cultural Values* (University of Michigan Press, 1989), p. 25.

[120] Caplan, Choy, and Whitmore, *Children of the Boat People*, p. 47.

[121] Kenja Ima and Ruben G. Rumbaut, "Southeast Asian Refugees in American Schools: A Comparison of Fluent-English-Proficient and Limited English-Proficient Students," *Topics in Language Disorders*, 9 (June 1989), p. 68.

[122] Ibid., p. 70.

[123] Rumbaut, "The Agony of Exile," p. 82.

[124] Ima and Rumbaut, "Southeast Asian Refugees in American Schools," p. 70.

[125] Ibid., pp. 69–70.

[126] Rumbaut, "The Agony of Exile," p. 82.

[127] Ibid., p. 87.

[128] Ibid., p. 88.

[129] Harry Kitano, "Changing Achievement Patterns of the Japanese in the United States," *Journal of Social Psychology*, 58 (1962), pp. 263–264.

[130] McDonnell and Hill, *Newcomers in American Schools*, p. 57. See also Table 32, same page.

[131] Nathan Caplan, Marcella H. Choy, and John K. Whitmore, "Indochinese Refugee Families and Academic Achievement," *Scientific American*, (February 1992), p. 41.

[132]See note #105.

[133]See note #107.

[134]Caplan, Whitmore, and Choy, *The Boat People*, p. 87.

[135]Ibid. p. 162.

[136]McDonnell and Hill, *Newcomers in American Schools*, p. xii.

[137]Ima and Rumbaut, "Southeast Asian Refugees in American Schools," pp. 62, 64.

[138]Mark A. Grey, "Immigrant Students in the Heartland: Ethnic Relations in Garden City, Kansas, High School," *Urban Anthropology*, 19 (Winter 1990), p. 419.

[139]Peter Nien-chu Kiang, *New Roots and Voices: The Education of Southeast Asian Students at an Urban Public University* (Doctoral dissertation, Harvard University, 1991), p. 70.

[140]Ibid., p. 219.

[141]Grey, "Immigrant Students in the Heartland," p. 419.

[142]Heather A. Peters, *A Study of Southeast Asian Youth in Philadelphia*, 1988 (ERIC ED 299 371), p. 64.

[143]Ibid., p. 164.

[144]Terrence G. Wiley and others, *Refugee Resettlement in Long Beach* (City of Long Beach, Department of Public Health, Refugee Technical Assistance Project, February 22, 1983), p. 49.

[145]Ibid., p. 54.

[146]Donna G. Davis and Janet L. McDaid, "Identifying Second-Language Students' Needs. A Survey of Vietnamese High School Students," *Urban Education*, 27 (April 1992), p. 36.

[147]Ibid., p. 39.

[148]Barbara J. Dillinger, *Adolescent Refugees: An Ethnographic Study of Vietnamese in U.S. Schools* (Master's thesis, Michigan State University, 1990), p. 64.

[149]Ibid., pp. 175–176.

[150]Thomas A. Du Bois, "Constructions Construed: The Representation of Southeast Asian Refugees in Academic, Popular, and Adolescent Discourse," *Amerasia Journal*, 19 (1993), p. 11.

[151]Grey, "Immigrant Students in the Heartland," p. 420.

[152]Ibid., p. 421.

[153]Ibid., p. 423.

[154]Chor-Swang Ngin, "The Acculturation Pattern of Orange County's Southeast Asian Refugees," *Journal of Orange County Studies*, 3/4 (Fall 1989–Spring 1990), p. 49.

[155]Ibid., p. 51.

[156]Peters, *A Study of Southeast Asian Youth in Philadelphia*, p. 69.

[157]See Len Reiser, *A Short History of Y.S. v. School District of Philadelphia* (Education Law Center, July 1990).

[158]Thayer, *Who Killed Heng Lim?*, p. 28.

[159]Ibid., p. 26.

[160]See chapter 2, Bigotry and Violence Against Asian Americans and chapter 4, Access to Educational Opportunity: Asian American Immigrant Children in Primary and Secondary Schools in U.S. Commission on Civil Rights, *Civil Rights Issues Facing Asian Americans in the 1990s* (The Commission, February 1992).

[161]Kiang, *New Roots and Voices*, p. 65.

[162]Ibid., p. 198.

[163]Ibid., pp. 214–215.

[164]Ibid., p. 173.

[165]Ibid., p. 211.

[166]Ibid., p. 213. This statement would seem to contradict the assertion by Caplan and associates, *Children of the Boat People*, p. 137: "Yet the refugees, while acknowledging a degree of bias against them, do not seem to let the discrimination become a prime focus of their attention or burden their efforts."

[167]Ibid., p. 160, footnote 25.

CHAPTER SEVEN

Cambodia

Unlike China, Korea, and Vietnam, government-sponsored education in Cambodia played virtually no part in its early history. Some 800 years ago, state education in Cambodia was reserved for children of the elite.[1] During the 1880s, years after the country became a colony—technically, a protectorate[2] of France —some Chinese and Vietnamese children in the country's capital, Phnom Penh, attended a French-managed school. Many Cambodian parents kept their children out of the school.[3] Only in 1904 did Cambodian authorities begin to establish a national system of education. The following year, officials reported 750 pupils attended protectorate schools in the capital city. These numbers included 29 princes and 25 princesses.[4] Not until some 25 years later was the country's first *lycée* (high school) built.

Ordinary people had to depend, for their education, on pagoda schools attached to Buddhist temples and taught by the *bonzes,* or monks. These schools, which were to be found throughout the country, were open only to boys and men. No institution existed for girls and women. It was common practice for males to enter the temples for some months or even years before marrying. As Bilodeau contended, however, the educational content of this traditional schooling was scant:

> The pagoda schools . . . were schools only in name. The pupils' chief role was to act as servants to the bonzes, accompanying them on their morning begging expeditions and cleaning the temple buildings. The pagoda schools had no curriculum, time table, inspectors or examinations. . . . Their only instruction was during part of the afternoon, when they learnt to read the sacred texts (which were inscribed

on palm leaves) and copied out the written characters. . . . A Cambodian boy leaving the pagoda school had his memory stocked with edifying passages, but could neither read, write nor count. . . . The sacred script was not employed outside the pagodas.[5]

Steinberg noted that "the students were little more than servants of the bonzes, learning only religious precepts and, perhaps, a little carpentry."[6]

Not least of the attractions of the traditional pagoda school was, to the state, its almost costless nature because no separate building was needed nor were teachers paid; and to the students' families, who were spared tuition and fees. The price paid by the local communities, however, was far greater. "In 1920 a reliable observer reported that French administrators were frequently unable to find in municipalities of several thousand people even one person who could read and write Cambodian [i.e., Khmer]."[7] After 1918, a dual school system existed: the pagoda schools, which were not, strictly speaking, a public-school system, and the French-sponsored official school system. To some extent, especially in the lowest grades, the two were in competition.

The inadequacy of Cambodian education was clear from the fact that in 1940, after some 75 years of French colonization, "Cambodia had only three trained doctors, one hospital, and a single high school to serve its three million people."[8] In 1931, a year after its establishment, the high school produced seven students who received the French *baccalaureat*, a high-school diploma. (Twenty three years later, the number had risen only to 144.)[9] In 1941, enrollment in the pagoda schools outstripped that in the French-directed public schools, as not a great deal had changed in Cambodian education.[10] Five years earlier, all the primary schools enrolled only 50,000 to 60,000 students.[11] Between 1938 and 1951, educational expenditures rose from 984,900 to 127,873,672 piastres, seemingly an enormous increase. In fact, however, these were depreciated piastres as the index of retail prices between 1939 and 1952 increased 41-fold.[12] Although these figures applied to middle-class Cambodians in Phom Penh, they were recorded in the city that was most extensively supplied with schools.

Peasants, who made up some 80% of all Cambodians, saw little educational progress. Three minority groups—Vietnamese as well as Chinese and Sino-Khmers—experienced considerably more. Large numbers of their children attended French-language public schools, thereby preparing to gain employment as members of the colonial bureaucracy and in French enterprises. Those most benefited were the children of the colonial indigenous elite whose parents lived in cities and who, over the years, developed a kind of claim on positions in the army and civil bureaucracy. Both in rural and urban areas, Chinese and Sino-Khmers monopolized wholesale commerce and retail trade as well as finance.

The advent of independence in 1949 set off a great expansion in education, this time far beyond the reach of depreciated money. Between 1955 and 1968, the following growth in enrollment was recorded:[13]

	1955	*1968*
Primary schools	300,000	1,000,000+
High schools	5,000	1,000,000+
Universities	0	Nearly 11,000

In the primary schools, a gross disparity existed between the numbers of boys and girls enrolled. During 1951 to 1952, for example, the numbers were 185,000 and 30,000, respectively, while enrollment rates were 77 and 12%.[14] Disparities moderated somewhat as expansion proceeded. Writing in 1955, Bilodeau observed that "extension of education is . . . primarily a question affecting girls."[15]

At first, most new university graduates became teachers in the lower schools. After a time, however, such positions became less available and graduates of universities and high schools searched for jobs in government employment. In 1961, the head of state announced, "that the administration was full and could not possibly accommodate the 600,000 or so students then in school."[16] Dissatisfaction spread among the educated unemployed and focused on the upper reaches of the central government. The army, heavily financed through U.S. military aid, increasingly functioned as an autonomous political force. Commanding officers engaged in illegal trade, at times selling arms gained through U.S. aid to Vietnamese opponents of the United States.[17] In the country at large, and especially in Phnom Penh, economic difficulties were magnified by growing social differences. "The pursuit of wealth through rackets and illegalities of the most complex and varied sort was part and parcel of life in Cambodia from the highest circles of the royal family and the government down."[18] By the late 1960s, the Vietnam War drew nearer to Cambodia as the Sihanouk regime permitted armed Vietnamese communist forces to conduct operations on Cambodia without declaring war against that country. Indeed, the bombing remained a secret inside the United States. In 1970, the second year of bombing, the Sihanouk government was overthrown by a militarist dictatorship under Lon Nol, supported by the United States. A full-scale civil war, waged by the communist Khmer Rouge (the red Cambodians) and the Lon Nol forces, tore the country apart.

The civil war closed a constructive chapter in the history of Cambodian education. In 1955 only one third of school-age children were in primary schools. By 1970, more than three fourths were students.[19] During the same years, the number of high schoolers skyrocketed from 5,000 to 118,000 as the number of teachers in the country rose from 7,000 to 18,000.[20] As opportunities for urban and professional employment widened, fewer Khmer boys enrolled in pagoda schools inasmuch as the latter provided little more than a religious education. This happened especially during the 1960s whereas in the countryside, enrollment failed to slump. Despite the movement away from pagoda schools, monasteries grew apace. From 1953 to 1969, their number expanded from 2,763 to 3,369, or by 65 a year.[21] The number of monks rose accordingly between 1961 and 1969 from 53,509 to 65,062.

Basic to the continued expansion of monasteries and monastic personnel were academic improvements implemented in response to demands of the monks, who felt the intense competition from secular schools. In addition to traditional theological and craft education, monks now took courses in mathematics, physics, social sciences, and English.[22] Preliminary steps in such directions had begun as early as 1954 when, with the aid of the government, the first Buddhist University was formed.[23] Later, a Buddhist Institute was built in Phnom Penh. Although strengthened academic preparation brought more recognition to the monks, their credentials were not as highly valued as those of secular institutions. This extended to pay and other matters.[24] By 1973, monks demonstrated publicly against such discrimination.[25] In any case, relatively few monks completed training at the Buddhist University that usually had an entering class of around 40 students.[26]

Buddhist monks played an important role in the expanding public school system:

> In nearly all villages in the countryside, the heads of monasteries and dignitary monks were elected as heads of the school committees, assuming responsibilities in requesting permission from the authorities to set up [secular] schools in their villages, and conducting fund raising for the construction of school buildings. By the end of 1970 almost every village, even in remote areas, had primary schools. The majority of these schools were located within the monastery compound in the countryside and in the city as well.[27]

The Buddhist clergy thus wholeheartedly promoted the cause of public education. A number of monks worked in public schools as paid teachers.

The civil war and American bombing from 1969 to 1973 undermined much of the progress in schooling recorded in the preceding decade. "From March 1970 to June 1973," said Sam, "a total of 997 monasteries, which constituted one third of the total number of all monasteries as of 1970, were reportedly destroyed."[28] Because many of the new secular primary schools were built inside the monastery property, they were not spared from the bombing. The same thing held true for the religious schools. Because "monasteries were used by all factions as strategic sanctuaries,"[29] all became objects of armed attack. The sweeping nature of the bombing can be discerned from Kiernan's characterization, "rural Cambodia was destroyed."[30] It should be recalled that at the outset of hostilities, at least four out of five Cambodians were peasants who lived in rural areas. Many of them sought refuge from the bombing by going to Phnom Penh, the capital. By 1971, the number of schools in the country had plummeted to fewer than half the figure at the end of the 1960s.[31]

During the Lon Nol years, government policy became more ethnically chauvinist toward Chinese and Vietnamese residents of Cambodia. Through an official organization called the Khmer-Mon Institute, Khmer were proclaimed as superior to allegedly inferior peoples such as Chinese and Vietnamese. Thousands of Vietnamese were massacred by the regime's troops.[32] In 1971, the use of minority languages was formally discouraged. In Phnom Penh, only Khmer

billboards were allowed. Business records could no longer be in Chinese or
Vietnamese. Even under Sihanouk, Lon Nol's predecessor, Vietnamese were
excluded from certain employment. School curricula embodied a hostile attitude
toward Vietnamese.[33] Apparently, few of these overt actions and policies were
adopted at the instance of popular opinion. Although a Chinese elite largely
monopolized commerce and banking, this fact did not lead to grass-roots
Khmer protest movements.[34] This was especially striking in view of the spread-
ing socioeconomic despair that pervaded the capital in 1974, when the population of Phnom Penh stood defenseless against Khmer Rouge attack.[35]

In the Spring of 1975, the end of the Vietnam War closed a generation of
warfare in Southeast Asia. For Cambodia, however, no respite ensued. Instead,
the 5-year civil war was quickly resolved in favor of the Khmer Rouge, which in
April occupied Phnom Penh and initiated a new and even more destructive
conflict. During the following 4 years, the new regime headed by Pol Pot sought
to revolutionize Cambodian society by eliminating the old ruling class. Also,
objects of the policy were persons with a higher education who had been able to
live a comfortable and secure life under the old order. Persons who had been ab-
sentee landowners or private employers were to be liquidated. Hundreds of
thousands of residents of Phnom Penh were forced to relocate to rural areas
where they worked as forced labor, clearing land or similar tasks. Many died.
Some, however, escaped to neighboring Thailand. State terror was freely utilized against persons suspected of planning resistance. Executions in this land of
the killing fields were widely employed and imprisonment was common.
Whereas some of these techniques had been employed earlier under the Sihanouk and Lon Nol regimes, none had approached the systematic character
and wide scope of measures employed by the Khmer Rouge in power. Although
much of the government's program was stated to be in the interest of the poorest peasants, many dissenting peasants in the Eastern zone of the country were
also subjected to extreme measures.[36]

During 1975 to 1979, education suffered grievously. For one thing, intellectuals were dishonored as devotees of foreign rule and bourgeois civilization.
"People with any education or a managerial background were singled out for
harsh punishment or were subject to execution."[37] The production of new intellectuals was precluded by ending all schooling beyond a few primary-school
classes. Universal literacy continued to be voiced by authorities as a goal of the
regime, but little or nothing was done to attain the objective. The government
directed that illiteracy be eradicated by lessons in factories and cooperatives but
this proved "notoriously unsuccessful."[38] McCormack reported that "education
arrangements . . . seem to have varied, from the complete abandonment of
schooling in some places, to a couple of hours basic language instruction of
three or four days a month in others. . . ."[39] However intensely Khmer Rouge
central leaders inveighed against schooling, they did not neglect the education
of their own children, who attended a privileged school.[40]

Late in 1978, Vietnamese military forces invaded Cambodia. In a few months, the government of the Khmer Rouge was defeated. A new regime of Cambodian rulers was installed by the Vietnamese and a new era in the country's history began.

The cost of the old era was high. Out of Cambodia's 1970 population of somewhat more than 7 million, 1½ million had been lost. About half a million left the country and a million more people died with "up to 500,000 deaths by execution and the rest from starvation, disease, and overwork."[41]

Some ethnic groups sustained greater losses than others, especially the Chinese. As Kiernan wrote, "The Chinese ... suffered the worst disaster ever to befall any ethnic Chinese community in Southeast Asia. Of the 1975 population of 425,000, about 200,000 Chinese survived the next four years."[42] On the same matter, Chandler noted:

> Chinese and Sino-Khmers were treated poorly, not because they were Chinese but because they were thought of as capitalists. . . . By and large, the regime discriminated against enemies of the revolution rather than against specific ethnic or religious groups.[43]

Wilmott made a parallel comment:

> There is some argument among Western observers over whether or not the Chinese were subject to discriminatory policies during the four-year period of Democratic Kampuchea (1975–1980). I have found no evidence to indicate that they were. . . . It was not ethnicity but class that counted against them under the regime of the Communist Party of Kampuchea.[44]

Little or no evidence to the contrary is presented in accounts that conclude otherwise.[45]

Another, smaller group that suffered disproportionately large death rates were the Buddhist monks. Some 50,000 of the country's 80,000 monks died in the war.[46] Boua found that "of a total of 2,680 Buddhist monks from eight of Cambodia's monasteries . . . only 70 . . . survived in 1979."[47]

The People's Republic of Kampuchea (PRK), which took office in 1979, governed amidst ruined resources, scattered authority, inadequate finances, and insufficiently trained personnel. In addition, the armed forces of the Khmer Rouge continued to operate against the PRK until the present writing. Experienced bureaucrats and professionals were few in number because of executions and escapes from the country. Nevertheless, the government announced its intention of making education a prime area of activity. Whereas before 1975, some 25,000 active teachers worked in schools, in 1979, only 7,000 showed up. Five years later, only 5,000 were recorded as working for the Ministry of Education.[48] Because in 1981 there were some 37,000 teachers at work, many were untrained and unregistered. As late as 1986, adult literacy stood at 48%.[49] Some of the illiterate adults took part-time courses; more than 140,000 completed this work by late 1981 and 250,000 more were enrolled after them.[50]

TABLE 7.1
Number of Students Enrolled 1979–1980, 1981–1982, and 1983–1984[52]

	1979–1980	1981–1982	1983–1984
Level one (years 1–4)	947,317	1,508,985	1,542,825
Level two (years 5–7)	5,104	39,434	146,865
Level three (years 8–10)	301	1,521	6,969

Illiterate children constituted a great challenge. At the end of the 1970s, "the bulk of children 6–14 years of age lack[ed] any basic education."[51] Schooling facilities were extremely rudimentary, with many children being gathered under a tree with an elder person serving as teacher. In time, more conventional facilities were provided. The number of children served rose rapidly. Throughout this 6-year span, Level one students comprised 99.4, 97.1, and 90.9% of precollege enrollment. Vickery noted that enrollment in secondary schools (especially Level three) was far lower than in 1969.[53] The quality of instruction is difficult to judge. In 1981, Summers reported:

> Children . . . now have only two hours of classroom instruction in language and arithmetic each day. Otherwise they receive "on the job" apprentice-style instruction or are assigned menial tasks in cottage industries and agriculture. Thus, children pay for their education by creating some value in the process.[54]

In the 1981 to 1982 school year, class sizes were enormous and children attended schools in three shifts, thereby sharply abbreviating the time spent with a teacher.[55]

Although official statistics recorded high percentages of school attendance by school-age children, illiteracy persisted; indeed, grew. As indicated earlier, adult illiteracy in 1986 was 52%. In 1979, a national total of 1½ million illiterates was reported.[56] In 1990, a UNESCO compilation showed an illiteracy rate of 64.8% and the presence of 3,479,000 illiterates.[57] (Illiteracy rates in 1990 for men and women were 51.8 and 77.6%.) Part of the illiteracy problem consisted of persons who had been of school age during the turbulent 1970s but had not been able to attend school.

Access to schooling was not the sole or even the most important problem confronting Cambodia's children. The challenge of life itself remained. In 1989, 12% of all children died before their first birthday. "Malnutrition is a serious problem in many parts of the country," wrote Chandler in 1991, "and is the major illness treated in the children's hospital in Phnom Penh."[58] Referring to the same year, he continued that, "all but a few thousand have a difficult time finding enough food for themselves and their families and proper medical attention." Orphans, of which there were a great many, were declared by the government to merit special protection under the law.[59] During the late 1980s, however, economic reforms stressing private enterprise rather than collective protection produced greater social inequality. During the early 1980s, for example, collective farms apportioned their incomes like this: "Before the groups divide up their produce, they must give some to teachers and nurses according to the number of days they worked; to old people, to pregnant women and to children. This must be done first."[60] By the opening of the 1990s, collective farming had ended.[61]

Government policy toward minorities changed greatly after 1979. Vietnamese armed forces who had overthrown the Khmer Rouge regime were not popularly regarded as conquerors. Nor did they act as such. The result was an important modification of the traditional anti-Vietnamese sentiment. During the 1980s, perhaps 300,000 Vietnamese settlers entered—in many cases, reentered —Cambodia. The latter had been forced out of the country in 1975. Now, their status as legitimate residents is protected by constitutional stipulation.[62] Writing in 1981, Wilmott declared that, "today no one identifies themselves as Chinese in Kampuchea."[63] With the advent of economic liberalization policies in the late 1980s, the cooperation of Chinese businessmen became crucial. But this greater economic role did not spill out into the cultural realm. There are no longer any Chinese schools. Summarizing official thinking on minorities, Vickery wrote:

> There is . . . no question of any systematic official discrimination, nor any doubt of PRK sincerity in treating all such groups equally, but there is an assumption that all minorities will gradually be transformed into "modern" agriculturally-settled Khmer, retaining only those features of their traditional cultures which are not in conflict with the transformation. . . . Certainly the PRK has a better record than any previous Cambodian regime in giving responsible positions to non-Khmers.[64]

The close of the 1980s and the onset of the 1990s saw Cambodia's economic growth taking a turn for the better. Its benefits, however, were heavily skewed in favor of new elite groups. School dropout rates remained high. According to the UNESCO representative in the country, in October 1991 "there were 460,000 pupils in grade one, but only 125,000 in grade five."[65] Teachers often waited long periods for their pay. In 1989, only 35.2% of adults were classified as literate and adults as a whole averaged only 2 years of schooling.[66]

IMMIGRATION

Few Cambodians moved to other countries before World War II. As late as the 1950s and 1960s, only about 200 lived in the United States.[67] In 1971, the civil war started to drive some of the country's elite elsewhere. "Cambodia's doctors, intellectuals, and other professionals left for the safety of France."[68] When, 4 years later, the Khmer Rouge prepared to take power, hundreds of other well-to-do Cambodians had already left on "spurious missions or seeking medical attention."[69] An emergency number—about 4,700—were admitted into the United

States in 1975 as the end of the Vietnam War endangered Cambodians closely identified with the American cause.[70] Although such refugees were nowhere near as numerous as in the case of Vietnam, nevertheless it was an unprecedented quantity. By late 1978, as the Khmer Rouge regime came under Vietnam attack, there were about 14,000 Cambodians in the United States.[71] In December 1978, Congress declared them eligible to qualify as refugees under American law. Their numbers rose to nearly 145,000 by 1987. Many more moved to other countries including France, Canada, and Australia. An additional third of a million were located in camps in Thailand.[72]

The most important Thai camp was Khao-I-Dang, labeled by Vickery as "a refuge for members of the former [Cambodian] bourgeoisie;" according to Vickery, "over 70 percent were of this category, the rest being peasants."[73] Ngor wrote that "because of the chance of resettling abroad, most of Cambodia's old middle class and elite showed up in Khao-I-Dang."[74] Many of Cambodia's teachers fled to Thailand, but this did not assure the offering of a satisfactory education program at Khao-I-Dang. A youthful refugee who lived in the camp reported it had an "elementary school, secondary school, and a training school."[75] A historian reports that in 1980, the camp "could not yet . . . offer a full syllabus or school day for all children. . . ."[76]

Out of a total population of 7.3 million, about 75% did not emigrate, nor did they become a death statistic under Khmer Rouge rule. In a country where four fifths of the population were peasants, the great majority of nonemigrants were thus peasants. Exact figures are unavailable. One reason for this is extensive shifting of boundary lines between rural and urban residents. During the brunt of the American bombing, 1969 to 1973, in the countryside, great numbers fled to Phnom Penh and other cities. These included not only peasants but also Chinese Cambodians, many of whom were prominent in rural trade and finance. When, in 1975, the Khmer Rouge took power, Phnom Penh and smaller cities were virtually emptied, most inhabitants being sent to farm areas. During the 1980s, many returned undeterred to their city of choice. Later, when Cambodians were enrolled for emigration purposes, their immediate background for the preceding decade or less could support a designation of urban as well as rural. In another sense, neither experience was authentically one or the other. For many Cambodians, they were merely alternative places to die. In neither case was it possible for individuals to develop life cycles based on stable, autonomous expectations.

THE UNITED STATES

Between 1975 and 1979, the Khmer Rouge period, fewer than 15,000 Cambodians entered the United States as refugees.[77] About one third of these were "urban, middle and upper class, educated city dwellers."[78] French speakers, many learned English readily. In the Boston area, they tended to locate in suburbs.[79] The nearly 130,000 Cambodians who arrived between 1980 and 1986 were a very different matter. On the average, they had attended school for fewer than 5 years.[80] A number lacked any schooling. Some had been enrolled in refugee camp schools where they had received instruction in Khmer and, to a small degree, in English. Fewer than 1% of the Cambodian newcomers had gone beyond high school.[81] Over three fourths (77.3%) claimed to be literate in Khmer and nearly one fourth (24.5%) in English.[82]

Most Cambodians lived in high-crime neighborhoods characterized by dilapidated, crowded housing. In Long Beach, California, where the nation's largest concentration of Cambodians lived, dangerous conditions forced Cambodian children to remain indoors. In Oakland and San Francisco, informants told one researcher that "women and children do not leave their small apartment complex alone even in daytime . . ."[83] The picture was not different in a Midwestern location:

> Violence was routine. Car windows were broken, cuts made into the paint, tires slashed. One girl told me they couldn't leave the children outside unsupervised because the neighbors threw chairs and garbage at them. During the summer of 1990 garbage cans were overturned, windows smashed . . . and human waste was thrown into the apartments . . . and into the smashed cars.[84]

In the Boston area, the situation met by the Cambodians was familiar: "Families have the windows of their homes broken, garbage dumped in their yards and their car tires slashed. Pedestrians must endure insults and other harassments as they walk through their own neighborhoods. . . . Motorists [are] harassed on the highway.[85] Hope beat a tortuous path through these obstacles. As a Long Beach city planning official commented when informed that a neighborhood was experiencing a decline in crime, "It is very likely due to the fact that the residents have given up reporting crime and have taken to barricading themselves inside their homes."[86]

Southeast Asian refugees as a whole met with similar receptions, especially in public housing facilities. As pointed out in the preceding chapter, other poor people resented the new arrivals as interlopers who violated their turf rights. This was true whether the older residents were Hispanic, African-American, or White. Heightening the ill will was a false impression among many Americans that the refugees had economic opportunities not available to themselves.

The bulk of the Cambodians in the United States, however, were a desperately poor people. Early in 1981, as the first large-scale movement of Cambodians into the country got underway, a survey in Long Beach "indicated that 95% of the refugee clients were on aid."[87] A decade later, it was reported that 51% of the city's Cambodians lived "in families with income below the poverty level . . ."[88] This was nearly double the level among Koreans and Chinese living in the Los Angeles inner city. In Boston's inner city, one third or more of Cambodians were unemployed by the early 1990s.[89] Between 80 and 90% of Cambodians in Stockton, California were unemployed.[90]

One aggravating factor was the difficulty many adult Cambodians had with English. A study by the General Accounting Office of the U.S. Congress found that "59 percent of Cambodians . . . spoke English 'not well' or 'not at all.'"[91] Sagara and Kiang reported that "over 90 percent of Cambodians in Massachusetts have problems understanding English."[92] Yet, school authorities in areas of high demand failed to provide sufficient instruction:

> In 1986, at the time of Proposition 63—the initiative declaring English as the state's official language—was being passed in California, over forty thousand immigrant adults were being turned away from English as a Second Language (ESL) classes in the Los Angeles Unified School District alone. . . . Available classes remain to date filled to capacity, and similar strong demand for English instruction has been reported in other immigrant concentrations.[93]

In the decade or so since the above was written, the situation worsened as the general economy deteriorated.

In the schools, Cambodian children responded positively to instruction in a strange tongue. A San Diego study found that their grade point averages matched "the white Anglo norm and their math scores . . . [were] at about the national average."[94] Analyzing a sample of 46 Cambodian senior students in an Oregon high school, Sack found that three fourths of them had GPAs of over 2.0 and a C average or higher. Often, these grades dropped when students were mainstreamed out of ESL classes. "At the end of the 1983–1984 academic year," reported Sack, "less than a quarter of the students could pass the high school graduation standards test of Oregon high schools (a test comparable to roughly the 7th grade achievement in reading, language, and mathematics)."[95]

Frequently, Cambodian students were placed under great strain in the school. Horng Kouch, who arrived in the United States late in 1980, recalled, "When I walked to school . . . I would say 'Hi' or I would give a grin to every American student I encountered, but they paid no attention to me at all. . . . At school I was like a person from another planet."[96] Vibora Lim, a member of an elite family that had arrived in 1975, recounted that "everyone in class would laugh when it was my turn to answer questions."[97] Sokunthy Pho, in Stockton, California, wrote:

> I hated my parents for bringing me and my sisters . . . to America because we were always being picked on by the white kids at our school. . . . They spat at us, sneaked behind us and kicked us with their leather sole shoes. . . . We didn't respond. . . . Instead, we kept quiet and walked home with tears running down our brown cheeks.

Now, however, he was determined to change. "If someone ever uses racist comments toward me, I would shut them out and tell them that I'm staying in America whether they like it or not."[98] In Long Beach, taunting of Cambodian classmates subsided after a time.[99]

The atrocities of the Khmer Rouge period continued to prey on the memories of the children. In an Oregon high school:

> The parents of all but one of the students said that they had talked with the student about their experiences during the Pol Pot regime. But when we asked students this same question . . . less than 50% said they had discussed Pol Pot with their parents.[100]

Parental reluctance to discuss these matters was communicated with force to the children. An observer in Philadelphia reported, "The Cambodian families have not yet come to terms with the Khmer Rouge experience. Very few observers report either the parents or the youth talking about it."[101] Although the students suffered silently, psychiatric disorders were common. Yet medical specialists were surprised "there were no cases of drug or alcohol abuse, and no antisocial or conduct disorders."[102] Teachers observed that children diagnosed as psychiatrically disordered tended to be withdrawn or daydreamers in class.[103]

The basic stability of expectations in the classroom helped the Cambodian children thrive, despite their violent heritage. But federal authorities seemed all too ready to relinquish any responsibility for meeting special needs of the stricken children. As Westermeyer wrote, "Refugee youths are essentially abandoned by the federal government within months of arrival, and thrown on the not-so-tender mercies of state, county, and city government. . . . An inhumane gap in services results. . . ."[104] Although in the main they seem to have risen above their circumstances, they also remained isolated and invisible in the schools.

Among teachers, one of the most enduring stereotypes of Cambodian children was their supposedly passive character. This orientation tended to accentuate their invisibility as teachers tended to spare the children the necessity of attracting attention. This fundamentally paternalistic attitude was a defect of teacher training rather than any shortcoming of students. Sin, an educational researcher who had taught high school in Cambodia during 1966–1972 and had been on fellowship in France in 1972 through 1974, addressed issues like this in her doctoral dissertation written at the University of Oregon. Speaking of the alleged passivity of Cambodian students in American schools, she stated:

> This stereotype of the Khmer students' attitude was not evident in this study. . . . Once they knew enough English to communicate, they became aggressive, outspoken, and strived their best to pursue their educational goal instead of dropping out of school.[105]

Many of the children, however, who had academic problems that remained unattended became gang members and soon dropped out of school. For whatever reason, in Lowell, Massachusetts during 1986 and 1987, nearly one sixth (15%) of Cambodian students in high school dropped out.[106] The rate for girls exceeded that for boys, suggesting that gang activity was not an adequate principal explanation.

Schools did little to take account of the children's cultural and historical backgrounds. From the first day onward, this omission shook the self-confidence of

Cambodian students. "I was lost and felt strange in the unknown world."[107] A bilingual school psychologist (rare in any language) noted that many children are referred to him even though they are normal. "[School personnel] cannot communicate with the children because of this language handicap, so they refer them to me."[108] A state education administrator complained:

> As students are mainstreamed from a Cambodian bilingual class . . . they are dropped—thud!—on the floor, because we have sort of an all or nothing thing, where either they're in a full-time bilingual program, or they get no support at all.[109]

ESL classes proved valuable to Cambodian students. Sometimes, this was because of some personal attribute of the ESL teacher. "They helped me, encouraged me, and supported me."[110] Although ESL teachers who knew Khmer were scarce, ESL aides who were bilingual worked in many classrooms. Unfortunately, the schools frequently failed to employ sufficient numbers, even when they were required by law to do so. In Stockton, California, for example, 178 mostly part-time aides were employed when under federal regulations, 426 full-time aides were obligatory.[111] Generally, the aides had little or no training, nor did school districts provide much.

Hopkins described the workings of ESL as it operated in the schools she studied:

> Most of the children are together in an ESL class for half the day, then are "mainstreamed" into regular classes for the other half. Federal funding will support this for a maximum of five years, so the children who are not "up to level" after five years enter the high school unprepared to function well in regular classes; as the teachers say, they just don't have "student behaviors." The teachers feel that the restrictions are unrealistic for children who hear no English at home and have no patterns of literacy or schooling in the family; they feel that such children or some of them may need as many as seven or nine years in special classes.[112]

Although Hopkins found the Cambodian children did well enough under this regimen, "they do not do as . . . strikingly well as the [Asian] . . . 'Whiz Kids.'"[113] Children who failed to thrive academically through ESL often were transferred to special education classes. This insured more individual attention by teachers. It did not, however, assure having a teacher who was any more adequately trained in the culture, language, and history of Cambodian children. Nor did it provide these children with a climate that fostered normal educational development.[114]

Relatively few Cambodian students attended higher education institutions. During Fall 1982, California State University, Long Beach enrolled 861 Vietnamese and Sino-Vietnamese but only 31 Cambodians.[115] In a decade, the latter figure rose significantly and Cambodian college graduates formed an organization to help recruit Cambodian high school graduates. In Fall 1990, among 223 Southeast Asian students at the University of Massachusetts, Boston, 194 were Vietnamese, 26 Cambodians, and 3 Lao.[116] Larger numbers could be found in community colleges but precise figures were lacking.

Both at CSU, LB, and UMass-Boston, as well as in colleges elsewhere, Cambodians and other Southeast Asian students most frequently majored in engineering, electrical engineering, computer science, business, and math.[117] In the 1980s, these were rapidly-growing fields for which ample employer-demand existed. Cambodians, along with many non-Asians whose facility with numbers exceeded their command of English, streamed to these fields. One did not need to be Cambodian to know that salaries in the fields were comparatively high. Many other Cambodian students did not enter these fields and dropped out of college altogether or were ensnared in a daily grind of full-time work and part-time study.

As pointed out in the preceding chapter, Southeast Asian students, including Cambodians, found little support at the University of Massachusetts, Boston. According to Kiang, they "seem to be neither academically nor socially integrated within the university."[118] The refugee students' accounts of their escape from death "reveal both profound suffering and an immense capacity to survive."[119] Isolation at the university strains the capacity to the utmost because the frequent absence of parents and siblings deprives the students of their accustomed succor found in the bosom of the family. Kiang concluded, "Without institutional support . . . student motivation to persist in college becomes critical. The findings of this study suggest that Southeast Asian student motivation is largely based on reference points external to the college experience."[120] Hopkins reported that by June of the first year of her study, 11 Cambodian high school graduates were accepted by local collegiate institutions. By Christmas, all those who entered had dropped out. A number disliked large classes and the overall anonymity.[121] To help Cambodian students and others, the Philadelphia Community College offered ESL instruction.[122]

Although Cambodian American communities were highly concentrated, the children attended schools and colleges in which parents had little to say. This was often attributed to a cultural practice derived from home-country experience. Undoubtedly, in part, such an explanation was valid in pagoda schools operated by Buddhist monks. These institutions were primarily religious and it would have seemed irreligious to have interfered with the established direction of the school. As we saw earlier, however, during the 1950s and 1960s, a state-sponsored educational system took form and many, probably most, parents chose government schools over religious schools. Although monks taught in the former, here they were state employees and no longer especially authoritative figures. Indeed, they came to be regarded by parents—and rightly so—as inadequately trained for their new positions. Many needed, and received, additional schooling. Such new stirrings were felt especially in urban areas where white-collar jobs were relatively plentiful and parents strove to qualify their children for such positions.

When Cambodians arrived in the United States, they encountered unfamiliar school systems taught in a strange language. These and other challenges sufficed to quiet any parental doubts. At the same time, however, they observed evidences of activist parent movements in many of the urban school systems that their children attended. These movements directly confronted school authorities and demanded changes.

During the 1980s, when Cambodians emigrated to the United States in large numbers, some began to participate as active parents. What was novel about this role was the directness with which parents encountered authority, the organized character of the action, and the cooperation with non-Cambodian parents. Because many of the schools involved were located in inner-city areas, they enrolled a broad range of children from ethnic and racial groups whose parents were dissatisfied with the education being provided their children. In Philadelphia, Asian parents, including Cambodians, filed a lawsuit against the board of education, which was charged with a long list of educational failings. A settlement was reached in the case.[123] In Lowell, Massachusetts, the second-largest Cambodian community in the United States, Puerto Rican, Cambodian, and other parents combined to protest against inadequate language policies and programs of the city's school board.[124] Massachusetts, which was the first state to enact a bilingual education law had, a decade later, become a center of the English-only movement. By the early 1990s, Cambodian families began a large-scale move away from Lowell.[125]

CONCLUDING REMARKS

Cambodians have been largely submerged as parts of two groupings: Indochinese and Southeast Asians. The first term was invented in 1886 by the French to cover Cambodia, Vietnam, and Laos, the French colonial empire in Southeast Asia.[126] The second term stood for Indochina and surrounding countries, including Thailand and Burma. Although Indochina disappeared in 1954 when the French armies were defeated by Vietnam, the term continues confusedly to describe present-day countries. For example, in 1993, a researcher wrote that, "Overall, Indochinese students are performing admirably in American schools"; unfortunately, this is followed immediately by a caution that "it is important to recognize that there is considerable between-group and in-group variation."[127] No specific groups are mentioned and the reader is left to speculate whether Vietnamese, Cambodians, or Lao are meant. Undoubtedly, the second assertion is quite correct but is difficult to apply in the absence of subgroup data. In the previous chapter and the present one, the span of social class and education was seen to be very large as between Cambodian and Vietnamese. (The cases of the Lao and Hmong are examined in the next chapter.)

NOTES

[1] David P. Chandler, *The Land and People of Cambodia* (Harper Collins, 1991), p. 61. See also May Ebihara, "Societal Organization in Sixteenth and Seventeenth Century Cambodia, *Journal of Southeast Asian Studies*, 15 (1984), p. 286.

[2] Milton E. Osborne *The French Presence in Cochinchina and Cambodia. Rule and Response (1859–1905)* (Cornell University Press, 1969), p. 203.

[3] See Milton E. Osborne, *Politics and Power in Cambodia. The Sihanouk Years* (Longman, 1973), p. 25: "By the early 1920s . . . the French . . . did not hesitate to use the expression 'colony' when referring to Cambodia."

[4] Osborne, *The French Presence*, p. 256. Serge Thion suggested there were no more than 500 children in attendance. See Thion, "The Cambodian Idea of Revolution," p. 14 in David P. Chandler and Ben Kiernan, eds., *Revolution and Its Aftermath in Kampuchea: Eight Essays* (Yale University Southeast Asia Studies, 1983).

[5] Charles Bilodeau and others, *Compulsory Education in Cambodia, Laos and Viet Nam* (UNESCO, 1955), p. 21.

[6] David J. Steinberg and Chester A. Bain, *Cambodia: Its People, Its Society, Its Culture* (HRAF Press, 1959), p. 253.

[7] Ibid., p. 252.

[8] Chandler, *The Land and People of Cambodia*, p. 108.

[9] Michael Vickery, *Cambodia: 1975–1982* (South End Press, 1984), p. 18.

[10] Osborne, *Politics and Power in Cambodia*, p. 28.

[11] Vickery, *Cambodia: 1975–1982*, p. 18.

[12] Bilodeau, *Compulsory Education*, pp. 56–57.

[13] Osborne, *Politics and Power in Cambodia*, p. 72.

[14] Bilodeau, *Compulsory Education*, p. 30.

[15] Ibid., p. 32.

[16] Vickery, *Cambodia: 1975–1982*, p. 19.

[17] Osborne, *Politics and Power in Cambodia*, pp. 104–105.

[18] Ibid., p. 84.

[19] Elizabeth Becker, *When the War Was Over. The Voices of Cambodia's Revolution and Its People* (Simon Schuster, 1986), p. 24.

[20] Ibid., p. 24.

[21] Yang Sam, *Khmer Buddhism and Politics from 1954 to 1984* (Khmer Studies Institute, 1987), p. 19.

[22] Ibid., p. 27.

[23] Ibid., p. 26.

[24] Milada Kalab, "Study of a Cambodian Village," *Geographical Journal*, 134 (1968), p. 534.

[25] Sam, *Khmer Buddhism*, p. 27.

[26] Kalab, "Study of a Cambodian Village," p. 535.

[27] Sam, *Khmer Buddhism*, p. 31.

[28] Ibid., p. 58.

[29] Ibid., p. 59.

[30] Ben Kiernan, "The American Bombardment of Kampuchea, 1969–1973," *Vietnam Generation*, 1 (1989), p. 4. Gavan McCormack, in "The Kampuchean Revolution 1975–1978. The Problem of Knowing the Truth," *Journal of Contemporary Asia*, 10 (1980), p. 77, wrote that "the tonnage [of U.S. bombs] dropped in six months of 1973 exceeded by half the entire tonnage dropped on Japan in the Second World War." See also Craig Etcheson, *The Rise and Demise of Democratic Kampuchea* (Westview Press, 1984), p. 99.

[31] Donald P. Whitaker and others, *Area Handbook for the Khmer Republic (Cambodia)* (U.S. Government Printing Office, 1973), p. 105.

[32] Haing Ngor, with Roger Warner, *A Cambodian Odyssey* (Macmillan, 1987), pp. 61, 71, and 394. See also Chou Meng Tarr, "The Vietnamese Minority in Cambodia," *Race and Class,* 34 (October–December 1992), p. 33–34. Whitaker, *Area Handbook,* p. 108.

[33] Tarr, "Vietnamese Minority," p. 36.

[34] W. E. Wilmott, "The Chinese in Kampuchea," *Journal of Southeast Asian Studies,* 12 (1981), p. 38.

[35] David P. Chandler, *The Tragedy of Cambodian History. Politics, War, and Revolution Since 1945* (Yale University Press, 1991), pp. 230, 233.

[36] Ben Kiernan, "Kampuchea's Ethnic Chinese Under Pol Pot: A Case of Systematic Discrimination," *Journal of Contemporary Asia,* 16 (1986), p. 27.

[37] Karl D. Jackson, ed., *Cambodia, 1975–1978. Rendezvous with Death* (Princeton University Press, 1989), p. 228.

[38] See Ben Kiernan, "Kampuchea 1979–81. National Rehabilitation in the Eye of An International Storm," *Southeast Asian Affairs* (1982), p. 179; and Vickery, *Cambodia 1975–1982,* p. 171.

[39] McCormack, "The Kampuchean Revolution 1975–1978," p. 96.

[40] Vickery, *Cambodia: 1975–1982,* p. 173. See also Elizabeth Becker, *When the War Was Over,* p. 45: "Travel, reading, writing were outlawed for all but the privileged people."

[41] Kiernan, "Kampuchea 1979–81," p. 167. Estimates of deaths made by other researchers vary. Those by Kimmo Kiljunen, ed. *Kampuchea: Decade of the Genocide Report of a Finnish Inquiry Commission* (Zed, 1984), p. 33 are close to the Kiernan estimate as are those by Chandler, *The Land and People of Cambodia,* p. 3.

[42] Ben Kiernan, "The Genocide in Cambodia, 1975–79," *Bulletin of Concerned Asian Scholars,* 22 (April–June 1990), p. 39. See also Kiernan, "Kampuchea's Ethnic Chinese," pp. 18–20, 25, 27.

[43] Chandler, *The Tragedy of Cambodian History,* p. 285.

[44] Wilmott, "The Chinese in Kampuchea," p. 43.

[45] Becker, *When the War Was Over,* p. 253, referred collectively to persons who were "targeted for elimination because of their race" but did not specify who they were or what their ultimate fate was. Chou Meng Tarr, "The Vietnamese Minority," p. 45, wrote somewhat vaguely that "ethnic minorities, especially the Cham Muslims, suffered disproportionately from the excesses of the late 1970s." It is noted by Tarr that the Chams were particularly cool to the revolution and may have suffered because of it rather than for their religion. In a book published after this chapter was completed, Kiernan wrote that the Khmer Rouge policy on the Chinese "could be construed as genocide," *The Pol Pot Regime* (Yale University Press, 1996), p. 296. This less than unconditional conclusion is at odds with that of Wilmott, whose own forthright conclusion to the contrary quoted earlier, is not mentioned by Kiernan. On the other hand, Kiernan cited a good deal of evidence to support his characterization of Khmer Rouge policy on Chams as genocidal; see *The Pol Pot Regime,* pp. 252–288.

[46] Kiljunen, *Kampuchea,* p. 41.

[47] Kiernan, "The Genocide in Cambodia, 1975–79," p. 39.

[48] Michael Vickery, *Kampuchea. Politics, Economics and Society* (Lynne Reinner Publishers, 1986), p. 155.

[49] Chandler, *The Land and People of Cambodia,* p. 1.

[50] Kiernan, "Kampuchea 1979–81," p. 179.

[51] Kiljunen, *Kampuchea,* p. 39.

[52] Data for columns one and three from Vickery, *Kampuchea,* p. 155; data for column two from Kiljunen, *Kampuchea,* p. 41.

[53] Michael Vickery, *Kampuchea: Politics, Economics, and Society* (Lynne Rienner Publishers, 1986), p. 155.

[54] Laura J. Summers, "Democratic Kampuchea," pp. 409–436 and Bogdan Szajkowski, "Post-

scriptum: People's Republic of Kampuchea," pp. 437–442 in B. Szajkowski, ed., *Marxist Governments. A World Survey*, Vol. 2, *Cuba–Mongolia* (St. Martin's Press, 1981).

[55] Kiljunen, *Kampuchea*, p. 39.

[56] Kiernan, "Kampuchea 1979–81," p. 179.

[57] *World Education Report 1991* (UNESCO, 1991), pp. 100–136.

[58] See Chandler, *The Land and People of Cambodia*, p. 167.

[59] Ibid., pp. 34, 161, and 179.

[60] Chanthou Boua, "Observations of the Heng Samrin Government 1980–1982," p. 267 in David P. Chandler and Ben Kiernan, eds., *Revolution and Its Aftermath in Kampuchea: Eight Essays* (Yale University Southeast Asia Studies, 1983).

[61] Chandler, *The Land and People of Cambodia*, p. 169. See also Börje Ljunggren, ed., *The Challenge of Reform in Indochina* (Harvard Institute for International Development, Harvard University, 1993), pp. 111, 161.

[62] Tarr, "The Vietnamese Minority in Cambodia," pp. 40, 42.

[63] Wilmott, "The Chinese Kampuchea," p. 45.

[64] Vickery, *Kampuchea*, p. 169.

[65] Ljunggren, *The Challenge of Reform in Indochina*, p. 363.

[66] Ibid., p. 385.

[67] Cynthia M. Coleman, p. 362 in David A. Ablin and Marlowe Hood, eds., *The Cambodian Agony* (Sharpe, 1987).

[68] Becker, *When the War Was Over*, p. 33.

[69] Chandler, *The Tragedy of Cambodian History*, p. 235.

[70] See Bill Ong Hing and Ronald Lee, eds., *The State of Asian Pacific America: Policy Issues to the Year 2020* (LEAP and UCLA Asian American Studies Center), p. 170.

[71] Coleman, *The Cambodian Agony*, p. 367.

[72] Chandler, *The Land and People of Cambodia*, p. 164.

[73] Vickery, *The Cambodian Agony*, p. 312.

[74] Ngor, *A Cambodian Odyssey*, p. 419.

[75] Hong Taing, p. 131 in Lucy Nguyen-Hong-Nhiem and Joel M. Halpern, eds., *The Far East Comes Near* (University of Massachusetts Press, 1989).

[76] Vickery, *The Cambodian Agony*, p. 313.

[77] *The State of Asian Pacific America*, p. 170.

[78] Coleman, *The Cambodian Agony*, pp. 363–364.

[79] Nancy J. Smith-Hefner, "Education, Gender, and Generational Conflict among Khmer Refugees," *Anthropology and Education Quarterly*, 24 (1991), p. 138.

[80] Ruben G. Rumbaut, "The Agony of Exile: A Study of the Migration and Adaptation of Indochinese Refugee Adults and Children," p. 70 in Frederick L. Ahearn, Jr. and Jean L. Athey, eds., *Refugee Children. Theory, Research and Services* (Johns Hopkins University Press, 1991).

[81] Paul J. Strand and Woodrow Jones, Jr., *Indochinese Refugees in America* (Duke University Press, 1985), p. 108.

[82] Ibid., p. 103.

[83] Shiori Ui, "'Unlikely Heroes': The Evolution of Female Leadership in a Cambodian Ethnic Enclave," p. 165 in Michael Burawoy, Joshua Gamson, and Josepha Schiffman, *Ethnography Unbound* (University of California Press, 1991).

[84] Mary Carol Hopkins, *Learning Culture: A Cambodian (Khmer) Community in an American City* (Doctoral dissertation, University of Cincinnati, 1991), p. 275.

[85] Carlton Sagara in *Voices Across America: Roundtable Discussions of Asian Civil Rights Issues* (U.S. Commission on Civil Rights, 1989), p. 167.

[86] Gordon Dillow, "Crime, Distrust Keep Cambodians Living in Fear," *Los Angeles Times*, July 5, 1992

[87] Terrence G. Wiley and others, *Refugee Resettlement in Long Beach* (City of Long Beach, Department of Public Health, Refugee Technical Assistance Project, February 22, 1983), p. 36.

[88] Paul Ong and others, eds., *The New Asian Immigration in Los Angeles and Global Restructuring* (Temple University Press, 1994), p. 120.

[89] Carlton Sagara and Peter Kiang, *Recognizing Poverty in Boston's Asian American Community* (The Boston Foundation, February 1992), p. 43.

[90] Ui, "'Unlikely Heroes,'" p. 165.

[91] Sagara and Kiang, *Recognizing Poverty*, p. 47.

[92] Ibid., p. 48.

[93] Alejandro Portes and Ruben G. Rumbaut, *Immigrant America. A Portrait* (University of California Press, 1990), p. 202. See also Hopkins, *Learning Culture*, p. 316.

[94] Ruben G. Rumbaut, "The Agony of Exile," p. 82. See also Rumbaut, "The Refugee Adaptation Process," p. 169 in David W. Haines, ed., *Refugees as Immigrants. Cambodians, Laotians, and Vietnamese in America* (Rowman and Littlefield, 1969) for the distribution of GPAs by ethnic group.

[95] William H. Sack and others, "The Psychiatric Effects of Massive Trauma on Cambodian Children: II. The Family, the Home and the School," *Journal of American Academy of Child Psychiatry*, 25 (1986), p. 380.

[96] Lucy Nguyen-Hong-Nhiem and Joel M. Halpern, eds., *The Far East Comes Near* (University of Massachusetts Press, 1989), p. 148.

[97] Ibid., p. 154.

[98] Sokunthy T. Pho, "No More Tears Will Run Down Our Brown Cheeks," *Asian Week* (May 28, 1993), pp. 14–15.

[99] Wiley, *Refugee Resettlement in Long Beach*, p. 19.

[100] Sack, "The Psychiatric Effects," p. 379.

[101] Heather A. Peters, *A Study of Southeast Asian Youth in Philadelphia* (January 1988), p. 114. ERIC ED 299 371.

[102] J. David Kinzie and William Sack, "Severely Traumatized Cambodian Children: Research Findings and Clinical Implications," p. 94 in Ahearn and Athey, *Refugee Children*.

[103] Ibid., p. 95.

[104] Joseph Westermeyer, "Psychiatric Services for Refugee Children: An Overview," pp. 156–157 in Ahearn and Athey, *Refugee Children*.

[105] Bo Chum Sin, *Socio-Cultural, Psychological and Linguistic Effects on Cambodian Students' Progress Through Formal Schooling in the United States* (Doctoral dissertation, University of Oregon, 1991), p. 240. In the early 1990s, she served as an educational adviser to the government of Cambodia.

[106] Nancy Smith-Hefner, "Education, Gender, and Generational Conflict," p. 137. See also Mary Ouk and others, *Handbook for Teaching Khmer-speaking Students* (Folsom Cordova Unified School District and Southeast Asia Community Resource Center, 1988), p. 50.

[107] Sin, *Socio-Cultural . . . Effects*, p. 146.

[108] Prem Suksawat in Joan McCarthy First and John Willshire Carrera, *New Voices—Immigrant Students in U.S. Public Schools* (National Coalition of Advocates for Students, 1988), p. 54.

[109] Charles Glenn in ibid., p. 50.

[110] Sin, *Socio-Cultural . . . Effects*, p. 189.

[111] See Ui, "'Unlikely Heroes,'" p. 169.

[112] Hopkins, *Learning Culture*, p. 287.

[113] Ibid., p. 288.

[114] See Kenja Ima and Ruben G. Rumbaut, "Southeast Asian Refugees in American Schools: A Comparison of Fluent-English-Proficient and Limited-English-Proficient Students," *Topics in Language Disorders*, 9 (June 1989), pp. 56, 74. Other writers on the subject see even fewer positive features in the practice.

[115] Wiley, *Refugee Resettlement in Long Beach*, p. 115.

[116]Peter Nien-chu Kiang, *New Roots and Voices: The Education of Southeast Asian Students at an Urban Public University* (Doctoral dissertation, Harvard University, 1991), p. 65.

[117]See ibid., p. 41 and Wiley, *Refugee Resettlement in Long Beach*, p. 54.

[118]Kiang, *New Roots and Voices*, p. 160.

[119]Ibid., p. 213.

[120]Ibid., p. 218.

[121]Hopkins, *Learning Culture*, p. 290.

[122]Peters, *A Study*, p. 66.

[123]Ibid., p. 74. The name of the class action case was *Y.S.* v. *School District of Philadelphia*. See Len Reiser, *A Short History of Y.S. v. School District of Philadelphia* (Education Law Center, Inc., July 1990).

[124]See Peter Nien-chu Kiang, "Southeast Asian Parent Empowerment: The Challenge of Changing Demographics in Lowell, Massachusetts," *Asian American Policy Review* 1 (Spring 1990), pp. 29–38 and ERIC ED 320 997. See also Carlton Sagara in *Voices Across America*, p. 168; Hai B. Pho, "The Politics of Refugee Resettlement in Massachusetts," *Migration World*, 19 (1991), pp. 4–10; and James Higgins and Joan Ross, *Southeast Asians. A New Beginning in Lowell* (Mill Town Graphics, 1986), p. 38.

[125]Sagara and Kiang, *Recognizing Poverty*, p. 12.

[126]*The American Heritage Dictionary*, 3rd edition, includes Vietnam, Laos, Cambodia, Thailand, Burma and the mainland territory of Malaysia in Indochina. The last three places never were part of the French empire.

[127]Smith-Hefner, "Education, Gender, and Generational Conflict," pp. 152–153.

CHAPTER EIGHT

Laos

Institutionalized education first appeared in Laos in the traditional pagoda schools operated in tandem with Buddhist temples. In most respects, they closely resembled their counterparts in traditional Cambodia. When Laos was colonized by France in the late 19th century, these were the sole educational institutions in the country and were staffed by monks (*bonzes*), who were aided by novices. Only during the first decade of the 20th century, when French-sponsored schools began to appear in provincial towns and elsewhere, were trained, secular teachers employed. They received their training in a Franco-Laotian school in the capital city of Vientiane.[1] A number of monks who were trained in this manner instead of accepting teaching positions "sought civil service posts for personal advancement and better pay."[2]

The traditional structure of the country embraced a small elite of native-born Lao and a large group of Lao villagers who lived and worked in lowland areas. Another half of the population consisted of assorted minorities, most of whom resided in highland areas, including mountain tops. These latter were known as *tribals*. Because most populated places were ethnically homogeneous, and the tribals were not Buddhists, they were excluded from pagoda schools. As a consequence, their children had no access to any schooling whatever. This continued into the second half of the 20th century for most tribal children.

Chinese and Vietnamese more or less controlled economic life, education, and the lower reaches of government administration. Vietnamese made up more than half the population in six larger towns, where their children had access to the best and most advanced schools.[3] As Toye wrote, Laos "depended largely on

Vietnamese immigrants for its educated class."[4] As late as 1945, Vietnamese constituted two thirds of the country's primary and assistant teachers.[5] Because they had been educated in French, they were well-prepared to perpetuate the language in Laos.

A French law in 1917 decreed the opening of a primary school in every village. The central government was to provide a teacher and supplies and local government was expected to provide a school building and housing for the teacher. Over the next 30 or so years, enrollment rose modestly for children in the first six grades:[6]

1915	713	1936	6,537
1920	1,687	1942	6,106
1925	2,429	1944	7,961
1931	6,181		

These grades were taught in Lao whereas the seven secondary grades were in French. During the early 1940s, six mobile schools served tribal minorities but by 1945, all had been closed.[7] Most Lao youngsters preferred the pagoda schools over secular French schools. There being no pagoda secondary schools, the comparative handful of Lao youth who wished to, and qualified for, entrance into the French-speaking institution had to be extremely well prepared. Scholarships were given to the top three graduates of each grade school.[8]

Neither the indigenous elite nor the French colonialists sought to create mass education. The latter's goal was simply to cultivate "a loyal 'feudal' elite imbued in the administrative mores of empire,"[9] and this is what it achieved. Laos had comparatively few economic resources that French businessmen could profitably exploit, and so the government invested little in the country. As Chan observed, the French "built few roads and no railways in Laos, as they had elsewhere in French Indochina."[10] The same was true in the field of education. Gunn pointed out that "in 1935 . . . only 8.45 percent of total public expenditure in Laos was allocated for education, versus 18 percent in Annam [Central Vietnam], 15 percent in Cochinchina [South Vietnam], 12.87 percent in Tonkin [North Vietnam] and 11.60 percent in Cambodia."[11] The quality of the schools operated under French supervision was quite poor. "The schools in Laos, compared to those in Cambodia, were regarded as notorious for poor attendance, low standards, and with low professional quality of the monks as educators."[12] The number of students who went beyond primary school was minuscule. In 1925, only 15 secondary students were enrolled in the entire country and by 1944, the year before the end of World War II, the figure had risen only to 197. As early as 1922, a public high school was opened in Vientiane but Lao youths in attendance were less numerous than children of colonial administrators and of Vietnamese officials.[13] Only after the end of World War II was the first authentic *lycée* (high school) opened in Laos.[14]

In 1946, Laos received a measure of self-rule and the following year, a constitution was written. In fact, however, the French remained in control. During World War II, French authorities had decided to loosen some colonial restrictions on Laos extending to self-government, if not outright independence. To implement this new policy, it would be necessary to educate and train many more indigenous specialists. Thus, between 1940 and 1945, more schools were built than in all the previous 47 years.[15] The long-term educational significance of this rush of construction was very slight and did almost nothing to change the heritage of illiteracy and truncated schooling produced under the French.

In 1945, Laos had the highest illiteracy rate in Southeast Asia; all but 5% were illiterate, according to one source.[16] At the same time:

> Only 15,000 Lao had ever attended primary school, and the majority of these for merely three or four years. . . . Fewer than one hundred Lao completed French-style education in the decade before World War II. An even smaller number had received university education, available only abroad, during the several decades of colonial rule.[17]

Both total illiteracy and lack of schooling were almost universal among the hill people.

After attainment of full independence in 1953, the new government undertook an expansion program in education. The next decade or so saw genuine progress, especially in the number of lowland Lao children attending school. Educational opportunities for minority children also expanded somewhat, as they also did for girls. However, profound inequalities continued to characterize the schooling of independent Laos, as they had of the colony. Around 1970, for example, the active population between 15 and 55 years old numbered 1,268,000 people. For socioeconomic purposes they were divided into three groups of unequal numbers: 2,000; 18,000; and 1,248,000. A count was then made from each group who attended selected schools. This is a listing of the percent of each group enrolled in such schools:[18]

Group I	24.0
Group II	12.0
Group III	0.4

Group I, the highest economic class, had about 60 times greater educational opportunity than Group III, or, substantially the rest of the country. Persons who remained basically untouched by the schools were adult illiterates, women, and tribal peoples. Occasional progress was made in short-term literacy campaigns. One source reported that in the early 1960s, illiteracy rates were declining by 4% a year as a result of the organization of rural training centers for adults and children.[19] Literacy programs were instituted in the military in 1967. Schools for dependents of soldiers were said to enroll about 40,000 around 1970.[20]

Another factor making for educational inequality was the socially differential nature of enrollment among the various curricula. For example, students coming from Group I families enrolled heavily in secondary curricula, as graduation from these qualified one to enter a university. Very few studied in technical curricula, as these were terminal. The same was true of teacher training. Even when students from lower social groupings registered for secondary courses, few completed the program. Many of them were disqualified from university entrance because they were unable to pass the extremely difficult examination in the French language.

Indigenous minorities continued to be all but excluded in disproportionately large numbers. The most numerous of these were the Kha, who made up one fourth of the total Laotian population; they were followed by the Tai (separate from Thai who populated neighboring Thailand) who made up another one sixth of the population. Hmong and Yao together were numerically small and slightly outnumbered by various foreign minorities such as Vietnamese and Cambodians. Laotians, who numbered half of the population, constituted 88.7% of students enrolled in secondary, technical, and teacher-training programs. Minorities ranked as follows:[21]

Minority	Percent in Population	Percent in Schools
Kha	25	0.3
Tai	16	1.2
Hmong and Yao	5	3.8 (Hmong)
Foreign minorities	6	6.0

Hmong, who made up less than 4% of the population in school and 8% of the total population, constituted 6.3% of students in teacher-training programs. The Kha and Tai, together 41% of the population, represented only 0.3 and 1.2% of the same specialty.

By the mid-1960s, a balance-sheet of Laotian schooling was drawn by Halpern and Tinsman:

> In a system where in 1964, 97 percent of the total school enrollment was at primary level, 80 percent of which was in the first (three-year cycle), not even basic literacy can be achieved. . . . An official Laotian government report of 1963 acknowledged that 75 percent of the total population had never attended any kind of formal school. It is currently [1966] reported that only one-half of the school-age population is enrolled in schools of any kind.[22]

Eight secondary schools existed in the entire country but "only one percent of the age group was enrolled in secondary schools in 1959."[23]

In 1950, a political event occurred that ultimately brought wholesale change in Laos, including education. This was the organization of the Pathet Lao movement. Backed in part by indigenous communists, the group aimed to eject the

French from Laos, establish a government that was representative of the broad population, and introduce socialism into the economy. Perhaps the most significant feature of Pathet Lao was the fact that it consisted largely—some 60%— of indigenous minorities such as the tribal groups. Pathet Lao became a military force and by 1962 exercised military control over one third to one half of the country.[24] To a considerable degree, many upland tribal people were attracted to the movement because of Pathet Lao's pledge to open schools for the children of the tribals. This was unprecedented in Laotian history. The same was true of the promise of public policy being determined by cooperation of lowland Laotians and tribal people.

In a decade or so after 1950, an educational structure existed in Pathet Lao country. In some cases, it was possible to draw comparisons and contrasts between education in Pathet Lao areas and those still governed by the royal regime. In 1964, Pathet Lao authorities reported that over 36,200 children were attending primary schools in their—liberated—zone. This contrasted with the 1945 enrollment in all of Laos of 11,400.[25] Also claimed was a secondary school enrollment of 250 whereas none had attended previously; the operation of four teachers' training schools and two adult complementary schools; and a supply of 380,000 textbooks as compared with a 1963 total of only 40,000.[26] By the end of the decade, "Communist efforts to provide some kind of rudimentary educational facilities [were] meet[ing] with a strong and positive response among the population."[27]

Educational progress in the Pathet Lao areas was striking because United States military aircraft bombed these areas very heavily as part of operations in the Vietnam War. "By 1971," wrote Summers, "approximately one-quarter to one-third of the entire Lao population were refugees, their villages and farmlands razed or destroyed by the combined effects of bombing and artillery."[28] Laotians were the most heavily bombed people in the Vietnam War. After the late 1960s, when the bombing became ever more intense, instruction in the Pathet Lao schools tended "to be conducted in less vulnerable locations such as in caves or in the jungle."[29] Langer stressed the Pathet Lao innovation of widespread adult education.

> It is quite likely that at least in some areas the Communists . . . outperformed the RLG [Royal Lao Government] with regard to adult literacy. . . . The [RLG] . . . never launched an effort comparable to that of the adult education drive in the Communist zone, except for some literacy programs in the armed forces.[30]

Yet, in 1969, reportedly all but 15 percent of villagers in the RLG were illiterate.[31] The Pathet Lao did not, however, have a magical touch. In the field of elementary education, Langer writes, they lagged behind the RLG.

The year 1975 saw the end of the Vietnam War. Late in that same year, the Pathet Lao forces proclaimed the Lao People's Democratic Republic (LPDR). The accession of the new regime set off a great emigration; one tenth of the population (375,000 out of 3,750,000) left. Forty percent of the emigrés consisted of Hmong, some of whom had several years of formal education, but most were unschooled. Vietnamese emigrés included nearly all the country's secondary school teachers as well as a large number of lower state officials. Among the Chinese emigrés were businessmen who had been in trade and commerce. Finally, there were lowland Laotians of middle- and upper class backgrounds. This group "included most of the former Lao elite and a substantial proportion of the educated middle class. Laos lost most of its middle managers, accountants, mechanics, and teachers."[33]

Undoubtedly, this loss of professional and technical personnel was serious. On the other hand, it provided numerous openings that were filled by minorities and poorer Laotians found in and near the ranks of the Pathet Lao. This wave of replacements would likely have occurred even in the absence of the emigration because the LPDR was committed to these changes by reason of ideology. The most startling of the new faces were those of the minorities. Batson wrote:

> A visitor to any of the major cities, including the nation's capital in the years following 1975, would have found many members of ethnic minorities running departments, schools, vet centres and so forth. This was not so, however, at the ministerial and central committee level.[34]

By the early 1980s, some comparatively better educated persons were selected to replace less competent officials, and political criteria were less frequently observed. In provincial and district governments, however, minorities were well represented. In areas where there was a heavy concentration of minorities, they held all the jobs, including top ones. An observer reported, "During my husband's 1985 visit to Nong Het, a Hmong stronghold on the Xieng Khouang border with Vietnam, negotiations for a variety of local aid projects were handled entirely by local Hmong government officials."[35]

Schooling expanded greatly in the LPDR. In minority areas, schools sprang up far beyond any token scale. By the mid-1980s, at least one third of minority children finished 3 years of primary schooling, a level attained by lowland Lao children just a generation earlier.[36] Teacher-training institutions prepared students who had completed five primary grades to teach in grades one to three. Special ethnic minority schools were organized; presumably these taught in indigenous languages rather than Lao, which was the language of instruction throughout other schools. Meng summarized the achievement recorded during the years 1976 to 1985:

> The total number of students receiving general education increased from 346,300 to 584,600 (68.8 percent), with primary school enrollment increasing by 56.2 percent, lower secondary enrollment by 160.0 percent and upper secondary enrollment by nearly 700 percent. . . . Primary enrollment reached 85.4 percent in 1983–4 compared to 67.5 percent in 1974–5, and secondary enrollment increased form 4.2 percent to 16.8 percent for the same period. . . . University and higher level ed-

ucation enrollment, including those studying abroad, represented only about 1.2 percent of the population aged 20–29 . . . in 1985.[37]

These figures clearly established that the LPDR had begun to close the gap between elementary education on the one hand and secondary and higher education on the other.

Great problems remained, wrote the Iresons. Many were physical. "Primary schools in most villages are only one-room shelters."[38] Both lowlands and upland areas were stricken by budgetary and personnel shortages. Rural villages in this overwhelmingly rural country were poorly supplied with primary schools. The Iresons visited schools for minorities that had grave shortcomings:

> [These schools] are characterized by ramshackle classrooms and dormitories constructed from bamboo; shortages or lack of blankets, mosquito nets, and cooking pots for the students; and rudimentary or nonexistent water and sanitary facilities. That the students lack books, writing materials, and teaching aids is axiomatic. The ethnic schools also lack qualified staff due to the low education of potential minority teachers and the unwillingness of lowland Lao to stay in the mountains, working for low pay, and growing their own upland rice without the help of relatives.[39]

Most of these shortcomings were consequences of the poverty of the nation and the state.

Program planners had set a goal of complete eradication of illiteracy by 1985. In 1975, the government estimated that 65% of persons aged 15 to 45 were illiterate. Five years later, 85% of the same age group was said to be literate. In 1984, a year early, the end of illiteracy was proclaimed. Widespread scepticism greeted the announcement. More realistically, UNESCO estimated in 1984 and 1985 that 56% of the 15 to 45 group was still illiterate.[40]

Twenty years after the end of the Vietnam War, little had been done to rehabilitate the country, which was "the most heavily bombed . . . in the world's history on a per capita basis."[41] Laos was also one of the poorest countries in Asia. In 1990, for example, the Gross National Product of Laos on a per capita basis was $170, or less than 47 cents a day per person.[42] By the same year, the country had overtaken its population of 1970. Malnutrition of the young called for urgent solutions. The country's dependency ratio—the number of children aged 14 and under in relation to the population aged 15 to 64 years—was one of the highest in Asia.[43] A minimum of international aid was available to enable Laos to overcome financial barriers to educational equality. Educational assistance from the United States, which had been significant, was cut off after the Pathet Lao victory in 1975.

THE HMONG IN LAOS

The Hmong, who numbered some 300,000—or 8% of the country's population—are an ancient people who fled China during the 19th and 20th centuries.[44] In Laos, they have lived exclusively in mountainous areas, preferably between 3,000 and 5,000 feet high. Their communities are organized along clan lines. Over the centuries, they maintained a distinctive society despite frequent attacks by the Chinese. Lacking a written language, they did without one altogether or learned to use that of the dominant society. "Many Hmong . . . mastered foreign languages with relative ease."[45]

Overwhelmingly a farming people, in Laos the Hmong practiced slash-and-burn agriculture whereby their fields remained fertile for only a few years. Thereupon they moved to new fields. They had little to do with lowland people or town dwellers. The French had considered "the hill-tribe minorities as savages."[46] and the Hmong well knew that "the majority of city dwelling Lao despised them."[47] Laotian officials under French rule took delight in treating Hmong with contempt. Thus, "the Hmong in particular, were not permitted to stand in . . . [the] company [of Lao officials], and if they approached an official they had to literally crawl, head down, and wait patiently until he saw fit to recognize their presence."[48] The encounter was all the more bitter because both participants knew that the Lao themselves were restricted by the French to third-rate official positions. (Many of the second-rate ones were occupied by Vietnamese.) The French became expert in playing one minority against another or against the Lao.[49]

The Hmong were a rebellious people who challenged superior power when they felt its sting. Long exploited by the neighboring Tai (another, larger minority in Laos), the Hmong exploded when local Tai rulers levied extraordinarily heavy taxes and other obligations on them. From 1918 to 1921, the rebellion spread. At its high point, "units of crack colonial troops [were tied down] over an expanse of 40,000 square kilometres spanning northern Laos and northwest Vietnam. . . ."[50] In the end, however, the movement was suppressed. Hmong leaders never gave up their search for allies, either among other minorities or French forces. They occasionally worked with lowland Lao elites where common interests dictated.

In general, mountain folk were among the poorest people in the country. This was also true of the Hmong, who were basically subsistence farmers. They raised crops that were consumed on their own farms. Corn, their main crop, was fed to the farm animals while the Hmong themselves ate the fruit and vegetables they produced.[51] In cases of emergency, such as when a move to new lands was necessary and a first crop had not yet been grown, money to tide them over could only come from the sale of two products: farm animals or opium.

Opium had been used as a pain killer for many centuries in the Far East and elsewhere. As Quincy reported, "from the ninth to the sixteenth century, Chinese treatises mention opium only in connection with medicine."[52] The British in India produced great amounts of opium in the 19th century and fought two wars with China to compel that country to permit further imports of opium. In the course of the century, the demand for opium in China had led to a sizable expansion in its production there. The Hmong—who lived in the mountainous areas that were favorable to opium cultivation—thereupon acquired a new cash crop that fed the growing national habit. Aside from selling the output of their own farms, however, they had nothing to do with the regional or world trade in the product where really vast profits were made. In the French empire, the government monopolized opium and strenuously merchandised it, as we saw in chapter 6. Until World War II, at least one sixth of the French government budget in Laos came from opium receipts.[53] Assuring a supply of this deadly but profitable commerce made the French somewhat more open to Hmong demands for social services, including education. For 8 years, a Hmong representative sat on the French Opium Purchasing Board that facilitated the expansion of opium production.[54]

Although great differences of wealth did not exist among the Hmong, class differences were discernible. One source refers to the parents of four prominent Hmong political figures as having belonged "to the Hmong aristocracy."[55] A Hmong who had lived in Vientiane, the capital, described his father's family as "rich." Lo Bliayao, a clan leader early in the 20th century, was "the richest Hmong in Laos."[56] Another mark of wealth was the ease with which a narrow circle of Hmong were able to send their children to schools located in Vientiane or to be taught by private tutors in the absence of local schools. Nevertheless, Hmong society remained basically egalitarian. Land, the foundation of agriculture, was available to all, in sharp contrast to the situation among the Lao in lowland areas. A poor crop year might press Hmong farmers to seek wage work in large towns. "In lowland towns their wages were invariably half of what a native Lao received for the same work."[57] It was very unlikely that such temporary residents of towns could afford to send their children to the town schools.

Hmong had a fearsome reputation as fighters dating back to early years in China. The rebellion just after World War I added to that record. Immediately after World War II, while Laos was still a colony, the Hmong became military supporters of the French. Under the leadership of Vang Pao, the first Hmong commissioned officer in the Royal Lao Army, Hmong were given military training and began to play active roles in French operations. This lasted until 1954 when the French were defeated at Dien Bien Phu by Vietnamese forces. This battle ended the French Empire in Indochina. Near the close of the decade, "the Laotian army gained the dubious world-wide distinction of being totally financed by the United States."[58] But the army ignored minorities when it came to recruiting soldiers. American military forces, however, were far more direct and made connections with Vang Pao. By 1961, the U.S. Green Berets had organized 9,000 Hmong soldiers into a guerrilla army.[59] This force was placed under the supervision and control of the U.S. Central Intelligence Agency (CIA).

The U.S. national administration kept American military participation in Laos a secret, both from Americans and the rest of the world. Secrecy also surrounded the Hmong fighters. The CIA conducted the campaign with no publicity. Although formally designed to give only economic and educational aid, the U.S. Agency for International Development (USAID) actually was also deeply involved in military affairs.[60] In the 1960s and early 1970s, the U.S. Embassy in Vientiane operated as the peak center of U.S. Military planning in Laos, with the Ambassador in charge.[61] Vang Pao was "the conduit for U.S. military and CIA aid" to the Hmong forces.[62]

Originally, the secret Hmong army was conceived of as guerrilla units. In time, however, they were converted into 300-men battalions, three to six of which then formed Mobile Groups. As time went on, "the Hmong were increasingly involved in conventional actions against sizable North Vietnamese forces."[63] This led to enormous casualties that by the end of the war in 1975 numbered some 30,000 or one tenth of all Hmong in the country. (The percentage may have been greater than that since by war's end, only half the Lao Hmong were supporters of the Vang Pao forces. The other half backed the Pathet Lao.) Historian Quincy wrote that, "nearly one-third of the Laotian Hmong perished during the conflict, which included close to half of all males over the age of fifteen."[64]

Yet the war also introduced thousands of Hmong to the modern urbanized and commercialized life of Laos. Hmong soldiers received admittedly brief training, but they mastered much technical equipment, including airplanes. In two large lowland towns, Long Cheng and Sam Thong, Hmong farmers switched from opium farming to raising corn and rice on a commercial basis.

> Some enterprising Hmong built an ice factory at Long Cheng, while others built restaurants. Hmong also took up new professions. There were Hmong photographers and Hmong dentists; Hmong became tailors, bakers, cobblers and radio repairmen. A new cottage industry, the fabrication of brooms, blossomed in the outlying villages giving employment to over 200 Hmong families.[65]

An advanced staging area of the CIA, Long Cheng was a crowded town of 30,000 as early as 1964 and served as Vang's headquarters.

Even before the wartime prosperity of the 1960s, Hmong schooling had begun to expand. At no time, however, was it sponsored by the Lao government. Expansion was actuated by the Hmong themselves and, later on, by the Americans. During the 1920s and 1930s, heads of various Hmong clans began sending their sons and male relatives to French elementary schools. Of this handful, only two are known to have graduated from a *lycée*. As Vang Pao rose in rank and responsibility, he made education a major policy concern:

> In the region under his command, he set up schools for the highlanders, paid the teachers when money was not forthcoming from the government, and organized nurse education through the . . . [USAID]. He built dormitories for minority students in Vietiane so that they could pursue higher education in the capital.[66]

Hmong built just about all the schools erected during the 1960s that were financed by USAID funds.[67]

On the American side, the key person in this school-building program was Edgar "Pop" Buell:

[This unofficial school system] brought one-room school houses to hundreds of mountain villages, and was later expanded to include nine junior high schools, two senior high schools, and a teacher training school. By 1969 three hundred Hmong were attending the most prestigious high schools in Vientiane, and twenty-four Hmong went on to attend universities in Australia, France, and the United States.[68]

In Xieng Khouange Province, the person who actually made the primary schools workable educational enterprises was Moua Lia, who had been trained as a teacher in France and was later to complete his training in Singapore.[69]

Military events soon overtook school building. At its peak, the Hmong secret army in 1969 enrolled some 40,000 soldiers.[70] From then on, however, a sweeping decline in Hmong fortunes set in. Air and ground artillery fire destroyed many Hmong villages, completely disrupting agriculture and other activities. Within several years, as many as 100,000 civilian Hmong were refugees, wandering over the countryside in search of a new home. During 1971 and 1972, the secret army began to disintegrate. "No longer a functional army, the Hmong soldiers of northeastern Laos had become merely a dispirited throng of war-weary people urgently seeking safety for their families."[71] Early in 1973, their numbers had fallen to 25,000.[72] As part of a general cease-fire movement in Indochina, in February 1973 the war in Laos came to an end. A year later, a new national government was formed. It was a coalition of left and right, but one tilted toward the Pathet Lao. By that time, Hmong forces numbered only 5,000. In May 1975, Vang Pao resigned his commission in the Royal Lao Army and was flown by the CIA to Thailand. In the days prior to the general's departure from Laos, he arranged for the air evacuation of 2,400 of his field officers and their families.[73] Apparently, they followed him to the United States.

Many Hmong were chagrined about the apparent haste with which the United States abandoned the Hmong secret army in particular and the Laotian theater in general. Reported Castle, "Since 1968 a growing split had developed between some CIA veterans and younger, recently arrived CIA case officers. The 'new breed' seemed insensitive to escalating Hmong casualties and the growing hill tribe refugee populations."[74] The viewpoint of the younger group may have been based, in part, on the fact that Hmong soldiers "could be put into the field for less than ten cents per man per day."[75] Because relations between the Hmong and the CIA were extralegal and thus not embodied in written and ratified documents, the question of American obligations to the Hmong remained an open one.[76]

Within 3 months of Vang Pao's departure, some 25,000 Hmong arrived in Thailand, en route to the United States and elsewhere. By 1983, between 60,000 and 65,000 lived in the United States. According to the U.S. Census of 1990, just under 100,000 lived here. Of the 150,000 who had fled Laos, only 17,000 ever returned between 1975 and 1988.[77]

HMONG IN THE UNITED STATES

Between 1975 and 1984, the bulk of the Hmong refugees arrived in the United States. Following is a statistical summary of their presence during these early years. The sample numbered 500 adults.[78]

Hmong who arrived in 1975 averaged fewer than 2 years of schooling and just under three fourths were unable to write in their native language. Nine out of 10 adults were either farmers, fishers, or members of the military. As of 1983, the religion of nearly half was ancestor worship, less than 5% were Buddhist. Nearly three fourths experienced family separation and by 1984, one sixth could still not communicate with the family left behind. A quarter were assaulted while trying to escape. During the years 1975 through 1983, nearly 90% had gone without food during their escape. Whereas Vietnamese refugees spent only 6 months in camps before coming to the United States, Hmong spent nearly five times as long. Between 1975 and 1984, the number who could not speak English dropped from 99.1% to 28.4%. This was a sharper drop than the Cambodians, Vietnamese, and the Hoa experienced during the same years. During the same span of years, the number who could not write English dropped from 99.1% to 77.0%. Hmong who arrived in 1975 typically spent some 30 months in ESL classes, but only 1.5 months in job training. In 1984, one sixth of the Hmong were employed, very much lower than the Vietnamese (46.5%). The unemployment rate for the former was more than double that of the latter. Of those Hmong employed, fully 45% had temporary jobs in 1984 and in three fifths of those jobs, there were no fringe benefits paid. Many of the enterprises were small.

During 1983 and 1984, the average Hmong household was around nine persons, six of these constituting the nuclear family. More than half the household was made up of children under 18 years of age. In nearly three fourths of the families, there were no wage earners and over 88% of the families were living in poverty. Welfare payments constituted over 72% of total Hmong family income.

On the whole, the Hmong community was extremely poor from the outset and remained that way. Lost in the averages are the exceptional families who, in Laos, had gained education and a middle-class occupation. Some, of course, had gone to other countries, especially France. The 1.8% of 1975 arrivals who were high-school graduates corresponded more or less to the 5% who listed themselves as former white-collar employees. The 31.3% classifying themselves as military represented many more than the 2,400 former army officers and their dependents who had been airlifted that year to the United States.

These general trends and tendencies held true in locations across the country. In California, with the greatest concentration of Hmong, during the mid-1980s, about 80% were without jobs whereas in the rest of the country, the figure ranged under 50%.[79] Some 80% of Hmong households in St. Paul were still living below the poverty line in the early 1990s.[80] In a Western town, 92% were at least partly dependent on public aid.[81] Elsewhere, 85% of the families received some government aid and upwards of 70% of household heads were unemployed.[82] Scott pointed to the occupational implications of the persistent failure of many communities to offer sufficient English-language and vocational training to Hmong adults

> The majority of the present adult population, in addition to the generation immediately to follow, is likely to fall backwards into a more permanent lower-class, or even "under-class," position, watching with envy, and perhaps with rancor, as the more successful among them, even some of their own children and grandchildren, move away into the higher levels of American society. Told to "sink or swim," they will surely sink, carried under, but given some solace, by the weight of an overly emphasized ethnicity.[83]

Goldstein noted that many Hmong boys were discovering, to their dismay, that a high-school diploma did not assure them an opening to desirable jobs.[84]

The federal government provided refugee aid to the Hmong for the first 3 years of residence. In San Diego County during the early 1980s, for example:

> Each family receives a monthly payment of at least $408. [With children the payment] . . . goes up to . . . a maximum of $1087 [a month] with eight [children], in addition to food stamps and medical assistance. [After three years recipients could switch to other programs such as AFDC.][85]

While on the 3-year program, recipients were required to enroll in ESL classes as well as in vocational training. If recipients worked for pay for more than 100 hours in a month, their cash and medical benefits were cut off. The burden of this rule fell especially hard on Hmong families with many children. On the other hand, the federal origin of most Hmong benefits convinced landlords in San Diego that these families were good tenants whose monthly rents would ordinarily be paid on time.[86] This contrasted with nonrefugee poor people seeking the same housing accommodations.

The Hmong were probably the most socially homogeneous refugee or immigrant group in the United States. As noted earlier, in Laos, the Hmong elite was tiny and may have sought a refuge in France. Nevertheless, there were instances of downward social mobility. Researcher Lopez-Romano reported the experience of a Hmong refugee in Northern California: "Back home, his father was a man of means and very high in the social hierarchy. In this country, he is a gardener, and the young man says it's just something his parents won't talk about."[87] A Hmong adult explained her feelings about the American economy's workings:

> The good part is we don't have to sweat over a piece of land to produce food for every meal. The bad part is, even though I am told that the United States is a land of freedom, I feel no freedom at all. Freedom, to me, is being able to farm our own land, raise our cattle, and own our own homes without obligation to anyone.[88]

This conception was far removed from the sense of dependency that enveloped the life of the refugee.

It is difficult to ascertain whether there were more misconceptions by Hmong about non-Hmong or the reverse. Race was one such arena. When Maijue Xiong entered kindergarten in Isla Vista, CA:

> I was shocked to see so many faces of different colors. The Caucasian students shocked me the most. I had never seen people with blond hair. The sight sent me to a bench, where I sat and watched everyone in amazement.[89]

Lee Fang, in Thailand while awaiting processing to the United States, was fascinated by the Americans' blond hair and light skin. "I used to go to their offices to stare at them for hours."[90] On the other hand, on arriving in San Francisco, he recalled that, "I was most amazed at the color of the Afro-Americans."[91] A number of younger Hmong remembered conflicts of one kind or another with African-American students but there were also those most of whose friends were African-Americans.[92]

Never before had the mass of Laotian Hmong children faced the possibility of gaining a comprehensive education from elementary through higher education. How did they fare? Hmong GPAs were unexpectedly high, despite their meager educational heritage from Laos. Most striking, they received the smallest portion of the lowest grades. Although a direct measurement is not possible, other data indicate that Hmong GPAs even outstripped those of White students.[93] How can this apparent anomaly be explained?

For one thing, many Hmong are enrolled in ESL classes in which subject-matter content is secondary to English-language understanding.[94] Thus, a high grade in ESL courses is not comparable with one in courses in which subject matter is primary. For another, tracking is regularly used in the San Diego schools. In such systems, high grades in a top-rated track are more meaningful for later entry into college than is a high grade in a low-rated track. Until we know the actual distribution of enrollment by track and ethnic group, it is not possible to judge the educational significance of GPAs.[95] These points are illustrated by Goldstein in a school she studied:

> For students who were quiet in class and did their assignments to the best of their ability, a passing "D" was guaranteed by these teachers regardless of the correctness of their work. A typical consequence was that LEP students would be their best in class, fail tests but still get a "D" while their American classmates would pass the tests but be demoted for poor behavior.[96]

In effect, the LEP students were rewarded for their so-called passivity.[97]

In the course of Walker's study of schools in Providence, RI, and Merced, CA, she found that Hmong community leaders were quite aware of the problem just discussed. "The Hmong were concerned about inferior education in ESL programs. Chou Tou regarded ESL classes as a trap because it tracks children in the lowest levels and does not enable them to compete with other students."[98]

She further found that "Hmong parents believe schools do not teach their children what they need to know to get into good high schools or colleges."[99] They were also aware that their children were not enrolled in college tracks. The federal Office of Refugee Resettlement brought a related situation to light:

> In the Twin Cities [St. Paul and Minneapolis], although the quality of ESL provided is generally considered to be quite good, observation of variations in teachers' qualifications gave rise to the serious charge from two separate groups of Hmong household heads that adult ESL programs deliberately hire poorly qualified American teachers so that refugee students will learn slowly and thus allow the programs to continue to receive funding.[100]

Some of the mechanisms producing unequal education of Hmong children became clear in a study of two high schools by Goldstein. Although the researcher did not reveal the location of the schools, they were possibly in Wisconsin. Called Ashmont and Logan, the former school was one in which "academically oriented and successful students who behaved like college students were valued," while in the latter the curriculum had "a preponderance of lower track classes and a well-developed vocational/technical education program."[101] About 20 Hmong students attended each school.

The principal of Logan stressed social integration rather than separate classes. He also made discipline a central concern of this lower-class school that was accorded a low status in the community. Teachers were sensitive about this:

> Because discipline was such an administrative priority, the faculty culture at Logan placed high value on students who cooperated with teachers. Teacher status was accorded not only to those teachers with academically-talented students but also to those with well-behaved students. Therefore, the Hmong students were welcomed by many teachers because their good behavior enhanced their teachers' status.[102]

Students were well aware that they were not valued for their academic prowess, but more as a matter of teacher convenience.

At Ashmont, the same result eventuated. Goldstein explained:

> For the majority of students and teachers in the school those students who were not "high academic achievers" posed a threat to the identity of the school. They were only welcomed in the school if they did not interfere with the serious business of preparing students for college entry. . . . The ESL/Bilingual program was acceptable . . . for precisely the reason that it did not make financial or faculty demands on the school. It provided a way to keep the high school's LEP students out of the mainstream classes, thus enabling the school to increase its quota of minority students, and qualification as a desegregated school, without cost to its reputation for academic excellence. Thus, structural means were used by Ashmont's administration to protect the school's culture.[103]

Teachers who taught advanced classes notified school staff that LEP students were not desired in those classes.

Thus, although the physical presence in the schools of students from different ethnic and class groups gave the impression of integration, the deeper reality was functional separation. The same outcome was achieved by high school rules barring students of a certain age—ranging from 19 to 21. Hmong and others who had come to the United States as late adolescents were thereby precluded from graduating after several years. A crowning insult to many Hmong and other students was the practice of some high schools awarding them "certificates of attendance or modified (meaningless) diplomas."[104]

Both within individual classrooms and in the rest of the school, Hmong interacted very little with other students. "Though students are reluctant to talk about it, in the Twin Cities and in Fresno harassment by American students is a common problem, both at elementary and secondary levels."[105] Much of the purportedly cultural passive classroom behavior of Hmong and others turns out to be actuated by this widespread antagonistic attitude that is their lot. Numerous Hmong have commented bitterly on the subject. In South Providence, RI, complains one, "Very few people say 'hi' on the streets; even when I try to say 'hi' to them, they don't answer."[106] In the same city, a young man, Thek Moua, said, "They called us names, imitated our talk, and shoved us around."[107] The future cofounder of the Hmong Club at the University of California, Santa Barbara, Lee Fang, on entering elementary school, "Experienced for the first time what it was like to be discriminated against and hated simply because we looked different. . . . It made me realize I would be surrounded by hatred and hostility."[108] Vu Pao Tcha, a young male Hmong, arrived in Fresno with his parents. Very soon he confronted antagonistic attacks. "Racism was the first shocking thing I observed after my arrival. . . . Racism was probably the hardest challenge and most difficult obstacle that I've encountered in the United States."[109] In the Minneapolis schools, early in the 1980s, anti-Indochinese incidents were numerous and "fights along racial lines are increasing among the students."[110]

Although in school the Hmong had almost nothing to do with White students, outside school there was even less interaction.[111] Wherever it was enacted, Hmong students came to the same conclusion: "They don't like us."[112] Goldstein supported this impression:

> Discrimination did occur. It frequently occurred subtly as in the social distance and silent isolation imposed intentionally and unintentionally in school by Americans on Hmong students. . . . [There were] numerous instances in which Hmong were treated as inferior outsiders. And at times . . . American students intentionally used rapid speech, plays on words or sarcasm at the expense of LEP students.[113]

A moderating effect on anti-Hmong feeling resulted from geographical differences. In larger communities marked by persistent problems—such as Long Beach and Minneapolis—Hmong met with greater hostility than in smaller communities such as Isla Vista, CA.[114] Whether this was also true of difficulties within schools is not clear.

Teachers have not seemed to play a prominent role in changing schools so as to accommodate Hmong students. As pointed out earlier, many teachers adopted a variety of strategies to avoid having Hmong students. Among the most desperate of these was the creation of imaginary classes. (Mr. Rodriguez was an ESL teacher in the school.)

> The teachers were willing to be flexible about rules and had the [Hmong] students register in their classes but attend classes taught by Mr. Rodriguez. In this way, on paper the Hmong were mainstreamed and meeting graduation requirements, while in practice they were segregated into LEP classes that did not officially exist.[115]

In Fresno, one study reported that "comments by teachers . . . are both favorable and encouraging."[116] In Minneapolis, on the other hand, community rumors included one that the school district had "experienced significant anti-Indochinese participation by school teachers. . . ."[117] In Goldstein's study of two schools, Hmong students "recognized and resented patronizing attitudes among teachers, and in fact assumed that a teacher was patronizing until she or he proved otherwise."[118]

In schools the country over, researchers found teachers of Hmong students who knew almost nothing of Hmong history and culture. In Walker's words, this resulted in "a patchwork education for the children."[119] Even those who were officially labelled "bilingual Hmong" teachers "knew nothing of . . . [Hmong] culture, life experiences, family background or language."[120] In Merced, CA, "until 1987, the administration did not feel as though mainstream teachers needed in-service training on cultural background of Hmong."[121] Such "in-service training of principals and school administrators is negligible or non-existent."[122] Instead of regarding this lack of knowledge as a shortcoming, many teachers and administrators viewed it as irrelevant to good teaching.

Teacher aides were generally required by law. Because they were assumed—often, quite correctly—to lack any specialized training, they were relegated to the most elementary tasks requiring adult personnel. According to one estimate, corridor or lunchroom duty absorbed the labor of three fourths of the aides.[123] In a Southern California school, wrote Jacobs:

> The aides are mandated by their funding to work with the lowest-reading students. One consequence of this is, in the mode of being efficient, the teacher tends to give less time to these neediest students, since they are already getting time with the adult aide.[124]

Jacobs also observed that although aides in bilingual classes spoke Spanish, in predominantly Indochinese classes, all the aides were Anglos who were unable to speak any of those languages.[125] School districts paid close attention to aides' salaries and length of the work day:

> The school district only allows aides to work three and a half hours a day at five dollars an hour to avoid fringe benefits. The fringe benefits cost three times as much if a person works over eighteen hours a week.[126]

The 1980s were a time of declining federal expenditures on education that aggravated the reluctance of school districts to spend money on language-minority students.

Few Hmong students had the advantage of bilingual education. A federal study found, "The closest approximation to bilingual education is provided in the Twin Cities areas, especially in Minneapolis schools. Hmong staff have been used to teach special sections of some subjects in Hmong, particularly social studies." [127] In Providence, wrote Walker, "almost all of the teachers I spoke to . . . are against bilingual education." [128] Even the meaning of bilingual education was in dispute in various places. Walker discovered that "in Merced, Hmong 'bilingual' education means ESL, as it does in most northern and central California school systems." [129]

Within Hmong communities, learning English is the central task of young people and many adults. The latter crowd onto long waiting lists to study with teachers who may know very little of Hmong life, past or present. [130] Contrary to expectations of refugee officials, few Hmong who were employed learned English on the job. [131] In part, this was because not many Hmong worked alongside non-Hmong. Also, at least early on, a sense of separation permeated the ranks of non-Hmong workers.

Hmong students varied in their command of English. Youngsters for whom an American school is their first formal educational institution do well. Older, adolescent children, on the other hand, are often assigned by age, despite the fact that they had no previous schooling in Laos. Too frequently, the result is— as in Fresno—that "the average reading level of Hmong students tested in the 11th grade was 4th to 5th grade." [132] In Minneapolis, 1 to 2 hours a day are devoted to study of English, complemented with about an hour a day for bilingual study of science, math, health, and social studies. Here, too, placement by age is one of the goals for mainstreamed classes. [133] Certain school practices seemed to have unintended consequences. In a Southern California school, for instance:

> The school . . . has a different reading program which requires all students in one grade to use the same reading text. The school can therefore report that all students in third grade are reading third grade level. For the ESL students, and low and high readers, this has potential for disaster, since a third grade class . . . incorporates reading levels from preprimer to fifth grade. [134]

Hmong students in Fresno also had an urgent problem. "Even the most successful Hmong high school students . . . feel they need much more writing instruction to continue their education effectively. Once they are mainstreamed out of ESL, they receive no further special help with their English writing skills." [135] Clearly, this was not an exclusively Hmong issue. After examining instruction in English in San Diego, Walker concluded that, "it is in reading comprehension, reading vocabulary, and spelling that the Hmong have particular problems." [136]

The research literature on Hmong education states frequently that literacy in Hmong (or other languages) is a positive influence in learning English. Green and Reder reported on Hmong adults that, "for the most part, the educated group scores higher than the noneducated and the literates higher than the non-literates."[137] They go on to cite three factors that have the greatest impact on English proficiency: ability to read Hmong, age, and previous education in Laos.[138]

Between 1952 and 1964, four writing systems were created in Laos. The first one, the Romanized Popular Alphabet (RPA), was produced by Christian missionaries during 1952 and 1953.[139] Its primary users were Christianized Hmong, of whom there were very few in the early 1950s. The second and third writing systems were produced by a Hmong, Shong Lue Yang, in 1959. The former system he called the Pahawh Hmong. In honor of his mother, a Khmu, he also created a writing system for that group. Five years later, a fourth writing system was invented in territory controlled by the Pathet Lao. (It is presently used by the Hmong still in Laos.[140]) In addition, separate writing systems exist for Hmong Daw (White Hmong) and Hmong Leng (Blue/Green Hmong) dialects. The RPA was not used in Lao public schools so, aside from some Christianized Hmong, it was a rare Hmong in the United States who arrived knowing how to use the RPA. In Vientiane schools attended by Hmong, French and Lao had been the languages of instruction.

If Hmong Americans were to learn to read and write Hmong, they would have to learn it themselves. This is almost wholly what they did. A study of Hmong high-school students in Fresno found that "47.5 percent had acquired the minimal proficiencies in reading and writing Hmong."[141] The researcher noted that "many Hmong have learned to read and write their mother tongue by themselves."[142] Some were helped by friends, or relatives, or others in their church. Hmong literacy had little or no economic significance; it did not improve one's standard of living nor qualify one for new occupations. Learning Hmong was basically a new way to be Hmong. In Laos, Hmong culture did not require Hmong literacy, but in the United States, the two were intertwined.[143] As McGinn put it, "The writing system is seen as the new mode of transmitting culture."[144] The circulation of letters and other written statements served to bind together far-flung Hmong settlements in the new country. Older Hmong greatly regretted the growing disuse of traditional culture in parent-child relations. They must also have been at least slightly confounded by the sight of young Hmong asserting their heritage at the same time.

Hmong writing did not spread uniformly. In the Minneapolis area, only about 20% of Hmong junior high school students had learned it.[145] Yet, such an incidence was far higher than had been the case back in Laos when the families of these students had lived there. Because of the virtual absence of bilingual education in Hmong and English in the United States and the complete lack of Hmong in Laotian schools, these Hmong youngsters had never experienced the use of written Hmong in their schooling. Many Hmong students in Laos, however, were quite able to converse in Lao and, to a lesser degree, Thai.[146] It was well-known that the Hmong script invented by foreign missionaries was largely used by Christian converts in Laos. For example, among the 1983 Hmong arrivals from Laos, 18.4% were either Catholics or Protestants. In addition, others may have been in mixed families or households that included at least one Christian. In the United States, where conversions to Christianity accelerated, the ground was laid for religion-linked writing. Because literacy in one language generally aids in the acquisition of a second one, the learning of English was facilitated by the simultaneous mastery of written Hmong.

In Laos, as we saw earlier, because the Hmong were not Buddhists, they could not attend the pagoda schools. Girls were seldom found in Lao- or French-language public schools. Wealthy Hmong were able to employ tutors to teach girls at home, but these were few in number. Illiteracy rates were much greater for women than for men. Even when occasional girls managed to enter schools, they did not remain for long in deference to their brothers, who had first call on family resources. In addition, early dropout of girls was related to their early marriage, which customarily ended any hope of further education.

In the United States, many more Hmong girls entered schools. Early marriage, however, had its usual effects. By the mid-1980s, the Office of Refugee Resettlement was reporting that, "with the exception of a few school districts, the dropout rate for girls ranges from 80–95 percent."[147] The report added that in St. Paul, "up to 90 percent of Hmong girls are dropping out . . . prior to graduation."[148] Curiously, however, another report covering the same city during 1985 and 86 to 1988 and 89 stated that data "showed no marked difference in Hmong dropout rates between the sexes. . . ."[149] Because no specific figures were listed, it was not possible to gauge the extent of marked differences. A possible resolution of this issue may rest on the development of a new Hmong pattern: More girls who marry do not automatically drop out of school. This seems to be happening. Walker, referring to Grades 7 through 12 in Fresno during 1987, wrote that, "the relatively equal number of Asian boys and girls suggests there was no apparent dropout problem among Asian [Hmong?] girls. . . ."[150] She attributed this to a rising number of school programs for pregnant minors in Fresno as well as Boulder and Merced. Yang recently commented that for the Hmong, "early marriage now is not as important as it used to be."[151]

The numerous Hmong women who enter the labor market rather than remain in school are compelled by circumstances to accept low-wage jobs. Mason pointed out that, "despite the stipulation of the 1980 Refugee Act that women must have the same employment training opportunities as men, training programs accessible to women have been inadequate and inequitable."[152] Job openings after training are largely restricted to positions in houseclearning and home sewing. A training course in Apparel Arts, which highlights sewing, resulted in immediate jobs:

> At the end of each term recruiters from the garment industry and other manufacturing companies come directly to the school to sign up Hmong women who have

completed the training. . . . Several companies have hired as many as forty Hmong women to work under a Hmong foreman. With this arrangement the women need only a minimum level of English proficiency.[153]

Mason contends that such policies "can only create a permanently disadvantaged group of women."[154] Their wages are so meager that a full-time worker earns an income below the poverty line. The same is true, of course, for many low-paid, non-Hmong workers.

Among the 1975 arrivals from Laos, fewer than 2% were high school graduates, a tiny reservoir for a college population. In addition, many—perhaps most—Hmong in high school were not enrolled in college-preparatory programs, nor were they well-served by guidance and counseling personnel. Although their parents were largely unschooled, nevertheless college attendance became a family goal.

During the mid-1980s, between 300 and 350 Hmong were attending college, most of them in the Fresno area.[155] Some 7 years later, "an attempt to create a Southeast Asian club . . . at the . . . [Calfornia State University, Fresno] failed in part because the other groups felt that they would be outvoted by the more numerous Hmong students."[156] Variation in enrollment was great in California. For example, in 1982, Isla Vista had seven Hmong students in college while Long Beach, with a Hmong population 10 times greater, had none.[157] Only about 5% of the Hmong college-age population (18–24 years old) was in college, whereas 31.8% of that age group in the general population were college students.[158]

At the University of Minnesota, Hmong students numbered as follows:

1984–1985	51
1988–1989	67
1990–1991	84
1991–1992	103[159]

During the early 1980s, Asian-American students tended to enter the General College, which had the lowest entrance requirements on campus. At the opening of the 1988 to 1989 academic year, however, the minimum passing grade for the Michigan English Language Assessment Battery (MELAB) was raised from 55 to 65. The number of Hmong students dropped as a result. Soon the old level was surpassed. By the early 1990s, the College of Liberal Arts replaced the General College as the main college of matriculation for Asian-Americans. In 1991 and 1992, "the Lao have 39 percent of their population in the General College, while the Cambodians and Hmong each have 18 percent of their population in this open admission college."[160] Although the Hmong numbers increased steadily, they and others found the academic going rough.

A recent study by Holt of the Minnesota English Center found:

Southeast Asian students seem to be at greater risk than the other populations in both lower-division and upper-division writing classes. Also, Southeast Asian students in the professional schools are writing poorly. . . . Although these [Southeast Asian] students generally have very good academic transcripts, it appears that their level of English fluency is not adequate when they must compete with native speakers of English.[161]

Hmong alumni created, in 1991, the Hmong Youth Association of Minnesota, which attracted enough grants to organize a project for Hmong high-school juniors to receive training in taking the ACT test and participate in a summer program in mathematics and Hmong history.[162] On campus, a Hmong Student Association was organized, one of seven Asian-American groups.

Individual Hmong parents visited their children's school on matters related to academic work or misbehaviors. Seldom, however, did the Hmong community as a whole participate in school matters. In two Wisconsin towns—La Crosse and Wausau—such intervention did occur when the entire town chose sides on a proposed elementary school desegregation plan. Virtually all the Hmong favored the plan, as did a sizable minority of Whites. The opposition consisted principally of White residents.

Hmong constituted about 4% of La Crosse's population but about 10% of school enrollment. Their children tended to be assigned to a few schools where their presence were prominent. Typically, the families had seven children each.[163] In a 1987 telephone poll, members of the larger community were split nearly evenly on their attitude toward continued growth of the Southeast Asian community, most of which consisted of Hmong.[164] In 1992, the school board adopted a plan to bus children for socioeconomic integration. Poor children, who made up from 4 to 68% of the schools, were to be redistributed so that "they would make up no fewer than 15 percent and no more than 50 percent of any school's population."[165] Opponents of the plan formed the Recall Alliance to recall board of education members who had voted for the plan. This move succeeded and four members were recalled. Nevertheless, the school board failed to dismantle the plan as citizens testifying before the board—including one Hmong, Thai Vue—were unanimous in their support for the plan.

In 1993, a similar desegregation plan became an issue in Wausau, a town about 100 miles from La Crosse. Five school-board members were targeted for a recall. Six elementary schools were to exchange students by busing. Opponents of the plan had succeeded in forcing the superintendent, the author of the plan, to resign. Hmong, whose children constitute about one sixth of enrollment, favored the plan.[166] Ya M. Yang, a Hmong, was recently elected to the board and had voted for it. (State law protects board members from recall during their first terms.) Yi Vang, executive director of the Wausau Area Hmong Mutual Association, affirmed his community's support for the plan. He noted, however, that only 130 Hmong were eligible to vote. About 80% of the Wausau Education Association, a teachers' group, favored the plan. Nevertheless, late in 1993, voters ousted five school-board members. Five months later, the desegregation plan was withdrawn—and replaced by a plan to "reshuffle attendance zones slightly to distribute Limited-English-Proficient students, who will account for between 21 percent and 46 percent of the enrollment of schools near their homes."[167] A magnet program was placed in a heavily minority school. Yang, the Hmong board member, voted against the compromise measure.

In 1991 a writer on the Hmong testified before a Congressional subcommittee, "The Hmong are unique in that they may be the only refugees in the world that do *not* want to resettle in the United States. Most Hmong in Thai camps want to return to their homelands in Laos."[168] This view was contradicted 3 years later by Hein, who wrote that, "unlike Cuban refugees . . . Hmong refugees arrived in the United States for permanent settlement."[169] As early as 1985, however, it was being reported that "thousands of Hmong in the [Thai] refugee camps have been approved for U.S. resettlement are no longer interested in coming.[170] More pointed was "the fear of losing the Hmong culture is a primary reason why forty-six thousand Hmong remained at Ban Vinai refugee camp in northern Thailand until 1986, despite opportunities to resettle since 1980."[171] (An additional, rumored reason for the failure to resettle was that Hmong were awaiting word from Vang Pao to invade Laos and overthrow the Pathet Lao government. This did not happen.) Scott attributed reluctance to seek refuge in the United States to "the difficulty in adjusting to life here."[172] Undoubtedly, overseas Hmong heard plenty from their U.S. compatriots about the persistent poverty they confronted. Finally, in 1988, historian Quincy contended that "only the very old continue to cling to the dream of repatriation."[173] Although in some Hmong circles it was rumored that Hmong who repatriated themselves to Laos had met with harassment from the government, a U.S. State Department spokesperson reportedly declared that, "there never has been one verifiable story of anybody being persecuted for having been repatriated."[174]

All in all, little suggested that American community life bore down on Hmong any more onerously than on others. Their growing propensity to enter community affairs was a strong indicator of future achievement. Historically, the Hmong had overcome even more serious challenges, including forced long-distance moves.

CONCLUDING REMARKS

The history of Hmong in Laos and the United States is inconsistent with stereotypical views of the Hmong as a preliterate, passive people. In both countries, most Hmong spoke Lao as well as their own language. Many spoke others as well. This departs greatly from a view of Hmong as peasants who are prisoners of purely local institutions and practices. During the years after 1945, Hmong played an increasingly active role in national politics. Advances in education followed from political bargains struck by Hmong and Americans in pre-1975 Laos.

In the United States, Hmong parents did not regard local schools as beyond criticism, as posited by amateur anthropologists. Instead, they formed critical judgments on teaching and other inadequacies. They learned, too, to demand structural changes to benefit their children. This was most evident in the Wisconsin desegregation cases.

An increasingly critical activism by parents suggested that Hmong were learning how to contend for improved schools in the American mode. Civil rights approaches were being utilized by Hmong. In Laos, the problem for parents was to get governmental authorities to build and conduct schools for Hmong children. In the United States, the schools existed but operated unequally.

NOTES

[1] Somlith Pathammavong, "Compulsory Education in Laos," p. 83 in Charles Bilodeau and others, *Compulsory Education in Cambodia, Laos and Viet-Nam* (UNESCO, 1955).

[2] Bounlieng Phommasouvanh, *The Preparation of Teachers and Its Role in the Laosization of Public Secondary Schools in Laos* (Doctoral dissertation, Southern Illinois University, 1973), p. 41.

[3] Hugh Toye, *Laos. BuVer State or Battleground* (Oxford University Press, 1968), p. 60.

[4] Ibid., p. 61.

[5] Ibid., p. 45.

[6] Phommasouvanh, *The Preparation of Teachers*, p. 42.

[7] Ibid., p. 43.

[8] Wendy Batson, "After the Revolution: Ethnic Minorities and the New Lao State," p. 141 in Joseph J. Zasloff and Leonard Unger, *Laos: Beyond the Revolution* (St. Martin's Press, 1991).

[9] Geoffrey C. Gunn, *Political Struggle in Laos (1930–1954): Vietnamese Communist Power and the Lao Struggle for National Independence* (Editions Duang Kamol, 1988), p. 33.

[10] Sucheng Chan, ed., *Hmong Means Free. Life in Laos and America* (Temple University Press, 1994), p. 7.

[11] Gunn, *Political Struggle in Laos*, p. 32.

[12] Ibid., p. 32.

[13] Phommasouvanh, *The Preparation of Teachers*, p. 77.

[14] Gunn, *Political Struggle in Laos*, p. 33.

[15] Ibid., p. 106.

[16] Paul F. Langer, *Education in the Communist Zone of Laos* (RAND Corporation, 1971).

[17] Ibid., p. 4, footnote 6.

[18] Phommasouvanh, *The Preparation of Teachers*, p. 117.

[19] Khamphao Phonekeo, "Literacy in Laos," *Bulletin of the UNESCO Regional OYce for Education in Asia*, 5 (1970–71), p. 48.

[20] Ibid., p. 49.

[21] Phommasouvanh, *The Preparation of Teachers*, pp. 120–121.

[22] Joel M. Halpern and Marilyn Clark Tinsman, "Education and Nation-Building in Laos," *Comparative Education Review* 10 (October 1966), p. 502.

[23] Ibid., p. 502.

[24] See maps of conflicting land-control claims in Chan, *Hmong Means Free*, pp. 34–35. For a Pathet Lao view of recent history, see Kaysone Phomvihane, *Revolution in Laos. Practice and Prospects* (Progress Publishers, 1981)

[25] *Vietnam Courier*, October 7, 1965, quoted in Halpern and Tinsman, "Education and Nation-Building in Laos," p. 50.

[26] Ibid., p. 50.

[27] Langer, *Education in the Communist Zone of Laos*, p. 6.

[28]Laura J. Summers, "Lao People's Democratic Republic," p. 475 in Bogdan Szajkowski, ed., *Marxist Governments. A World Survey,* Vol. 2, *Cuba-Mongolia* (St. Martin's Press, 1981). See also Sandra C. Taylor, "Laos: The Escalation of a Secret War," pp. 73–90 in Elizabeth J. Errington and B. J. C. McKercher, eds., *The Vietnam War As History* (Praeger, 1990).

[29]Langer, *Education in the Communist Zone of Laos,* p. 5.

[30]Ibid., p. 33.

[31]Summers, "Lao People's Democratic Republic," p. 480.

[32]Langer, *Education in the Communist Zone of Laos,* p. 35.

[33]Batson, "After the Revolution," p. 143.

[34]Ibid., p. 143.

[35]Ibid., p. 145.

[36]Ibid., p. 149.

[37]Ng Shui Meng, "Social Development in the Lao People's Democratic Republic: Problems and Prospects," pp. 163–164 in Joseph J. Zasloff and Leonard Unger, *Laos: Beyond the Revolution* (St. Martin's Press, 1991). See also Arthur J. Dommen, *Laos. Keystone of Indochina* (Westview Press, 1985), p. 157.

[38]Carol J. Ireson and W. Randall Ireson, "Ethnicity and Development in Laos," *Asian Survey,* 31 (October 1991), p. 92.

[39]Ibid., p. 92.

[40]Meng, "Social Development in the Lao People's Democratic Republic," pp. 161–163.

[41]Batson, "After the Revolution," p. 135.

[42]For data, see *World Education Report 1991* (UNESCO, 1991). In 1994, Laotian government sources claimed per capita annual income of $250 to $335, or from 68 to 92 cents a day, but this was widely doubted. See Henry Kamm, "Communism in Laos: Poverty and a Thriving Elite," *New York Times,* July 30, 1995, p. 6.

[43]Ibid.

[44]A full-length background can be found in Keith Quincy, *Hmong. History of a People* (Eastern Washington University Press, 1988). A shorter piece, devoted primarily to recent political history, is Sucheng Chan, *Hmong Means Free. Life in Laos and America* (Temple University Press, 1994), pp. 1–60.

[45]Quincy, *Hmong,* p. 164.

[46]Timothy N. Castle, *Alliance in a Secret War: The United States and the Hmong of Northeastern Laos* (Master's thesis, San Diego State University, 1979), p. 16.

[47]Ibid., p. 65. See also J. Mottin, *History of the Hmong* (Odeon Store Ltd., 1980), p. 51.

[48]Quincy, *Hmong,* p. 68.

[49]See Geoffrey C. Gunn, "Minority Manipulation in Colonial Indochina: Lessons and Legacies," *Bulletin of the Concerned Asian Scholars,* 19 (July–September 1987), pp. 20–28 and Gunn, *Political Struggles in Laos (1930–1954): Vietnamese Communist Power and the Lao Struggle for National Independence* (Editions Duang Kamol, 1988), p. 297.

[50]Geoffrey C. Gunn, "Shamans and Rebels: The Batchai (Meo) Rebellion in Northern Laos and North-West Vietnam (1918–1921)," *Journal of the Siam Society,* 74 (1986), p. 107.

[51]Quincy, *Hmong,* p. 74.

[52]Ibid., p. 101.

[53]Gunn, *Political Struggles in Laos,* p. 33.

[54]Quincy, *Hmong,* pp. 141–142. Compare Jane Hamilton-Merritt, *Tragic Mountains. The Hmong, the Americans, and the Secret Wars for Laos, 1942–1992* (Indiana University Press, 1993), p. 8: "Hmong . . . were not involved in . . . international drug trafficking. Those in control would never allow minorities to participate."

[55]Chan, *Hmong Means Free,* p. 66.

[56]Katsuyto K. Howard, *Passages: An Anthology of the Southeast Asian Refugee Experience* (Southeast Asian Student's Services, California State University, Fresno, 1990), p. 114.

[57] Quincy, *Hmong,* p. 121.

[58] Ibid., p. 135.

[59] Castle, *Alliance in a Secret War,* pp. 37–38.

[60] Ibid., p. 52.

[61] Timothy N. Castle, *At War in the Shadow of Vietnam: United States Military Aid to the Royal Lao Government, 1955–75* (Doctoral dissertation, University of Hawaii, 1991), p. 149.

[62] Ibid., p. xix.

[63] Castle, *Alliance in a Secret War,* p. 61.

[64] Castle, *At War in the Shadow of Vietnam,* p. 255.

[65] Quincy, *Hmong,* pp. 163–164.

[66] Ibid., p. 183.

[67] Gary Yia Lee, "Ethnic Minorities and Nation-Building in Laos: The Hmong in the Lao State," *Peninsule,* Nos. 11–12 (1985–1986), p. 228.

[68] Quincy, *Hmong,* p. 183.

[69] Ibid., p. 176.

[70] Hamilton-Merritt, *Tragic Mountains,* pp. 125, 199, 331.

[71] Chan, *Hmong Means Free,* p. 32.

[72] Castle, *At War in the Shadow of Vietnam,* p. 256.

[73] Castle, *Alliance in a Secret War,* p. 86.

[74] Ibid., p. 92.

[75] Castle, *At War in the Shadow of Vietnam,* p. 266, footnote 30.

[76] Victor Marchetti and John D. Marks, *The CIA and the Cult of Intelligence* (Dell, 1974), p. 111.

[77] See Castle, *Alliance in a Secret War,* p. 116: "The fact remains that the United States did offer to care for the Hmong. This obligation remains largely forgotten and unpaid." This statement was written in 1979.

[78] W. Courtland Robinson, "Laotian Refugees in Thailand: The Thai and U.S. Response, 1975 to 1988," p. 231 in Zasloff and Unger, *Laos.* Data in this section are taken from tables 8.1, 8.2, 8.3, 8.4, and 8.5 in David W. Haines, ed., *Refugees as Immigrants. Cambodians, Laotians, and Vietnamese in America* (Rowman and Littlefield), pp. 144, 146, 148, 150, and 152.

[79] Shur Vang Vangyi, "Hmong Employment and Welfare Dependency," p. 195 in Glenn L. Hendricks, Robert T. Downing, and Amos S. Deinard, eds., *The Hmong in Transition* (Center for Migration Studies, 1986).

[80] Miles McNall and others, "The Educational Achievement of the St. Paul Hmong," *Anthropology and Education Quarterly,* 25 (March 1994), p. 52.

[81] Stephen Reder, "A Hmong Community's Acquisition of English," p. 277 in Bruce T. Downing and Douglas P. Olney, eds., *The Hmong in the West* (Southeast Asian Refugee Studies Project, Center for Urban and Regional Affairs, University of Minnesota, 1982).

[82] Beth Goldstein, *Schooling for Cultural Transition: Hmong Girls and Boys in American High Schools* (Doctoral dissertation, University of Wisconsin, 1985), p. 58.

[83] George M. Scott, Jr., *Migrants Without Mountains: The Politics of Sociocultural Adjustment Among the Lao Hmong Refugees in San Diego* (Doctoral dissertation, University of California, San Diego, 1986), p. 290.

[84] Goldstein, *Schooling for Cultural Transition,* p. 110.

[85] Scott, *Migrants Without Mountains,* p. 152, footnote 1. See also Joan Strouse, *Continuing Themes in U.S. Educational Policy for Immigrants and Refugees: The Hmong Experience* (Doctoral dissertation, University of Wisconsin, 1985), pp. 156–157.

[86] Scott, *Migrants Without Mountains,* p. 33, footnote 11.

[87] Sylvia S. Lopez-Romano, *Integration of Community and Learning among Southeast Asian Newcomer Hmong Parents and Children* (Doctoral dissertation, University of San Francisco, 1991), pp. 56–57.

[88] Chan, *Hmong,* p. 116.

[89] Ibid., p. 123.

[90] Ibid., p. 154.

[91] Ibid., p. 155.

[92] See, for example, ibid., p. 221.

[93] See top panel of Table 8.8 in Ruben G. Rumbaut, "The Refugee Adaptation Process," p. 169 in David W. Haines, ed., *Refugees as Immigrants. Cambodians, Laotians, and Vietnamese in America* (Rowman and Littlefield, 1989).

[94] See discussion of this matter in the preceding chapter, pp. 145–147.

[95] See Wendy D. Walker, *The Other Side of the Asian Academic Success Myth: The Hmong Story,* December 1988, p. 8. ERIC ED 302 609.

[96] Goldstein, *Schooling for Cultural Transition,* p. 180. This school was not in San Diego.

[97] Ibid., p. 192.

[98] Wendy D. Walker, *The Challenge of the Hmong Culture: A Study of Teacher, Counselor and Administrator Training in a Time of Changing Demographics* (Doctoral dissertation, Harvard University, 1989), p. 138.

[99] Ibid., p. 178.

[100] Literacy and Language Program, Northwest Regional Educational Laboratory and others, *The Hmong Resettlement Study,* Volume 1 (Office of Refugee Resettlement, U.S. Department of Health and Human Services, April 1985), p. 146.

[101] Goldstein, *Schooling for Cultural Transitions,* pp. 64–65.

[102] Ibid., p. 136.

[103] Ibid., p. 146.

[104] Literacy and Language Program, *The Hmong Resettlement Study,* p. 180.

[105] Ibid., p. 176.

[106] Amy Catlin, *The Hmong from Asia to Providence* (Center for Hmong Lore, Roger Williams Park Museum, Providence, Rhode Island, 1981), p. 30. See also Scott, *Migrants Without Mountains,* p. 179.

[107] Chan, *Hmong,* p. 230.

[108] Ibid., p. 157.

[109] Ibid., p. 202.

[110] Eddie A. Calderon, "The Impact of Indochinese Resettlement in the Phillips and Elliot Park Neighborhoods in South Minneapolis," p. 368 in Bruce T. Downing and Douglas P. Olney, eds., *The Hmong in the West* (Southeast Asian Refugee Studies Project, Center for Urban and Regional Affairs, University of Minnesota, 1982), p. 368.

[111] Goldstein, *Schooling for Cultural Transitions,* p. 216.

[112] Ibid., p. 220.

[113] Ibid., p. 232.

[114] Catherine S. Gross, "The Hmong in Isla Vista: Obstacles and Enhancements to Adjustment," p. 152 in Glenn Hendricks and others, eds., *The Hmong in Transition* (Center for Migration Studies, 1986).

[115] Goldstein, *Schooling for Cultural Transitions,* p. 138.

[116] Shareen Abramson and Gordon Lindberg, *Report on the Educational Progress of Hmong Students in Fresno Unified School District,* November 1982, p. 7. ERIC ED 224 574.

[117] Downing and Olney, *The Hmong in the West,* p. 368.

[118] Goldstein, *Schooling for Cultural Transitions,* p. 192.

[119] Walker, *The Challenge of the Hmong Culture,* p. 1.

[120] Ibid., p. 2.

[121] Ibid., p. 84.

[122] Ibid., p. 177.

[123] Ibid., p. 73.

[124] Lila Jacobs, *Differential Participation and Skill Levels in Four Hmong Third Grade Students:*

The Social and Cultural Context of Teaching and Learning (Doctoral dissertation, University of California, Santa Barbara, 1987), pp. 90–91.

[125] Ibid., p. 269.

[126] Walker, *The Challenge of the Hmong Culture*, p. 92.

[127] Literacy and Language Program, *The Hmong Resettlement Study*, p. 165.

[128] Walker, *The Challenge of the Hmong Culture*, p. 77.

[129] Ibid., p. 90.

[130] Catlin, *The Hmong from Asia to Providence*, p. 31. See also Literacy and Language Program, *The Hmong Resettlement Study*, p. 247.

[131] Ibid., p. 31.

[132] Literacy and Language Program, *The Hmong Resettlement Study*, pp. 169–170.

[133] Renee E. Lemieux, *A Study of the Adaptation of Hmong First, Second and Third Graders to the Minneapolis Public Schools* (Doctoral dissertation, University of Minnesota, 1985), p. 16.

[134] Jacobs, *Differential Participation and Skill Levels*, p. 97.

[135] Literacy and Language Program, *The Hmong Resettlement Study*, p. 192.

[136] Walker, *The Other Side*, p. 23.

[137] Karen R. Green and Stephen Reder, "Factors in Individual Acquisition of English: A Longitudinal Study of Hmong Adults," p. 314 in Glenn Hendricks and others, eds., *The Hmong in Transition* (Center for Migration Studies, 1986).

[138] Ibid., p. 317.

[139] Finian J. McGinn, *Hmong Literacy Among Hmong Adolescents and the Use of Hmong Literacy During Resettlement* (Doctoral dissertation, University of San Francisco, 1989), p. 17.

[140] *Life of Shong Lue Yang: Hmong "Mother of Writing." Keeb Kwm Soob Lwj Yaj: Hmoob "Niam Ntawu,"* translated by Mitt Moua and Yang See. Southeast Asian Refugee Studies, Occasional Papers, Number 9 (Center for Urban and Regional Affairs, University of Minnesota, 1990); and Halpern and Tinsman, "Education and Nation-Building in Laos," *Comparative Education Review*, 10 (October 1966), p. 505.

[141] McGinn, *Hmong Literacy*, p. 59.

[142] Ibid., p. 76.

[143] Ibid., p. 87.

[144] Ibid., p. 83.

[145] Literacy and Language Program, *The Hmong Resettlement Study*, p. 186.

[146] See Jeremy Hein, "From Migrant to Minority: Hmong Refugees and the Social Construction of Identity in the United States," *Sociological Inquiry*, 64 (August 1994), p. 288 and Literacy and Language Program, *The Hmong Resettlement Study*, p. 12 and p. 6, Appendix 4.

[147] Literacy and Language Program, *The Hmong Resettlement Study*, p. 172.

[148] Ibid., p. 179.

[149] Miles McNall and Timothy Dunnigan, "Hmong Youth in St. Paul's Public Schools," *CURA Reporter*, 23 (March 1993), p. 12.

[150] Walker, *The Challenge of the Hmong Culture*, p. 160.

[151] Mao Yang, "The Education of Hmong Women," *Vietnam Generation*, 2 (1990), p. 66.

[152] Sarah R. Mason, "Training Hmong Women: For Marginal Work on Entry Into the Mainstream," p. 101 in Glenn L. Hendricks and others, eds., *The Hmong in Transition* (Center for Migration Studies, 1986).

[153] Ibid., p. 109.

[154] Ibid., p. 118.

[155] See Literacy and Language Program, *The Hmong Resettlement Study*, p. 198; and Franklin Ng, "Towards a Second Generation Hmong History," *Amerasia Journal*, 19 (1993), p. 55.

[156] Ng, "Towards a Second Generation Hmong History," p. 63.

[157] Gross, "The Hmong in Isla Vista," p. 153.

[158] Literacy and Language Program, *The Hmong Resettlement Study*, p. 198.

[159] Carolyn S. Nayematsu, "Asian-Pacific Learning Resource Center," p. 22 in John Nobuya Tsuchida and others, *Culturally Sensitive Academic Support Services. A Successful Retention Model at the University of Minnesota* (Office of the Associate Vice President for Academic Affairs and Associate Provost, University of Minnesota, June 1993).

[160] Ibid., p. 23.

[161] Ibid., p. 27.

[162] Ibid., p. 24.

[163] William Ruefle, William H. Ross, and Diane Mandell, "Attitudes Toward Southeast Asian Immigrants in a Wisconsin Community," *International Migration Review*, 26 (Autumn 1992), p. 878.

[164] Ibid., p. 885.

[165] Peter Schmidt, "La Crosse To Push Ahead With Income Based Busing Plan," *Education Week*, August 5, 1992. See also Muriel Cohen, "Wisconsin City Will Mix Students by Family Income," *Boston Globe*, December 26, 1991.

[166] Peter Schmidt, "Bold Busing Plan Leads to Deep Divides in Wausau," *Education Week*, December 15, 1993.

[167] Peter Schmidt, "New Board Members in Wausau Ditch District's Controversial Busing Scheme, *Education Week*, May 18, 1994. For general comments, see Ray Beck, "The Ordeal of Immigration in Wausau," *Atlantic Monthly*, 273 (April 1994), pp. 84–97; and Jack Griswold, "Hmong in Wausau," *Atlantic Monthly*, 274 (July 1994), pp. 6–8, with reply by Beck, p. 9.

[168] Hamilton-Merritt, *Tragic Mountains*, p. 519.

[169] Hein, "From Migrant to Minority," p. 285.

[170] Strouse, *Continuing Themes*, p. 152.

[171] Walker, *The Challenge of the Hmong Culture*, p. 24.

[172] Scott, *Migrants Without Mountains*, p. 486, footnote 1.

[173] Quincy, *Hmong*, p. 203.

[174] Beck, "The Ordeal of Immigration in Wausau," p. 88.

CHAPTER NINE

Hong Kong

Hong Kong became a British Crown colony in three phases. Between 1840 and 1842, Britain seized the Chinese island as part of the Opium War, so-called because the immediate occasion was the confiscation of British merchants' opium that had been shipped into China in violation of Chinese laws. As early as 1800, China had prohibited importation of opium, but European and American shippers continued the lucrative trade. The Treaty of Nanking in 1842 made Hong Kong a British possession. In 1860, another British-initiated military adventure led to the acquisition of Kowloon and Stonecutters Island. These became part of Hong Kong. Finally, in 1898, the British forced the Chinese to lease to them the New Territories for 99 years; these were administered as Hong Kong territory.

Until 1842, Hong Kong had been Chinese, but it played only a marginal role in national affairs.[1] Populated by peasants and fisherpeople, all but a few lived in small villages in traditional Chinese fashion. Many of these villages had tiny schools financed by local people who were sufficiently wealthy to contribute. There was no tuition and fees were minimal. Children attended when they could and remained, typically, for 2 or 3 years. They gained an unsteady grasp of reading and writing. One did not need either for success in fishing or farming although the elementary numeracy they commanded was of practical use.

More than opium profits attracted the British to Hong Kong. They sought to make the colony into the principal port of entry for the world's trade with China. Constituting at the time the greatest naval and economic power in the world, Britain was well equipped for the task. It needed laborers who were in plentiful supply in Canton and surrounding territory; this great Chinese city lay less than 100 miles from Hong Kong. British companies contributed capital and selected Chinese-speaking agents—compradors—who could represent their interests with governments and other firms.

Britain did not intend to make Hong Kong into a settlement of Englishmen. Not only was the island small; more important, trade and political relations with the China market required businessmen who themselves were thoroughly Chinese. By 1894, the ratio of adult Chinese to English adults in Hong Kong was 160:1.[2] The great majority of the former were laborers, a small minority compradors and related persons, and the latter consisted of every class except a proletariat.[3] Between 1855 and 1900, a total of 1,830,572 Chinese arrived from China.[4] Yet the population of Hong Kong in 1937 was only about 750,000.[5] The explanation of this trend is that few Englishmen or Chinese considered Hong Kong to be their permanent home. Chinese shuttled back and forth between China and Hong Kong according to economic need and cultural and family obligations. As long as the needed labor could be had, the colony's rulers were content with a fluctuating population. For one thing, under such a circumstance there was less pressure for community and family infrastructure and correspondingly less need for government to spend on such facilities.

Hong Kong was governed by European businessmen and English-educated bureaucrats who consulted closely with the wealthiest, most powerful businessmen in the Chinese community. "By the last two decades of the nineteenth century," said Lethbridge, "means of communication between Governmental and influential Chinese community leaders had become official, organized, and institutionalized, to the mutual benefit of both groups."[6] Chinese leaders did not customarily consult with the mass of poorer Chinese. The ties of interest and ideology that bound the governmental leaders and the leading Chinese were stronger than any traditional cultural connections with the mass of Chinese. During the 1920s, when the new University of Hong Kong began producing large numbers of professionals, some of these additions to the Chinese middle class were able to compete with Europeans. A few moved nearer the circles of power.

A century after the British became the proprietors of Hong Kong, government policy remained unchanged in one respect: The protection and encouragement of business interests formed the core of government action. Little, if anything, was done by law in the areas of labor, social welfare, or education. Almost unending flows of Chinese labor provided low-cost workers. Because few brought families along with them, neither the government of Hong Kong nor private employers needed to finance the building of schools, hospitals, and housing installations. Tax policies favored the very rich, and the government rarely investigated private activities even if commanded to do so by regulation or statute.

The ruling combine shared a common ideology that included a profound personal racism:

> The Chinese were despised and treated with contempt as inferior beings. . . .
> There was no social mixing. . . . Chinese could not walk abroad after nine o'clock
> in the evening without a note from their employers, and had to carry lanterns after
> dark.[7]

Early on, Chinese were not permitted to serve on juries nor be employed as attorneys. This prohibition was lifted in 1858.[8] Sir John Pope Hennessy, who served as governor of the colony between 1877 and 1882, was exceptional in his opposition to racism:

> [He] was the first Governor to be shocked by the unequal treatment of the Chinese.
> . . . He took the first steps to translate into reality the sentiment of non-discrimination between races which had appeared in the Governor's instruction in 1866
> and in British colonial policy even earlier. He treated the Chinese as partners, and
> largely because of this he was hated by the Europeans.[9]

In 1897, nocturnal Chinese strollers no longer needed their employer's permission to walk.[10] More basic attitudes, however, persisted. As Lethbridge observed, British "attitudes to Chinese were . . . close to middle-class attitudes to servants in Britain, for servants in that country were perceived as members of another race—dank, incomprehensible, illiterate troglodytes."[11]

The working alliance contracted between the colony's rulers and the Chinese elite did not extend to informal social interaction. Housing, for example, was restricted, even to the wealthiest Chinese. The Peak, an area of opulent housing for the colony's leaders, was open to Chinese "so long as Chinese conformed to certain residential standards."[12] In 1941, however, the district was barred altogether to Chinese residence. Five years later, the exclusion was lifted.[13] Naturalization was another area where Chinese were de facto penalized. Britain had no general naturalization statute. Persons wishing to become British citizens had to convince Parliament to pass a law relating to those specific persons. Between 1880 and 1900, when such requests failed, the Hong Kong government enacted measures declaring 53 persons as British citizens only in the colony.[14] A more explicit assertion of the lack of Chinese worth was not required.

The meager education imparted in village schools led to low literacy, although the numbers were puzzling. In the early 1920s, Endacott wrote, "it was estimated that 90 percent of the peasants of the colony could neither read nor write."[15] Barely a decade later, however, according to Agassi, in 1931, "51 percent of the population aged 10 and upward could read, 74 percent of the men and only 19 percent of the women."[16] It is difficult to reconcile these statements. Placing them in the context of changes in schooling may help explain the differences. Unfortunately, the schooling figures are not an improvement over those for literacy. Thus, for the year 1865, two sources agree that there were 14,000 school-age children in Hong Kong. But one reports 1,870 attended school whereas the other states there were 514 students.[17] Around 1880, about 28% of school-age were reportedly attending school.[18] In 1947, the figure had risen to

63%.[19] (Just two years later, Communists in China took power and a new chapter in Hong Kong's history began.)

Defects riddled the entire system of schools, even when the government contributed funds. Endacott wrote:

> The government-maintained and assisted schools were often mere hovels, particularly in the villages, and in 1887 it was reported that only ten or twelve schools out of 204 in the colony were in decent buildings. Standards of attainment remained low.[20]

Overcrowding was the norm. Although teachers were honored, those working in small private schools were not as well trained and received very low salaries. One historian states that teachers were paid only a bit more than coolies.[21] In many village schools—renamed district schools in 1882—English was taught, primarily in the Sixth and Seventh Forms (i.e., grades). "Data given in 1900 showed that of the total number of students who attended these schools, over 90% never got beyond the fourth standard and less than 3% ever succeeded in reaching the seventh standard."[22] Thus, exceedingly few poor Chinese students gained a firm foundation in their study of English. Even when they did, those who lived in the countryside had hardly any opportunities to practice their English with others. Schools organized by Christian missionaries were another institution aimed at poorer Chinese children. These schools used Chinese as the main language of instruction. About 1870, 30 mission schools educated some 40% of Hong Kong's students.[23] These schools received government funds in the form of grants-in-aid. Their curriculum consisted of the three Rs with instruction in needlework added for girls.[24]

In 1862, Hong Kong authorities created the Central School, an elite institution designed primarily for wealthy Chinese students. Admission was by examination only. Chinese classic texts were the core of the curriculum during a 7-year course of study. The essentials of English were also taught:

> The students were satisfied with their education in Chinese as soon as they were able to repeat from memory the maxims of the ancient sages, and left school immediately after they had acquired sufficient knowledge of English to enable them to find a position in the commercial firms.[25]

Many of the students were children of traders who were well acquainted with the educational requirements of this employment. Whether out of fear of competition with their children or simple snobbishness, wealthy traders sought endlessly to gain special educational privileges for their sons. In 1901, "eight leading Chinese petitioned for schools where children of the better classes could be sent so as not to mix with those of the lower classes."[26] The request was granted. British parents also requested separate schools apart from Chinese. This, too, was approved. Wealthy Chinese frequently sent their sons to China for secondary schooling. Advanced training in Chinese as well as the making of contacts on the mainland were commercially advantageous.

Because relatively few women emigrated to Hong Kong during the early years of Hong Kong history, family formation lagged. The trend shifted decisively during the years 1901 through 1931: "In 1901, for every 1,000 males there were 387 females, while in the years 1911, 1921, and 1931 the increases in order were 433, 642 and 749 per thousand males."[27] In 1870, girls constituted only 8.5% of all children in schools.[28] Just 4 years before, Frederick Stewart, a major figure in Hong Kong education, had declared:

> I should be glad if more could be done for girls in the Colony in the way of giving them a purely Chinese education . . . without turning their heads by teaching them English or any other so-called accomplishment which would give them a distaste for their humbler sphere in life.[29]

Whether immodest or not, during the last years of the 19th Century, the number of girls going to school rose significantly: From 8.5% in 1870, it increased to 18% in 1880 and 32% in 1890.[30] In 1900, the figure reached 41.3%.[31] During the same years, however, they were subject to discrimination. In the 1880s, for example, "government schools tended to have few girls, who were sent to the mission schools, where they were taught by ladies."[32] The likelihood of having a trained teacher was greater in government schools than in mission schools. When a few girls did attend government schools, they were placed in an all-Chinese track. Anglo-Chinese schools, ones that used English as an instructional language, were reserved for boys. Per-pupil government grants were less for girls than for boys. This was still true in the late 1920s.[33] When the University of Hong Kong began enrolling students in 1912, it refused to accept women applicants. This did not change until 1921.[34]

Exceedingly few students attended Hong Kong University. One who had been there between 1930 and 1934 recalled, "In those days we only had about 400 students in the entire University. And most came from the upper crust of the society. I would say that 90% of them were children from the wealthy families."[35] Nor was the University much of an academic center: "Until World War II . . . [the] Faculty of Arts [was] more a finishing school for young ladies and a teachers' training college of sorts than a center of intellectual and cultural activity. . . ."[36] During the years 1928 to 1933, women students were primarily enrolled in the Arts and about one third were in Medicine; few could be found in Science and fewer still in Engineering.[37] At a time when even leading countries like the United States had only a fledgling industrial-research structure, there was little call for training a scientific research workforce in a port of entry.

Because Hong Kong's main business was the moving of goods for long distances and the servicing of such shipments, numerous workers were needed in shipping, warehousing, insurance, finance, and related fields. Except for a thin layer of decision makers and specialists at the top, a great mass of wage workers operated the port. Employers, the largest of whom also had predominant political power in the port city, valued obedience and passivity in their employees.

When workers attempted to compel wage increases and working conditions improvements, the police could be counted on to stop such efforts. Employers and colonial officials also feared possible influences emanating from China that could mobilize the colony's Chinese residents into a nationalist movement for independence from Britain. Also, when left-wing influences permeated internal Chinese politics, they could be confidently expected to pour over an international boundary.

In 1925, a general strike broke out in Hong Kong and continued for some 16 months. From the viewpoint of the colony's elite, the action took on the appearance of a revolution. Joining the demonstrating workers were students and other Chinese. Although force was used successfully to suppress the movement, public authorities sought other means to prevent similar explosions of protest from occurring. Governmental promotion of the doctrines of Confucianism was one such means. These doctrines had no room for class conflict nor nationalism. Instead, they stressed social stability, the identity of the ruler as the father of the family of the Chinese people, and a search for a common philosophical truth that was equally binding on ruler and ruled. One writer advocated the incorporation of Confucian doctrine into the schools. He called this doctrine, "probably the best antidote to the pernicious doctrines of Bolshevism [i.e., Communism], and is certainly the most powerful conservative force, and the greatest influence for good."[38] Tsai commented that, "in the revival of Confucianism the main objective of both the Chinese elite and the colonial authorities coincided—to revive a conservative ideology for better social control."[39] He concludes that "it proved only a vain, quixotic attempt."[40]

This did not end the matter as the colonial government pressed on. Under Governor Sir Cecil Clementi, the Chinese literati of Hong Kong were showered with jobs and honors and in Hong Kong University and in the secondary schools, the study of Chinese history and language took on a new importance. As Luk observed:

> By patronizing the literati, Clementi sought to uphold for the Chinese people of Hong Kong and elsewhere, an approach to China and Chinese culture that would be socially credible and viable and, at the same time, provide a political alternative to the nationalistic appeal of the modern intelligentsia, the protestors, and the revolutionary parties supporting the general strike. Thus, he tried to balance Chinese cultural tradition against contemporary Chinese nationalism.[41]

This attempt to politicize the curriculum had little effect as its goals were all too transparent.

Some 12 years later, toward the end of 1941, Japan invaded and occupied Hong Kong. As these events unfolded, many looters appeared on the scene. Sweeting reported:

> At least one civilian noted that opportunity was taken to settle old scores, as mobs of relatively poor and disadvantaged local Chinese ransacked the homes of the lo-

cal Chinese and Eurasian elite, accusing them of being the running dogs of British colonialism and gleefully roaring *"Sing Lei! Sing Lei!* [Victory! Victory!]" to mark their own long-awaited victory.[42]

The use of English in the schools was outlawed and replaced by Chinese. Japanese was taught in the schools and Japan's history and culture entered the curriculum. To a small degree, the poor made certain gains as the restricted character of British-designed education was discarded.[43] As the occupation wore on, however, fewer and fewer Japanese resources were devoted to education with the result that the number of students shrank drastically.[44] Under these conditions, any advantage accruing to poor children simply faded away.

The end of World War II in 1945 unleashed a civil war in China that lasted for 4 years. In 1949, the Chinese Communist Party took power. Hong Kong was deeply affected by these events.

Every major Communist advance on the road to power heightened the anxiety of the propertied classes in China. In many industrial areas, this took the form of shipment of capital overseas, including dismantled machinery and raw materials as well as money in Chinese banks. Reportedly, 10 to 30 billion Chinese dollars were shifted from Shanghai to Hong Kong during a 4-month period in 1946.[45] Other capital came from Guangdong Province, adjacent to Hong Kong. Emigration was another response. During 1947, Hong Kong's population increased from 600,000 to 1,600,000.[46] This stream of refugees originated in China and consisted of a number of skilled persons:

> Many had middle class origins, having been civil servants, teachers and small entrepreneurs. In Hong Kong they had to take menial jobs in order to survive, but they did not consider themselves to be working class, and they lacked industrial militancy more likely to be found in a well-established urban proletariat.[47]

By 1953, public authorities in the colony were moved to limit the flow of refugees from China. Never before had Hong Kong taken such a measure.

By the early 1950s, the refugees had effected a great change in Hong Kong. It had become an industrialized colony, one of the few such in Asia or elsewhere. Refugee capital and low-wage labor were employed in numerous small factories of fewer than 20 workers. Hong Kong became an exporter, thereby complementing its role as a port of entry. As employment opportunities grew, both legal and illegal immigration also expanded. Entire families arrived for lifelong residence rather than adult males whose wives and children remained in China. Although unemployment remained low, working conditions and pay rates lagged grievously. As Halliday wrote:

> [In 1974, there was] no mimimum wage . . . no sickness benefits, no unemployment insurance; no pensions; no insurance provisions with young children; no guaranteed free medical aid. In 1968 Hong Kong workers had the longest working day and the longest working week of city dwellers in Southeast Asia: 58 percent worked 7 days a week, and 52 percent 10 hours or more per day. The 1971 Census showed

174,439 workers working a least 75 hours per week, while 13,792 of these were working at least 105 hours per week.[48]

Partly offsetting these conditions was a rise in industrial workers' real wages, which "doubled from the late 1950s to the mid 1970s."[49] In the country as a whole, great inequality in the distribution of income prevailed.[50]

The governance of Hong Kong remained unaffected by economic expansion. A historical alliance of business and bureaucracy perpetuated its control of all levels of government. The general population, numbering 6 million by the 1980s, had no vote. After the mid-20th century, one British government after another strengthened the hand of the Hong Kong alliance by releasing its government from various imperial financial controls. Advisory bodies to the government of Hong Kong were lopsidedly composed of the most favored elements in society. As Leung found in a study:

> 69.15 percent of the members of the . . . [appointive] Councils and of a number of important advisory boards and panels in 1975 were made up of representatives of the major business concerns and organizations. . . . Organized labor and low-income groups constituted only 0.5 percent.[51]

Members of the managing boards of the largest corporations in the colony were intricately interlocked both in the firms and government committees.

Within such a political context, public education fared poorly. Expenditures on establishing and supporting public schools were extremely meager although their rate of increase was "glacial."[52] A double dual school system was created. Among the public schools, great differences in quality existed, depending principally on the language of instruction—English or Chinese. Outside the public schools, a private system existed that was generally acknowledged to be inferior. Especially in the realm of secondary and higher education, the private enrollment far exceeded that of the public realm. The government only reluctantly yielded to public demand for improved education after World War II but employed a variety of ruses to postpone full implementation of the policy.

The development of free, compulsory, primary education was long and laborious. During the late 1960s, it was reported that "150,000 children between the ages of six and twelve do not get even primary education."[53] In 1968, the government responded weakly to this challenge by cutting fees in some existing schools and facilitating the acquisition of textbooks at no cost to selected students.[54] Neither of these measures actually placed children in schools. After many promises, in 1978, primary schooling was made free and compulsory. The basic motivation for this step lay more in the area of business advantage than in educational policy. European competitors of the Hong Kong textile and other industries had sought to exclude Hong Kong exports to the European Common Market on the ground that the colony employed great numbers of child laborers at the cost of their education.[55]

Before 1978, entrance examinations were given to applicants for primary school. Especially valued were primary schools that had a connection with a secondary school, private or otherwise. Primary schools operated by the government that were tuition free were usually built in or near poor neighborhoods. None had connections with secondary schools. Some 10% of graduates from Chinese-language primaries succeeded in entering the highly valued Anglo-Chinese secondary schools. Kindergartens, operated privately for tuition, were becoming training grounds for children preparing to take the entrance exams for primary school. Poorer people were less able to take advantage of this aid in moving up the educational ladder. The primary entrance exams, for example, covered the same subjects as the crucial Secondary School Entrance Examination (SSEE). Kindergartners are drilled to a point of familiarity with "300–500 Chinese characters, a similar number of English words, and arithmetic up to addition and subtraction of two-digit numbers."[56]

A substantial number of children dropped out of primary school by the sixth grade, which ended primary school. A number of parents complained that government primaries promoted students automatically every year. At the same time, in all primary schools, students were permitted to repeat a maximum of a year's work once in 6 years. In addition, only as many as 6% of enrolled students in primaries could be held back each year. Alternatives to government primaries were government-assisted or outright private schools. Tuition was not nominal. In fact, tuition for private primaries approached that for private secondaries.[57] Government promises made during the early 1970s to improve primary education remained unfulfilled. "[Primary schools remained] overcrowded, often with two schools sharing the same building on a "bi-sessional" basis, and with non-graduate teachers. What were supposed to be temporary measures are still commonplace in 1993, more than twenty years later."[58] Rises in gross enrollment tended to cloak these persistent problems.

Historically, secondary education in Hong Kong was available to a small sector of youth. Before World War II, 37,355 students were in secondary education but in 1948, 3 years after the end of the war, there were only 20,802.[59] The deficit was largely accounted for by the failure of private schooling to recover from the war. During the 1960s and 1970s, almost one third of primary-school graduates succeeded in entering secondary schools.[60] Accomplishment of this goal required the passing of the SSEE. One's grade on the exam determined which specific school one would attend, as well as the degree of scholarship aid to be received. In 1973, over three fifths (62%) of primary graduates failed to score high enough on the SSEE to gain entrance to a government-financed secondary school.[61] About half of this number went to private schools with their families paying tuition. Two researchers noted, "If a child failed in the SSEE, he failed forever no matter what had been his overall performance throughout his primary school career."[62]

In 1978, when primary schooling was made free and compulsory, junior secondary schools (Forms I–III) were included. The following year, as we saw

previously, the government announced a 9-year period of compulsory schooling. Whereas the decision was of considerable import, it seemed to have little to
do with a carefully thought-out policy. There was no prior notice of the action,
nor was any planning done. The Education Commission "was not informed,
still less consulted."[63] This added verisimilitude to the charge that the policy
change had more to do with export policy than education. Once the authorities
had decided to extend the span of schooling—for whatever reason—and incur
greater financial obligations, other steps followed. In 1978, the SSEE was dis-
continued. By no means, however, did this open the floodgates to mass secondary education. The portion of the entire population that had completed secondary education was as follows:[64]

1976	29.2%
1981	36.3%
1986	39.5%

The movement to expand secondary education did not abate.

In 1980, the government introduced the Junior Secondary Education Assessment (JSEA). It was administered at the end of the first 3 years of secondary education and was used to allocate places in Form IV and, thus, government scholarships. This ensured continuation in the college preparation track.[65] A maximum of 40% of Form III students were permitted to pass into Form IV. When
demands arose to add 2 more years of compulsory education, through Form V,
authorities objected. They feared increasing school costs by US $171 million
through the provision of added places in upper secondary (Forms IV–V). (The
ending of JSEA would qualify many more Form III leavers for advanced
schooling than the present 40%.)[66] The colonial government could hardly plead
poverty. Large budget surpluses were not unknown. Because the government
did little borrowing, it was not saddled with large public debt. In fact, interest on
its public debt constituted only 0.4% of the budget, as compared with Britain,
where the corresponding figure was 11.0%.[67]

As of 1980, nearly 9 out of 10 students completing the period of compulsory
schooling chose to go further.[68] Of that number, 40% studied in government-
financed or aided schools and 60% had to depend on private schools. Four years
earlier, when the SSEE was dropped, the percentages were 30 and 70.[69] The private schools were sponsored by private parties ranging from church groups to
individual entrepreneurs seeking personal profit. As a whole, they were held to
be inferior to government and government-aided schools.

Historian Sweeting declared that after World War II, "Hong Kong's educational reconstruction depended . . . heavily on private enterprise schooling
which was declared by government spokespersons to be characteristically ineffi-
cient and corrupt. . . ."[70] Crozier, an education agent, asserted that, "in many of
these schools, trained, semi-trained, and untrained teachers are working for

starvation salaries and are being exploited in several ways."[71] By far, most teachers in these primary and junior secondaries were graduates neither of universities nor teacher-training establishments. Director of Education Kenneth Topley held that, "it would not basically be right for the Government to subvent or otherwise financially assist the private independent schools since they are legally business ventures and to assist them financially is to subsidize profits."[72] Ross wrote that these for-profit schools "generally cut corners as they please."[73] A young woman in Hong Kong pointed to the widespread practice of for-profits to advance students "no matter how they performed on the tests."[74]

During the early 1990s, college graduates in Hong Kong earned salaries from 4 to 10 times larger than the average worker.[75] The pecuniary attraction of a university education grew as the colony became a more important industrial and financial center, and as lower and middling positions in government became more available to Chinese persons. Public opinion polls discovered that "the proportion of the parents who wished their sons to receive higher education rose from about 22 percent in 1951 to 50 percent in 1964, and to 70 percent in 1977."[76] Apparently, this was true of a broad reach of classes, but more so among the wealthiest. "In 1972, 74 percent of those from blue collar and other lower class families wanted very much to attend university, although the proportion was higher among pupils from upper class families (92 percent)."[77]

Around the mid-1980s, from 2 to 3% of Hong Kong's college-age population was attending a university.[78] At the University of Hong Kong alone, in 1984, "over 15,000 applications were received for 1,600 freshmen places. . . ."[79] This Harvard-like level of acceptance–rejections for an institution of the status of UHK was most restrictive. A certain number of UHK students reflected lower-class origins, despite the great selectivity of students in general. Also in their favor was the provision of free places for about 15% of the students. In addition, grants were available to some degree. Unfortunately, the trend was downward during the 1980s. Thus, during the 1979 and 1980 academic year, grants were received by 39.5% of university students in Hong Kong as a whole. Ten years later, the figure was only 20.4%.[80] Over the same period, loans fell from 63.5% to 25.5%. In addition, until 1987 the loans were interest-free but a 2½% interest rate was charged from that date forward.

The Chinese University of Hong Kong, which opened in 1963, enrolled a less selective student body. Ross wrote:

> Over 40% of the students' fathers and over 70% of their mothers had not gone beyond primary school. More than 70% of the fathers had not gone beyond the third year of middle school; for mothers the figure is over 85%.[81]

The occupations of the parents of Chinese UHK were fairly typical of the colony. It was far different in the older UHK.

In 1989, the government announced an expansion program for higher education. A basic reason for the measure was the impending reversion of Hong Kong to China in 1997. Since the reversion had been formalized in 1984, numerous wealthy, educated Hong Kongers had left the colony. Many more planned to do so. The expansion program was designed, among other things, to educate a new governing class to replace the British and Hong Kong Chinese who had administered the colony's affairs for a century and a half. By 1995, the number of first-degree places were to expand from some 7,000 to about 15,000 in both universities, a new institution of science and technology, and two existing colleges. When implemented, about 25% of the college-age group would be accommodated. (As of 1989, the time of announcement, about 8% attended some form of higher education.)

A large contingent of the Hong Kong propertied class, however, did not depend completely on the colony's universities, either present or proposed. Instead, almost as many students attended overseas institutions as students attended at home. For example, as the 1995 goal of 15,000 places approached, in 1993, 13,752 Hong Kong students attended higher education institutions in the United States.[82] A number of others were college students in Britain, Canada, Australia, and elsewhere.

These overseas students had, with almost no exception, attended the best secondary schools in Hong Kong, which were taught in English and whose curricula were largely geared toward preparation for university work. Their parents were among the wealthiest in the colony. One reason for the dominant choice of American colleges or universities was that their entrance requirements were often less formidable than those of similar institutions in the British Commonwealth.[83] By the early 1990s, there were at least 50,000 alumni of American universities in Hong Kong.[84] Elite families who were exploring a possible move to the United States—a large number during the late 1980s and early 1990s—had all the more reason to send their older children to scout out possibilities. As Skeldon wrote in 1994, "Ten to twelve thousand poeple have left Hong Kong annually for the United States over the last two decades."[85] During the 1950s, the number was about 15,500 over the decade but 75,000 during the 1960s. During the years 1982 to 1992, 135,449 Hong Kong residents entered the United States as immigrants.[86] In Hawaii alone, during 1991 and 1992, some 500 Hong Kong students were in higher education.[87]

Undoubtedly, the annual short-term movement of wealthy students overseas reduced somewhat the pressure for admission into Hong Kong universities. It did not, however, lead to the admission of unqualified aspirants who had not passed the required examinations.[88] On the other hand, the growing exodus of entire upper-class families from Hong Kong into the early 1990s did serve to diminish the availability of high-scoring secondary graduates. According to Morris and associates, in higher education, "modal entry qualifications in 1992 were already close to the borderline for acceptability."[89] Hong Kong, however, had never lacked for bright, poor students. The problem had always been rather to find the physical places to enroll them.

For working-class students who were unable to gain entrance to higher education, there were few good alternatives. Technical training was one, but opportunities for such training were scarce. One reason for this was the failure of the Hong Kong economy to develop high-tech industries as a number of neighboring economies were doing (Singapore and Malaysia). Economic planners in Hong Kong were not accustomed to prodding the economic elite into departing from traditional ventures.[90] During the late 1960s, an observer reported that, "the demand for technical training exceeds the vacancies for training by no less than eight to one."[91] At the outset of the 1990s, the situation was no better. "But at present there are an insufficient number of technical colleges and industrial training centers in Hong Kong. The ratio of qualified applicants to full-time vacancies is 10:1."[92] This comment was written by a visiting educator from China where higher education opportunities were also not plentiful but industrial training was expanding rapidly in community colleges and elsewhere.

Language of instruction has been a major problem of schooling in Hong Kong. The Cantonese dialect was the first language of the 98% of the colony's population that is Chinese. Once Hong Kong became British property, English formed a central priority in the colony's schooling. Aside from shipping and financial records, however, very little English literacy was required to carry on the work of the port. Cauldwell wrote recently:

> As long as workers know enough of the language to take an order in English, to follow directions, or to paste a "Made in Hong Kong" label right-side up on a box of . . . toys manufactured for export, then the educational system has done its part in serving the corporate-industrial machinery."[93]

Outside the workplace, few Hong Kongers felt a need to be bilingual in Cantonese and English. Many, perhaps most, community needs could be met by institutions utilizing one or the other language. Schools, newspapers, recreational services, and necessities of life could be obtained with the aid of Cantonese or Mandarin alone. According to Lee, for example, "there are eight English and 54 Chinese-language newspapers being published every day in 1983."[94]

Knowledge of English, however, was critical for obtaining one of the best-paid and most secure jobs.[95] Parents knew this well and could most often be found urging their children to master English. Although the same parents might also press schools to find a place in the curriculum for at least some classical Chinese subjects, they could be depended on to advocate the superiority of English as a language of instruction. British educators came to the same conclusion but by another pathway. Frederick Stewart was for 17 years the inspector of government schools in Hong Kong. He advocated the learning of English as a means of introducing Hong Kongers to the values of Western civilization.[96] Allied to this view was that of an early governor of Hong Kong who urged government schools to, "ensure that their students became Chinese Englishmen."[97] The ideology of English civilization endured in the secondary-school curriculum where English literature and history played a prominent role.

Through the years, the government spent far more on teaching English than on instruction in Chinese, particularly in secondary schools. The examination system and student selectivity in general operated as a means of promoting English. As late as 1990, education authorities decided to track graduates of primary schools on the basis of their proficiency in Chinese and English, a measure that created an additional structural encouragement for English.[98] Another institutionalized practice enabled an interested person to discover whether the graduate had taken his or her examinations in English or Chinese. Secondary schools were called Anglo-Chinese when their instructional language was English except for Chinese language and history courses. In reality, much Cantonese crept into a variety of courses, out of necessity if not design.[99] Kanwit reported that, "some schools . . . [use] public address systems to monitor classes to check that teachers are not slipping into Chinese too often."[100]

The educational consequences of learning in a foreign language were clear. In 1990, an Education Commission report concluded:

> that just 30% of the territory's students are capable of learning via English medium instruction (and thus recommends that 70% of the students be taught in Cantonese, with vaguely defined bridging courses used to prepare such students for examinations in English).[101]

Another study, by Brimer, found that "the language of instruction makes no significant difference in the case of the top 30 percent of the ability range. . . ."[102] Little historical evidence exists to suggest that the educational bureaucracy was much concerned about English-language difficulties in the lower 70%. What do appear repeatedly in that literature, however, are references to widespread and continuing problems. "Grossly inadequate,"[103] is Gibbons's characterization of the English commanded by entering secondary-school students. University courses confront students with great difficulties, is a parallel observation. The students are relatively slow readers.[104] Osgood, writing about an island community of 9,000 people, noted that "primary school graduates who have had all the prescribed course work in English cannot necessarily understand the language, to say nothing of speaking it readily."[105] (Because the study of English in island schools began in the third grade and the schools extended only through sixth grade, "all the prescribed course work" was offered during 4 years. Fewer than 2% of the population of school age or more on the island had gone beyond the sixth grade.)[106] A Chinese educator–observer was told by an education official that "only 20 percent of the students are able to understand courses taught in English."[107] Many observers also frequently report a generally low level of competency in English speech by teachers. All in all, difficulties with English must have played a major role in the high dropout rate among secondary school students.

Among the Chinese in Hong Kong, their native language was not considered a pariah tongue. Parents almost always used it at home. More recently, "within at least some sectors of the student community . . . the use of the English language . . . has become a cause of social rejection or at least of adverse comment." [108] In the past, especially early in the 20th century, the absence of Westerners who were able to speak and write Chinese underscored the need for an instructional language the Western teachers could handle. More recently, however, "most of the teachers of content subjects in Hong Kong are . . . Chinese." [109] This raises a realistic possibility of Chinese as a general language of instruction. Educationally, the move has much to support it. Tung reported that "evidence has consistently shown that, for the majority of the students, teaching through the medium of Chinese produces better academic results." [110] Yu and Atkinson pointed out that "pupils could write better in Chinese than in English." [111] The comparative lack of sufficient Chinese-language textbooks for various subject matters is already a matter of planning. A government grant to publishers to assist in creating Chinese-language materials has been made.[112] Few secondary schools manifested support for the movement toward Chinese-medium schools. In 1986, when the Education Department queried 316 schools on whether they were willing to convert to complete Chinese-language education, fewer than 13% replied in the affirmative.

Since World War II, women in Hong Kong have become better educated and more broadly employed in an expanding economy. Yet, as Salaff contended, "the gap between men and women in education, employment, and earnings remains nearly as wide today as in the past." [114] In the early 1980s, women earned wages that were 70% of those earned by men.[115] During the 1970s, more women entered the labor force, the number of children per married woman fell by nearly one third, the percent of women completing secondary school rose from 19.5% to 35.3%, and the portion of women lacking any education dropped from 28.5% to 18.3%. Women university graduates greatly increased their participation in the labor market, from 23.6% to 66.3%. Yet, "the main increase in women's employment has been in clerical jobs." [116] Thus, in 1986 two thirds of all clerical workers were women although they constituted only one fifth of managerial and administrative workers.[117] Turner and associates, in a survey of employment, found that women made up more than 40% of professional and technical workers, "but this appears to be due to a particular concentration of females with upper secondary education in the lower ranks of these jobs." [118]

Women made their greatest advances in the field of education. By 1988, they constituted 50.1% of enrollment in secondary schools, 48.0% in primary schools, and 42.2% in universities.[119] The progress was somewhat diluted, however, by the fact that a given amount of education earned more income for men than for women.[120] Women were most numerous in less remunerative positions. Thus, they made up 99% of kindergarten teachers, 51% of secondary-school teachers, but only 28% of postsecondary teachers.[121] At the University of Hong Kong in 1986, women faculty were least represented in the highest ranks.[122]

Obstacles to further advances were resistant. Pearson, writing in 1990, reported there was "still some prejudice against girls pursuing an education beyond the compulsory limit [that is, at age 15 and older]."[123] Until 1981, women civil servants were denied certain family benefits (housing allowances and medical or dental treatment) that their male counterparts received.[124] Many mothers who were working frequently relinquished their jobs in order to remain at home to supervise their children's homework.[125] Historically, government grants for the schooling of girls were smaller than those for boys.[126] Boys continued to receive priority on family finances for schooling and their sisters had to remain content with inferior schooling.[127]

In a real sense, contemporary Hong Kong was created by the Chinese revolution that culminated in 1949. An industrial society migrated from Shanghai and Canton and transformed an entrepot. Meanwhile, China itself underwent a change into the fastest-growing poor country in the world. In the process, both Hong Kong and neighboring South China became increasingly integrated as a regional economic zone. Unlike 1949, however, during the 1980s and 1990s, Hong Kong capital was invested heavily in the Guangdong area adjacent on the north to China. The great attraction was high profits derived from plentiful low-wage labor and land prices far lower than in Hong Kong. Capital also flowed in from Taiwan, Japan, and the United States. By 1992, two thirds of all foreign investment in China originated in Hong Kong. Only about one fourth of the industrial workers employed by Hong Kong factories worked in the colony; the rest worked in the Guangdong region.[128] Midway in the same year, "Taiwan manufactures in south China industry burgeoned, involving some 5,517 enterprises and $4.75 billion. . . ."[129]

At the same time, a contrary movement was underway: Hong Kong was losing large parts of its middle class. They were fleeing out of fear of the fate that awaited them in 1997 when Hong Kong reverted to China.[130] In 1988, a Task Force of the Legislative Council characterized them: "Emigrants consisted of a disproportionately high percentage of people in the economically active group aged 25–44, with university degrees, and were professional, technical, administrative and managerial workers."[131] They were also wealthier than average. A number of those who remained did so alone, having left their families in new permanent quarters overseas. Many middle-class Hong Kongers tried to get permission to move to England but were turned back. Some 3.25 million who held British Dependent Territory Citizen passports were denied the right to settle there.[132] In 1990, the British Parliament passed a nationality bill.

> [It] granted full citizenship or the "right of abode" [in Great Britain] to only fifty thousand elite Hong Kongers and their families (about one-quarter of a million out of a total population . . . [of 6 million]. This special subcategory of Chinese is carefully chosen from among householders (presumably predominantly male) who have British connections in government, business, or some other organization. A point system for different occupations like accountancy and law discriminates among the applicants, who must have a higher education and presumably speak fluent English. They are mainly in the thirty-to-forty-years-of-age bracket.[133]

Nevertheless, despite the continuing loss of experienced middle managers, the Hong Kong economy seemed able to replace them. As Overholt, a close observer of Hong Kong affairs, observed, "High-level skills are flowing into Hong Kong to a greater degree than they are flowing out."[134]

American educational institutions do not ordinarily keep records of children from Hong Kong (or Taiwan) separately from those from China. Therefore, it is not possible to trace systematically their educational experiences.

NOTES

[1]G. B. Endacott, *A History of Hong Kong* (Oxford University Press, 1958), p. 3.

[2]Henry Lethbridge, *Hong Kong: Stability and Change* (Oxford University Press, 1978), p. 135.

[3]Ibid., p. 181.

[4]Jung-Fang Tsai, *Hong Kong in Chinese History. Community and Social Unrest in the British Colony, 1842–1913* (Columbia University Press, 1993).

[5]Bernard Hung-Kay Luk, "Chinese Culture in the Hong Kong Curriculum: Heritage and Colonialism," *Comparative Education Review*, 35 (November 1991), p. 661.

[6]Lethbridge, *Hong Kong: Stability and Change*, p. 5.

[7]Endacott, *A History of Hong Kong*, p. 70.

[8]Ibid., p. 96.

[9]Ibid., p. 244.

[10]Lethbridge, *Hong Kong: Stability and Change*, p. 167.

[11]Ibid., p. 174.

[12]Judith Agassi, "Social Structure and Social Stratification in Hong Kong," p. 79 in Ian Jarrie and Joseph Agassi, eds., *Hong Kong: A Society in Transition* (Praeger, 1968).

[13]Endacott, *A History of Hong Kong*, p. 245.

[14]Endacott, *A History of Hong Kong*, p. 295.

[15]Judith Agassi, "Social Structure and Social Stratification in Hong Kong," p. 74.

[16]See Endacott, *A History of Hong Kong*, p. 143; and Ng Lun Ngai-ha, *Interactions of East and West. Development of Public Education in Early Hong Kong* (The Chinese University Press, 1984), p. 157. The relative percentages are 13.6 and 3.7.

[17]Endacott, *A History of Hong Kong*, p. 171.

[18]Ibid., p. 306.

[19]Ibid., p. 239.

[20]Ngai-ha, *Interactions of East and West*, pp. 51–52.

[21]Ibid., p. 74.

[22]Ibid., p. 56.

[23]Anthony Sweeting, *Education in Hong Kong Pre-1841 to 1941: Fact and Opinion. Materials for a History of Education in Hong Kong* (Hong Kong University Press, 1990), p. 43.

[24]Ngai-ha, *Interactions of East and West*, p. 67.

[25]Endacott, *A History of Hong Kong*, p. 250.

[26]Ngai-ha, *Interactions of East and West*, p. 13.

[27]Grace C. L. Mak, "The Schooling of Girls in Hong Kong: Progress and Contradictions in the Transition," p. 168 in Gerard A. Postiglione, ed., *Education and Society in Hong Kong. Toward One Country and Two Systems* (Sharpe, 1991).

[28]Sweeting, *Education in Hong Kong*, p. 222.

[29]Endacott, *A History of Hong Kong*, p. 240.

[30]Mak, "The Schooling of Girls in Hong Kong," p. 168.

[31] Endacott, *A History of Hong Kong,* p. 238.

[32] Mak, "The Schooling of Girls in Hong Kong," p. 168.

[33] Ibid., p. 169.

[34] Ibid., p. 169.

[35] Sweeting, *Education in Hong Kong,* p. 465.

[36] Agassi, "Social Structure and Social Stratification in Hong Kong," p. 132.

[37] Mak, "The Schooling of Girls in Hong Kong," p. 169.

[38] Sweeting, *Education in Hong Kong,* p. 402.

[39] Tsai, *Hong Kong in Chinese History,* p. 256.

[40] Ibid., p. 256.

[41] Luk, "Chinese Culture in the Hong Kong Curriculum," p. 659.

[42] Sweeting, *Education in Hong Kong,* p. 343.

[43] See G. B. Endacott, *Hong Kong Eclipse,* edited by Alan Birch (Oxford University Press, 1978), p. 164.

[44] Ibid., pp. 310–311.

[45] A. G.-O. Yeh and M. K. Ng, "The Changing Role of the State in High-Tech Industrial Development: The Experience of Hong Kong," *Environment and Planning, Government and Policy,* 12 (1994), p. 450, footnote 1.

[46] Ibid., p. 450.

[47] Mark Bray and W. O. Lee, "Education, Democracy and Colonial Transition. The Case of Hong Kong," *International Review of Education,* 39 (November 1993), p. 546.

[48] Jon Holliday, "Hong Kong: Britain's Chinese Colony," *New Left Review,* Nos. 87–88 (September–December 1993), p. 546.

[49] Steven C. Chow and Gustav F. Papanek, "Laissez-Faire Growth and Equity—Hong Kong," *Economic Journal,* 91 (June 1981), p. 476.

[50] Ibid., p. 481. See also Benjamin K. P. Leung, ed., *Social Issues in Hong Kong* (Oxford University Press, 1990), pp. 36, 71, 81.

[51] Leung, *Social Issues in Hong Kong,* p. 18.

[52] Anthony Sweeting, *A Phoenix Transformed. The Reconstruction of Education in Post-War Hong Kong* (Oxford University Press, 1993), p. 120.

[53] Richard Hughes, *Hong Kong. Borrowed Place—Borrowed Time* (Praeger, 1968), p. 45. In 1961, the same number of children of school age (5–15) were not attending any school; see Jarvie and Agassi, *Hong Kong: A Society in Transition,* p. 233.

[54] Lee Wing-on, "Decades of Educational Expansion, The Expansion of a Dual System: The Case of Japan and Hong Kong," *CUHK Education Journal,* 17 (June 1989), p. 40.

[55] For an account of the prevalence of child labor, see Robin Porter, "Child Labour in Hong Kong and Related Problems: A Brief Review," *International Labour Review,* III (May 1975), pp. 427–439. On the issue of child-labor exploitation and education policy see Anthony E. Sweeting, "Hong Kong Education within Historical Processes," p. 49 in Gerard A. Postiglione, ed., *Education and Society in Hong Kong. Toward One Country and Two Systems* (Sharpe, 1991); and Walter Easey, "Notes on Child Labour in Hong Kong," *Race and Class,* No. 18 (Spring 1977), pp. 377–387.

[56] Mark J. M. Ross, *Competition for Education in Hong Kong: The Schools, the Entrance Examinations, and the Strategies of Chinese Families* (Doctoral dissertation, University of Texas, 1976), p. 31.

[57] Material in this and the preceding paragraph is based on ibid., pp. 2, 28, 29, 31, 33, 38, 57, 60–64, 153–154, 207.

[58] P. Morris, J. A. G. McClelland, and Yeung Yat Ming, "Higher Education in Hong Kong: The Context of and Rationale for Rapid Expansion," *Higher Education,* 27 (1994), p. 130.

[59] Endacott, *Hong Kong Eclipse,* p. 311.

[60] Ching-kwan Lee and Tak-sing Cheung, "Egalitarianism and the Allocation of Secondary School Places in Hong Kong," p. 151 in Gerard A. Postiglione, ed., *Education and Society in Hong Kong. Toward One Country and Two Systems* (Sharpe, 1991).

[61] Janet W. Salaff, *Working Daughters of Hong Kong. Filial Piety or Power in the Family?* (Cambridge University Press, 1981), p. 28.

[62] Lee and Cheung, "Egalitarianism," p. 152.

[63] Morris, "Higher Education in Hong Kong," p. 131.

[64] Ian Scott, *Political Change and the Crisis of Legitimacy in Hong Kong* (University of Hawaii Press, 1989), p. 244.

[65] Institute of International Education, *Regional Education Profile: Asia. China, Hong Kong, Macau, Thailand, Indonesia, Malaysia, Brunei*, March 1986, p. 18.

[66] Ibid., p. 18.

[67] Norman Miners, *The Government and Politics of Hong Kong*, 4th ed. (Oxford University Press, 1986), p. 136.

[68] Gerard Postiglione, "The Decolonization of Hong Kong Education," p. 11 in Postiglione, ed., *Education and Society in Hong Kong. Toward One Country and Two Systems* (Sharpe, 1991).

[69] Wing-on, "Decades of Educational Expansion," p. 42.

[70] Sweeting, *A Phoenix Transformed*, p. 130.

[71] Ibid., p. 156.

[72] "Even 'Learning Shops' Must Have Standards," *Bridge*, 5 (Winter 1977), p. 14. See also Appendix 1, "A Young Teacher's View," pp. 211–216 in Mark Ross, *Competition for Education in Hong Kong;* and A. J. Youngson, ed., *China and Hong Kong. The Economic Nexus* (Oxford University Press, 1983), p. 292.

[73] Ross, *Competition for Education in Hong Kong*, p. 66.

[74] Salaff, *Working Daughters of Hong Kong*, p. 100.

[75] Anita S. Mak, "From Elites to Strangers: Employment Coping Styles of New Hong Kong Immigrants," *Journal of Employment Counseling*, (December 1991), p. 147. See also Salaff, *Working Daughters of Hong Kong*, p. 23.

[76] Wing-on, "Decades of Educational Expansion," p. 39.

[77] Ibid., p. 39.

[78] See Mark Bray, "Strategies for Financing Higher Education: Perspectives from Hong Kong and Macau," *Higher Education*, 21 (1991), p. 12; and Morris, "Higher Education in Hong Kong," p. 131.

[79] Institute of International Education, *Regional Education Profile*, p. 22.

[80] Maureen Woodhall, *Student Loans in Higher Education: 2 Asia* (UNESCO, 1991), p. 47.

[81] Ross, *Competition for Education in Hong Kong*, pp. 106–107.

[82] See table in *Chronicle of Higher Education*, September 1, 1995, p. 18.

[83] Frank Welsh, *A Borrowed Place. The History of Hong Kong* (Kodansha International, 1993), p. 482.

[84] Glenn Shive, "Educational Expansion and the Labor Force," p. 220 in Gerard A. Postiglione, ed., *Education and Society in Hong Kong. Toward One Country and Two Systems* (Sharpe, 1991).

[85] Ronald Skeldon, "Hong Kong in an International Migration System," p. 29 in Skeldon, ed., *Reluctant Exiles? Migration from Hong Kong and the New Overseas Chinese* (Sharpe, 1994).

[86] Ibid., p. 43.

[87] Richard Chabot and others, "Hong Kong Chinese in Hawaii: Community Building and Coping Strategies," p. 272 in Ronald Skeldon, ed., *Reluctant Exiles? Migration from Hong Kong and the New Overseas Chinese* (Sharpe, 1994).

[88] Ross, *Competition for Education in Hong Kong*, p. 10.

[89] Morris, "Higher Education in Hong Kong," p. 137.

[90] Yeh and Ng, "The Changing Role of the State in High-Tech Industrial Development," p. 460.

[91] Hughes, *Hong Kong*, p. 163.

[92] Li Yixian, "On the Characteristics, Strong Points, and Shortcomings of Education in Hong Kong: A Mainland Chinese Educator's View of Education in Hong Kong," p. 258 in Gerard A. Postiglione, ed., *Education and Society in Hong Kong. Toward One Country and Two Systems* (Sharpe, 1991).

[93] Brit N. Cauldwell, *Made in Hong Kong. An Imperialist Rhetoric and the Teenage Mutant Ninja Turtles*, July 11, 1990, p. 7. ERIC ED 322 503.

[94] Chin-Chuan Lee, *The Partisan Press in Hong Kong: Between British Colonial Rule and Chinese Politics*, August 1985, p. 19. ERIC ED 258 247.

[95] See John Gibbons, "The Issue of the Language of Instruction in the Lower Forms of Hong Kong Secondary Schools," *Journal of Multilingual and Multicultural Development*, 3 (1982), p. 121.

[96] Gillian Bickley, "Plus ça change, plus c'est la même chose: Attitudes towards English Language Learning in Hong Kong—Frederick Stewart's Evidence," *World Englishes*, 9 (Winter 1990), pp. 289–300.

[97] Ibid., p. 291.

[98] Julian Y. M. Leung, "Education in Hong Kong and China: Toward Convergence?" p. 269 in Gerard A. Postiglione, ed., *Education and Society in Hong Kong. Toward One Country and Two Systems* (Sharpe, 1991). See also Nigel J. Bruce, *Prioritizing Equality of Outcome in Hong Kong Secondary School Education*, 1991, p. 2. ERIC ED 354 755.

[99] Ora W. Y. Kwo, "The Teaching of Putonghua in Hong Kong Schools: Language Education in a Changing Economic and Political Context," p. 206 in Gerard A Postiglione, ed., *Education in Society in Hong Kong. Toward One Country and Two Systems* (Sharpe, 1991).

[100] Elizabeth Kanwit, "Chinese Without a Country," *Times Educational Supplement*, August 23, 1974.

[101] Alan Hirvela, "Footing the English Bill in Hong Kong: Language Politics and Linguistic Schizophrenia," *Journal of Asian Pacific Communication*, 2 (1991), p. 130.

[102] Anthony E. Sweeting, "Hong Kong Education within Historical Processes," p. 64.

[103] Gibbons, "The Issue of the Language of Instruction," p. 123.

[104] Jarvie and Agassi, *Hong Kong*, pp. 328–329.

[105] Cornelius Osgood, *The Chinese. A Study of a Hong Kong Community*, 3 vols. (University of Arizona Press, 1975), vol. 3, p. 1055.

[106] See ibid., vol. 2, p. 836 and vol. 3, p. 1057.

[107] Yixian, "On the Characteristics," p. 256.

[108] Bickley, "Plus ça change," pp. 290–291.

[109] Ibid., p. 295.

[110] Peter C.S. Tung, "Why Changing the Medium of Instruction in Hong Kong Could be Difficult," *Journal of Multilingual and Multicultural Development*, 11 (1990), p. 523.

[111] Vivienne W. S. Yu and Paul A. Atkinson, "An Investigation of the Language Difficulties Experienced by Hong Kong Secondary School Students in English-Medium Schools: I. The Problems," *Journal of Multilingual and Multicultural Development*, 9 (1988), p. 271.

[112] Bickley, "Plus ça change," p. 295. See also Tung, "Changing the Medium of Instruction," p. 533.

[113] Mau-Siu Yau, "The Controversy Over Teaching Medium in Hong Kong—An Analysis of a Language Policy," *Journal of Multilingual and Multicultural Development*, 10 (1989), p. 291.

[114] Salaff, *Working Daughters of Hong Kong*, p. 13. See also Veronica Pearson and Benjamin K. P. Leung, eds., *Women in Hong Kong* (Oxford University Press, 1995).

[115] Suk-Ching Ho, "Women's Labor-force Participation in Hong Kong, 1971–1981," *Journal of Marriage and the Family*, 46 (November 1984), p. 952.

[116] Ibid., pp. 948–950.

[117] Mak, "The Schooling of Girls in Hong Kong," p. 174.

[118] H. A. Turner and others, *The Last Colony: But Whose?* (Cambridge University Press, 1980), p. 75.

[119] Mak, "The Schooling of Girls in Hong Kong," p. 172.

[120] Ibid., p. 176.

[121] Ibid., p. 175.

[122] Leung, *Social Issues in Hong Kong*, p. 125.

[123] Veronica Pearson, "Women in Hong Kong," p. 121 in Benjamin K. P. Leung, ed., *Social Issues in Hong Kong* (Oxford University Press, 1990).

[124] Ibid., p. 124.

[125] Ibid., p. 128. See also Turner, *The Last Colony,* pp. 48–49.

[126] Mak, "The Schooling of Girls in Hong Kong," p. 169.

[127] Salaff, *Working Daughters of Hong Kong,* p. 43.

[128] Statement by William H. Overholt, Governor, American Chamber of Commerce in Hong Kong, April 2, 1992, "U.S. Relations With Hong Kong," p. 5 in U.S. Congress, 102nd, 2nd session, House of Representatives, Committee on Foreign Affairs, *U.S. Policy Toward Hong Kong. Markups of S.1731* (Government Printing Office, 1991).

[129] Nancy B. Tucker, *Taiwan, Hong Kong, and the United States, 1945–1992* (Twayne, 1994), p. 161.

[130] See Ian Scott, *Political Change and the Crisis of Legitimacy in Hong Kong* (University of Hawaii Press, 1989), p. 320.

[131] Yeh and Ng, "The Changing Role of the State," p. 467.

[132] Joseph Y. S. Cheng, "The Democracy Movement in Hong Kong," *International Affairs,* 65 (1989), p. 445.

[133] Aihwa Ong, "On the Edge of Empires: Flexible Citizenship among Chinese in Diaspora," *Positions,* 1 (Winter 1993), pp. 749–750.

[134] U.S. Congress, 102nd, 2nd session, Senate, Committee on Foreign Relations, Subcommittee on East Asian and Pacific Affairs, *Hearing. Hong Kong's Reversion to China and Implications for U.S. Policy* (Government Printing Office, 1992), p. 39.

CHAPTER TEN

Taiwan

The last dynasty of China conquered Taiwan and for several hundred years, it was a valued colony. As a result of the Sino-Japanese War of 1894 and 1895, Japan took possession of Taiwan in 1895 and held it under the name *Formosa* for the next 50 years. Together with Korea in 1910 and Manchuria during the 1930s, these three colonies were the core of the Japanese Empire until 1945. To an unusual degree, the colonies were more integrated into the overall economic design of Japan itself. For the Japanese, their colonies carried a larger burden of production than was the case with European colonies. This extended even to industrial output, a realm usually considered off-limits in other colonies. A broad range of products and materials lacking in the home country was to be provided by the colonies. As Aseniero observed, "Japanese colonialism, rapacious as it was like any other, was not interested in Korea and Taiwan merely for pillage and extraction of value."[1]

Taiwanese were not entrusted with significant governmental authority. A small number became higher civil bureaucrats.[2] Many more were employed as heads of townships; few could be found as district counselors, a step above township heads. Both township heads and district counselors received economic privileges from the Japanese.[3] Although many Taiwanese passed the requisite civil service examinations, they did not receive appointments to which they were entitled.[4] Wealthy Taiwanese who collaborated with the colonial government were rewarded with lucrative opportunities and extraordinary wealth as well as occasional governing responsibilities. Thus, "in 1937, seven years after the number of Taiwanese councilors had been increased from 9 to 14, all Taiwanese council seats were occupied by big businessmen and industrialists."[5] Positions in the colonial military service, however, were denied to Taiwanese until the closing years of Japanese rule.[6]

Japanese tended to regard the Taiwanese as inferiors and excluded them from arenas other than governance. In economic life, ordinary Taiwanese were employed principally as manual workers. They were not permitted to marry Japanese.[7] In education, they were managed so as to minimize their progress.

Aborigines made up another group of Islanders who were treated as unequals. Numbering about 150,000 in 1895—as compared with 2.5 million Taiwanese—they were subjected to repeated military attacks by Japanese soldiers who sought to tame them.[8] Gates pointed out that even when some were assimilated, they still bore signs of inferiority. "The Chinese surname that many 'sinified' Aborigines were given in the past—Pan—is a character meaning 'barbarian', with another beside it indicating the category 'insect'. . . ."[9] Between 1906 and 1909, the Japanese military conducted 18 separate campaigns against the aborigines.[10] Between 1916 and 1918, "Japanese planes were dropping bombs on aborigine villages."[11] (This was during World War I when Japan tried to use the distractions of the European theater of war to acquire further land in China. As an ally of Britain's, it declared war on Germany, which controlled Shantung, in China. Protests against the Japanese moves led to the May 4th Movement of 1919, a nationwide protest in China.) In 1930, the aborigines raised an armed rebellion against the Japanese but were defeated once more. "The Japanese forced them militarily into a vast reservation that they were not permitted to leave, though Japanese could enter, mostly as policemen and school teachers."[12] Aborigines continued to suffer discrimination in the community and in job seeking after the end of the colonial period.

Sugar production became the single most important industry in colonial Taiwan. Organized by a handful of Japanese giant corporations encouraged by subsidies paid out of tax revenues levied on Taiwanese, the Japanese capitalists reinvested ample profits in other industries in the colony.[13] Taiwanese businessmen were not permitted to organize firms that were competitive to the large sugar companies. Instead, they were forced to invest their capital in other businesses.[14] By 1919, "the Taiwanese owned 85% of the enterprises employing 5 to 49 workers, 74.9% of those employing 50 to 99 workers, 38% of those employing 100 to 199 workers, and only 3% of those employing more than 200 workers."[15] At the end of the first decade of colonial rule, the Island not only was self-supporting, it was running a surplus.[16]

At first, Taiwanese who resented the Japanese overlordship reacted with violence. Between 1898 and 1902, over 11,000 were killed while engaging in revolts.[17] Eleven more revolts were recorded between 1907 and 1916.[18] The colonial government was only a little less disturbed by peaceful protests. The Assimilation Society, which advocated equality between Taiwanese and Japanese, was dissolved by the Governor General in 1914, the year it was formed. Colonial authorities were displeased by the Society's denunciation of Japanese discrimination against Taiwanese. After this, protests centered on demands for home rule in Taiwan but the Diet (Japanese parliament) rejected 15 petitions on the subject between 1921 and 1934. A similar fate was accorded to a proposal to establish a Taiwanese parliament. Over the period 1914 to 1936:

> Reformist anti-colonialism commanded strong support from the native bourgeoisie. . . . Yet the physicians, lawyers, clerks, journalists, teachers, technicians, and entrepreneurs who occupied the ranks of mainstream anti-colonialism were from a class that was largely a creation of Japanese colonialism. Educated in Japanese schools both in the colony and in the ruling country for occupations which Japanese development of their island had created, they were as much products of Japanese colonialism as the sugar refineries and the coal mines. . . . The major thrust of their demands was toward equality in economic competition, political franchise, and social status.[19]

Independence from Japan was publicly advocated only by the Taiwanese Communist Party, formed in Shanghai in 1928.[20]

The Japanese established a triple school system in Taiwan: a first-rate one for Japanese children of families living in the colony, a second-rate one for Taiwanese children, and a third-rate one for children of the Aborigines. (From 1902, aborigine affairs were under the charge of the police, some of whom acted as teachers.[21]) Japanese children attended primary schools whereas Taiwanese were enrolled in common schools. The police installations for aborigines were not even called schools. Colonial authorities did not hurry to educate anyone except Japanese children. After 10 years of colonization, 72.9% of Japanese children and 4.66% of Taiwanese children attended public school.[22] Most of the latter came from carefully selected children of literati whom the Japanese courted for their influence over the mass of Taiwanese.[23] Twenty-five years after the Japanese accession, barely 25% of Taiwanese school-age children were in school. By 1938, 43 years into colonization, still less than half of the children attended public schools. As was true of the French in Vietnam, only the advent of World War II pressed the Japanese to expand Taiwanese enrollment: A year before war's end and the departure of the Japanese, over 70% attended school. Enrollment figures need to be discounted liberally by annual dropouts. These suggest that exceedingly few Taiwanese students were still around to attend secondary schools, at least during the years between 1906 and 1918. The poor educational quality of the common schools was a frequent cause of complaint by parents. Educational authorities, on the other hand, were seeking to make children "unquestioningly loyal to Japan."[24] The colonial government's strategy of educational provision went far beyond quality or loyalism. It included:

> Winning support for the new regime; developing a stratum of Taiwanese sufficiently well educated to service the administrative and clerical apparatus of the colonial government; educating Japanese nationals living in Taiwan; popularizing

formal education for girls; producing Taiwanese teachers and medical personnel; and making the islands' school system as financially self-sufficient as possible.[25]

The last-named goal was assiduously pursued. For the first 4 years of Japanese rule, the colonial government paid all the expenses of schooling. With the creation of common schools, wealthy local taxpayers were required to pay for the schools. By 1906, localities paid three fourths of the expenses; the remainder was paid by the central administration. Because all but a few of the students in these schools at first came from well-to-do families, the matter of financial support was not of great interest to many Taiwanese. As, however, broader circles of families sent their children to school, and municipal taxes rose to support the schools, grievances grew. "Taiwanese taxpayers supported well-endowed schools for Japanese," wrote Tsurumi, "while their own children studied in inferior facilities."[26] During the 1930s, per-pupil expenditures in three different types of schools were highly unequal. In primary schools, nearly twice as much was paid than in common schools, and nearly eight times as much in aborigine centers.[27] The figures for earlier years were comparable.

Secondary and higher education was financed mainly by the central administration, out of Japanese funds. The vast majority of secondary school students were Japanese. "Virtually all Japanese applying to middle school or higher girls' school were accepted in some secondary institution."[28] In 1928, Taihoku Imperial University was opened as an all-but Japanese preserve. The curriculum was drenched in political concerns. "Japanese colonial authorities had strongly discouraged Taiwanese from studying law, politics, and the like fearing that higher education in these fields would breed discontent and even rebellion."[29] It was for the opposite kind of reason, however, that many Japanese students studied law and politics. Following is a compilation of the number of students who enrolled in various courses of study or faculties at Taihoku between 1928 and 1944:[30]

	Literature and Political Science	Science	Medicine	Agriculture	Engineering
Taiwanese	173	124	513	1	2
Japanese	1,167	1,085	523	176	47

Taiwanese graduates had few opportunities to practice their specialties inasmuch as Japanese applicants almost always were given special consideration. Because of the island government's commitment to a large-scale, public-health program, there was room for indigenous physicians as well. Another result was that physicians were the largest group of Taiwanese graduates of Taihoku. Perhaps a zeal for higher education was at least as important as an enthusiasm for medical practice.

Taiwanese parents resented the exclusivity of schooling for Japanese. The first-rate schools were not available to Taiwanese on the frank basis of nationality. Yet, the few Taiwanese children who were admitted only to the common schools seemed to have done well. In 1923, for example, Island-wide academic achievement tests were administered to 8,000 primary- and 4,000 common-school students. The results surprised many. "In arithmetic, common school students did much better than primary schoolers in the same grades. Moreover, their overall academic performance in all subjects was also rated higher than that of primary school pupils in the same grades."[31] (Around the same time, Puerto Rican children tested generally higher than their mainland contemporaries, which confounded many U.S. educators.[32]) Japanese authorities argued that the Taiwanese students were a more selective group—97.3% of Japanese students attended primary schools but only 28.6% of Taiwanese school-age children were in common schools. Also, the Taiwanese children were a year older and thus more mature. Taiwanese critics retorted that whereas the Japanese students were taking tests in their first language—Japanese—the Taiwanese were using it as a second language. (The Taiwanese language was barred from the schools.) Also, the primary schools were far better financed, the teachers better trained, and supplies and equipment highly favorable.[33] The colonial government settled the controversy by suppressing it; education authorities were not permitted to sell the test report to the public and circulation of it was allowed only to administrative personnel.[34]

From time to time, the colonial government made concessions on educational matters. These steps had a minimal impact because of their limited scope or simply because they were largely spurious. The education rescript of 1922 was an example of both the former and the latter. It provided that the common schools were to be reserved for non-Japanese-speaking students whereas the primary schools were to be open to Japanese-speaking students, whatever their nationality.[35] Exceedingly few Taiwanese students entered the primary schools. Moreover, "although fluency in the Japanese language was the only legal requirement for entrance to the first grade of a primary school, an unofficial quota system made sure that Taiwanese made up no more than 10 percent of the primary school population."[36] Other crucial reforms were not granted. Thus, authorities repeatedly rejected demands for the enactment of compulsory attendance. In 1943, 48 years after the inception of Japanese rule, it was finally granted. Two years later, the Japanese left Taiwan.

Wealthy Taiwanese could sometimes maneuver within narrow limits and manage to arrange a better-than-average education for their children. For the most part, however, such opportunities could be had only by sending their children to attend schools in Japan. In 1922, for example, some 2,400 Taiwanese students were studying in Japan; half of them attended colleges or universities.[37] No ethnic quota existed in Japan, nor were limitations placed on subjects of specialization. Indeed, it was easier for Taiwanese to enroll in Japan's schools than in corresponding schools inside Taiwan.[38]

Before 1895, women partook of extremely little formal education. In 1920, only 9.36% of girls of school age were enrolled in elementary schools; the figure for boys was 39.11%. By 1944, the percentages were 60.94 and 80.86.[39] For both sexes, the education was quite rudimentary. "In general, these colonial schools were primarily aimed at developing farmers who could read the directions on fertilizer bags, clerks who could keep Japanese records, low ranking policemen who could understand their superiors' commands, and so on."[40]

In 1945, World War II ended but in China a bitter civil war between the Nationalist government and the Chinese Communists resumed in full force. After 4 years, the Communists took power and the Nationalists escaped to Taiwan. Already in 1945, the Nationalists had occupied the island and established themselves as Japan's successors. They ruled as conquerors, regarding the Taiwanese as unfit to rule themselves. In 1947, while the civil war still raged on the mainland, Taiwanese rebelled at the refusal of the Nationalists to apply a new Chinese constitution to Taiwan. Other grievances also played a part in the uprising. Troops were brought in from the mainland and they "brutally smashed the demonstrations."[41] When, in 1949, the Nationalists' forces fled to Taiwan, a full-scale military dictatorship, headed by Chiang Kai-Shek, was ensconced there. Chiang brought with him the gold reserves of his former government.

For the next 25 years or so, the Nationalist government actively prepared to invade mainland China and end Communist rule. Three groups of material resources were critically important in building up Taiwan's capacity to exist independently or to prepare an economic base for a continental invasion: (a) Chiang's treasure of China's gold supply and other funds once held by the Bank of China; (b) Japanese property in Taiwan, including factories, farms, and extensive infrastructure in transportation and communication; and (c) economic and military aid from the United States. Most important and priceless was the role of the United States in pledging the military protection of Taiwan. Between 1950 and 1965, the United States gave Taiwan an annual average of $100 million. Between 1951 and 1955, all the funds were in the form of grants that did not require repayment. After 1955, low interest rates were charged, and the period of repayment was extended for long periods.[42]

The state, rather than private individuals played a major economic role in Taiwan. Largely discredited on the mainland for its corruption, cronyism, and incompetence, the ruling Kuomintang restrained itself somewhat on the island. Preparing ultimately to reign once more over China, Chiang and his close associates knew they needed to overhaul their reputation. Consequently, persons placed in charge of the day-to-day economic policy tended to be technically apt rather than simply well-connected.[43] Instead of key personnel milking every economic opening for their own gain, extreme differences in income did not prevail as they had in pre-Communist China. Unlike South Korea, generals played no part in official economic machinery.[44] In one respect, at least, Kuomintang policy did not change during transit to Taiwan: labor policy. The dictatorship clamped down mercilessly on labor unions and strikes. Genuine collec-

tive bargaining was all but unknown. There was little chance of a labor movement developing any independent political power.[45] Martial law, which was in
operation continuously from 1949 to 1987, placed the armed forces in a state of
readiness to be used against unions as well as other targets. Income inequality in
Taiwan declined during the late 1960s and all of the 1970s but was on a rising
trend during the early 1990s.[46] Compared with many other countries, Taiwan's
concentration of income, however measured, was low. Unfortunately, data on
the distribution of wealth in Taiwan were not available. Customarily, ownership
of wealth is nearly always more concentrated than income. In any event, a significant group of Taiwanese considered extreme income disparities as serious or
very serious problems.[47]

Throughout the years after 1949, mainlanders continued to hold their edge in
employment. For example, in 1967:

> Mainlanders . . . held 82 percent of all jobs in the national security sector, includ-
> ing the police force, and more than one-third of positions in public administration
> and the professions even though they made up but 15 percent of the population.[48]

In 1985, despite the disparity in population numbers, mainlanders had a disproportionately large representation of managers. This was especially the case in
all levels of government.[49] Nevertheless, over 70% of mainlanders were members of the working class.[50] One may imagine that this large group of workers
was not relegated to the most unpleasant, low-paid work.

During over half of the colonial period, 1905 to 1935, the percentage of Taiwan's population that lived in cities of 20,000 or more were 4.92 and 15.91. Later
figures were as follows:[51]

$$
\begin{array}{ll}
1952 & 47.6\% \\
1962 & 52.0\% \\
1972 & 66.3\% \\
1980 & 70.3\%
\end{array}
$$

Lesser levels of urbanization during colonial times reflected, of course, the
widespread persistence of small-scale agriculture. After 1949, however, agricultural reforms led to sharp drops in the number of farm workers. The single
greatest factor making for urbanization was the immigration of mainlanders,
most of whom worked in government offices and military posts, both located
predominantly in or near cities. In 1955, for example, only slightly more than
one fifth of mainlanders lived in nonurban areas.[52]

In 1951, just 6 years after the Japanese left, the average Taiwanese had attended school for only 2.75 years.[53] This was the heritage of Japan's educational
policy in its colonies. Once an independent government was in place, popular
discontent with Taiwan's school system mounted as parents sought to make up
for lost time. By 1962, 95% of elementary-school-age children were attending
school.[54] At the same time, dropouts from elementary schools started to fall

from their 1951 rate of 16.5%.[55] Examinations for entrance into junior high school were failed by more students than ever. The streets of Taipei and other cities were filled with young people whose education had ended and who were unemployed because they lacked vocational training. Representatives of industry clamored, meanwhile, for better educated and trained workers. In 1968, the government responded by extending compulsory education from age 12 to age 15 and thus establishing a 9-year period of free, compulsory education.

Wishing to minimize corresponding problems in more advanced education, authorities expanded facilities in secondary and higher education, although less so in the latter. The rate at which students entered junior high school had been 31.99% in 1950. By 1985 it had reached 99.38%.[56] At higher levels:

> The number of students in senior vocational schools increased from 11,226 in 1950 to 421,784 in 1985, and in 5-year [junior] colleges, from 1,729 in 1959 to 150,779 in 1985. . . . The absolute number of students in the senior high school had an increase from 18,866 in 1950 to 194,757 in 1985, but its relative share in secondary education was declining.[57]

The labor force in 1988 approached an average schooling of 9 years; 27 years earlier, it had been 4.8 years.[58] Similarly, illiteracy dropped from 42.1% in 1952 to 8.4% in 1985.[59]

The least expansion occurred in higher education. Entrance into higher education was regulated by examinations given to graduates of secondary schools. Only graduates of a comparatively small number of high schools could look forward to successful completion of their course of study and entrance into a university. Education authorities channeled students according to the curricula in official favor. Thus:

> The average passing rate of the entrance examination for universities and colleges in 1975 was 26.36%. . . . For applicants in the fields of humanities and social studies, the passing rates were 14.98% and 22.03%, and for medical and agricultural studies, 39.73%. . . . In 1985, the average passing rate for all applicants was 31.84%, but that for the science group was 41.48% and for liberal education, 24.58%.[60]

Shortages of places in the senior high schools were a continuing problem that excluded numerous qualified students.

Nevertheless, higher education in Taiwan proceeded as an amalgam of restriction and advancement. In a study by Chan and Chan, the educational history of a sample population was analyzed into three groupings: students born 1925 to 1939, 1940 to 1955, and 1956 to 1965. In the oldest cohort—those born 1925 to 1939—56% had received no more than a primary education and fewer than 10% of the youngest cohort had received only that much schooling.[61] Clearly, over a period of time, educational standards had risen with reference to the primary level of education. The picture was quite different, however, with respect to higher education or beyond. Following are the percentages of the studied population who received undergraduate education or beyond:[62]

1925–1939   10.8%
1940–1955   13.2%
1956–1965   12.2%

A very moderate increase in university-going had occurred.

Viewed from the stance of class, the greatest beneficiaries of the increase were the two top classes that the researchers call service classes, who constituted a little over one fifth of all the students:

> Throughout the whole period, an extra thirty-five service class children for every 100 received higher education, but for the working class the increment was about four per 100. Although there was a narrowing trend in the service-working distance in the later stage of expansion, the picture of unequal access to higher education has not changed much over time.[63]

The working class, however, numbering nearly two thirds of the population of Taiwan (64.0%), contributed a small percentage of the total but a very large one in gross numbers. Thus the researchers can conclude that, "a great majority of those who received higher education came from homes where both parents had no experience" of having attended a university.[64]

Taiwan's economic development took off especially during the 1960s and 1970s and continued briskly in the succeeding decade. This was the basic factor behind the educational expansion of the same years. It also paved the way for considerable change in the role of women in the Taiwanese economy and in education.

A year before the Japanese left Taiwan, in 1944, 80.86% of boys and 60.94% of girls of school age were enrolled in elementary schools. It took over 40 more years before substantially all boys and girls of school age were in elementary school. Barrett noted that

> between 1960 and 1970, the proportion of women who had completed junior high school jumped from 5.3 to 9.4 percent, high school graduates in the female population rose from 2.7 to 8.9 percent, and the proportion of those with college or university training rose five-fold, from 0.6 percent to 3.0 percent.[65]

A decade later, by 1980:

> a Taiwanese woman was only about half as likely to be a college graduate . . . and while almost 25 percent of all men were high-school graduates, less than one fifth (19.8 percent) of all women were. Junior high school completion rates ran about 5 percent higher among men.[66]

Illiteracy was declining differentially for both women and men. Thus, in 1952, female and male illiteracy was 56.7 and 28.2%, respectively; in 1980, the figures were 19.2 and 5.9%.[67] Measured another way, however, the female-male discrepancy had grown from 2 to 1 to more than 3 to 1.

Sex differential pervaded a number of aspects of higher education. Between 1960 and 1990, total enrollment rose from 34,623 to 515,515. Women's representation increased during these years from 21 to 43%.[68] During this period also, private higher education expanded greatly. Indeed, from 1960, when 19% of total enrollment was in private institutions, until 1990, the figure rose to 73%. Clearly, mass higher education in Taiwan was heavily dependent on private rather than governmental auspices. Funds depended upon student fees, gifts, and occasional governmental contributions. Over time, the public sector became an elite redoubt for men whereas parts of the private sector were characterized by a large representation of women.[69]

In the midst of much educational change, the relative economic position of women in Taiwan remained stagnant. With reference to wages, for example, in 1966:

> Female workers were at a disadvantage in every educational group. Moreover discrimination was higher for the low educational categories, which absorbed almost 90 percent of female workers. . . . Discrimination against female workers also prevailed for every age group, and the severity of discrimination increased with age.[70]

Twenty-five years later, Chang wrote that "average unadjusted female salaries stayed well below the average salaries of equally educated males."[71] Although it was true that some Taiwanese women with a higher education were able to work as professionals, they were not accorded equal status. Jan, an American-trained mechanical engineer, returned to Taiwan to work at her profession but left after only 6 months. "There is a lot of sexual discrimination," she told an interviewer. "People don't respect a woman engineer. . . . I hate the way women are treated here."[72]

The distribution of men and women in the class structure reflected the above material. Thus, in 1985 the following distribution was obtained.[73] Clearly, women

TABLE 10.1
Class Distributions Within Sexes

Row pct Col pct	Male	Female
Capitalists	88.6%	11.4%
	3.6	0.8
Petty Bourgeoisie	77.5	22.5
	15.0	7.5
Managers	88.7	11.3
	6.2	1.3
Workers	59.0	41.0
	60.0	70.8
Small Farmers	56.7	43.3
	15.2	19.7
Col Total	100.0	100.0

were relatively more prominent in lower classes (workers and small farmers) than men were (capitalists, petty bourgeoisie, and managers). At the same time, some women at least were consolidating their rising-class positions by gaining a higher education. In 1980, for example, 33.6% of married couples had a college education or more. By 1993, the figure had grown to 44.4%.[74] In the latter year, a college-educated person in Taiwan earned around 2½ times the annual income received by a person with primary school or less.

Under the Japanese, it will be recalled, a number of elite Taiwanese sent their children to be educated in Japanese schools and colleges. After 1945, as American influence grew, elite Taiwanese began using educational institutions in the United States. By the early 1960s, fewer than half of Taiwanese holders of American doctorates had returned home.[75] This demonstration that marked emigration was a real possibility stimulated further departures. Between 1965 and 1969, the movement of Taiwanese students to institutions in the United States broadened. Their numbers rose from 6,780 to 12,029 in that period.[76] From 1971 to 1982, 69% of Taiwanese students going overseas at their own expense went to colleges or universities in the United States and only 25% went to Japan.[77] The stream broadened rapidly. Thus, during 1990 and 1991, 33,500 left for the United States and in 1993 and 1994, 37,581.[78] By the latter date, Taiwan was the third largest provider of foreign students, being outstripped only by China and Japan.

Nevertheless, internal developments within Taiwan were also generating a reverse movement. The central government, eager to encourage the growth of domestic high-technology industries, had begun stimulating the development of science and technology curricula in the common schools. At the other end of the scale, government-sponsored measures were undertaken to attract back to Taiwan holders of American doctorates in science and technology to staff research and teaching positions in higher institutions. As Tucker observed: "By 1989 advanced programs graduated four times as many engineers per capita as in the United States."[79] The government built the Hsin-chu Science-Based Industrial Park that was populated by numerous private industrial organizations. Supplied by the government were first-rate support services, including housing and excellent schools. Between 1988 and 1991, "some 2,250 high-technology specialists left jobs in the United States to work at Hsin-chu."[80] Many returnees, however, left their families overseas.

Only seldom in the literature of the subject are distinctions made between Chinese, Taiwanese, and Hong Kongers. Consequently, it is all but impossible to distinguish institutional events among the three groups. The educational attainment of Taiwanese immigrants is highest of the three, with 56% having 4 or more years of college.[81] Clearly, this far exceeded the rate on the island itself and is another evidence of the selectivity of Taiwanese immigrants. It is no wonder, therefore, that they "seem to fare better in the job market than the Hong Kong immigrants."[82] Chen reported that "Taiwan immigrants in the United

States told me that the United States is a paradise for children because of light homework, the absence of physical punishment in school, and easy entrance into college."[83] To children of workers and small businessmen, however, the prospects are less than paradisiacal. Their parents often know little English and their working hours keep them apart from their children. Especially for older children, school progress is grinding.[84] Class factors play a large role among the Taiwanese immigrants.[85]

CONCLUDING REMARKS

The educational histories of Hong Kong and Taiwan underscore the deleterious effect of colonialism. Although in both cases the imperialist power introduced modern schooling, it was presented as a privilege for a chosen few and as a near-charade for the many. The resulting system produced highly unequal results. Advanced schooling was a taunt rather than an opportunity.

A free, compulsory, common-school system did not yet exist in Britain when Hong Kong became a colony, nor in Japan when Taiwan was first colonized. At no time before 1945 were educational opportunities in Hong Kong or Taiwan anywhere near what they were in Britain or Japan. That one or the other of the colonies was more extensively schooled at any given time was due to varying needs of the colonizing power. As was pointed out earlier, the Japanese integrated Taiwan much more into its home affairs than did Britain with Hong Kong. To that extent, schooling served as an imperial imperative, especially in Taiwan. Throughout the 19th century, on the other hand, mass schooling in Hong Kong was neither an economic or a strategic imperative.

NOTES

[1] George Aseniero, "South Korea and Taiwanese Development. The Transnational Context," *Review*, 17 (Summer 1994), p. 287.

[2] Ching-Chih Chen, "Impact of Japanese Colonial Rule on Taiwanese Elites," *Journal of Asian History*, 22 (1988), p. 25.

[3] Ibid., p. 33.

[4] Ibid., p. 39.

[5] Ibid., p. 44.

[6] Ibid., p. 49.

[7] Hill Gates, *Chinese Working-Class Lives. Getting By in Taiwan* (Cornell University Press, 1987), p. 42.

[8] E. Patricia Tsurumi, *Japanese Colonial Education in Taiwan, 1895–1945* (Harvard University Press, 1977), p. 231.

[9] Gates, *Chinese Working-Class Lives*, p. 32.

[10] Wen-hsiung Hsu, "Anti-Japanese Colonialism in Taiwan, 1907–1916," *Chinese Studies in History*, 25 (Spring 1991), p. 76.

[11] Tsurumi, *Japanese Colonial Education in Taiwan*, p. 231.

[12] Gates, *Chinese Working-Class Lives*, p. 32.

[13] E. Patricia Tsurumi, "Mental Capacity and Resistance. Lessons from Taiwanese Anti-Colonialism," *Bulletin of Concerned Asian Scholars*, 12 (April-June 1980), p. 13, footnote 56.

[14] Chen, "Impact of Japanese Colonial Rule," p. 40.

[15] Ibid., p. 42.

[16] Hsu, "Anti-Japanese Colonialism in Taiwan," p. 73.

[17] Ibid., p. 73.

[18] For a tabular summary of these actions, see ibid., Table 1, pp. 78–79.

[19] Tsurumi, "Mental Capacity and Resistance," p. 9.

[20] Ibid., p. 9.

[21] Tsurumi, *Japanese Colonial Education in Taiwan*, p. 232.

[22] Hsu, "Anti-Japanese Colonialism in Taiwan," p. 75.

[23] Tsurumi, *Japanese Colonial Education in Taiwan*, p. 12.

[24] Ibid., p. 11.

[25] Ibid., p. 18.

[26] Ibid., p. 82.

[27] Ibid., pp. 239–241.

[28] Ibid., p. 116.

[29] Chen, "Impact of Japanese Colonial Rule," p. 39.

[30] Tsurumi, *Japanese Colonial Education in Taiwan*, p. 254.

[31] Ibid., p. 96.

[32] See Meyer Weinberg, *A Chance to Learn*, 2nd edition (University Press, California State University, Long Beach, 1995), p. 237.

[33] Tsurumi, *Japanese Colonial Education in Taiwan*, pp. 96–97.

[34] Ibid., p. 97.

[35] Ibid., p. 99.

[36] Ibid., p. 111.

[37] Chen, "Impact of Japanese Colonial Rule," p. 35.

[38] Tsurumi, *Japanese Colonial Education in Taiwan*, p. 103.

[39] Sang-Bok Han and Kwang-Ok Kim, eds., *Traditional Cultures of the Pacific Societies. Continuity and Change* (National University Press, 1990), p. 476.

[40] Ibid., p. 476.

[41] Nancy B. Tucker, *Taiwan, Hong Kong, and the United States, 1945–1992* (Twayne, 1994), p. 28.

[42] Ibid., p. 54.

[43] Peter Evans and Chien-kuo Pang, "State Structure and State Policy: Implications of the Taiwanese Case for Industrializing Countries," p. 7 in Hsin-Huang MichaelHsiao and others, eds., *Taiwan. A Newly Industrialized State* (Department of Sociology, National Taiwan University, 1989).

[44] Ibid., p. 11.

[45] See Hagen Koo, "The State Industrial Structure and Labor Politics: Comparison of Taiwan and South Korea," p. 573 in Hsin-Huang Michael Hsiao and others, eds., *Taiwan. A Newly Industrialized State* (Department of Sociology, National Taiwan University, 1989).

[46] *Report on the Survey of Personal Income Distribution in Taiwan Area of the Republic of China* (Directorate-General of Budget, Accounting and Statistics, Executive Yuan, Republic of China, 1993), p. 2. This report deals with family income. Hagen Koo, ibid., p. 570, uses household income. See also Tucker, *Taiwan, Hong Kong, and the United States*, p. 107. See also Hou-sheng Chan and Ying Chan, "Origins and Destinations: The Case of Taiwan," p. 217 in Hsin-Huang Michael Hsiao and others, eds., *Taiwan, A Newly Industrialized State* (Department of Sociology, National Taiwan University, 1989); and Hsin-Huang M.Hsiao and Yung-Mei Tsai, "Social Structural Changes in Post-War Taiwan: A Macrosocial Analysis," p. 178 in Sang-Bok Han and Kwang-Ok Kim, eds., *Traditional Cultures of the Pacific Societies. Continuity and Change* (National University Press, 1990).

[47] Wei-yuan Cheng, "Economic Dependency and the Development of Taiwan: Cross-Sectional and Longitudinal Analysis," p. 523, footnote 1 in Hsin-Huang Michael Hsiao and others, eds., *Taiwan. A Newly Industrialized State* (Department of Sociology, National Taiwan University, 1989).

[48] Tucker, *Taiwan, Hong Kong, and the United States*, p. 114.

[49] Jia-you Sheu, "The Class Structure in Taiwan and Its Changes," p. 140 in Hsin-Huang Michael Hsiao and others, eds., *Taiwan. A Newly Industrialized State* (Department of Sociology, National Taiwan University, 1989).

[50] Ibid., p. 140.

[51] Hsiao and Tsai, "Social Structural Changes in Post-War Taiwan," pp. 169, 174–175.

[52] Ibid., p. 175.

[53] Chun Chig Jim Chang, *The Nine-Year Compulsory Education Policy and the Development of Human Resources in Taiwan* (Doctoral dissertation, University of Maryland, 1991), p. 9.

[54] Ibid., p. 16.

[55] Ibid., p. 50.

[56] Chan and Chan, "Origins and Destinations: The Case of Taiwan," p. 218.

[57] Ibid., p. 218.

[58] Chang, *The Nine-Year Compulsory Education Policy*, p. 215.

[59] Chan and Chan, "Origins and Destinations: The Case of Taiwan," p. 218.

[60] Ibid., p. 220.

[61] Ibid., p. 228.

[62] Ibid., p. 229.

[63] Ibid., p. 253.

[64] Ibid., p. 240.

[65] Richard E. Barrett, "The Changing Status of Women in Taiwan," p. 478 in Hsin-Huang Michael Hsiao and others, eds., *Taiwan. A Newly Industrialized State.*

[66] Ibid., p. 478.

[67] Ibid., p. 477.

[68] John C. H. Fei, Gustav Ranis, and Shirley W. Y. Kuo, *Growth With Equity. The Taiwan Case* (Oxford University Press, 1979), p. 136.

[69] See table in Ruth Hayhoe, "An Asian Multiversity? Comparative Reflections on the Transition to Mass Higher Education in East Asia," *Comparative Education Review*, 39 (August 1995), p. 301.

[70] Ibid., p. 304.

[71] Chang, *The Nine-Year Compulsory Education Policy*, p. 245.

[72] Quoted in Karl Schoenberger, "Breathing Life Into Southland," *Los Angeles Times*, October 4, 1993.

[73] Hsin-Huang Michael Hsiao and others, eds., *Taiwan. A Newly Industrialized State* (Department of Sociology, National Taiwan University, 1989), p. 137, Table 7A. Read the table as follows: 88.6% of capitalists were men and 11.4% were women, while 3.6% of all men were capitalists and 0.8% of all women were capitalists, and so on.

[74] *Report on the Survey of Personal Income Distribution in Taiwan Area of the Republic of China* (Directorate-General of Budget, Accounting and Statistics, Executive Yuan, Republic of China, 1993), p. 5.

[75] Tucker, *Taiwan, Hong Kong and the United States*, p. 80.

[76] Ibid., p. 120.

[77] Ibid., p. 188.

[78] Ibid., p. 188; and *Chronicle of Higher Education*, September 1, 1995, p. 18.

[79] Tucker, *Taiwan, Hong Kong, and the United States*, p. 188.

[80] Ibid., p. 189. See also Kwoh-ting Li, *Economic Transformation of Taiwan, ROC* (Shepherd-Walwyn, 1988), p. 220.

[81] Luciano Mangiafico, *Contemporary American Immigrants: Patterns of Filipino, Korean, and Chinese Settlement in the United States* (Praeger, 1988), pp. 145–146.

[82]Lawrence R. Hong, "Recent Immigrants in the Chinese-American Community: Issues of Adaptation and Impacts," *International Migration Review,* 10 (1976), p. 510.

[83]Hsiang-shun Chen, *Chinatown No More. Taiwan. Immigrants in Contemporary New York* (Cornell University Press, 1992), p. 66. This item seems to be the only English-language, book-length study of Taiwanese in the United States.

[84]See ibid., pp. 249–250, 252.

[85]See ibid., p. 41.

Micronesia

Micronesia, a grouping of islands in the northwest Pacific, entered modern history as a place for ships to pause in trips between the Asian mainland and elsewhere. There they took on supplies of coal and fresh water supplies. During the 17th, 18th, and 19th centuries, Spain was the dominant imperialist power in the Pacific, as it occupied a number of Micronesian islands. Dividing up the area in the 20th century were Great Britain, France, Germany, Japan, and the United States. Only after World War II did some of the island-states become independent. Many more, however, remained outright colonies or sparsely self-governing entities. The imperialist powers in Micronesia shared at least one characteristic in common: They ruled as if forever, and thus expended no effort in preparing the indigenous people to exercise political power. Other than strategic location, few economic resources attracted the attention of outside countries. Native products included fruit- and vegetable-bearing plants and trees; a market existed for copra, the white meat of coconuts; and sugar was grown in some of the Northern Mariana Islands. Fishing was a major source of food. Altogether, the vast majority of people lived as subsistence farmers and fisherfolk. Continued outside rule, however, destroyed the economic independence of Micronesia and transformed most of the islands into a state of economic dependency.

Spanish rule lasted from 1521 to 1898, but the government undertook very little education in these years. Missionaries organized village schools whose principal purpose was to facilitate religious conversions. These were highly successful and by the mid-19th century, it was claimed by one source that "a large majority of the indigenous peoples of the South Seas were professed Christians."[1] The missionaries also sought to undermine the basic values of native life.[2] In large part, this, too, succeeded. As Antilla wrote, "The Chamorro learned to look upon his own culture as inferior and to hide from Europeans whatever vestiges of it he still treasured. The native who had the greatest prestige was the one living in proximity to the Spaniard."[3] The missionaries employed native languages in village schools although Spanish was the official language of instruction. (It will be recalled that the same was true in the Philippines.) Most of the priests were Spanish Basques "who taught a rigid, medieval Christianity. They were deeply conscious of class distinctions."[4]

Spanish efforts in education were somewhat more extensive on Guam, the largest island in Micronesia. The first missionary school was open only to young men of the elite group; later, women were accepted. Reading and writing in Chamorro was taught, but those of the elite who wished to learn studied Spanish. As Aguon explained, "membership in this elite was based on intermarriage with the Spaniards, residency in Agana [the capital town], and . . . wealth."[5] An educated elite could aid the Spanish in governing the island. But to attempt to educate the indigenous people as a whole, the Spanish feared, would "render them unfit for future usefulness."[6] Only in the 19th century did the schools of Guam teach a smattering of Spanish to ordinary pupils.[7]

Indigenous boys in Guam were trained as aides to priests in a seminary built during the 1670s. Gifts from Spanish individuals helped finance the institution as they received glowing reports of widespread conversions. At first, parents were warned to attend mass regularly as well as enroll their children in village schools. By the 1670s, however, "either they accepted Christianity, or they were killed by the Spanish military."[8] Around the same time, soldiers began the practice of seizing children and handing them over to priests attached to military units for purposes of baptism. After many such incidents, "much of Guam remained unsafe for the missionaries unless escorted by armed soldiers."[9] As of 1689, fewer than half of the Chamorros had been converted. Resistance to the Spanish conquest continued despite the loss of 100 Chamorros for every Christian killed.[10]

Intermarriage with the Spanish moderated the tension between conquerors and conquered. By no means, however, did Chamorros on Guam simply acquiesce in the defeat. As Rogers explained:

> Chamorros were not just passive victims of foreigners . . . but agents of their own transformation. . . . The Chamorros were neither totally Hispanicized nor replaced by a hybrid nonindigenous population, as occurred in Cuba and Puerto Rico. Instead, the Chamorros absorbed immigrants into a neo-Chamorro society with new attributes but still permeated by a distinctive univocal Chamorro consciousness at the grassroots level.[11]

They retained their distinctiveness while yielding to superior armed power. In other parts of Micronesia, outcomes varied.

During the last century of Spanish rule, schooling, already extremely modest, deteriorated further. The village schools received no funds from local people nor were Chamorros taxed or tithed for school purposes. In 1839, a school that had operated for years "was now used by the *curé* to raise fighting cocks."[12] The ravages of typhoons and epidemics were difficult to overcome. In the smallpox epidemic of 1856, over three fifths of the people of Guam died.[13] According to a Spanish official, during the 1880s, "Guam's schools were so poor that students 'wrote with little sticks on banana leaves.' Nearly 90 percent of the population was partially or completely illiterate."[14] Nevertheless, defenders of the Spanish regime repeatedly observed that in 1898, the regime's last year, every village had a school.

Between 1899 and 1918, Germany became the principal ruling power over parts of Micronesia. The first school was opened in 1906 and German was the language of instruction. In general, however, schooling was left entirely to church missions. There were no public schools. Apparently, the German civilizing mission was to be discharged without benefit of education.

At the outbreak of World War I in 1914, the Japanese moved quickly to occupy German colonies in Micronesia. Britain supported the action. For the following 31 years, Japan applied its customary colonial techniques that had operated in Taiwan and Korea for some years. In education, this meant the creation of a segregated dual system of public schools, one for Japanese children resident on the islands and the other for indigenous children. Japan now presided over the Carolines, the Marshalls, and the Northern Marianas.

Peattie summarized the central features of Japanese-sponsored schooling in Micronesia:

> Formal Japanese education for many Micronesians was at worst a cultural humiliation; for most it was of limited permanent value; and at best—for the minority who gained some facility in the Japanese language—it was good training for certain useful but subordinate roles as clerks, interpreters, assistant teachers, personal servants, labor supervisors, and village scribes. . . . There was no institution to train Islanders to assume leadership responsibilities or to direct Micronesian destinies, even for some distant day.[15]

Schooling was formalized in 1922 when two sets of public schools were organized. Japanese children received 8 years of elementary school, just as they would in Japan itself. Micronesians, on the other hand, were entitled only to 3 years of schooling, plus an additional 2 if they were among the more able.[16] Ramarui, a Micronesian who had attended a school for indigenous, characterized the school as one "designed to make Micronesians understand the Japanese and obey their orders."[17]

All instruction was in Japanese, a language far removed from any indigenous language. Ramarui recalled, "Vernacular was completely eliminated from the curriculum. Students were punished if they spoke their native tongue."[18] As a consequence, wrote Antilla, "no Micronesian learned to read, write, spell, or study the grammar of his own tongue except for a handful of scholars in mission schools."[19] Because most native children attended school only for 3 years, extremely few learned much Japanese, either. Despite spending half the school day studying Japanese, after 5 years of instruction, "the graduate cannot read a Japanese newspaper and finds a magazine or book quite impossible."[20]

Japanese contempt for Micronesians was expressed in many ways besides inadequate education. Sachuo, a native of Truk, the most populated Micronesian island, wrote in his doctoral dissertation that "the Japanese treated natives as sub-humans."[21] Among Japanese, a common topic was the natives' "low level of civilization."[22] Similarly, "Micronesians . . . were always viewed by Japanese colonial administrators as lesser peoples."[23] The Yapese, "stubbornly resistant to Japanese institutions, values, and ministrations, were singled out as 'savages' who were 'rather difficult to keep in order.'"[24] During the late 1920s and afterward, "reports came to refer to Micronesians as a lazy, uncivilized, inferior people, whose barbaric and objectionable habits would take a long time to overcome."[25] Japanese administrators regarded the Chamorro of the Marianas as the most adaptable and advanced of all Micronesians.[26] This may have been related to the success of sugar production in the Northern Marianas. The Japanese were deeply concerned with turning a profit in their colonial ventures.

By 1936, 8,000 Micronesian students had completed their 3-year elementary course and an added 3,000 finished a supplementary 2-year course.[27] Ten years earlier, a Woodworkers' Apprentice Training School had been established. It was the highest-level educational institution in Micronesia. Advanced courses in agriculture as well as woodworking enrolled from 50 to 60 young men a year, a tiny proportion of those qualified to attend.[28]

In 1927, the percentage of school-aged children actually attending school varied by island. That year, 86.7% in Palau and 14.2% in Truk attended. In Micronesia as a whole, 43.6% were in attendance.[29] Only the schools for Japanese were compulsory.[30] By 1936, attendance on Truk had risen to somewhat over half and that on Yap registered 98%.[31] Ease of transportation was a basic factor in attendance. Schools were free, as were supplies and even food occasionally. The curriculum was based on the supposition that the students were Japanese. As a result, there were no reading materials relating to the history and contemporary life of Micronesia. "In large classes, often of eighty or more students, with one teacher for all subjects, Micronesian children were drilled, pushed, pummeled through a few years of schooling that stressed their subordinate role in a Japanese system."[32] Throughout the years of Japanese rule, mission schools continued to use vernacular languages, but they were primarily religious institutions. The colonial authorities frowned on all private schools but especially objected to use of any language other than Japanese.

Japan governed Micronesia as it did its other colonies. Resistance to its policies were not tolerated, nor did authorities hesitate to use force against protestors. When chiefs in Palau resisted orders, they were deposed "and replaced . . .

with puppets."[33] In Ponape, the islanders continued their historic pattern of resistance to invaders. The Japanese met these rebellions by killing some leaders and deporting others.[34] Petitions from Micronesians requesting that Japanese not be required as a language of instruction were rejected without exception. In any event, the occupiers refused to grant Micronesians any of the constitutional rights that Japanese citizens enjoyed in the home country.[35]

The Spanish-American War ended in 1899 with the signature of the Treaty of Paris. From that date until 1941, the United States occupied Guam as a colony. During the years 1898 through 1941, 40 governors—most of them naval captains—held office. Captain Richard P. Leary, in Order II, admonished U.S. naval personnel that "the natives of Guam are not 'damned dagoes,' nor 'niggers'. . . ."[36] (This failing was reminiscent of the behavior of American troops in the Philippines.)

During the first 6 years of American rule, there were practically no schools open in Guam. Although a public school system had been created on paper, a shortage of secular teachers precluded any actual instruction. At this early date, the Navy decided on English as the language of instruction. The use of Chamorro on school premises was barred. Not even during baseball games were students permitted to speak in their native language.[37] Nevertheless, by 1917, Executive General Order 243 specified, "Chamorro must not be spoken except for official interpreting."[38] The *Guam News Letter* of April 1917 complained that "very few inhabitants had learned to speak English."[39] "Frequently," wrote an observer, "governor reports to the Secretary of the Navy measured educational progress not in terms of English acquisition, but rather in terms of how little Chamorro was being used in some homes."[40]

The Navy refused to yield before popular dissatisfaction on language and other issues. The law was on its side, according to the U.S. Supreme Court's ruling in *Downes* v. *Bidwell*, one of the 1901 *Insular Cases*. Involved was whether or not inhabitants of colonies were entitled to protection of the federal Constitution. Speaking for the Court, Justice Henry B. Brown declared, "If these possessions are inhabited by alien races, differing from us in religion, customs, laws, methods of taxation and modes of thoughts, the administration of government and justice, according to Anglo-Saxon principles, may for a time be impossible."[41] A dissenter, Justice Harlan, criticized the majority—the vote was 5 to 4—for opening the road to a violation of the Constitution by the government itself. Another such violation occurred in 1922 when Navy commanders ordered the collection and burning of whatever copies of a Chamorro–English dictionary could be found.[42] The directive was carried out.

In 1922, the island-wide public school system was reorganized. The state curriculum of California and New Mexico became the model for the Island's schools.[43] Teachers were informed, in true Navy-style: "No teacher or principal is permitted to deviate from this course of study."[44] To conserve space, coeducation was to be practiced. In addition, a rigid form of segregation was enjoined. Separate schools were reserved since 1929 for Continental Americans and Guamanians.[45] Segregation deprived the Chamorro children of one certain avenue to a knowledge of English by interaction with children who spoke it. As Paloma wrote, however:

> The American naval government . . . did not want Americans to mix with the natives. American children went to a separate school, taught by people like themselves. Their military personnel were forbidden to live with the natives and were punished if they were caught. Furthermore, they had their own premises—with fences with barbed wire facing out, stores, movies, theaters, markets, gas stations. There was an unspoken policy and attitude of the American side versus the native side.[46]

When, in 1919, the naval governor barred interracial marriage, that is, of Whites with either Chamorros or Filipinos, the Secretary of the Navy revoked the order.[47] Twelve years earlier, as pointed out previously, a similar order apparently had gone unchallenged.

As the largest employer by far on Guam, the Navy exercised great economic power. The color line was strictly enforced. Thus, for example, the Navy permitted Chamorros to serve, but only as mess attendants. (The same policy also held for African-Americans and Filipinos.) In spite of that, the job was attractive if only for a pension paid in American money. The educational system was not capable of preparing indigenous children for any kind of skilled, technical, or professional employment. The first secondary school, built in 1930, was a junior high school. In 1936, it was replaced by Guam's first high school. Parents who wanted more and improved education for their children, however, had few venues to pursue. In 1938, the colony's first citizens' board of education was established, "but it was only advisory to the governor and had no authority over personnel or the curriculum."[48] When the 1940 Census was taken, it was discovered that the Navy's battle against the Chamorro language was only half-won. Three fourths of Chamorros over age 10 spoke English but Chamorro "remained the main language in nongovernmental activities."[49]

Underwood recalled the long campaign against a language:

> For the first 70-odd years of American rule, individuals remember paying fines and being punished for speaking Chamorro in the classroom and on the school campus. They remember stern warnings of teachers and administrators that the speaking of Chamorro was of little value in life and would hinder intellectual development.[50]

To promote the use of English, "'English-Speaking Area' signs [were posted] around the school campuses, . . . recognition [was given] to students who spoke only English and . . . English-speaking clubs [were formed]."[51]

Within several hours after the December 1941 Pearl Harbor bombing by Japanese aircraft, Guam also came under attack and was readily defeated and occupied. Schools reopened after 4 months, taught in Japanese by some Japanese soldiers. Only after 2 more months did civilian teachers arrive. Most class-room time was taken up by instruction in the language and many families had fled the towns where most schools were located, so comparatively little was accomplished. For one year, the Japanese kept the schools going but were soon overwhelmed by the tide of battle. In mid-1943, schools were closed and all Chamorros other than children were drafted to work as slave labor. After another year of fighting, the Japanese were defeated in August 1944.[52]

The naval administration of Guam changed considerably during the first months of reoccupation. This was especially so with respect to education. A new spirit of cooperation led to the opening of three elementary schools within 2 months. When the war ended, more than 7,000 students attended 21 new schools, taught by 167 Chamorro teachers.[53] Early in 1945, the high school reopened. One year later, its first class graduated. Most startling was the scene of children of U.S. personnel and Chamorro youngsters attending the same schools, public or parochial. In these first postwar months, there was still no institution of higher education in Guam. Elite families, however, sent their children to the mainland for such schooling.

The years after 1945 saw a greatly heightened significance of the Pacific region in American national and foreign policy. In 1949, the Chinese Communists took power and the Soviet Union tested its first atomic bomb. The Korean War (1950–1955) and the Vietnam War (1955–1975) deeply involved the United States. Economic competition with Japan rose to a new level of intensity. Micronesia was frequently used as a jumping-off place for airborne missions, including flights from Tinian carrying the Hiroshima and Nagasaki atomic bombs. The CIA secretly trained Chinese Nationalist troops on Saipan preparing to invade Communist China.

Guam was deeply affected by the militarization of the Pacific Islands. Its population grew beyond any previous level, as follows:[54]

	Chamorros		Non-Chamorros		Total
1940	20,177	91%	2,113	9%	22,290
1960	34,762	52%	32,282	48%	67,044
1980	47,845	45%	58,134	55%	105,979
1990	57,648	43%	75,504	57%	133,152

Construction of housing and military infrastructure absorbed great numbers of laborers. An expanding governmental bureaucracy placed a premium on English literacy. After Navy rule ended in 1950, Micronesians joined military ranks in a broad range of positions.

In 1950, Congress passed an Organic Act that still left Guam as a colony but granted its people some of the rights that Americans enjoyed.[55] Guamanians now became citizens, after a fashion. They still lacked protection from denial of habeas corpus—supplied 18 years later—and certain political rights. One freedom they acquired without reservation was the right to move to the American mainland. A number exercised this promptly. The new legislation also emboldened educators so that Chamorro was no longer forbidden in schools. In fact, after 1950, "people spoke Chamorro freely anywhere on the island. . . ."[56] In 1972, the island legislature made Chamorro the second official language. By the mid-1980s, according to Spencer, Guam was "considered the most advanced school system in the Micronesian Region. . . ."[57] Unfortunately, the superlative held true only by reference to a very low standard.

Outside Guam, Micronesia had undergone significant political changes since the end of World War II. Guam had been a U.S. colony since 1898 but much of the rest of Micronesia had been under Japanese control as a League of Nations Mandate. (This meant hardly more than a requirement for periodic reports to the League.) With the creation of the United Nations in 1945 as a successor to the League, the mandated areas now became known as Trust Territories. The United States signed a Trusteeship document embodying U.N. conditions that the areas be administered with a view toward preparation for eventual independence and economic development. Created in 1951 by the United States was the administrative arrangement known as the U.S. Trust Territory of the Pacific Islands (T.T.P.I.). It included the Marshall Islands, Ponape, Truk, Northern Marianas, Yap, and Palau. Because of various conflicts, T.T.P.I. dissolved and in 1972 a group of Micronesian islands (Kosrae, Yap, Truk, and Pohnpei [formerly Ponape]) formed the Federated States of Micronesia (FSM). Three years later, an agreement between the United States and the Northern Mariana Islands brought about the formation of the Commonwealth of the Northern Mariana Islands (CNMI). The people of CNMI became citizens of the United States as of 1986; in certain areas of government, CNMI exercised self-rule.

These new governing relationships usually entailed increased U.S. financial contributions. Although federal money was welcomed by island authorities, especially in the field of education, the flow of funds accentuated a fundamental problem: The more self-rule the islands received, the more dependent they became on the United States. Prospects for genuine independence thus receded. American policy makers viewed Micronesia as a great military asset rather than as prospective independent nations. Accordingly, they were not concerned about helping the islands develop new industries nor in protecting island sovereignty over valuable natural resources.[58] In 1990, the United Nations ended the U.S. Trusteeship over Micronesia. By that time, the United States had anchored its dominant position in formal agreements with individual Micronesian states.

Apparently only on one occasion had the U.N. intervened in trusteeship issues concerned with Micronesian education. In 1961, a Visiting Mission reported after a first-hand investigation on "inadequate schools, health facilities and medical care and criticized the neglect of economic development."[59] Kanost described the response by Trust officials who acted under U.S. pressure:

Overnight, elementary education ceased to be a responsibility of the local community and became a responsibility of the high commissioner. The goal became a minimum of twelve years of education for every child, instead of the previous goal of six years. English replaced the local languages as the language of instruction. . . . An American standard school system became the goal. Crash programs for construction of schools and teacher housing began in every district. A classroom a year was to be added to the intermediate schools in each district, until a full twelve-year system was completed. Recruitment began for an initial complement of one hundred forty American contract teachers to help man the elementary schools throughout the territory.[60]

Kanost, who directed a teacher-personnel program in Micronesia during the late 1960s, further reported that administrators of the new TTPI measures "suddenly judged hundreds of Micronesian teachers completely unqualified for jobs they had held for years."[61] They were not discharged, however. Many ignored the English-language policy and continued to teach in the vernacular languages.[62]

As a result of the U.N. criticism, budget expenditures on education rose from $7.5 to $149 million a year in 1984.[63] In 1966, the Peace Corps was financed sufficiently so as to engage in 166 separate programs costing an additional $35 million. "Education," wrote Kiste, "became the largest industry in the TTPI."[64] Certain aspects of Micronesian education continued to fester. Chief among these was the English language. During the mid-1980s, 92.1% of Micronesian public-school students were Limited English Proficient (LEP), as follows:[65]

	Total Enrollment	Total LEP	% LEP
Guam	25,168	21,262	84.5
CNMI	4,774	4,634	97.1
Belau	3,512	3,508	99.9
Marshall Islands	11,399	11,304	99.2
Yap, FSM	2,439	2,233	99.8
Pohnpei, FSM	7,557	6,572	87.0
Kosrae, FSM	1,854	1,807	95.9
Truk, FSM	15,609	15,287	97.9
	72,312	66,607	92.1

Under the old Navy definition, these figures were not alarming provided the same children were known not to be using Chamorro. To U.S. officials, ending the use of Chamorro and other indigenous languages was far more important than improving English. Unfortunately, it was too easy to mistake the former for the latter. Yet, it was self-deception to imagine that orders from on high enjoining the use of English could be seriously implemented in view of these figures. Teachers and students thereupon chose the only practical way out—they used a native tongue throughout the schooling cycle. Children of military personnel and more affluent Micronesians who wanted an English-language education and could afford to pay for it simply enrolled in growing numbers in private, including parochial, schools.

The first Micronesian bilingual program was established in the CNMI in 1968. The next year, the Micronesian Congress called "for the use of vernacular languages in all public schools of the Region." [66] In 1970, the public schools of Guam undertook their first bilingual program. As Spencer noted, however, progress came slowly:

> 70 percent of all students enrolling in the University of Guam and 96% of Trust Territory students [in the mid-1980s], must take basic ESL classes to develop English speaking, listening, reading, and writing skills sufficient to carry them through freshman introductory courses. [67]

In the 1950s and 1960s, according to Flinn, those who attended this institution, "represented the most intellectually able of the high school graduates." [68] It seems doubtful that the same was true a generation later.

Quantitative progress in schooling was undoubted. This was especially clear in secondary education. High-school graduates numbered 400 in 1961, 732 in 1964, and 1,160 in 1971. [69] Other than openings in military services, however, few other jobs existed for the graduates. During these same years, the teaching force changed greatly. Many more Americans were employed as teachers. "While in 1950–51 such teachers accounted for only 16 percent of the education staff in Guam, by 1970–71 only a quarter of all teachers were Chamorros. . . ." [70] Nor in these years was the curriculum adjusted so as to show how improved education could be useful in changing the social reality of colonial Guam. Instead, mainland culture remained the touchstone of island education.

Higher education in Guam was no different. During the 40 years preceding World War I, an average of only two Chamorro a year attended mainland colleges, and barely one fourth of the total returned to Guam. [71] Children of elite families had frequently gone to the United States for higher education. During the 1980s, middle-class families were using stateside universities as finishing schools before emigration to the mainland. Yet on the island, economic opportunities were expanding during the same decade. For one thing, a real estate boom brought large Japanese capital investments to Guam as tourism engulfed the island. Some who profited from rising land values cashed in and left for the mainland. Others remained to participate in new-found economic opportunities. The Census of 1990 revealed that speaking Chamorro at home was no longer an economic handicap, as it had been 10 years earlier: "The mean individual income of those who spoke Chamorro at home was recorded to be $18,572 . . . as opposed to the next highest group (those who spoke only English at home) which recorded a mean individual income of $18,372." [72]

Spencer described with discernment the language situation in Micronesia's schools around 1984:

> Although English is the predominant language of the schools in Guam, and is rapidly assuming this position in the Commonwealth of Northern Marianas, the vernacular language continues to be the medium of instruction in public elementary schools everywhere else in the Region. In the few high schools within the Micronesian Region (beyond Guam and CNMI), English is officially designated as the language of instruction; however, in actual practice, the vernacular languages are used extensively in these settings as well. Except in Guam, English is a second and usually non-dominant language for the majority of school teachers. Except for Guam and the CNMI, English is present in the community only as a government and tourist language, or a *lingua franca* amongst Micronesians of diverse linguistic groups. Thus, students will develop in a linguistic community in which the indigenous language of their culture is the primary linguistic input, with English and other languages of the Region heard as rare or only occasional inputs.[73]

This characterization seems valid also for the years since 1984. In 1992, for example, she wrote that, "achieved literacy is not widespread in the home language or in English in most parts of the region."[74]

In addition to its role in schooling, the larger cultural role of language is not without its problems. "The fact that Chamorro is still held in high esteem," wrote Underwood, "is remarkable given the experience of Chamorro in Guam's schools."[75] Chamorros have embraced English not because of repugnance at their native tongue but for the obvious economic value of English. Underwood believes that Chamorro attraction to American culture has played a lesser role than the practical advantage of English. Spencer builds on a study by Odo who found that:

> Adults spoke . . . [Chamorro] to one another in the presence of children, but adults speak English when directly communicating with Chamorro children. This is language acquisition by eavesdropping, as Underwood has said elsewhere. . . . Odo's subjects were almost all in favor of stable bilingualism for their children. They wanted their children to speak "good Chamorro and good English." But in saying that they expect to pick it up somewhere along the way, they seem to have underestimated the fragility of the current state of the Chamorro language in Guam.[76]

Between the celebration of Chamorro by Underwood and the scepticism by Spencer lay a large gulf.

Between 1946 and 1958, the United States tested 66 atomic and hydrogen bombs in various Marshall Islands.[77] During the first year, the 170 inhabitants of Bikini Atoll consented to be moved to a new home island. The Governor of the Marshalls had told them that the forthcoming tests were to be done for the good of mankind and would lead to an end to world wars. Chief Juda responded that if the tests "with God's blessing will result in kindness and benefit to all mankind," his people would be pleased to move.[78] As the time of departure approached, "the community's cemetery was cleaned and decorated with flowers and palm fronds, and a ceremony was held to bid farewell to the Bikinians' ancestors and to entrust their souls to the care of God."[79] They moved first to Rongerik, then Kwajalein, then Kili, and in 1968, back to a horribly changed Bikini. Parts of islands as well as several entire ones no longer existed; the beaches were strewn with rusting equipment; in addition, "most coconut palms and other plants of economic value had been removed or destroyed, and the atoll was engulfed by a dense layer of scrub vegetation."[80] Marshallese travelled far to find space for new communities. In Costa Mesa, California, such a community was established and by the beginning of the 1990s, some 400 persons lived there. Plans were underfoot to organize a Marshallese Consulate and a Cultural Center.[81] In Hawaii, on the other hand, two local communities rejected Marshallese initiatives.

Kwajalein Atoll became the test target area for intercontinental missiles launched from Vandenberg Air Force Base in California. Throughout Micronesia, similar installations were located, making it an exceedingly dangerous area for inhabitants. In 1983, when a study group of the World Council of Churches visited the Marshalls, they found that "there is widespread distrust by Marshallese of United States scientists involved in radiation monitoring and health surveillance programs."[82] Such suspicion was fueled by government secrecy and lack of candor in admitting the hazards of radiation. (Until 1990, "Guam had more nuclear weapons per capita than any other place in the world."[83])

Kwajalein and Ebeye islands illustrate how militarization of the Marshalls had far-reaching effects on the two communities. The two places are separated by 3 miles of lagoon. In 1984:

> No Micronesian, with the exception of the ranking Trust Territory Representative and his family, is allowed to live on Kwajalein. All others must commute in by boat, and unless given special permission, must be off Kwajalein by 5:30 p.m.
>
> Residents in Kwajalein live in air-conditioned housing. They have free transportation, free recreation, including movies, a bowling alley, a library, a golf course, tennis courts, tended beaches, swimming pools and use of boats from the marina. They also have high quality schools and a well-equipped air-conditioned hospital. . . . American employees of Kwajalein Missile Range . . . may shop at all stores on Kwajalein. Micronesian employees may not.[84]

Ebeye's principal export is laborers to Kwajalein. Its 7,500 or so inhabitants live in one tenth of a square mile. All food is purchased in stores in Ebeye. Only the Paramount Chief has the right to shop in Kwajalein stores. Land is not owned by any laborer in Ebeye. There is no high school on the island as there is in Kwajalein. Children from Ebeye are barred from that high school.[85] Ebeye, wrote Connell, "is perhaps the worst urban area in the Pacific region."[86]

Alexander, who was writing a doctoral dissertation about Ebeye at the New School for Social Research, told a U.S. House of Representatives hearing about much evidence of discrimination against Micronesian workers and favoring non-

Micronesian workers. "There are," he wrote, "discriminatory practices [as] regards vacation time, equal pay, benefits, and the advancement or training for higher positions which is not granted."[87] Discrimination against Micronesians also existed in hospitals.[88] Although Ebeye laborers received low wages, the grocery stores to which they were restricted charged higher prices than did grocery stores on Kwajalein.[89] Alexander's research work, based on field work during July 1975 to July 1976, concluded:

> The history of the Marshalls under United States Trusteeship is a disgraceful record; including the various results of the Bikini and Enewetok nuclear tests, the irradiation of the Rongelap and Uterik people and last, Ebeye, which may be the focal point for the ultimate destruction of Marshallese society."[90]

Pohnpei had been a Japanese Mandate and in 1945 became part of the American Trust territory. In both cases, the affiliation resulted from military action; the people of Pohnpei were not given an opportunity to choose or declare their independence. Missionary and Japanese schooling promoted "the subtle, often unconscious, process of learning inferiority through compulsory participation in foreign schools."[91] Under the United States, the process continued. Such, at least, was a dominant view among scholars of the matter.

During the 1970s, however, a political movement for independence arose in Pohnpei. These same people who had learned inferiority increasingly viewed themselves as equally entitled to a nation state. In 1975, a referendum took place in which voters were given a choice of independence or free association with the United States. (The latter relationship would still subordinate Pohnpei to the United States but give its people the right to travel to any part of the U.S. area. Also, financial payments to Pohnpei would be stepped up.) As Vitarelli reported, "In every district there was a majority who voted in favor of independence over Free Association."[92] Because Pohnpei was outvoted by others of the Northern Mariana Islands, the FSM free association was implemented. In 1983, Pohnpei once more voted in favor of independence but did not receive it. In both votes, Peterson observed, "the people of Pohnpei called for independence from the U.S., even though they believed that this would cut off American funding and leave them effectively broke."[93]

The schooling the children of Pohnpei received paid little heed to nationalist strivings of the people. Indeed, children were taught to regard the United States as the very model of democracy, and separation from it as a step backwards in history. Clearly, Pohnpeians knew how to select their options whether or not these were taught in school. The islands' resistance to American pressure had more to do with the nature of its economy than with its schooling. Unlike many other Micronesian islands, Pohnpei has a thriving subsistence economy that operates communally. Most people own their land. It is not wholly dependent on imports or U.S. subsidies. Its people "believe that they can feed themselves should U.S. funding be cut off. What is more, many . . . believe that their economy will thrive only when that funding is ended."[94] Food is produced to be shared by all through a series of exchanges, especially large-scale feasts. They thus "see themselves as actively creating a political community in which everyone plays a role. Consequently . . . [they] have never, despite their colonial history, lost a sense of the importance of governing themselves."[95] When, in 1983, a majority of the member states of the FSM approved the principle of free association with the United States, Pohnpei was dragged into the new arrangement when it was ratified by the United States in 1986.

Belau, formerly Palau, was one of the six administrative districts of the U.S. TTPI, created in 1951. Twenty-one years later, the United States informed Belau that it wanted to reserve land and/or harbor rights in three places, including Belau. The request was granted. In 1979, however, a proposal by the United States that it be allowed to store nuclear bombs on Belau was rejected. (A majority voted in favor but not the three fourths majority required for approval.) Great pressure by the United States was exerted on Belau voters to support the measure. In 1990, for example, after the proposal had been rejected six times, the island government declared that unless voters approved the measure that "money would not be released for local projects—roads, hospitals, schools, etc."[96] It was then rejected for a seventh time. In 1992, however, by a vote of 62 to 38%, Belauans agreed to eliminate the constitutional provision for a three fourths majority, and the next year, they consented by a margin of 68% to join the Compact of Free Association. In 1994, the Compact came into full operation.[97] The United States thereby gained certain military rights that Belau had resisted for a number of years.

William Vitarelli, who had been an educational administrator in Belau from 1949 to 1954 and then served as a vice president of the University of Guam, spoke at the Modekngi School in Belau. (In 1982, Belau had become an independent republic.)

> Almost anywhere in the world it is now known that the brave little Republic called Belau is the first nation in the world to include a non-nuclear clause in its constitution. . . . By this wise act Belau has become an inspiration for many nations throughout the world as they struggle for their independence. . . . You have become international leaders and have contributed toward the survival of this place. . . .[98]

Many Belauans have emigrated to other countries.[99] In one study, it was found that one fifth of all Palauans lived abroad, Similarly, in 1980 one fourth of their women of childbearing age resided outside the territory. By no means, however, did they become permanent expatriates. As Nero and Rehuher observed, "Many Palauan women return not only for The First Child Ceremony, but bring their young children to spend time in Palau to ensure they will learn the language and get to know their relatives."[100]

The Micronesian experience with the United States was not a happy one:

> The U.S. was not interested in developing the islands economically, but rather in

keeping other countries out. . . . In what has been called the "zoo theory" of administration, the islands languished with little input from the United States, without even replacement of indigenous and Japanese infrastructure destroyed by . . . [World War II]. The "administrators" of the islands didn't even reside there, but far off in Hawaii until the 1960s.[101]

The "zoo" extended far beyond a single colony.

CONCLUDING REMARKS

Whether in a Pacific island or a colony of millions, no conquest is complete without a process of cultural devaluation. Unlike armed encounters that are more readily won by conquerors, a people's language, history, and grass-roots economic power are far more resistant to foreign manipulation. In Guam, the United States outlawed the use of the native language, but it did not die out. The Japanese in Korea were no more successful at suppressing an indigenous language than they were in forbidding study of Korean history. The island state of Pohnpei successfully resisted the most powerful country in the world on a matter of nuclear policy, secure in its long-run capacity to live on its own traditional means. Belau resisted from 1979 to 1992.

NOTES

[1] R. Murray Thomas and T. Neville Postlethwaite, eds., *Schooling in the Pacific Islands: Colonies in Transition* (Pergamon Press, 1984), p. 4.

[2] Elizabeth K. Antilla, *A History of the People of the Trust Territory of the Pacific Islands and Their Education* (Doctoral dissertation, University of Texas, 1965), p. 120.

[3] Ibid., p. 95.

[4] Ibid., p. 93.

[5] Katherine B. Aguon, "The Guam Dilemma: The Need for a Pacific Island Education Perspective," *Amerasia Journal*, 6 (1979), p. 80.

[6] Willard Price, *Japan's Islands of Mystery* (John Day, 1944), p. 60.

[7] Charles F. Reid, *Education in the Territories and Outlying Possessions of the United States* (Teachers College, Columbia University, 1941), p. 317.

[8] Robert F. Rogers, *Destiny's Landfall. A History of Guam* (University of Hawaii Press, 1995), p. 57.

[9] Ibid., p. 62.

[10] Ibid., p. 71.

[11] Ibid., p. 104.

[12] Ibid., p. 98.

[13] Ibid., p. 101.

[14] Ibid., pp. 104–105.

[15] Mark R. Peattie, *Nan'yo. The Rise and Fall of the Japanese in Micronesia, 1885–1945* (University of Hawaii Press, 1988), p. 95.

[16] Donald R. Schuster, "Schooling in Micronesia During Japanese Mandate Rule," *Educational Perspectives*, 18 (May 1979), p. 21.

[17] Ibid., p. 22.

[18] Ibid., p. 24.

[19] Anttila, *A History*, p. 346.

[20] Price, *Japan's Islands of Mystery*, p. 168.

[21] Sweeter Sachuo, *Cultural and Educational Imperialism: An Examination of the Consequential Impacts of Externally Designed and Imposed Educational Systems on the Children of Truk and Other Trukese Culture* (Doctoral dissertation, University of Oregon, 1992), p. 12.

[22] Anttila, *A History*, p. 272.

[23] R. Peattie, *Nan'yo*, p. 111.

[24] Ibid., p. 112.

[25] Ibid., p. 113.

[26] Ibid., p. 112.

[27] Anttila, *A History*, p. 233.

[28] Schuster, "Schooling in Micronesia," p. 24.

[29] Ibid., p. 22.

[30] Price, *Japan's Islands of Mystery*, p. 45.

[31] Ibid., p. 167.

[32] Peattie, *Nan'yo*, p. 94.

[33] Anttila, *A History*, p. 246.

[34] Ibid., p. 276.

[35] Peattie, *Nan'yo*, p. 104.

[36] Rogers, *Destiny's Landfall*, p. 120.

[37] Ibid., p. 133.

[38] Ibid., p. 140.

[39] Ibid., p. 141.

[40] Aguon, "The Guam Dilemma," p. 82.

[41] Rogers, *Destiny's Landfall*, p. 125.

[42] Rogers, *Destiny's Landfall*, p. 147. See also Rosa S. Paloma, "American Policies and Practices Affecting Language Shift on Guam: 1898–1950," p. 25 in Mary L. Spencer, ed., *Chamorro Language Issues and Research on Guam. A Book of Readings* (University of Guam, Mangilao, Guam, 1987).

[43] Aguon, "The Guam Dilemma," p. 82. According to Rogers, *Destiny's Landfall*, p. 147, the model was California; New Mexico is not mentioned.

[44] Rogers, *Destiny's Landfall*, p. 147.

[45] See Laura Thompson, *Guam and Its People*, 3rd edition (Princeton University Press, 1947), p. 220 and Paloma, "American Policies," p. 34.

[46] Paloma, "American Policies," pp. 34–35.

[47] Rogers, *Destiny's Landfall*, p. 145.

[48] Ibid., p. 159.

[49] Ibid., p. 159.

[50] Robert A. Underwood, "Language Survival, the Ideology of English and Education in Guam," p. 5 in Mary L. Spencer, ed., *Chamorro Language Issues and Research on Guam. A Book of Readings* (University of Guam, 1987).

[51] Ibid., p. 9.

[52] See chapter 10 of Rogers, *Destiny's Landfall*, pp. 163–181.

[53] Ibid., p. 201.

[54] Ibid., p. 283.

[55] See ibid., pp. 225–232 for a summary and commentary on the Organic Act of 1950.

[56] Ibid., p. 225.

[57] Mary L. Spencer, *History and Status of Vernacular School Materials and Instruction in the Micronesian Region, with Comments on Literacy and Emerging Local Educational Needs* (Department of

Behavioral Sciences, College of Arts and Sciences, College of Education, University of Guam, December 1986), p. 13. ERIC ED 297 583.

[58] See Victoria King, "The Commonwealth of the Northern Mariana Islands' Rights Under United States and International Law to Control Its Exclusive Economic Zone," *University of Hawaii Law Review*, 13 (Fall 1991), pp. 477–504 and John Connell, "The New Micronesia: Pitfalls and Problems of Dependent Development, *Pacific Studies*, 14 (March 1991), pp. 87–120.

[59] Richard F. Kanost, "The American Performance in Micronesia: A Retrospective Appraisal," *American Journal*, 12 (1985–1986), p. 67.

[60] Ibid., p. 68.

[61] Ibid., p. 68.

[62] Ibid., p. 68.

[63] Robert C. Kiste, "New Political Statuses in American Micronesia," p. 71 in Virginia S. Lockwood, Thomas G. Harding, and Ben J. Wallace, eds., *Contemporary Pacific Societies. Studies in Development and Change* (Prentice-Hall, 1993). See also Karen M. Peacock, "Robert E. Gibson, Educator and Advocate of Justice," *Contemporary Pacific* 5 (Fall 1993), p. 387.

[64] Kiste, "New Political Statuses," p. 72.

[65] Spencer, *History and Status*, p. 42.

[66] Ibid., p. 8.

[67] Ibid., p. 16. See also Mary L. Spencer, "Literacy in Micronesia," *ISLA: A Journal of Micronesian Studies*, 1 (1992), p. 69.

[68] Juliana Flinn, "Transmitting Traditional Values in New Schools: Elementary Education of Pulap Atoll," *Anthropology and Education Quarterly*, 23 (March 1992), p. 48.

[69] Leland Bettis, "Colonial Immigration on Guam. Displacement of the Chamorro People Under U.S. Governance," p. 287 in Grant McCall and John Connell, eds., *A World Perspective on Pacific Islander Migration. Australia, New Zealand and the U.S.A.* (Center for South Pacific Studies, University of New South Wales, 1993).

[70] Ibid., p. 288.

[71] Ibid., p. 288.

[72] Ibid., p. 293.

[73] Spencer, *History and Status*. p. 7.

[74] Spencer, "Literacy in Micronesia," quoted in Ellen Boneparth and M. James Wilkinson, "Terminating Trusteeship for the Federated States of Micronesia and the Republic of the Marshall Islands: Independence and Self-Sufficiency in the Post-Cold War Pacific," *Pacific Studies* 18 (June 1995), p. 69.

[75] Underwood, "Language Survival," p. 12.

[76] Spencer, *Chamorro Language Issues*, p. 203.

[77] Glenn Alcalay, "Pax Americana in the Pacific," *Covert Action Information Bulletin*, Spring 1992, p. 48.

[78] Robert C. Kiste, *The Bikinians: A Study in Forced Migration* (Cummings, 1974), p. 28.

[79] Ibid., p. 33.

[80] Ibid., p. 175. For more extensive findings on a series of bomb explosions, see A. Costandina Titus, *Bombs in the Backyard. Atomic Testing and American Politics* (University of Nevada Press, 1986).

[81] Karen L. Nero and Fausino K. Rehuher, "Pursuing the Dream. Historical Perspectives in Micronesian Movement Patterns," p. 248 in Grant McCall and John Connell, eds., *A World Perspective on Pacific Islander Migration. Australia, New Zealand and the USA* (Center for South Pacific Studies, University of South Wales, 1993).

[82] World Council of Churches Delegation to the Marshall Islands, 20 May–4 June 1983, *Marshall Islands: 37 Years After* (Commission of the Churches on International Affairs, World Council of Churches, 1983), p. 15.

[83] Peter De Benedittis, *Guam's Trial of the Century. News, Hegemony, and Rumor in an American Colony* (Praeger, 1993), p. 5.

[84] William Vitarelli, "United States Educational Policies in Micronesia," p. 14 in Catherine Lutz, ed., *Micronesia As Strategic Colony* (Cultural Survival, Inc., June, 1994).

[85] See Giff Johnson, *Collision Course at Kwajalein. Marshall Islanders in the Shadow of the Bomb* (Pacific Concerns Resource Center, 1984), p. 22.

[86] Connell, "The New Micronesia," p. 107.

[87] William J. Alexander, *Wage Labor, Urbanization and Culture Change in the Marshall Islands: The Ebeye Case* (Doctoral dissertation, New School for Social Research, 1978), p. 45.

[88] See ibid., pp. 52–57.

[89] Ibid., p. 47.

[90] Ibid., p. 174.

[91] Nat J. Colletta, *American Schools for the Natives of Ponape. A Study of Education and Culture Change in Micronesia* (University Press of Hawaii, 1980), p. 43.

[92] Vitarelli, "United States Educational Policies," p. 94.

[93] Glenn Petersen, "Some Pohnpei Strategies for Economic Survival," p. 189 in Victoria S. Lockwood and others, eds., *Contemporary Pacific Societies. Studies in Development and Change* (Prentice-Hall, 1993).

[94] Vitarelli, "United States Educational Policies," p. 95. See also Ellen Boneparth and M. James Wilkinson, "Terminating Trusteeship for the Federated States of Micronesia and the Republic of the Marshall Islands. Independence and Self-Sufficiency in the Post Cold-War Pacific," *Pacific Studies* 18 (June 1995), pp. 61–77.

[95] Ibid., p. 96.

[96] Bob Aldridge and Ched Myers, *Resisting the Serpent: Palau's Struggle for Self-Determination* (Fortkamp Publishing Co., 1990), p. 182.

[97] Samuel F. McPhetres, Julie Olsson, and Donald R. Shuster, "Micronesia in Review: Issues and Events, 1 July 1993 to 30 June 1994," *Contemporary Pacific,* 7 (Spring 1995), p. 126.

[98] Vitarelli, "United States Educational Policies," p. 80.

[99] Connell, "The New Micronesia," p. 108.

[100] Nero and Rehuher, "Pursuing the Dream," p. 252.

[101] Ibid., p. 244.

Polynesia

SAMOA

Samoa was an independent country until 1889 when it came under a colony-like supervision of Great Britain, Germany, and the United States. A decade later, it was divided outright into two colonies, one American and the other German. Britain was compensated elsewhere. American Samoa, which included the superb port of Pago-Pago, was less than one tenth the size of Western Samoa, the German colony. In 1914, on the outbreak of World War I, the latter became a colony of New Zealand until 1921, when it was transformed into a Mandated Territory of the League of Nations and assigned to New Zealand. At the end of World War II, Western Samoa was made part of the new United Nations Trusteeship System; it remained under New Zealand's rule. In 1962, it became independent. American Samoa has remained an American colony since 1899.

During all these shifts and turns in world politics, neither the people nor the governments of Samoa were consulted other than perfunctorily.

Before the advent of colonialism, Samoans lived in a subsistence economy in which land was owned communally. The traditional system operated effectively:

> Village gardens and community fishing supply food for all; the labor and distribution being under the direction of the village and family chiefs. No one is rich in the sense of owning property or stores of goods, but no able-bodied man or woman is devoid of useful employment and no one goes hungry so long as there is a mouthful to be passed around.[1]

In its essentials, this system remained in force during the 19th and 20th centuries.

Formal education was introduced into Samoa by Christian missionaries who first arrived in numbers during the 1830s and 1840s. Literacy was made a prerequisite for church membership. Because there was no written Samoan language, the missionaries created one. By 1839, 12,300 children were attending mission schools. Of this number, fully 1,000 soon learned to read the new script.[2] Another source reports that there were "10,000 literate Samoans" by that same year.[3] Only 5 years earlier, the first printed book in Samoan—a Bible— had been printed. The first Samoan dictionary followed in 1862 and a syntax of Samoan grammar in 1875. By century's end, almost all Samoans were literate in their own language. This remains the case. In each village, the church contained a school that taught Samoan reading and writing. Besides religion, however, very little else was taught. Other than these institutions, no public schools were established by the native government during the remainder of the 19th century.

American rule was administered by the U.S. Navy, which exercised its authority with an iron hand. Chiefs and other native title-holders were left in office, but they could only protest when confronted with governmental actions based on Naval orders. During the entire period of Naval rule (1900–1951), Samoans implored the Navy to attract U.S. government funds as a subsidy for a public school system. The Navy refused. A Presidentially appointed governor explained that "it is debasing to the moral fibre of the people to obtain benefits in any other way than through their own efforts."[4] The Secretary of the Navy wrote that "government aid should be discouraged as far as possible and the people encouraged to do more for themselves."[5] (Little, apparently, was said about the historic American policy of making extensive land grants to states as a subsidy for public education.) When, in 1903, a group of native chiefs petitioned authorities to build a public school, the naval commandant offered to contribute $100 in government funds if the chiefs would cede their islands to the U.S. government. The offer was accepted. When a school was built, 68 scholarships were awarded. Fifty-two were given to Samoans whereas the naval commandant appointed 16 "children of white or part white blood."[6] Seven years later, Gov. William M. Crose wrote in a letter that "repeated requests for money to establish public schools have so far met with only silence."[7]

Meanwhile, mission education held its own. In 1912, the government proclaimed compulsory education for ages 6 to 13 years, for at least 4 days a week. Primer classes and three grades were required with Grade IV as an extra class. By 1914, six mission and two island-government schools existed. These latter, although secular in auspices, were taught by religious personnel. The school day was to last 3 hours. In fact, however, the new regulations were more or less ignored.[8]

After 20 years of American rule, in 1921 the island government finally installed a public school system. Eighteen public schools were opened, most of them extending only through four primary-school grades.[9] A school tax was levied on each taxpayer. Six persons were appointed to a school board, which, however, was merely advisory to the governor. Three Samoan chiefs sat on the board. More than half of the schools had plantations that were worked by students and teachers. Of 42 teachers, 38 were Samoan and 4 white. Besides the school tax, some island revenues were available, especially those derived from customs duties on exports and imports. No federal funds were spent on education, as before 1921.

Although the island government proudly published rising enrollment data in periodic reports, some Samoans were less impressed. Tuitele submitted a statement to a federal hearing that declared, "The public schools are the veriest makeshifts. The native teachers are entirely incompetent, beyond the barest rudiments."[10] Chief Magalei challenged authorities:

> If you are satisfied that these schools are very good schools and have very good teachers, why then are the children of [naval] officers not sent to the schools to be educated, but sent to other schools, such as the [Marist] Brothers' schools and other schools?[11]

Chief Satele emphasized:

> Our schools were not built by the Navy. We built them with our own money. Like this school here in Leone. We built that house as a school for the education of our children when the Navy wouldn't build the school. The Navy didn't spend a single cent on this school building.[12]

Defenders of the schools also were heard, but they were not numerous.

Commander C. C. Baughman of the U.S. Navy cautioned his hearers against overeducating the Samaoans:

> To teach anything beyond what is a necessity in Samoa would give the people a knowledge of and insight into things and phenomena (to them) that can only breed discontentment, a disinclination to work, and a desire only to go to the movies, drive a car, carouse, and in some cases to travel to America, where they do not fit. . . . The standard curriculum of education should comprise only the simple necessities of Samoan life and include only such subjects as public health, manual training, agriculture, reading, writing, and arithmetic.[13]

He did not discuss any of the criticisms made by the Samoans. Another 21 years were to pass before the Navy departed Samoa in 1951 and a new philosophy of education could be adopted.

Meanwhile, Samoans found other ways of making their sentiments known. Traditionally, parents were responsible for bringing food to the teachers. A very thin teacher was usually adjudged to be under parental stricture through being denied his rations. Entire villages sometimes withheld food.[14]

One indicator of some educational progress in the schools was a change in the distribution of the children among the primary grades. Between 1926 and 1953, public school enrollment by grades was as follows:[15]

Percent of Enrollment

Grade	1926	1953
1	58.1	24.8
2	11.6	19.0
3	11.0	15.4
4	9.5	10.2
5	5.1	8.1
6	2.6	8.2
7	1.1	5.4
8	0.8	4.7
9	0.2	4.2

In the earlier year, only 9.8% were in the upper grades (5–9) whereas in the later year, the figure had risen to 30.6%.

During the years of Naval rule, primary school teachers had no more than a junior-high-school education, and sometimes less. In fact, as late as 1961, "the vast majority of the elementary school teachers only have the equivalent of a sixth-grade [U.S.?] education."[16] That same year, according to a retrospective comment 4 years later, the governor was said to have found that teachers had an equivalent of a fifth-grade U.S. education.[17] Also in 1961, a Congressional Study Mission declared that "an untrained, poorly paid teaching force is laboring in unequipped, inadequate buildings which would be unrecognizable as schools in much of the rest of the United States."[18] The same group also discovered that teachers had not received a salary increase in 10 years; partly as a result, one third of the teaching force turned over each year. Although average family incomes in Western Samoa were much lower than in American Samoa, teachers in the former were paid one third more than in the latter. As a consequence, Western Samoan teacher-training courses attracted 10 times as many students as did those in American Samoa.[19] Congressional legislation that provided for federal aid to specified educational programs did not benefit American Samoa because the measures almost always exempted the colony. This was true, for example, for the Smith-Hughes and George-Barden Acts, vocational education measures, the Library Services Act, and the National Defense Education Act.[20] As late as 1961, there was no public library system in American Samoa.[21] Nor were there any in elementary or junior high schools. A small high-school library was the only one in operation.

School buildings were desperately scarce in American Samoa. According to long-time practice, each village was expected to build and maintain its own elementary school. The government of the islands was expected to build all other school buildings. In fact, however, the government did not build a single school structure in the 10 years after the Navy withdrew from American Samoa in 1951. By that time, the villages had also stopped building schools; they could no longer afford to do so. For a number of years, villages had borrowed building funds from the island-operated Bank of American Samoa. Because they had great difficulty in repaying the loans, the Bank stopped the loan program. Money from the small school tax could not be used for building schools.

By 1960, average schooling of indigenous Samoans was 7.3 years for males and 6.5 years for females.[22] At the same time, a separate elementary institution, called the Dependents' School, was established for English-speaking students—that is, White students. Male students in that school averaged 13.4 years schooling. Certified teachers from the mainland taught there and enforced educational standards comparable with those in the United States. During the late 1950s, enrollment in the junior high schools was permitted to rise; over a 5-year period, the number of students increased by one eighth each year. Nevertheless, few of the graduates could attend high school because school authorities established an annual cap of 105 students admitted to the high school. This was enforced by an academic entrance exam. In 1960 and 1961, the ceiling was raised to 135 new students.

In fact, the early 1960s saw an important increase in school building and educational expansion in American Samoa. Perhaps it resulted in part as a rebound from the U.N.-stimulated school changes in Micronesia. In any event, federal grants-in-aid to the colony rose from $984,800 in 1961 to $1,875,433 in 1962; it was proposed to rise in 1963 to $2,623,150. School construction expenditures increased from $1,286,800 in 1962 to $4,576,750 the following year. High school facilities were expanded so that all junior-high graduates could attend high school. By 1967, compulsory attendance was enjoined for ages 6 through 18 or until graduation from grade 12.

It was unclear as to how much educational quality improved as a result of these changes. The U.S. Department of Interior annual report for 1968 announced that "the size of classes [in secondary schools] had been reduced from 90 to approximately 35 pupils."[23] Interestingly, it had never been reported previously that the class size was so high. Neither Navy nor Interior annual reports had ever discussed class size as problematic. In addition, the Interior Annual Report for 1967 explained that classes were organized into four levels because "much of the curriculum for children who were in school before 1964 is remedial in nature."[24] Never had an annual report admitted as much. Nor did the Interior Department remind readers that it was the very agency administering such a curriculum before 1964, indeed, since 1951. In 1968, the Annual Report announced an evaluation of English reading and usage among current students on Level IV with students in 1964. No results were announced for other levels, nor were any quantitative data released. The reader was informed only that the Level IV scores were much higher in 1968 than earlier. At no time did Interior explain the criteria by which students were assigned to different levels. According to Rolff, "During the 1970s, most high school seniors in . . . American Samoa were insufficiently prepared to pass the military entrance examinations."[25] Levin and Ahlburg commented, "The school system in American Samoa seemed to be unable to prepare students for the exams for cultural or educational reasons." [26]

As of mid-1950, only two American Samoan graduates of the local public schools were attending college. In 1971, when the Community College of Samoa opened, 61.5% of the students dropped out during the Fall semester. Apparently, the tuition charges weighed heavily on students. During the Spring semester, when tuition was abolished, dropouts declined to 36.3%. [27] In 1955, the Church of Jesus Christ of Latter Day Saints founded the Church College of Hawaii and operated it largely as an open-door college. Some 20 years afterwards, however, cut-off points for admission were increased in tests of academic and language aptitude. The institution became Brigham Young University-Hawaii and enrolled a modest number of American Samoan students as follows: [28]

1975	12	1985	16
1980	19	1989	24

During the first 35 years after the close of World War II, "The Mormon Church provided a much more convenient access to college-level education than was available to any other group in the central Polynesian islands." [29]

The educational role of language and culture was a continuing issue in Samoa during the 19th and 20th centuries. In missionary schools, Samoan was the language of instruction. This facilitated the preparation of indigenous teachers—some of whom themselves became missionaries. As we saw earlier, Samoans became an almost completely literate society before the close of the 19th century. The British indulged their racism by establishing separate schools for Whites and half-castes. Native Samoans were not permitted in these schools. They deeply resented being excluded inasmuch as they wished to learn English in addition to their native tongue. A Samoan woman explained what lay behind the policy:

> I believe that they do not wish natives to learn the English language because they are afraid that they would learn too much about values, trade, commerce, and matters of business, and it would not be so easy [for the British] to get the advantage of them in many things as it is at the present time; but I know that it is a stumbling-block in the way of the advancement of the native Samoans, and a standing cause of offense to them. [30]

Once the United States established its rule over American Samoa, school-language policy changed. In 1903, English was decreed as the language of instruction for village schools. [31] When in 1922 the first public-school system began operation, it also adopted the English-only policy. The consequences of this policy became clear when in 1927 and 1919, "ranking chiefs . . . complained that their children were not being taught their own language and customs." [32] American authorities were not impressed because they viewed the decline of Samoan as a complement to the rise of English. As in Guam, one goal was confused with the other. Among Samoans, however, the very reverse logic prevailed: Both languages were valued and mastery of Samoan was regarded as a strong basis for mastery of English. When, therefore, Samoan parents sought to insure their children a chance to learn English, it was not out of derogation to Samoan. Rather, it was an affirmation of the goal of bilingualism.

In 1932, this was grasped by anthropologist Keesing:

> The big danger in a place . . .like Samoa . . . is that there will be a prolonged period of *cultural pauperization,* in which native ways and language will be despised but English ways and language will be really little grasped. . . . An emphasis on the vernacular would minimize this and provide a very desirable *cultural anchor.*[33]

Keesing cautioned that "a school system which disregards the native cultural setting and fails to use the vernacular language in which by now the Samoans are so fully literate is wasteful of a remarkable opportunity to enrich the native life and thought."[34] He called it artificial "for children who speak only the vernacular at home to struggle with English only in the school."[35]

Beginning in 1949, school authorities began to change their English-only policy. Samoan was not formally studied as a second language, but it was now deemed acceptable for teachers to use Samoan to explain aspects of the curriculum. Preschool, first, second, and third grades were conducted solely in Samoan.[36] Much of this had already been done for years. In 1951, the Navy Department reported:

> In the last two years greater emphasis has been placed upon the use of the vernacular as a means of instruction in the Primary section (grades 1, 2, and 3) with English taught as a subject. The transition from the vernacular to English takes place in the Intermediate section (grades 4, 5, and 6) with the Samoan language diminishing as the child goes up the grade ladder. English is the means of instruction in the upper section (grades 7, 8, and 9), but the Samoan language is occasionally used to facilitate the comprehension of ideas.[37]

These changes signaled a softening of the ideology of English-only.

The Governor's annual report to the U.S. Interior Department began in the 1950s to include the following sentence: "As English is the official language of the Government, it is essential that the children become literate in that language while *maintaining the bilingual nature of their society.*"[38] In 1960, a new Constitution for Samoa was approved in Washington. An amended Article 1, Section 3, revised in 1966, read, "It shall be the policy of the Government of American Samoa to protect persons of Samoan ancestry against alienation of their lands and the destruction of the Samoan way of life *and language,* contrary to their best interests."[39] Samoan was declared the second official language. Elementary schools gave instruction on Samoan culture and history. The same schools, however, gave increasingly less instruction in Samoan and more in English on each academic level, as follows:[40]

Year	Grade Levels	Percent in Samoan	Percent in English
1957	1–3 grades	75	25
	4–6 grades	50	50
	7–9 grades	25	75
1961	1–3 grades	40	60
	4–6 grades	25	75

High schools were taught in the English language only, but daily practice contradicted this. Thus, in the mid-1980s, "teachers were instructing in English at greater percentages, yet students continued to speak to them in Samoan 90% of the time."[41] By the late 1980s, the schools accelerated their move away from biliguality and back to English-only. In 1987, for example, it was reported that "Samoan curriculum materials developed through . . . bilingual programs are no longer in use in the classroom."[42] At the same time, increased English usage has been reported outside schools, including among extended family members and friends.[43]

In a 1961 investigation, it was found that "graduates of the elementary and district junior high schools are not generally proficient in English."[44] Even worse, "many pupils are not becoming fully literate either in Samoan or English."[45] In the years since these statements were written, the Samoan language endured as the dominant language of everyday affairs as well as an educational language of fluctuating significance. The average level of school attainment has risen considerably and thus it is difficult to believe that incomplete literacy in both languages has grown. Although the cultural content of the curriculum has developed unevenly, it is no longer accurately described as "teaching Samoan children about snow, supermarkets, railroads, rabbits, and apples, [and] . . . [confining] their formal learning to objects and ideas foreign to their community."[46]

More central to Samoan distinctiveness than language was the colony's socioeconomic system. Based on common ownership, it permitted the growth of a sense of collective welfare that precluded class differences and sizable inequalities in access to Samoan resoures. As Samoan writer Meleisea put it, "There was no substantial difference in the standard of consumption between the highest ranking chief and an untitled man."[47] Equal access to land was managed by a system of *matais* or chiefs. Each extended kin-group had a leader and trustee of its land and property.[48]

When American rule began, in 1900, the authority of *matais* was formally recognized and in 1906, all matais were required to register with the U.S. government.[49] In 1960, the Samoan Constitution, as approved by the U.S. Department of the Interior, provided for a two-house legislature. The Senate—the upper house—consists wholly of matais who are chosen by other matais. The lower house is elected by voters throughout American Samoa. Both houses are equal in power. According to Laughlin, "there is considerable public dissatisfaction with matai control of one house of the territorial legislature."[50] In addition, only matais can hold the Office of Secretary for Samoan Affairs, part of the American Samoa government. Customarily, only matais have become judges on the High Court even though most such appointees had no legal training.[51] Under the Naval government until 1951, many matais were appointed (and a number successfully coopted) to lesser governmental positions.

Although the Samoan way of life retained its hold in general, increasing dissatisfaction with the matais' political power was manifest.[52] Samoans, however, were not eager to abandon their system. Even when they move overseas, "Samoan migrants retain their rights to family lands and titles back home. Remittances are a means of maintaining and enforcing those ties."[53]

Before World War II, few Samoans migrated to the mainland. After the war, however, the numbers began to rise. A few Samoans who were in the U.S. Navy were transferred to Hawaii. This stream broadened in 1951 when the naval base at Pago Pago was closed down and personnel were shifted to Hawaii. By 1972, some 500 Samoans a year were moving to Hawaii or California. Reportedly, Samoans in the United States outnumbered those in Samoa by nearly two to one.[54] As these Samoans left their historic homes, they were replaced by migrants from Western Samoa, which had become independent in 1962. The principal attraction was a higher material standard of living. The language in both Samoas was identical, as was their religion and other cultural characteristics. Western Samoans were considered more traditional and had not come to depend as much on formal schooling. Part of the explanation of a persistent traditional culture in American Samoa lay with this large-scale eastward migration of Western Samoans. (The two Samoas are separated by some 70 miles of water.) By the early 1990s, three out of five American Samoans were living on the U.S. mainland.[55] In 1981, of 68,700 Western Samoans living outside their country, 42,000 were in New Zealand, 13,000 in American Samoa, 13,238 in Hawaii and the United States, and 500 in Australia.[56] The contingent in New Zealand would have been much greater had it not been for insistence by the government of that country in the mid-1970s that immigration of Samoans be reduced sharply. A decade later, the U.S. government lowered the ban on Western Samoans wishing to move to American Samoa.[57] According to the American census of 1990, the number of Samoans living in the United States rose from 1,948 in 1980 to 62,964. At this time, the total number of Samoans in both Samoas was 192,000 (160,000 in W. Samoa and 32,000 in American Samoa). As the 1990s began, the terms West and East were somewhat confusing as Western Samoans now made up a majority of inhabitants in American Samoa.[58]

The American Census did not count Pacific Islanders until 1980. That year, virtually 7 out of 10 Samoans lived in concentrations of 1,000 persons or more, as follows:[59]

Honolulu	13,811
Los Angeles–Long Beach	8,049

San Francisco–Oakland	4,239
San Diego	2,807
Orange County	2,008
Seattle-Everett	1,164
San Jose	1,037
	29,299

A survey by the National Office of Samoan Affairs found that Samoans and Americans nationally had graduated from high school in comparable percentages. They were far apart, however, in percentages who had graduated from college:[60]

	High-School Graduates	*College Graduates*
U.S.: Total	66.5	16.
Samoans	65.7	7.3
CA: Total	73.5	19.6
Samoans	63.5	6.6
Hawaii: Total	73.8	20.3
Samoans	51.0	3.3

In comparing schools in Samoa with those in Hawaii and the mainland, "most Samoans . . . believe the schools of American Samoa to be generally inferior. . . ."[61] One principal consequence of the inferiority can be found in the great difficulty many Samoan youth in mainland schools had in the field of English. Thus, in a survey of Samoans in Compton, California, 95% were found to be LEP.[62]

Data gathered in 1979 showed that "90 percent of the American Samoan children in the 12th grade are at least five grades below grade level in reading achievement."[63] During the academic year 1986 to 1987, among Seattle students, Samoans had the lowest overall scores in achievement tests. On reading, language, and mathematics tests, the following percentages scored below the 50th percentile: 76.9; 69.8; and 65.4. Samoan students also had the highest dropout rates during 1985 to 1986, triple the rate of all Asian-Americans.[64] "It is not uncommon," said Luce, "to find at least one dropout in practically all Samoan households."[65] Specialized educational programs are rare to the point of invisibility. "In the State of California, only one bilingual program for Samoans exists in Harbor City. Multicultural education for Pacific Americans is nonexistent."[66] Although the number of Samoans in the United States during the 1980s increased by half, the literature on their educational problems remained slim.

Minority children whose parents were poor experienced the greatest educational neglect. In Hawaii, for example, the 1979 median income of males was $7,577 and at times the state-wide average was $11,505.[67] A year later, the Samoan infant death rate was the highest of all ethnic groups in the state.[68] Only

15.4% of Samoans occupied housing that they owned; the statewide average was 51.7%.[69] In 1973, Samoans, who made up 2% of the population, constituted 5% of welfare recipients in Hawaii.[70] Samoan women concentrated in nursing and men tended toward such low-paid jobs as construction. In a study of academically successful and unsucessful Samoan students, however, it was found that:

> the greatest proportion of successful children came from families in which the general level of acculturation was high, there was mixed ethnicity, the parents spoke English well, the parents were highly educated and participated in ethnically mixed groups, the father had a skilled occupation, and parents were oriented toward upward mobility.[71]

The Samoan families who lived in such conditions were scarce. In addition, Samoans generally dwelled in areas of poor and public housing where few if any first-rate schools were located.[72]

NATIVE HAWAII

Europeans first came to Hawaii in 1788. Before that time, Hawaiians developed a distinctive language related to the Marquesan and Tahitian tongues. As Kimura pointed out, "Hawaiian shares 56 percent of its basic vocabulary with Marquesan and . . . 46 percent with Tahitian."[73] Hawaii was ruled by an aristocracy of chiefs who competed for regional supremacy. Although traditionally one monarch did not rule, a movement toward such a sovereign came into being less than 10 years after the first European incursion, by Captain James Cook, in 1788. Under the rule of Kamehameha I, Hawaii was first united as an autonomous nation state.

Land was the chief booty of war and after Kamehameha I selected the choicest parts for himself, the remainder was parceled out among his allies. They held it at the pleasure of the monarch who could—and did—retract it if he later wished. After the initial division, the chiefly holders owed allegiance to the king, who felt safer on his throne by requiring the holders to remain by his side. After Kamehameha I died in 1819, the aristocracy successfully diluted monarchical power by permitting its own lands to be inherited rather than continuing to be subjected to redivision by the king.[74]

In 1820, American missionaries arrived in Hawaii, uninvited but eager to establish Christianity there. Accurately sizing up the social structure, they saw the pivotal role that the chiefs played and promptly established connections with them. Missionaries and chiefs created a mutually beneficial relationship. "They were able to cooperate inasmuch as for the first, political power was the convenient means of propagating their religion, while for the second, religion was the traditional means of propagating their power."[75] Devising an Hawaiian alphabet, the missionaries printed religious reading materials by 1822 and then set out to create a system of mission schools. The prospect of a network of local institutions reaching throughout Hawaii, staffed by persons skilled in presenting a religious ideology, was bound to alert the chiefs to the political implications of the idea. Caution was advised and the missionaries accepted the advice.

But the chiefs were far from merely interested observers:

> Indeed, the political, the ritual, and the educational could hardly be distinguished. The original schools were set up under the aegis of the high *ali'i* [chiefs] at central places such as Honolulu. . . . The students consisted of the chiefs and their entourages. . . . Each such chief had a principal teacher, chosen from among the better students in his or her retinue. Other attendants who had become proficient enough in reading were sent to establish schools in the out districts, that is, in the *ali'i's* lands in the several islands.[76]

The chiefs neither needed nor received any directions from the missionaries.

> The local chiefs' men, the *konohiki* . . . were required to supply each teacher with a house, a schoolhouse, food, and clothing (tapa cloth). After a time, students from these initial schools were in turn dispatched to satellite lands of the chief where they founded more local schools. Within a few years the islands were covered with such quasi-ritual centers, corresponding in their organization to the hierarchy and segmentations of the system of chiefship. . . . The "teachers" were often *konohiki* of the place or other local people in the owning chief's service.[77]

It is difficult to imagine how the missionaries could have managed the same tasks unaided.

Neither adult commoners nor children were permitted to attend these early schools.[78] Only in 1824 were schools for the former organized. Four years later, children began to be admitted.[79] By 1831, wrote historian Kuykendall, "the bulk of the population—certainly more than half—had learned to read—somewhat haltingly it is true."[80] In that same year, "the number of common schools throughout the kingdom was about 1,100, and the number of pupils about 52,000, approximately two fifths of the entire population."[81]

Within several years, however, the school scene changed greatly. Instead of expansion, few new schools were built and attendance fell off. The missionaries had created a written form of Hawaiian as an aid to religious conversion rather than as a contribution to general education. They then made literacy a precondition to membership in the church. Yet in the early 1830s, church membership and literacy grew at very different and irregular rates. Between 1832 and 1834, for example, the number of persons able to read declined and the number of new members fluctuated, as follows:[82]

Year Ending June	Number of Readers	Number Admitted to Church Membership
1832	23,127	235
1833	20,184	72
1834	10,608	124

"In 1833–34," wrote Sahlins, "half of the mission stations failed to report any so-called readers for the reason that school attendance was derisory to nonexistent."[83] The 1830s were an economically depressed decade for all of Hawaii.[84] One reason is that the beginning of the 1830s saw the end of the once-lucrative sandalwood trade. The demand from China for this aromatic wood declined sharply. The ruling chiefs, who profited greatly from the trade, had compelled thousands of commoners to leave their regular pursuits and spend months felling and transporting the valuable lumber; few received any considerable pay for this work. When the sandalwood trade disappeared, the chiefs and their *konohiki* redirected the commoners back to their neglected farms, which, of course, engaged their attention for a number of years. It was to the self-interest of the chiefs and konohiki to revive food production. This took precedence over managing the school system, and so education lagged during the decade. For the common farmers, a return to the land was not an occasion for a relaxed pace of work. Instead, the pace of work intensified as farmers were pressed by konohiki to supply crops that could be sold on the market, to the profit of the landed chiefs and to the relief of their heavy debts still outstanding from merchants' financial advances to the chiefs.

The end of the 1830s completed the first phase of Hawaiian schooling. Some 15 or so years had shown that the chiefs need have no fear of any untoward political effects of schooling. Nor was their day-by-day tutelage any longer required. A corps of indigenous teachers and administrators existed. Control of schooling was transferred to the national government and in 1840, a national system of public schools was created by law. The new system incorporated within itself a two-tier arrangement of schools: common schools, which were taught by trained native teachers, and select schools instructed by missionaries and enrolling mainly children of chiefs.[85]

The school law of 1840 established a school in every community containing at least 15 school-age children. Male adults voted for local school boards. Teachers were employed by the board and the local missionary. Criteria for employment of teachers were modest:

> If a man could read, write and understands geography and arithmetic, and is a quiet and moral man, and desires a teacher's certificate, it shall be the duty of the school agent [on each of the five principal islands] to give him one, and not refuse."[86]

Later in the decade of the 1840s, teachers and school officials were exempted from the labor tax that otherwise applied to "male subjects born of native aboriginal mothers."[87] In 1850, the labor tax was replaced by a school tax levied on all male adults. Land was set aside for schools. In addition, public land was given to schools and teachers on the condition that they (and the students) put it into productive use and give any income to the schools. Because the government had no funds for salaries and school expenses, the teachers and students were in effect financing the schools. Between 1850 and 1888, tuition was charged for both common and select schools, although indigent persons were exempted from the charge. After 1888, select-school students still paid tuition, where English was the medium of instruction.

Odgers wrote that "The greatest weakness of the whole school system was the poorly prepared, practically untrained teachers of whom there were many. The mission boarding schools produced most of the teachers, but the standards were not high.[88] As early as 1831, missionaries had established the high-school level Lahainaluna Seminary for Boys to prepare teachers and preachers. During 1849 and 1850, the school was taken over by the government with the understanding that its higher academic level would be maintained. A survey conducted in 1850 found that of its over 400 graduates up to that time, some 112 were teachers, two were ministers, a few were lawyers, and one was the Governor.[89] In 1865, Lahainaluna operated within the government system as an ordinary select school. Presumably, it continued to offer a curriculum much like the one it taught during 1851 and 1852: algebra, geometry, trigonometry, surveying, navigation, natural and revealed theology, natural and moral philosophy, anatomy, Hawaiian laws, chronology, sacred geography, sacred history, geography, composition, punctuation, and music.[90] This was far from the meager curriculum of the common school.

Hawaiian remained the instructional language for the great majority of students in the common schools, with a much smaller number taught in English. Kuykendall wrote of "the craze among the Hawaiians for learning English" in the late 1840s and early 1850s.[91] In 1853, money was appropriated to set up English-language instruction in select schools already operating. In addition, the Oahu Charity School, conducted in English, was established in 1833 to educate part-Hawaiian children, that is, children of foreigners who had married Hawaiian women. Public funds were appropriated, but tuition was also charged. As the part-Hawaiian population expanded, the Oahu school also grew and was known as the Honolulu Town School or the Honolulu Free School.[92] In 1865, the board of education ceased its financial support of English day schools for Hawaiian children, but interest in such instruction continued to grow among Hawaiian parents. Mataio Kekuanaoa, Hawaii school board president, warned:

> that if we wish to preserve the Kingdom of Hawaii for Hawaiians, and to educate our people, we must insist that the Hawaiian language shall be the language of all our National Schools, and the English shall be taught whenever practicable, but only, as an important *branch* of Hawaiian education."[93]

Kekuanaoa, the father of two Hawaiian kings and the governor of Oahu, was deeply devoted to traditional ways.

Those traditional ways, however, were under great pressure during the second half of the 19th century. The native Hawaiian population declined catastrophically after the arrival of an appreciable number of European-Americans. At the minimum, an 18th century population of some 300,000 had by 1831 become a mere 130,000. More misfortune lay ahead:[94]

1831–1832	130,313
1835–1836	108,579
1850 (Jan.)	84,165
1853 (Dec.)	73,138
1860	69,800

The low point of indigenous population was reached in 1900, when it was recorded as some 38,000.[95] In 1778, the Hawaiians had constituted the total population; by 1900, their share had fallen to 24%.[96] Most of the decline was caused by lack of resistance to European-introduced diseases, including a disastrous smallpox epidemic in 1853. Recovery from population decline was greatly delayed by the persistence of small families and thus limited the potential for future growth.[97]

The demographic collapse may have helped prepare the way for a destruction of traditional culture. Hawaiians were struck down by diseases to which Europeans were already immune. This seeming selectivity could have undermined the normal self-confidence of the people. As Sahlins wrote:

> To "modernize" the people must first learn to hate what they already have, what they have always considered their well-being. Beyond that they have to despise what they are, to hold their own existence in contempt—and want then, to be someone else. . . . Coercion in itself does not seem a sufficient explanation.[98]

Another arena for the enactment of this kind of modernization was a revolution of the land system during the 1840s and 1850s.

In the Constitution of 1840, it was stipulated that the land belonged "to the chiefs and people in common and was not the personal property of the king."[99] One threat to this provision was the desire of foreign capitalists to purchase Hawaiian land in order to establish a large-scale sugar industry. Outright foreign ownership, however, was forbidden by law. During the mid-1840s, a great national movement arose in Hawaii that demanded that foreigners continue to be prevented from owning any of the land. Other issues were also brought forward in a stream of petitions and remonstrances. "There were protests against abusive taxes, the forced labor system, and the high-handed activities of Hawaiian tax collectors, magistrates, land commissioners, konohiki, and owning chiefs."[100] Protests were also lodged against foreigners' prominent role in government as well as excessive numbers of foreigners having become naturalized citizens of Hawaii.

Partly in response to the popular unrest, in 1845 the king appointed a Board of Commissioners to Quiet Land Titles, or land commissioners as the group was called. After much discussion, the Commission, the legislature, and the king promised the commoners "an undivided one third interest [of the land] in most of Hawaii."[101] During the first 3 months of 1848, however, the legislature enacted the Great Mahele (the division) that divided up the country's land very differently. Commoners received less than 1% of the land, or under 30,000 acres.

The king reserved just under 1 million acres; nearly 1.5 million acres became the property of the government, and the chiefs received somewhat more that 1.5 million acres.[102] On the average, each chief received over 500 times more land than each commoner.[103] Recipients of land rights received a legal title granting the owners unconditional control of the land. Foreigners did not receive land under the Great Mahele. They could, however, purchase land outright from any of the legal owners, which happened on a large scale. By 1886, Whites owned two thirds of the government land,[104] much of it organized into sugar plantations. In 1892 to 1893, "four fifths of the property of the Islands was owned by whites."[105]

The most fateful development of the 19th century was the ouster of an independent Hawaiian government in 1893. By that time, a tightly knit economic autocracy had enough political power to effectuate a transfer of power with the military aid of the United States. (Whereas the latter systematically denied responsibility for action, in 1993 the U.S. Congress finally acknowledged that it had provided the military assistance a century earlier. The measure, Public Law 103–150, was signed by President Clinton.) In 1898, Hawaii was annexed as a territory of the United States and became a state in 1959.

The great majority of native Hawaiians opposed American annexation, fearing it would complete their submergence in the larger culture. They also resented the often-repeated claim by Americans that they had more or less rescued Hawaii from economic disaster in the past. Much of the so-called American capital in Hawaii was misnamed. As the Hawaiian Patriotic League declared in 1893, "Those who are now independent run their plantations or business firms on money made here, out of the Hawaiian people and from Hawaiian soil, through coolie labor. . . ."[106]

During the early years of American rule, Hawaiians constituted a reservoir for public employment. Because Asian immigrants were not eligible for citizenship and relatively few mainland Whites lived in Hawaii, Hawaiians were the only sizable group who were both educated and eligible to work for local and territorial governments. They were all citizens and could and did vote. In 1902, for example, Hawaiians constituted 68.8% of registered voters and Whites made up 30%. Thirty years later, the figures were 33.8 and 39.8%.[107] In 1903, 71.1% of territorial legislatures were Hawaiians and in 1933, 51%.[108] Public-school teaching reflected a similar situation. In 1902, 30.4% of teachers were Hawaiians whereas Whites made up 69.3%. In 1926, the figures were 26 and 54%. Japanese represented only 7% in the latter year.[109] In 1920, Hawaiians constituted 3.2% of all male professional workers, exceeded only by Whites (5.9%).[110] Ten years later, the same relationship held true (5.2 and 5.5%). In 1940 and thereafter, however, Hawaiians were overtaken by Chinese and Japanese male professional workers. This was also the case in public school teaching, with Japanese in 1948 representing 46.4% and Hawaiians only 5.7%.[111] A sharp turnaround had occurred.

Culturally, Hawaiians had been left behind even earlier. As early as 1888, while the kingdom of Hawaii still existed and Hawaiian was the first language of school children, 84% were taught in English.[112] When the *coup d'etat* government fully established its rule in 1894, the few schools still teaching in Hawaiian were closed down. During the rest of its period in office—until 1900—and under Territorial rule by the United States:

> Hawaiian was strictly forbidden anywhere within school yards or buildings, and physical punishment for using it could be harsh. Teachers who were native speakers of Hawaiian . . . were threatened with dismissal for using Hawaiian in school. Some were even a bit leery of using Hawaiian place names in class. Teachers were sent to Hawaiian-speaking homes to reprimand parents for speaking Hawaiian to their children.[113]

The Territorial legislature enacted a law in 1919, however, that required Hawaiian to be taught in high schools and teachers' colleges. In 1935, another measure was passed mandating the daily teaching of Hawaiian in schools serving areas within the Hawaiian Homes program. Both laws were ignored by education authorities whereas territorial officials did not insist on compliance.[114]

During much of the 19th century, Hawaiians were more literate than Whites on the Islands. This was still true in 1900 and 1910.[115] (Probably during the 19th century, the Hawaiians were even more literate than Americans on the mainland.)[116] In the years after 1910, Island Whites were marginally more literate than Hawaiians. At all times, however, both Chinese and Japanese in Hawaii were less literate than Hawaiians. Adult Hawaiians depended on Hawaiian newspapers for much of their education in indigenous and Western culture. "Hawaiian traditions were serialized in the newspapers along with translations of famous European works, such as those of Shakespeare."[117] However, over time, the schools' treatment of Hawaiian as an outlaw language took its toll. Hawaiian-language newspapers died out for lack of readers. During the first 20 years of the present century, Hawaiian was largely replaced by pidgin English as a language of the streets. Kimura pointed out:

> Creolization of pidgin was the perfect tool for local children to resist the campaign to force them to speak English. Pidgin is English, and yet it really is not. Thus, the children were able to comply with the heavy campaign to make English the language of the territory and still not cooperate with what Hawaiians saw as persecution of their own language, nor identify linguistically with the *haole* group. . . .[118]

Yet, the rise of pidgin English did not interfere with the literacy of the Hawaiian people. In 1980, for example, 97.4% of Hawaiians completed five grades of school, just more than one percentage point under the Whites of Hawaii.[119] The "brokenness" of pidgin English did not affect the Hawaiians' ability to learn to read and write English.

In 1887, a well-financed group of private schools was organized for the sole benefit of Hawaiian girls and boys. Known as the Kamehameha schools, they continue to this day. "Especially until 1930," wrote Fuchs, "the boys' school emphasized vocational training and military drilling and the girls' concentrated on training future mothers and homemakers."[120] In 1929, one third of school-age Hawaiian and part-Hawaiian children attended these schools.[121] Fifty years later, a Hawaiian student at the University of Hawaii recalled her experiences at Kamehameha in 1969:

> We were offered Hawaiian language, but they did not really say "take it—you are Hawaiian—it is your language. . . ." What they said was "we want you to go to college so you ought to take Spanish because Hawaiian will not give you the credits you need.[122]

Ten years later, the situation had changed considerably. Cachola, a Kamehameha staff member, described aspects of the Hawaiian Studies program:

> We offer the Hawaiian language from kindergarten on, and we require two years of Hawaiian culture and language at the high school level; we are the only high school in the world requiring Hawaiian studies. In order to put these two studies into the curriculum, military science had to be discontinued.[123]

In 1948, when the speaker began teaching there, the schools had only three tracks: shop, commercial, and college preparatory.

In 1979, the schools enrolled only about 3% of Hawaiian children of school age.[124] In response to pressure from the Hawaiian community, however, an Extension department was instituted that reached about 30,000 children per year. A number of these contacts consisted of a visit to a school by three teachers for several hours on a single day.[125] In all, the Kamehameha schools spent under 18% of their budget on extension. For entrance to the full-time program, students had to pass through a very competetive admission process. Despite the work of the Extension department and various concessions made by the school administration, the highly selective character of the schools continued in force. Thus, in 1993, only 6% of school-aged native-Hawaiian children attended the Kamehameha schools. Six of every seven applicants were rejected.[126] This was not because of financial stringencies, however. The schools as a whole had an endowment of some 6 billion dollars, about equal to that of Harvard University. Hawaiian children who were accepted had more than 90% of their tuition and fees forgiven. Each of the five trustees is paid $860,653 a year.[127] Punahou, the ranking private prep school in Hawaii, enrolled relatively few Hawaiians. In 1979, from 6 to 10% of enrollment consisted of Hawaiians. In the school as a whole, three out of four applicants were rejected. The SAT test is used for admissions purposes.[128]

The great majority of Hawaiian students attended public schools where many did not experience success. Their dropout rate was "nearly double . . . [that] for the state as a whole. . . ."[129] During the late 1950s, "Japanese and Chinese parents sometimes . . . [took] their children out of public schools because of a high proportion of Hawaiian and Portuguese children, whose negative effects upon the academic and social behavior of their own children they fear[ed]." [130] The one fourth to one third of the part-Hawaiian population in public schools is not identified as such within the school system,[131] thus raising questions about statements regarding academic performance by ethnic groups. Melahn estimated that nonidentification may throw off the numbers of part-Hawaiians, especially from 25 to 30%. Because part-Hawaiians are more successful academically than "pure" Hawaiians, their omission may severely distort the academic status of Hawaiian students as a whole. Socioeonomic influences loom large in Hawaii's schools. In high socioeconomic status (SES) schools, Hawaiian and Caucasian students perform at "closely parallel" levels.[132] A study of Hawaii's elementary schools between 1975 and 1983 found that the school system was "functioning in a manner which 'narrows the gap' between schools." [133] This study, conducted by Mirikitani, sampled fourth and sixth graders in up to 170 schools.

In 1980, the various ethnic groups in Hawaii were somewhat closely aligned with respect to the proportion of persons 25 years or over who had completed 4 years of high school. Following is a listing of such groups, arranged by median years of education:[134]

13.3 years	Whites	12.4 years	Native Hawaiians
12.9 years	African-Americans	12.1 years	Filipinos
12.8 years	Chinese	12.0 years	Samoans
12.6 years	Japanese and Koreans		

In higher education, the picture was quite different. Here is a listing of persons having 4 or more years of higher education:[135]

28.2%	Whites	14%	African-Americans
27.6%	Chinese	10.8%	Filipinos
19.8%	Japanese	7.7%	Native Hawaiians
17.9%	Koreans	3.3%	Samoans

According to Okamura, the overall stratification order in Hawaii is highly consistent with that of occupational status. He gave the following as his reading of the stratification order: Chinese, Whites, Japanese and Koreans, African-Americans, Filipinos, Native Hawaiians, and Samoans.[136] In more recent times, Okamura noted, groups such as Native Hawaiians and Filipinos have turned toward political processes as a means of attaining greater upward mobility. "However," he wrote, "social status advancement through access to political power is a lengthy and arduous process that is made more difficult by the lack of economic resources." [137] Meanwhile, the educational system provided only limited opportunities to groups such as the Native Americans.

Because the entire State of Hawaii constitutes a single school district, the legislature appropriates the same amount of money per pupil in all schools. Yet, it has been difficult to verify empirically that equal per-pupil spending actually occurs. Physical facilities in the schools seem to be distributed quite unequally. "Some schools have swimming pools and other facilities, but a substantial percentage have substandard dining facilities, libraries, and other forms of educational infrastructure. Schools with predominantly Filipino and Hawaiian enrollment tend to be have-nots."[138] An expert building contractor observed after an extensive inspection, "We were struck by the quality differences in the physical aspects of the schools we saw."[139] He contrasted two groups of schools:

> Starting at the top of the socioeconomic scale, Radford High and Manoa Elementary were housed in modern buildings, excellently maintained with landscaped grounds. The classrooms, well designed, were bright and cheerful. . . . At the bottom of the scale, at Farrington and Kalakaua, the buildings are old, well beyond their prime, poorly designed, unkempt. The classrooms were neither well-lighted nor well-ventilated. The atmosphere . . . was dark and dank.[140]

A positive feature throughout the schools was the fairly uniform distribution of experienced teachers.

Apparently, state authorities did not monitor expenditures of individual schools. As a result, it was not possible to discern whether equal legislative appropriations were being translated into equal per-pupil expenditures on a school-by-school basis. In 1994, however, a study commissioned by the State Auditor found sweeping differences in per-pupil expenditures from school to school. Cooper of Fordham University, who conducted the study, reported per-pupil spending ranging from $3,839 to $9,706.[141] The state superintendent of education refused to adopt the Cooper research method and, instead, favored one constructed by the National Center for Education Statistics that does not report data for single schools.

Language continued to be a problem in the schools or at least among school authorities. As we saw earlier, they had for many years singled out the widespread use of Hawaiian Creole as an obstacle to learning. "In 1987, the Board of Education . . . adopted a policy to prohibit speaking Hawaiian Creole, since many teachers were doing so to communicate with students. . . ."[142] Nevertheless, by 1993, the Department of Education had shifted ground. It was now "recognized as a language in its own right"[143] rather than as another variety of broken English. Many young people who used the language viewed it as a protest against colonialism. Romaine described Creole English as a vital "language coming of age and gaining in status."[144] Part of its rising status derives from the increasing frequency with which it is starting to be incorporated in printed imaginative literature of contemporary Hawaii. On the other hand, many advocates of the Hawaiian language look suspiciously at Creole as an unworthy competitor. Another factor favoring the reception of Creole English is the "ruling by the Office of Bilingual Education and Minority Language Affairs of the U.S. Department of Education [which] recognizes HCE [Hawaiian Creole English] as a language qualifying for bilingual education funding under Title VII of the Elementary and Secondary Education Act."[145]

Hawaiians had no opportunity to attend a local institution of higher education during the 19th century. In the 1880s, however, when government policy was increasingly dominated by Americans, some few Hawaiians attended colleges overseas. In 1907, the College of Agriculture and Mechanic Arts was founded and was succeeded 4 years later by the College of Hawaii. In 1920, the University of Hawaii was organized. During these early years, Whites were the main beneficiaries of higher education. For example, between 1915 and 1918, the percentages of students who were White were 84.7, 75.2, 71.8, and 67.8.[146] During the same years, the percentages for Hawaiians were 1.4, 3.4, 4.5, and 4.2 and those for Chinese were 8.3, 13.7, 11.8, and 16.1. In Fall 1919, the entering class of the College of Hawaii contained 47 men and 7 women, and was distributed as follows:[147]

Caucasians	26
Chinese	20
Japanese	6
Hawaiians	1
Koreans	1

At the same time the entire enrollment of the College was as follows:

Caucasians	53
Chinese	36
Japanese	13
Hawaiians	2
Koreans	3

That so few indigenous Hawaiians entered the College in 1919 attests to the minimalistic secondary-school curriculum that existed at the Kamehameha schools, let alone the public schools.

During the 1920s and early 1930s, when native Hawaiians were comparatively well represented in the professions, their numbers increased significantly at the University of Hawaii. The next generation, however, witnessed a sharp drop of Hawaiians in the professions and the University. The low point was reached in 1979 when only 0.5% of enrollment was Hawaiian. By the 1980s, the level recovered to some 5%, more or less where they had been in 1917 and 1918.[148] At community colleges, the Hawaiians were always better represented. During the 1980s, they constituted somewhat over one tenth of enrollment.[149] Only about one fourth of the Hawaiians who transferred from a community college to a senior college ever graduated.[150] Haas reported that "in community colleges . . . counselors seldom give adequate information about admission requirements to . . . [the University], and Filipinos and Hawaiians are less likely to transfer to a four-year college than Japanese students [who made up about a quarter of community college enrollment]."[151] Yet, at the University of Hawaii, "One out of eight Hawaiian freshmen drop out, about half of all Hawaiian students are eventually dismissed, placed on probation, or are suspended . . . their overall graduation rate of 29 percent compares with the campus average of 49 percent."[152] It should be recalled that nearly all the Hawaiian students attending the University are graduates of the Kamehameha schools and that 80% of Kamehameha students go on to higher education.[153] Between 1975 and 1989, the percentage of faculty of an Hawaiian background ranged from 1.3 to 2.0 and those of a White background ranged between 70.0 to 73.8.[154] As recently as 1992, fewer than two thirds of one percent of the faculty consisted of Hawaiians while under 5% of students were Hawaiians.[155]

During the 1970s, a group of native Hawaiian activists gave rise to a movement of land rights for their people. Although the immediate issue involved a tract of land in the Kalama Valley on O'ahu, in time, older issues respecting much of Hawaii emerged.[156] Nearly one half of Hawaii was covered by land that, according to some land-rights leaders, belonged to the native people.[157] The land issue encouraged the emergence of certain aspects of the native Hawaiian culture, including a new interest in the Hawaiian language and history that soon came to influence education on all levels. A movement arose to establish Hawaiian language-immersion schools.[158] In 1987, only about 2,000 native speakers of Hawaiian could be located. Within the following few years, the number of Hawaiian-speakers under the age of 10 rose from nearly none to at least 500.[159] State education officials, however, seemed uninterested in supervising the movement. Although in 1978 the legislature directed that all schools offer courses in Hawaiian Studies, 5 years later, "only half the schools were following the mandate."[160]

CONCLUDING REMARKS

This chapter and the preceding one might support an incorrect impression that the history of colonies can be examined in isolation from events in mother countries. Equally erroneous is the misimpression that the negatives of colonialism—including destruction of native culture, language, and historiography, and the ending of traditional democratic political rights—were inflicted on societies overseas while sparing any group residing in the home country. In fact, however, these negatives were tried out first at home. Thus, before the Civil War, the federal government in the United States contracted with missionaries to operate schools, most of whose expenses were supplied by the Native Americans themselves. This was not far from the early practices both in Samoa and

Hawaii. Why any kind of schooling was provided was, from the government's view, a matter of pacification rather than religion or educational principle. It was hoped by U.S. officials that the schools might convince Indians not to oppose their own banishment across the Mississippi.[161]

Americans were not free to duplicate their home-grown practices overseas. Sometimes, geography stood in the way. In Samoa, the port of Pago-Pago was the main attraction. Americans, however, did not confiscate significant amounts of Samoan land and thus left the system of common ownership undisturbed. This was not because of U.S. respect for the principle of common ownership but simply because there was not much productive soil available. In Hawaii, on the other hand, much land was available and could be put to productive use promptly by the Americans. Within a few years, in fact, the traditional Hawaiian system of land ownership was legislated out of existence and by the 1890s, as we saw earlier, Americans owned most Hawaiian land. A great attraction of Guam to Americans was the presence there of comparatively much level cultivable land. Land whose location was valuable militarily was taken without a second thought.

NOTES

[1] Elizabeth K. Anttila, *A History of Education in American Samoa and Guam* (Master's thesis, University of Texas, 1953), p. 30.

[2] Thom Huebner, "Language and Schooling in Western and American Samoa," *World Englishes*, 8 (1989), p. 63.

[3] Edwin R. Embree, *A New School in American Samoa* (Julius Rosenwald Fund, 1932), pp. 8–9.

[4] Governor S. V. Graham to Mrs. Helen Wilson, quoted in Pedro Cruz Sanchez, *Education in American Samoa* (Doctoral dissertation, Stanford University, 1955), p. 103. See also Felix M. Keesing, *Modern Samoa. Its Government and Changing Life* (George Allen and Unwin, 1934), p. 430.

[5] Statement of September 14, 1922; quoted in *American Samoa, Naval Governor, 1910–1913* (Government Printing Office, 1927), p. 81.

[6] Ibid., p. 81.

[7] Ibid., p. 82.

[8] Ibid., p. 85.

[9] Ibid., p. 88.

[10] U.S. American Samoan Commission, *American Samoa. Hearings* (Government Printing Office, 1931), p. 52.

[11] Ibid., p. 113.

[12] Ibid., p. 137.

[13] Ibid., pp. 321, 325.

[14] See, for example, ibid., p. 467.

[15] *Annual Report. Governor of American Samoa to the Secretary of the Interior for the Fiscal Year Ended June 30, 1953*, pp. 24, 131.

[16] *Annual Report. Governor of American Samoa to the Secretary of the Interior for the Fiscal Year Ended June 30, 1961*, p. 67.

[17] *Annual Report. Governor of American Samoa to the Secretary of the Interior for the Fiscal Year Ended June 30, 1965*, p. 12.

[18] U.S. American Samoan Commission, *American Samoa. Hearings*, p. 138.

[19] Ibid., p. 138.

[20] U.S. Congress, 87th, 1st session, Senate, Committee on Interior and Insular Affairs, *Study Mission to Eastern [American] Samoa. Report* (Government Printing Office, 1961), p. 150.

[21] Ibid., p. 150.

[22] *Annual Report. Governor of American Samoa to the Secretary of the Interior for the Fiscal Year Ended June 30, 1960*, p. 68.

[23] *Annual Report. Governor of American Samoa to the Secretary of the Interior for the Fiscal Year Ended June 30, 1968*, p. 13.

[24] *Annual Report. Governor of American Samoa to the Secretary of the Interior for the Fiscal Year Ended June 30, 1967*, p. 18.

[25] K. Rolff, *Fa' a Samoa: Tradition in Transition* (Doctoral dissertation, University of California, Santa Barbara, 1978), p. 177, quoted in Michael J. Levin and Dennis A. Ahlburg, "Pacific Islanders in the United States Census Data," p. 110 in Grant McCall and John Connell eds., *A World Perspective on Pacific Islander Migration. Australia, New Zealand and the USA* (Centre for South Pacific Studies, The University of New South Wales, 1993).

[26] Levin and Ahlburg, "Pacific Islanders in the United States Census Data," p. 110.

[27] *Annual Report. Governor of American Samoa to the Secretary of the Interior for the Fiscal Year Ended June 30, 1971*, p. 13. See also *Pacific Islands Monthly*, 1974, p. 9.

[28] Max E. Stanton, "A Gathering of Saints. The Role of the Church of Jesus Christ of Latter-Day Saints in Pacific Migration," p. 26 in Grant McCall and John Connell, eds., *A World Perspective on Pacific Islander Migration. Australia, New Zealand and the USA* (Centre for South Pacific Studies, University of New South Wales, 1993).

[29] Ibid., p. 35.

[30] William H. Barnes, ed., *The Story of Laulii, A Daughter of Samoa* (Jos. Winterburn & Co., 1889), p. 132.

[31] Edward Beauchamp, "Educational Policy in Eastern Samoa: An American Colonial Outpost," *Comparative Education*, 11 (March 1976), p. 25.

[32] U.S. Congress, *Study Mission to Eastern [American] Samoa. Report*, p. 143.

[33] Felix M. Keesing, "Language Change in Relation to Native Education in Samoa," *Mid-Pacific*, 44 (October 1932), p. 312 (emphasis added).

[34] Ibid., p. 313.

[35] Ibid., p. 313.

[36] Felix M. Keesing and Marie M. Keesing, *Elite Communication in Samoa. A Study of Leadership* (Stanford University Press, 1956), pp. 257–258.

[37] *Annual Report. Governor of American Samoa to the Secretary of the Interior for the Fiscal Year Ended June 30, 1951*, p. 8.

[38] *Annual Report. Governor of American Samoa to the Secretary of the Interior for the Fiscal Year Ended June 30, 1956*, p. 41 (emphasis added).

[39] Heinz Kloss, *The American Bilingual Tradition* (Center for Applied Linguistics, 1997), p. 256 (emphasis added).

[40] See *Annual Report. Governor of American Samoa to the Secretary of the Interior for the Fiscal Year Ended June 30, 1957*, p. 46 and *Annual Report . . . 1961*, p. 59.

[41] Trudie Iuli Chun, *Bilingual Framework in American Samoa 1980–1985*, 1985, p. 4. ERIC ED 263 745.

[42] Anne R. Freese, *How American Educational Policy and Practices Impact the Language and Culture of an American Pacific Island*, April 1988, p. 8. ERIC ED 314 468.

[43] Ibid., p. 6.

[44] U.S. Congress, *Study Mission to Eastern [American] Samoa. Report*, p. 146.

[45] Ibid., p. 147.

[46] Ibid., p. 245.

[47] Malama Meleisea, *The Making of Modern Samoa. Traditional Authority and Colonial Administration in the History of Western Samoa* (Institute of Pacific Studies of the University of the South Pacific, 1987), p. 19.

[48] Ibid., p. 7.

[49] Stanley K. Laughlin, Jr., "United States Government Policy and Social Stratification in American Samoa," *Oceana*, 53 (1982), p. 31.

[50] Ibid., p. 35.

[51] Ibid., pp. 35–36.

[52] Ibid., p. 36.

[53] Leulu Felise Va' a, "Effect of Migration on Western Samoa. An Island Viewpoint," p. 351 in Grant McCall and John Connell, eds., *A World Perspective on Pacific Islander Migration. Australia, New Zealand and the USA* (Centre for South Pacific Studies, University of New South Wales, 1993).

[54] Gordon R. Lewthwaite, Christiane Mainzer, and Patrick J. Holland, "From Polynesia to California: Samoan Migration and Its Sequel," *Journal of Pacific History*, 8 (1973), p. 133.

[55] Paul Shankman, "The Samoan Exodus," p. 157 in Victoria S. Lockwood and others, eds., *Contemporary Pacific Societies. Studies in Development and Change* (Prentice-Hall, 1993).

[56] Ibid., p. 157.

[57] Ibid., pp. 165–166. The U.S. Immigration and Naturalization Service does not control immigration into American Samoa. See Edward J. Michal, "American Samoa or Eastern Samoa? The Potential for American Samoa to Become Freely Associated with the United States," *Contemporary Pacific*, 4 (Spring 1992), p. 141.

[58] Ibid., 157.

[59] Patosina H. Luce, *The Educational Needs of American Samoan Students*, March 15, 1985, p. 5. ERIC ED 257 886.

[60] Ibid., p. 9.

[61] Ibid., p. 5.

[62] Bradd Shore and Martha Platt, *Communicative Barriers to Samoans' Training and Employment in the U.S.*, July 1984, p. 4, ERIC ED 264 334.

[63] Stephen Thom in U.S. Commission on Civil Rights, *Civil Rights Issues of Asian and Pacific Americans: Myths and Realities* (The Commission, 1980), p. 368.

[64] Valerie Ooka Pang, "Asian-American Children: A Diverse Population," *Educational Forum*, 55 (Fall 1990), pp. 59–60. See also "Helping Samoan Students Beat Odds," *New York Times*, July 29, 1992.

[65] Patosina H. Luce in U.S. Commission on Civil Rights, *Civil Rights Issues of Asian and Pacific Americans: Myths and Realities* (The Commission, 1980), p. 364.

[66] Ibid., p. 364.

[67] Michael Haas, *Institutional Racism. The Case of Hawaii* (Praeger, 1992), p. 39.

[68] Ibid., p. 39, table 2.

[69] Ibid., p. 40.

[70] Luce in U.S. Commission on Civil Rights, *Civil Rights Issues*, p. 362.

[71] Mildred Bloombaum, *The Samoan Immigrant: Acculturation, Enculturation, and the Child in School* (Doctoral dissertation, University of Hawaii, 1973), p. 181.

[72] Ibid., p. 5.

[73] Larry L. Kimura, "Language Section of Native Hawaiians Study Commission Report" (Office of Hawaiian Affairs, February 1983), p. 174 in Native Hawaiians Study Commission, *Report on the Culture, Needs and Concerns of Native Hawaiians*, vol. I (The Commission, June 23, 1983).

[74] Ralph S. Kuykendall, *The Hawaiian Kingdom, 1778–1854. Foundation and Transformation* (University of Hawaii Press, 1938), p. 270. (This is known as Volume I although it carries no such notation.) See also Marshall Sahlins, *Anahulu. The Anthropology of History in the Kingdom of Hawaii. Volume One. Historical Ethnography.* With assistance of Dorothy B. Barriere (University of Chicago Press, 1992), p. 63.

[75]Sahlins, *Anahulu*, Vol. 1, p. 67.

[76]Ibid., p. 91.

[77]Ibid., p. 92.

[78]Ralph S. Kuykendall, "Education Prior to 1831," *Hawaii Educational Review* (November 1931), p. 61.

[79]Ibid., p. 62.

[80]Ibid., p. 67.

[81]Kuykendall, *The Hawaiian Kingdom*, p. 106.

[82]Sahlins, *Anahulu*, p. 124.

[83]Ibid., p. 124.

[84]Ibid., p. 105.

[85]Ralph K. Steuber, "An Informal History of Schooling in Hawaii," p. 21 in Marion Kelly and others, *To Teach the Children. Historical Aspects of Education in Hawaii* (University of Hawaii, 1982.

[86]Kuykendall, *The Hawaiian Kingdom*, pp. 348–349.

[87]George Allen Odgers, *Educational Legislation in Hawaii, 1845–1892,* (Master's thesis, University of Hawaii, 1932), p. 34.

[88]Ibid., p. 56.

[89]Kuykendall, *The Hawaiian Kingdom*, p. 364.

[90]Ibid., pp. 364–365.

[91]Ibid., p. 365.

[92]Ibid., p. 363.

[93]Ralph S. Kuykendall, *The Hawaiian Kingdom 1854–1874. Twenty Critical Years* (University of Hawaii Press, 1953), p. 112. (This is known as Volume II although it carries no such notation).

[94]Sahlins, *Anahulu*, p. 106.

[95]Haas, *Institutional Racism*, Table 1.1.

[96]See Sahlins, *Anahulu*, pp. 201–203. See also David E. Stannard, "Disease and Infertility: A New Look at the Demographic Collapse of Native Populations in the Wake of Western Contact," *Journal of American Studies*, 24 (1990), pp. 349–350; and Stannard, "Recounting the Fables of Savagery: Native Infanticide and the Functions of Political Myth," *Journal of American Studies*, 25 (1991), pp. 381–418.

[97]Marshall Sahlins, "The Economics of Develop-man in the Pacific," *RES*, 21 (Spring 1992), p. 24.

[98]Kuykendall, *The Hawaiian Kingdom, 1778–1854*, p. 272.

[99]Sahlins, *Anahulu*, p. 130.

[100]Neil M. Levy, "Native Hawaiian Land Rights," *California Law Review*, 63 (July 1975), pp. 855–856.

[10]Kuykendall, *The Hawaiian Kingdom, 1778–1854*, p. 294.

[102]Jocelyn Linnekin, "Structural History and Political Economy: The Contact Encounter in Hawaii and Samoa," *History and Anthropology*, 5 (1991), p. 219 (emphasis added).

[103]Lawrence H. Fuchs, *Hawaii Pono. A Social History* (Harcourt, Brace and World, 1961), p. 16.

[104]Ibid., p. 31.

[105]Statement of the Hawaiian Patriotic League; U.S. Congress, 53rd, 2nd session, House of Representatives, Exec. Doc. No. 47, *President's Message Relating to the Hawaiian Islands*, serial number 32224 (Government Printing Office, 1893), pp. 450–451, 453, 455, quoted in Meyer Weinberg, ed., *America's Economic Heritage*, Vol. I (Greenwood Press, 1983), p. 517.

[106]Haas, *Institutional Racism*, p. 42.

[107]Ibid., Table 2.11.

[108]Ibid., Table 5.8.

[109]Ibid., Table 2.6.

[110]Ibid., Table 5.8.

[111]Kimura, "Language Section," p. 195.

[112]Ibid., p. 196.

[113]Ibid., p. 196. The Hawaiian Homes program consisted of state lands that had been leased to Hawaiian families who were half or more Hawaiian.

[114]Haas, *Institutional Racism*, table 2.4.

[115]Kimura, "Language Section," p. 189.

[116]Ibid., p. 189.

[117]Ibid., p. 199.

[118]Haas, *Institutional Racism*, Table 2.4.

[119]Fuchs, *Hawaii Pono*, p. 77.

[120]Connor B. Stroupe, *Significant Factors in the Influx to Private Schools on Oahu Since 1900* (Master's thesis, University of Hawaii, 1955), p. 53.

[121]Helen and Harold Friedman, "Education in Hawaii," *Integrateducation*, 17 (May–August 1979), p. 53.

[122]Ibid., p. 12.

[123]Ibid., p. 13.

[124]Ibid., pp. 13–14.

[125]Millicent Lawton, "Embarrassment of Riches? Financial Realm Makes Private Hawaii School a Target of Criticism," *Education Week*, (September 29, 1993), p. 17.

[126]Ibid., p. 17.

[127]Friedman and Friedman, "Education in Hawaii," p. 22.

[128]Haunani-Kay Trask, "The Birth of the Modern Hawaiian Movement: Kalama Valley O'ahu," *Hawaiian Journal of History*, 21 (1987), p. 128.

[129]Bernhard L. Hormann, "Integration in Hawaii's Schools," *Social Process in Hawaii*, 21 (1957) p. 11.

[130]Christopher Lee Melahn, *An Application of an Ecological Perspective to the Study of Education Achievement among Native American Hawaiians* (Doctoral dissertation, University of Hawaii, 1986), p. 478. See also p. 557.

[131]Ibid., p. 561.

[132]Raymond T. Mirikitani, *A Longitudinal Study of Achievement in Hawaiian Public Elementary Schools, 1975–83* (Doctoral dissertation, Stanford University, 1988), p. 137. See also *Native Hawaiian Educational Assessment Project, Final Report* (The Kamehameha Schools/Bishop Estate Office of Program Evaluation and Planning, 1983), p. 12.

[133]Jonathan Y. Okamura, *Ethnicity and Stratification in Hawaii*, 1990, p. 11. ERIC ED 347 220.

[134]Ibid., p. 11.

[135]Ibid., pp. 11–12.

[136]Ibid., p. 12. Compare Andrew Lind, "Race and Ethnic Views: An Overview," *Social Process in Hawaii*, 29 (1982), pp. 130–150.

[137]Okamura, *Ethnicity and Stratification*, p. 14. See also Richard L. Rapson, *Fairly Lucky You Live Hawaii! Cultural Pluralism in the Fiftieth State* (University Press of America, 1980), p. 95; and Native Hawaiians Study Commission, *Report*, I, pp. 45–48, 123–134.

[138]Haas, *Institutional Racism*, p. 208.

[139]Friedman and Friedman, "Education in Hawaii," p. 21.

[140]Ibid., p. 21.

[141]Lonnie Harp, "Spending Disparities Found in Single District," *Education Week* (September 21, 1994), p. 14.

[142]Haas, *Institutional Racism*, p. 205.

[143]Suzanne Romaine, "Hawai'i Creole English as a Literary Language," *Language in Society*, 23 (1994), p. 549.

[144]Ibid., p. 551.

[145]Ibid., p. 549.

[146]Haas, *Institutional Racism*, p. 169.

[147] U.S. Department of the Interior, U.S. Bureau of Education, *A Survey of Education in Hawaii.* Bulletin No. 16 (Government Printing Office, 1920), p. 283.

[148] For enrollment figures covering 1915 to 1990 by ethnic group, see Haas, *Institutional Racism,* p. 169, Table 6.1.

[149] Ibid., p. 170.

[150] Ibid., p. 163.

[151] Ibid., p. 210.

[152] Ibid., p. 203.

[153] Friedman and Friedman, "Education in Hawaii," pp. 11, 15. See also David W. Gegeo, "Colonialism at the University of Hawaii: The Experience of a Pacific Island Student" in Majid Tehranian, ed., *Restructuring for Ethnic Peace: A Public Debate at the University of Hawaii* (Spark M. Matsunaga Institute for Peace, University of Hawaii, 1991); and Jaye Mercer, "Native Hawaiians Push to Extend and Deepen University's Diversity," *Chronicle of Higher Education* (August 4, 1994).

[154] Haas, *Institutional Racism,* p. 126.

[155] Haunani-Kay Trask, "An Hawaiian Activist's Fight," *Against the Current,* (May–June 1992), p. 10.

[156] Trask, "The Birth of the Modern Hawaiian Movement," p. 127.

[157] See Haunani-Kay Trask, "Natives and Anthropologists: The Colonial Struggle," *Contemporary Pacific,* 3 (Spring 1991), p. 163.

[158] Ibid., p. 163. See also Romaine, "Hawai'i Creole English as a Literary Language," p. 549.

[159] Haas, *Institutional Racism,* p. 196.

[160] Ibid., p. 208.

[161] For some details of the U.S. educational policy at home, see Weinberg, *A Chance to Learn,* pp. 181–182. See also Frederick E. Hoxie, ed., *Indians in American History* (Harlan Davidson, 1988).

CHAPTER THIRTEEN

India

After 4,000 years of history, India, the world's second most populous country, has not yet provided all its children with a simple elementary-school education. Its adult population is among the least literate in the world. Yet, as early as 500 B.C. or so, the Indian script had already evolved.[1] By A.D. 200 or even earlier, knowledge of reading and writing was "fairly widespread."[2] Learning, however, was locked within a political–religious structure that reserved opportunities to elite circles. Newly developing kingships were established and the monarchs sought to command the loyalty of their new subjects. Chief among their adherents were the Brahmins, the topmost caste, who were designated as the custodians of the Vedas, the holy scriptures of what came to be known as Hinduism. The Brahmins formulated a theory presenting kingships as sacred, thus investing the monarchs with a legitimacy beyond reproach. Brahmins "were the most ardent supporters of this new idea of sacred kingship because they expected from the king that he would uphold their own eminent position in the caste system."[3] This is just what happened.

Formal education—that is, study and teaching of the Vedas—was open only to the top three castes: Brahmins, Kshatriya, and Vaisya. After a time, the Brahmins came to monopolize formal education. Sudras, that is, the fourth estate, were excluded from study of the Vedas, but knowledge of these filtered down to them.[4] Students of the three castes could be taught only by others of the same castes. Sudras established apprenticeship programs for their children. During the early years of the caste system, women were accorded equal educational rights with men.[5] As the system matured, however, the place of women receded. In any event, women of the lower castes came to share the exclusion from any formal education. As Keay and Karve indicated, "Indian women for long centuries were excluded from any education except training in domestic and religious duties."[6]

Hindu elementary schools known as *pathshalas* were located in temples and regarded as village schools. Villagers set aside a part of their farm produce as contributions to the schools. Because no fees or tuition were charged, teachers depended on "the rich, the nobles, and the merchants for subsistence."[7] Children of privileged castes studied reading, writing, arithmetic, and Vedic texts. Here they received their first lessons in Sanskrit. Reportedly, "the Hindus were particularly proficient in mathematics."[8] Misbehavior was punished, sometimes by compelling the miscreant to "sit on his haunches on the tips of his toes and hold his ears with his hands from under his thighs."[9] Five was the age at which schooling began. Textbooks were unknown and memorization was the rule. None of the pathshalas received any governmental funds.

Higher education was offered on a highly selective basis during ancient and medieval times. The scene was dominated by the Brahmins who organized Nelanda University in the 5th century A.D.; it was destroyed in the early 13th century. Admission was by entrance examination to upper castes. According to Chopra, only 20% of applicants passed.[10] Entrance to the secondary course at Nelanda was easier. Nelanda University taught both Brahmanical and Buddhist doctrines. (Buddhism had begun its spread in India during the 6th century B.C.). This was true despite certain tensions between the two religious movements. Buddhism, for example, did not accept the caste system and preached the need for social justice to the poorest strata of Indian society. Aside from a small amount of heavily religious instruction in Buddhist temples, no specifically educational institutions were established by the Buddhists. Although Buddhist nunneries were widespread, their existence did not help "to any great extent to spread education amongst women."[11]

From the 8th century onward, Islam became a living presence in India. Although Muslims constituted no more than one fifth of the country's population during these pre-colonial times,[12] schools and colleges were founded on a large scale. The earliest Muslim invaders destroyed Hindu universities, temples, and monasteries, especially in the North.[13] Beginnning, however, in 1526 with the first of a line of Mughal Emperors, Islam became the state religion but Hinduism was not outlawed. The Mughals could not rule India unaided.

In every mosque, a primary school or *maktab* was established. Sometimes, one was located instead in a home. A higher school, the *madrasa*, was readily available. The greatest concentration of Muslims existed in the northwest of the country, which meant that the greatest number of Muslim schools followed suit. The schools were tuition free although contributions were accepted on behalf of the teachers. Religion played a central role in the curriculum. "Every child had to know the *Quaran* by heart."[14] Other subjects included reading, writing, and grammar; amongst the latter was Arabic and Persian grammar. (Between the 11th and 14th centuries A.D., Persians who fled their country to escape conquest by the Mongols brought their libraries to India and established colleges there. In time, Persian became the official language in governmental affairs. Arabic was the language of the religious faith and other limited uses. Numerous works from Arabic were translated into Sanskrit.) Nearly every madrasa had a library of some size. Girls of a young age were permitted to attend primary schools with boys but with an abbreviated curriculum. These girls, however, apparently came from families of middling circumstances. Daughters of wealthy Muslims used the services of private tutors. "Women belonging to the lower ranks of society such as housemaids, peasants, etc., were illiterate."[15] All in all, women, whether Hindu or Muslim, fared just as badly in education.[16]

Although separate school systems developed for Hindu and Muslim, neither one was hermetically sealed from the other; nor was the caste system enforced without exception in the field of education. In A.D. 1203, the University of Nadia came under Muslim control. Perhaps this was one reason why non-Brahmins were allowed to study in Sanskrit colleges there. As we saw earlier, Hindu and Muslim students studied together at the University of Nalanda. Mughal emperors regularly made large contributions to colleges that were principally Hindu. And sizable land grants were made by both kinds of rulers to Muslim and Hindu colleges and universities.[17]

Slavery continued to be practiced during Muslim rule. Some slaves were permitted to rise in Indian society as high as their talents dictated:

> Muhammed Ghiori (1174–1206) . . .really laid the foundation of the Muslim domination of India. . . . Among the slaves he . . . [adopted and] educated was Kutbud-din, who succeeded his master in 1210 at Delhi, and was the first of what is called the Slave Dynasty.[18]

With reference to Firuz Tughlak, a monarch who ruled during the latter years of the 12th century:

> Like some of the Muslim sovereigns of India before him he had a special interest in educating young slaves, though he carried it to a farther extent than any of his predecessors. It is said that he maintained no fewer than eighteen thousand of these lads, and large sums must have been spent by him for their support and education. He had some of them apprenticed to craftsmen, while others were set to learn the Koran or the art of copying manuscripts.[19]

This latter experience might have been described, in part at least, simply as a process of raising the skill level of the slaves.

During the last half of the 18th century, British forces defeated the French in India and by century's end had established their military superiority over indigenous Indian governments. By this time, education in the country was in disarray. Many indigenous village schools had been abandoned. Chopra noted the continuation of government failure to finance schooling. The traditional governments neither planned nor regulated the schools. Teachers, who Chopra described as "far from qualified," nevertheless "managed to exist on the meager gifts they received at irregular intervals from their village patrons."[20] Part of the reason for the plight of the indigenous schools lay with such internal failings. Another lay with the advent of the British. During the 1770s and 1780s, scattered British missionaries opened schools that offered instruction in English, but by 1800 a mere 1,000 students attended these mission schools.[21] Officials of the East India Company opposed the extension of schooling to Indians "lest it make them less docile."[22]

During the first quarter of the 19th century, British rule was becoming institutionalized. The labor requirements of the English bureaucracy were enormous and could not be met by English immigrants alone. Native Indians were needed to staff the lower ranges of government administration a well as the expanding colonial economy. For these positions, they needed training, especially in English. The pursuit of these goals led India into the world system of colonies. Education was a principal avenue of this enterprise. How should the schools of India be organized to serve British ends?

In 1835, T. B. Macaulay, recently appointed by the Governor of India as a Law Member of the Governor General's Executive Council, was directed to prepare an educational plan for India. The future Lord Macaulay responded with a long memorandum in which he contended that English must be the basis of the schools, because, in his opinion, Sanskrit and Arabic were the languages of error and falsehood. "A single shelf of a good European library," he wrote, "was worth the whole native literature of India and Arabic."[23] Many upper-class Indians already spoke English, a language that was likely to dominate commerce in the region. This was the class that Macaulay felt British educational policy should embrace. As for "the body of the people," they were too expensive to educate:

> We must at present do our best to form a class who may be interpreters between us
> and the millions whom we govern; a class of persons, Indian in blood and color,
> but English in taste, in opinions, in morals, and in intellect.[24]

As for what Macaulay called "the vernacular dialects" of the country, he would leave these to the interpreters to modernize so that these became "by degree fit vehicles for conveying knowledge to the great mass of the population."[25] As for Macaulay's assertion about the library, wrote the historian of Indian education, Mukerji, "this sophistic statement reveals the British snob at his worst and we have the menace of [the] color bar almost in sight."[26] Lord Acton, the well-known British historian, said of Macaulay's sparse knowledge that "he knew nothing respectable before the seventeenth century, nothing of foreign religion, philosophy, science or art."[27]

Macaulay's piece expressed the contempt with which Englishmen increasingly discussed Indian capacities and achievements. At least as important, it also served the economic and political needs of empire building. It was this latter goal that led to fundamental changes in the school system. Almost immediately, the British government endorsed Macaulay's recommendations.[28] Public funds were to be spent only on schools using English as the language of instruction. The money was to be used as grants-in-aid to privately operated schools rather than in schools operated by the government directly. Also, no public funds could any longer be used to publish works other than in English. Nineteen years later, Wood's Despatch laid out a more comprehensive design for Indian education. Vernacular languages were to be retained as a means of instructing the masses of people in the "diffusion of European knowledge."[29] Government-operated schools were to be completely dismantled in favor of more private schools. "The importance of female education in India cannot be overrated," wrote Wood.[30] While the time had arrived to establish universities in India, it was even more important, in Wood's mind, to consider the best education for "the great mass of the people."[31]

Some 28 years after Wood's Despatch, in 1882 and 1883, the Indian Education Commission was appointed to review the implementation of the Despatch. The Commission urged the expansion of State-financed-schooling primary education and that normal schools be increased accordingly. The grants system was strengthened. In 1904, a conference adopted the Resolution of Government on Educational Policy, which acknowledged that "only one girl out of forty attends any kind of school."[32] Again, expansion of State-financed primary education was called for. Resistance to compulsory and free primary education, however, remained strong. Between 1910 and 1912, Gokhale argued for such a measure in the Imperial Legislative Council, but it was defeated. Gokhale told his fellow members, "The Bill thrown out today, will come back again and again, till on the stepping-stones of its dead selves, a measure ultimately rise which will spread the light of knowledge throughout the land."[33] He was answered by the Government of India when it announced the next year that although the time was not yet ripe for free, compulsory primary education, the principle that primary education had a "predominant claim upon the public funds [was] no longer open to discussion."[34] The coming of World War I in 1914 delayed implementation of this latest resolve.

What were the realities of popular schooling in colonial India outside the realm of formal government reports? Nearly a century had passed since the Macaulay recommendations.

By 1900, indigenous village schools had all but disappeared.[35] Even as early as the 1830s when people in some areas failed to pay the teachers in these schools, the latter were abandoned.[36] Mukerji noted that "while in 1820 there was one Hindu boy in every ten of school-going age in an indigenous school, it was one in forty in 1882."[37] In the latter year also, only a bit over 1% of the entire population of India attended primary school.[38] Over the next 40 or so years, the enrollment figures of India's primary schools rose impressively and were cited frequently by education officials. In fact, however, they meant little, as was explained by a government report in 1919:

> In the primary system . . . the waste is appalling. So far as we can judge, the vast increase in numbers in primary schools produces no commensurate increase in literacy, for only a small proportion of those who are [in] the primary stage reach Class IV, in which the attainment of literacy may be expected. The wastage in the case of girls is even more serious than in the case of boys. . . .[39]

Likewise, Chopra reported that "out of every 100 boys in Class I in 1922–1923, there were only 19 reading in Class IV in 1925–1926."[40] In any event, even these meager figures were beyond the reach of most of India's children. In 1946 to 1947, the last school year under colonialism, no more than 30% of school-age children (6 to 11 years) attended school.[41] The schooling of girls rose slowly. In 1921 and 1922, they constituted only 17.2% of all students in primary schools. By 1946 and 1947, it had increased to 20.8%.[42] Over 25 years, the average rise was about .14 of one percent a year.

The mandatory use of English as a language of instruction had been the central Macaulay recommendation in 1835. But years before that, many middle-class Indians had begun studying English. Early in the 19th century, "rich citizens of Calcutta and Bombay came forward to set up English schools in collaboration with individual European officials and businessmen and in Calcutta [a number] founded Hindu College . . . in 1817."[43] In 1844, the government of India announced that Indians literate in English would be eligible for governmental employment. This whirlpool of careerism enveloped the Indian middle class in one city after another. The rest of the population remained unaffected. Meanwhile, middle-class and upper caste Hindus had no difficulty learning English. As Kulke and Rothermund put it, "Under Mughal rule they had mastered Persian as the language of administration; they now learned the language of the new rulers as well."[44] Acquisition of English constituted another barrier between the social elite and the great mass of Indians, thereby widening the gap between the two.

Most of the poor were denied not simply a chance to learn English—which would have seemed useless to most of them. Any kind of formal schooling was out of reach. Now and then, private charity enabled a talented few to gain an education. Very modest public funds on a provincial basis were occasionally made available to tribal peoples and outcaste groups. Despite formal government assertions of sympathy with the education of women, little was accomplished. Virtually all the published accounts of women's education during that time describe the schooling of women of elite families. Jotiba Govindrao Phuley, a Hindu gardener of modest circumstances, built the first school for Hindu girls in Bombay as well as an orphanage. In Poona during 1852, he opened a school for Harijans ("Untouchables") and then two more; these he supported from his own meager funds.[45] Phuley refused to accept the so-called Filtration Theory of education according to which the benefits of schooling would trickle down to the masses once the elite groups had been educated. Macaulay, of course, enthusiastically subscribed to this theory.

Muslims constituted another group that was accorded inferior public educational opportunities. Not until 1871 did the Government of India institute any specific measures on behalf of Muslim schooling. During 1871 and 1872, Muslims in Bengal made up 32.3% of the population but only 14.4% of students. In colleges and universities, about 4% of the students were Muslims. Generally speaking, Muslims seemed to prefer their own private Muslim institutions; yet, there was also an absolute shortage of public schools, so that it is difficult to determine which condition was the more basic. In addition, Muslims as a whole were poorer than Hindus. Finally, an element of discrimination against Muslims was discernible. As Haque wrote, "The Bengal educational department could be described as a Hindu establishment."[46] Thus, in Bengal itself, the department employed 148 Hindus and 4 Muslims as school inspectors.[47]

In 1886, Muslims founded the All-India Muslim Educational Conference to counter the inequalities and discrimination in public education on all levels.[48] To help increase the number of Muslim students, the Conference pressed for the appointment of Muslims on the governing bodies of universities. Another focus of protest was the anti-Muslim content of school textbooks approved by Hindu educational officials.[49] Islamic Studies were introduced at the instance of the Conference. Glaring failures of educational authorities were highlighted. For example, in 1911, Muslims in Jammu and Kashmir, a majority Muslim state, had inferior educational opportunities. Literacy figures for Muslims, Hindus, and Sikhs were 0.8, 61.0, and 94.0% respectively.[50] In India as a whole, between 1927 and 1932, few Muslim boys proceeded beyond primary school:

> In 1932, Muslims formed 30.5 percent of . . . Class I; in Class II they formed only 25.3 percent; in Class V only 19.4 percent. In the middle stage there were only . . . 15.0 percent of the total. In colleges and universities there were only . . . 13.6 percent of the total.[51]

Dropouts for Muslims were somewhat larger than those for Hindus. At the same time, the schools functioned poorly for children of both groups.

Education was distributed in colonial India overwhelmingly along class and caste lines. Compared with more developed countries such as Russia and Germany, India ranked very low in terms of affording its people a primary education. Early in the 20th century, literacy and primary education were available to nearly all in the two European countries, "while in India even in 1951 the majority of [the] population was illiterate and more than a half (58 percent) of children remained outside primary school."[52] This same sweeping backwardness, however, did not hold for educating the Indian elite. There, secondary and higher education was not only:

> concentrated within the propertied classes . . . but also . . . since the early 20th cen-

tury the propertied classes, particularly their upper crust, in India were provided with the secondary and higher education at least not to a much lesser extent than those in developed countries.[53]

Unlike in the West, industrial development in India was not accompanied by the growth of general literacy. Thus, in 1913, on the eve of World War II, two thirds of Russian industrial workers were literate. At the same time, India's industrial workers were in the main illiterate. Even the Bombay factory workers, relatively better paid than Indian agricultural workers, were only 30% literate.[54] India's social system bred an educational process that—almost uniquely— modernized its elite without sharing the fruits of that modernization with a large fraction of its people.[55]

Since the failure in 1912 of the Gokhale motion for free, compulsory primary education, the nationalist movement for Indian independence had made schooling for all a primary issue. Some headway was made on the province-wide level, but the British government resisted any national solution. In 1937 and 1938, under the leadership of Mahatma Gandhi, a conference of nationalist educators met to draw up a plan for a non-official system of schools that was to operate without fees or tuition for a period of 7 years. The mother tongue was to be the language of instruction. The expenses of operation would be supplied by income earned from the sale of products made by the students. A detailed syllabus was drawn up by the Zakir Hussain Committee and it was approved by the Indian National Congress, a body organized in 1885 to pursue the goal of independence.[56] Although the principle of self-sufficiency was consistent with Gandhi's philosophical outlook, the nationalist movement did not pursue this aspect of the proposal. Indeed, the entire matter was overtaken by events as, in 1947, India became independent

Three years later, a constitution was promulgated—in which education was given extensive attention.[57] In it, India was declared, a sovereign socialist secular democratic republic, resolved to secure to its citizens social, economic, and political justice. All persons were to be equal before the law and discrimination on the basis of religion, race, caste, sex, or place of birth was outlawed. The constitution made special provision "for the advancement of any socially and educationally backward classes of citizens or for the Scheduled Castes and the Scheduled Tribes" and for similar persons in the area of public employment. Language and cultural rights of minorities were to be protected. Minorities could establish and operate educational institutions. Within the next 10 years, free and compulsory education until age 14 years was to be attained. Another section provided: "The State shall promote with special care the educational and economic interests of the weaker sections of the people, and, in particular, of the scheduled castes and the scheduled tribes, and shall protect them from social injustice and all forms of exploitation." The Anglo-Indian community was guaranteed certain educational rights. Hindi was made the official language, but for 15 years from 1950, English could continue to be used for official purposes. States might elect to use languages other than Hindi for official purposes. Chil-

dren of linguistic minorities could be educated in primary schools with their
mother tongue. Fifteen languages were designated as official languages.

Since Independence, educational actualities have lagged seriously behind
Constitutional declaration of intention. As Sen pointed out:

> It is truly remarkable that in rural India in the age group 12 to 14 years, more than
> a *quarter* of the boys have *never* been enrolled in any school and more than *half* the
> girls have *never* been enrolled either. . . . More than two thirds of the girls between
> 12 and 14 [in the state of Uttar Pradesh] have never had the benefit of any school-
> ing at all.[58]

In the mid-1980s, Tilak wrote that "as many as 22 percent of the villages in India do not have even a single primary school" and that "not less than 20 percent
of the country's children have never been to school of any kind."[59] In 1993, according to Radhakrishnan and Akila, there were "more than 45 million out-of-
school children most of whom are compelled to work for a living."[60] (It is ger-
mane to note that when, in 1910, Gokhale introduced his motion for free, compulsory education, he included in it a proposal that child labor be outlawed.[61])

Although the Constitution spoke in terms of equality, the daily reality was
quite otherwise. As Galanter found, "Children from low status groups tend to
attend schools with the least-adequate facilitites, the least-qualifiied teachers,
and the least-advantaged fellow students."[62] The adverse impact of unfavorable
economic trends on education is thus especially destructive on the poorest children. Consider the following findings by Sen:

> Judged in "real terms," the percentage expansion of the number of teachers has
> actually fallen steadily from the 1950s, to the 1960s, to the 1970s, and through the
> 1980s. The trend has not been reversed recently—to some extent quite the oppo-
> site. The number of primary school teachers per unit of population has *fallen* be-
> tween 1980–81 to 1990–91. . . . Since the economic reforms, there seems to have
> been a decline in the absolute number of primary school teachers between 1991–
> 92 and 1992–93.[63]

(The "economic reforms" refers to policies of economic liberalization and the
removal of numerous governmental regulations that were effected during the
late 1980s and early 1990s.) As the general supply of primary teachers falls, the
poorest children are likely to suffer the greatest deprivation, either through
growing class sizes or the absence altogether of sufficient numbers of teachers.
In the light of growing teacher shortages, children who are now out of school
—again, the poorest—are in effect further excluded from an education. The
same social decisions that withdraw investments in teachers are the same ones
that regard mass education as unproductive.

Dropout rates at all levels of schooling have continued to be high. During
the school year 1986 to 1987, according to Radhakrishan and Akila:

> the dropout rates at the primary level were about 51, 66, and 49 [percent] among
> the [scheduled castes and scheduled tribes] and the general population respec-

tively; with 69, 80, and 61 [percent] as the corresponding figures at the middle level, and about 80, 87 and 74 [percent] at the high/post-basic level.[64]

Two years later, Upendranadh reported, "nearly half of the enrolled students dropped out without completing primary schooling. [In general,] 46.76 percent of boys and 49.69 percent of girls drop out of school before V class."[65] At the same time, children of scheduled castes and scheduled tribes were dropping out at rates higher than those cited.[66] Writing about the years 1952 to 1964, Zachariah stated that "the secondary school population consists mainly of children from the higher castes and/or the upper and middle classes."[67] Undoubtedly, the same statement could have been made 30 years later because dropping out was a phenomenon of the poorest children.

Literacy has grown since Independence but so, also, has the number of illiterates, as follows:[68]

Year	Literacy (%)			Illiterates
	General	Male	Female	Number
1951	19.7	29.0	2.8	241,640,000
1961	30.1	43.0	16.3	240,370,000
1971	36.5	49.0	23.0	274,870,000
1981	43.6	56.4	29.7	314,150,000
1991	52.1	63.9	39.4	335,830,000

The distribution of illiterates as between rural and urban areas is highly uneven. A national survey during 1986 and 1987 found the following illiteracy rates:[69]

Rural		Urban	
Male	47.61	Male	25.26
Female	68.39	Female	40.88
General	57.68	General	30.01

One Indian state, Kerala, was outstandingly successful in promoting literacy, even among women. "In adult female literacy rate, India's 39% is well behind China's 68%, but Kerala's 86% rate is much higher than China's. . . . In terms of female literacy, Kerala has a higher achievement than *every* individual province in China."[70] Because, however, Kerala's economic development has been far less favorable, its educated unemployed are very numerous.[71]

Higher education in India is the training ground for leaders in country-wide careers: "higher ranks of administrators, doctors, advocates, engineers, industrialists, businessmen, journalists, scientists, diplomats, and officers in the armed forces."[72] Recruited from a narrow social range, they are educated at public expense, because all universities are supported by tax revenues. Colleges are private or governmental, although the former also receive their principal funding from government. Minocha emphasized, "Nearly 135 government colleges have less than 100 students each. Quite a large number of colleges are substandard and non-viable."[73] Only recently have women become an appreciable presence in higher education. Between 1960 to 1961 and 1990 to 1991, women increased their representation in enrollment from 10.1 to 32.5%.[74] Although enrollment as a whole in Indian higher education increased by 23 times between 1950 and 1951 and 1988 and 1989, this order of magnitude was repeated in a number of other developing countries.[75]

Enrollment in higher education is overwhelmingly undergraduate. During the late 1980s, it stabilized at around 88% undergraduate. Few go on to graduate work (11.5%) and many fewer to research positions (0.8%) in higher education.[76] Raza, a geographer and prominent former administrator of a large university, has a low opinion of much undergraduate education in India and other developing countries: "Instead of giving doles to its unemployed as in the developed world, quite a few of the developing countries dole out the thin gruel of inferior undergraduate education to the unemployed youth."[77]

Student aid programs, however, are minimal, at best. During the early 1950s, government covered some 40% of all expenditures on higher education; these rose to 73% by 1980.[78] From 1963 on, national loan scholarships have been interest free; the term of repayment extends over 10 years. Among the states, the rate of repayment ranges from 1 to 73%. These loans have become decreasingly available because the total number of students has risen from 1.3 million in 1963 to 1964 to 9.2 million in 1988 to 1989. The number of scholarships, however, has not increased from their original 20,000. Worse yet, the maximum amount of loans has also not risen since 1963 to 1964. Meanwhile, the cost of living increased eightfold since that time.[79] As a result, the scholarships bore little relation to the real financial needs of poorer students. In the early 1990s, the highest court in India ruled that the Constitutional guarantee of education covered all levels and not just primary schooling.[80] Because under the existing system of scholarships these were more readily available to students from upper social groups, it was not clear how the new judicial ruling would be implemented.

Unemployment and underemployment are widespread in India. In 1990, some 30 million youth were unemployed. One fifth of these were educated, that is, college graduates or post-graduates.[81] Another report stated that "many B.A.s and M.A.s are . . . having to work as rickshaw drivers or bus-conductors."[82] India does have the world's third largest reserve of trained scientific and technical personnel. Yet the proportion of such manpower per 10,000 of the population comes to 6 in India as compared with 115 in the USSR and 190 in Japan.[83] This narrow layer of technical manpower is well-trained and available at low pay. Thus, "experienced [computer] programmers command salaries of $1,200 to $1,500 a month, compared with $4,000 to $6,000 . . . in the United States."[84] Many American computer firms have begun to employ Indian computer technicians who continue to work in their own country.

The Constitution had pledged the instituting of free and compulsory education in elementary schools no later than 1960. Further deadlines were set peri-
odically to no avail. The Five-Year Plans drawn up by the Indian government
beginning in 1950 to 1955 repeated the commitment, stating that, "the provision
of free and compulsory primary education is the first necessary step towards establishing equality of opportunity of every citizen."[85] The Sixth Plan, for 1980
to 1985, spoke of reaching "universalization (Class I–V) up to the age of 11
years, in the next five years. . . ."[86] Even this was a retreat because the original
pledge spoke of the age of 14. The Seventh Plan (1985–1991) declared resound-
ingly that "overriding priority will be given to realizing universalization"; age
14 was restored but little else changed.[87] The Eighth Plan (1992–1997) announced
unflinchingly, "Universalization of Elementary Education and complete eradication of illiteracy among the people in the age group 15 to 35 years have been
recognized as a priority objective. . . ."[88] This lamentable parade of good intentions was matched by Parliament in 1986 when it adopted a legal policy statement on "Education for Equality and Equality in Education."[89]

The national default in elementary education had serious economic consequences. A study conducted in 1981 found that "the mean level of education for
the workforce is 1.9 years of schooling."[90] Such a rudimentary level of education made it most unlikely that India could hope to match the economic progress
of other rapidly industrializing Asian countries. Compared with South Korea,
Hong Kong, China, and Thailand, India lagged seriously in adult literacy rates
over the years 1960 to 1980, as follows:[91]

	1960	1970	1980
India	28	36	52
South Korea	71	93	96
Hong Kong	70	90	100
China	43	69	76
Thailand	68	86	93

As Sen observed:

> The point is not that these countries have a much higher base of elementary edu-
> cation *now* than India currently has, but that they *already had* radically higher lev-
> els of elementary education in the 1970s, when they went rapidly ahead, compared
> with what India has *now*."[92]

India lacks more than common schooling, Sen stressed. Three of the four other
countries had also experienced a land reform that helped modernization. Also,
the rising level of living in those countries was broadly based. In India, too,
poverty receded somewhat. In urban areas, between the mid-1960s and 1989 to
1990, the percentage of persons living in poverty fell from 56 to 34.[93]

In 1995, the India correspondent of the *New York Times* referred to that country as one "having English as its common language."[94] This, however, was a

vast overstatement. Much more precisely, Gopal accurately called it, "the language of the ruling class."[95] In 1988, fewer than 5% of the Indian people could handle it.[96] English, according to Gopal, "is the language of communication of the civil services, of the managers and senior employees of the civil services, of the managers and senior employees of the public and private sectors of the economy, and of the professions."[97] Mohan characterized the role of English in India as "representing national state power, corporate power, the social elite and India's interface with the global [economic] system."[98]

The Constitution of 1950 had given English as an official language a breathing space of 15 years while directing the new government to energetically pursue the spread of Hindi throughout all levels of government. Instead, a dilatory process ensued during which English retained and even strengthened its hold in official circles. Although the use of Hindi also grew, it failed to attain the dominant position envisioned by the makers of the Constitution.[99] The 15 standard regional languages, given a special rank in the Constitution, flourished, although not uniformly. Within specific states, however, children who did not conform to the regional language, suffered for it. Saxena and Mahendroo reported their observations:

> We have constantly witnessed children and adults being ridiculed, humiliated and reprimanded for speaking in their own [village or tribal] language. In schools, there is no dearth of episodes where children are punished for failing to talk in the standard language or continuously lapsing back into their mother tongue.[100]

Saxena and Mahendroo compared these regional efforts at creating language uniformity to those exerted on great masses of people by the English-speaking elite. (Article 350 of the Constitution provides for "instruction in the mother tongue at the primary stage of education to children belonging to linguistic minority groups.")[101]

Five separate articles of the Constitution deal specifically with governmental authority to make special provisions for scheduled castes, scheduled tribes, and backward classes. (See articles 15, 16, 46, 338, and 340.[102]) Both national and state governments are covered. Very limited provisions such as these originated under British rule. Only the governmental sphere was affected; the private sector such as business, indusry, agriculture, and the like was excluded from such regulations. In 1872, the first legislation—the Caste Disabilities Act—was passed. In 1895, the State of Mysore government reserved certain posts to be filled by backward castes.[103] Similar laws were adopted elsewhere. By 1943, under the leadership of Ambedkar, 8.3% of reservations had been set aside for untouchables. This is in part a consequence of work of leaders such as Phule, "the founder of [the] revolutionary low-caste protest movement."[104] (See pp. 292–293.) By the late 1980s, the practice had spread widely:

> There are now 16 states and two union territories today which are providing special assistance of varying degrees to other backward classes, mostly on the basis of

caste, in addition to the all-India reservation policy of the government of India in favor of scheduled castes and tribes.[105]

In primary schools, children of scheduled castes and tribes now attend in much larger numbers. Many, however, are not very successful: According to Upendranadh, "59.2 percent of SC and 74 percent of ST students dropout from the school before reaching class V."[106] Because these two groups constitute a majority of the poor in India, this means that the reservations policy has not been able to overcome basic class deprivations in education.

In education as a whole, the share of scheduled castes rose between 1964 to 1965 and 1977 to 1978 as follows:

		Higher Education	
	All Education	*General*	*Professional*
1964–5	10.8	5.5	4.3
1972–3	10.8	7.1	5.5
1977–8	12.6	7.7	6.6

Scheduled castes make up 15% of the total population. Colleges and universities have resisted the increase, especially in curricula that prepare students for high-paying careers. Often, scheduled castes had to seek court orders to compel institutions to admit them. Raza and Aggarwal wrote that the institutions did not:

> in most cases, make any special effort to facilitate the proper adjustment of these deprived students into the sophisticated system of the alien world and their high failure rate was used as an additional argument to denigrate the system of protective discrimination itself.[107]

Extremely few Scheduled Caste students can be found in postgraduate courses in Medicine, Engineering/Technology, Education, and Law.[108] Yet, studies of sample populations of scheduled-caste students show more encouraging results. One concludes that aid to such students along with reservation of jobs "has, by and large, led to reasonably satisfactory outcomes, at least in the case of those residing in a metropolitan city like Ahmedabad."[109]

Overall evaluations of special aid and reservations arrived at positive conclusions. "The reservation policy has materially helped a substantial number of individuals of lower-caste background to gain entry into office and professional jobs."[110] Doubts raised about the solidity of academic preparation of students benefitting from special aid and reservations, are, according to Chalam, unmerited. "But no one has ever produced convincing evidence to show that engineers, doctors and administrators belonging to reserved categories have proved much worse than others."[111] Bitter-end opponents of reservations in academe sometimes conducted street warfare against scheduled-caste inroads at B. J. Medical College in Ahmedabad during 1981. The latter, however, "were no match for gangs of high- and middle-caste youths armed with knives, clubs, kerosene and fire."[112] Five years later, after the Gujarat state government widened the coverage of reservations in universities and government jobs, high- and middle-caste students rioted and attacked public property as well as Scheduled Caste areas. At an election, scheduled-caste candidates won a sweeping victory that resulted in the appointment of a prime minister who was a Scheduled Tribe member. Upper- and middle-castes protested and pillaged. In turn, "six thousand tribals attacked upper caste homes and shops in several small towns."[113] Among tribals and Scheduled Castes, devotion to the reservations policy continued to grow.[114]

ASIAN INDIANS IN THE UNITED STATES

During the first third of the 20th Century, some 7,000 Indians emigrated to the United States.[115] Nearly all came from a compact area in Punjab, a productive agricultural province in northwestern India. Most arrived during the years 1907 through 1908. Efforts to restrict their flow began almost as soon as they made their initial appearance. Meanwhile, however, they worked at railroad building, logging, and farming. Most lived in Southern California. Few had much formal education in India; their knowledge of English was rudimentary at best. About half were literate in their native language. The bulk were agricultural laborers and unskilled workers. Their religion was Sikhism, combining some elements of caste society; in the Punjab, they had been *jats*, the agricultural caste.

In 1907, when agitation in San Francisco was at its height in the school segregation issue—see p. 53—the Japanese and U.S. governments had agreed that Japan would no longer permit laborers to emigrate to the United States. Merchants, ministers, and students, however, were allowed to move to this country. In 1882, on passage of the Chinese Exclusion Act, the same arrangements had been made: Laborers were excluded but merchants, ministers, and students could still emigrate to the United States. In 1908, only a year after the Indians began to arrive, the U.S. Immigration Bureau declared them ineligible for naturalized citizenship because they were Mongolic people rather than Whites as the 1790 Naturalization Act required.[116] At the same time, the U.S. Department of Justice began to take steps to prevent the granting of citizenship to any Indians.[117] Two years later, the U.S. Bureau of the Census, "Began to classify Indians with Koreans and Filipinos as 'other.' U.S. attorneys were instructed to challenge any Indians seeking citizenship. . . ."[118] This step was taken to discourage any federal judges from granting citizenship to Indians, as some had done. Altogether, at least 59 such awards had been made in federal courts. (The judges had considered Asian Indians as Whites under the 1790 Naturalization Act and thereby eligible for citizenship.) Congressmen, especially those representing White constituencies in the West, were assiduous on the citizenship and exclusion issues. "From the 60th Congress (1907–1909) for a span of ten years

24 bills were introduced that named the Hindus directly or included them among those ineligible to citizenship and recommended their exclusion."[119] Congressmen Everis A. Hayes of California told the House of Representatives in 1913, "I believe that I have no race prejudice whatever, but I do believe in racial purity [applause]."[120] None of Hayes' bills ever came to a vote.

In 1917, however, the exclusionists won a major victory with passage of the Barred Zone amendment. India was one of the countries designated by location rather than name that hereafter could no longer send emigrant laborers to the United States. This measure was most effective and remained on the books until 1946. As was customary under the 1917 measure, merchants, ministers, and students could still be admitted. In 1924, the Immigration Act achieved a double exclusion by providing that no person could immigrate to the United States who was not eligible for naturalized citizenship. The ban was highly effective. Indians in the United States numbered about 6,400 in 1920. During the following 20 years, nearly half this number (3,000) left the United States for India. By 1940, 2,405 remained in this country; in another 6 years, only 1,500 still resided here.

It was in this climate of dwindling numbers and hostile intent that Asian Indians built a community, primarily in Southern California. Before World War II, not even a dozen Indian women had emigrated to the United States.[121] As a result, during the years 1913 to 1949, in Southern California, four out of five married male Asian Indians were wedded to Mexican American women.[122] Although children of those unions spoke Spanish with their mothers—as did their fathers, after a time—"in contrast to their mothers, most sons and daughters were intensely curious about their Indian heritage and remember[ed] vividly what their fathers told them."[123]

Punjabi-Mexican children living in the Imperial Valley—just north of the Mexican border—generally were assigned to the segregated schools attended by Mexican children or both Mexicans and African-Americans. They were not welcomed by Mexican children:

> Stories included harassment in the outdoor privies, taunts and shoves on the school bus, and name-calling and fighting at school. . . . Some Punjab-Mexican children had stones thrown at them by the children of their fathers' workers as they went down the lanes to school together. . . . Some Punjabi fathers protested the assignment of their children . . . others did not. . . . Punjabi-Mexicans and Anglos in Holtville attended the same schools (there were few Mexicans and no blacks in Holtville). Not only school systems but public facilities such as restaurants, barber shops, movie theaters, swimming pools, and even many churches were segregated.[124]

Even though by World War II a number of Punjabi-Mexicans had become well-to-do employers of farm labor, this did not buy them an exemption from racist penalties. On the other hand, as Leonard pointed out, prosperity enabled the employers to separate themselves from the bulk of Mexican American working-class persons. Also, Punjabi-Mexican children did not need to work as most of their peers did. The first Punjabi-Mexican children graduated from high school in Holtville between 1937 and 1940. A bit later and until 1951, Central Junior College became the local college in El Centro. A college degree was only a minor attraction to most Punjabi-Mexican parents, especially for their daughters.

Residence in the United States did not create a great forward movement in the schooling of Indians. According to the 1940 Census, one out of three Indians over age 25 had attended less than a year of schooling. Among Indians as a whole, the median years of schooling completed was 3.7, the lowest of any ethnic group. The next lowest was the Chinese, at 5.5 years.[125] Only 4% of all working Indians were employed as professionals. Discrimination was an important factor. "Some Indians who had difficulty finding jobs in cities claimed to be Mexican or black, believing the prejudice to be greater against Indians. . . . Some Indians . . . found that they could discard their turbans and pose as southern Italians or Portuguese."[126] Under the California land laws of 1913 and 1920, it became exceedingly difficult for Indians (and other Asians) to own any agricultural land. "The Punjabis were forced to rely upon Anglo lawyers, bankers, neighbors, and friends to lease and hold land for them."[127] The widespread American conception of Indians as incompetent was underscored in 1929 when Rabindranath Tagore, the Bengali writer who won the 1913 Nobel Prize for literature, was asked by a U.S. consul in Vancouver whether he could read and write.[128]

The 1950s were the last complete decade of the old order in Asian Indian community life. Still numbering only about 1,500 and concentrated around the remnants of Punjabi culture, the Asian Indians could not look forward to a fresh beginning. Due to a change in federal law in 1946 (the Celler-Dickstein immigration act), the bar to Indian immigration and Indian naturalization was removed. The following year, India became independent; natives of India received a small immigration quota to the United States. The increase in immigration resulting from Celler-Dickstein was considerable. Between 1946 and 1964, some 12,000 Indians entered the United States, effecting a 9-fold expansion in the number of Indians in the country. In 1965, however, a general immigration act was passed that revolutionized the immigration process from India. The old quota system that favored immigration from northern and western Europe was abolished. The new quota system applied impartially to all countries, which, in effect, gave Asia its first equal chance at emigration to the United States. Almost 600 Indians entered the United States in 1965, but nearly 10,000 arrived in 1970. Ten years later, over 20,000 immigrated.[129] By the time of the 1990 Census, a total of 815,447 Asian Indians lived in this country. In 1994, the nearly 500,000 foreign-born Asian Indians resided in the following regions: Northeast, 207,000; Midwest, 64,000; South, 92,000; and West 131,000.[130] By period, these immigrants had come as follows: before 1970, 34,000; 1970 to 1979, 101,000; 1980 to 1989, 210,000; and 1991 to 1994, 149,000.[131]

The new generation of immigrant Asian Indians was drawn from the middle and upper ranks of Indian society and thus differed greatly from its predecessor. Physicians were prominent among the newer immigrants. In the New York City area, according to Saran:

> 95 percent of those who had practiced medicine in India . . . [found] similar positions in the United States. Nonetheless, for these doctors, as for many other doctors, while the occupation might remain the same, the work itself often entailed an initial lessening in both responsibility and reward.[132]

As so frequently in the case of Filipino physicians in the United States, many Asian Indian physicans also worked at assignments usually rejected by White American doctors. (See p. 119.) Nevertheless, in one research study, "more than half of the immigrants said that they would like . . . [their children] to be medical doctors."[133]

Overcrowding of the professions in India created a large reserve of future expatriates. Thus, a graduate of Bombay Medical School in 1968 reported that 45 out of his graduating class of 120 moved to the United States. Similarly, "in the years 1968 to 1976, about half the members of the graduating classes of Indian Institutes of Technology have emigrated; for the Indian Institutes of Management, the totals have been 10–15 percent."[134] Within the past decade, the number of management institutes in Bombay grew from 1 to 15, thereby increasing the potential export of talent. Three-year diploma programs at Polytechnics have the same effect. An official of Motorola, the American computer and electronic firm, stated, "There's no question that when one looked at India, one is struck by the very, very great excess of graduates."[135] A study of the years 1988 to 1990 found that over 150,000 highly skilled people emigrated to the United States, more than half from Asia: "Engineers, mathematicians, and computer scientists are more likely to originate in India and Taiwan. . . . For the small number of natural scientists, India supplied the largest component."[136] Indian professionals usually move as a family.

Not all immigrants from India were well-to-do. In 1993, for example, 9.3% lived in poverty and 10.2% were unemployed. Bachelor's degrees were held by 137,000 and graduate/professional degrees by 132,000, but another 40,000 were not high-school graduates. Only about one fifth of 1% of the immigrants received any public assistance.[137] The most recent immigrants have represented somewhat decreased economic circumstances. Thus, between 1980 and 1994, 11.7% of Indian immigrants lived in poverty. Otherwise, the general features of immigrant status remained undisturbed. The younger poverty-households used practically no public assistance whereas only about one seventh of the elderly households did so.[138] In a study of New York City, Fisher found a "small enclave of impoverished Indians" in Manhattan, around Broadway and 113th Street.[139]

The post-1965 immigrants came primarily from Punjab (35%), Gujarat

(55%), and Kerala (10%).[140] Most were Hindus. In addition, a number emigrated from Uganda in East Africa after they were ejected from that country as part of a racist campaign by ruling groups. The new Punjabi immigrants arrived in intact families and looked down at the Punjabi Mexicans, especially as potential sons-in-law.[141] This friction was not the result of class bias because the Punjabi-Mexicans had prospered. Writing about Yuba City and Marysville, La Brack observed:

> In place of the relatively landless laboring class was a fairly wealthy owner-operator group of Sikhs who owned (as of 1976) over 7,000 acres of prime orchard crop land and whose members were entering mercantile, white collar, professional, and educational fields in increasing numbers.[142]

Nevertheless, for social and cultural reasons, the Punjabi-Mexicans were viewed by newcomers as unnatural and controversial.[143]

Between 1980 and 1982, Gibson conducted research among the California Punjabi-Mexicans. She found a strong climate of rejection in the schools:

> In school, Sikh children are told directly by white classmates and indirectly by their teachers that they stink. They are verbally and physically abused by majority students, who refuse to sit by them in class or on buses, crowd in front of them in lines, spit at them, stick them with pins, throw food at them, and worse. Only a handful of white youths participate actively in the harassment, but the majority either condones their classmates' behavior or feels powerless to alter the status quo. Teachers and administrators, although disturbed by the situation, seem almost equally powerless to turn things around. They deal with the most blatant hostilities, but otherwise encourage Sikh students to be understanding of their majority peers' "ignorance." Sikh students who seek to defend themselves fear that they will be labeled troublemakers.[144]

In one instance "a Punjabi girl's long braids were set on fire as she walked to class."[145]

The Sikh children also suffered for their traditional cultural practices:

> [They are] told in one way or another that India and Indian culture are inferior to Western and American ways. They are criticized for their values, their diet, and their dress. They are faulted because they defer to the authority of elders, accept arranged marriages, engage in group decision making, and place family ahead of individual interests. They are condemned most especially for not joining in majority-dominated extracurricular activities and for withstanding as best they can the pressure to conform to the dominant culture.[146]

No mention is made in Gibson's research of any distinction the Anglo children drew between children of Punjabi-Mexicans or the newer Punjabi immigrants.

In 1978, it became evident from a series of minimum competency tests in the high school of Valleyside, CA—a 2-hour car drive from San Francisco—that Punjabi students scored significantly lower than non-Punjabi students. On analysis, it emerged that the low scores belonged primarily to Punjabi children who had spent their first 4 years in Indian schools and then emigrated. Students who had had all their schooling in California, on the other hand, did as well as the Anglo students. Aside from the test-score differentials, school-district officials "and Punjabi community leaders also were deeply concerned by mounting tensions between Valleysiders and Punjabis, in school settings and in the community."[147] These concerns led to a series of inquiries.

One line of inquiry dealt with language training. It was found, for example, that ESL programs achieved little for Punjabi students who had received their first 4 years of schooling in India. Gibson reported that "almost 90 percent of . . . [such students] continued to be weak in English through high school."[148] She also noted that the ESL program in high school math, science, and English "was, at best, equivalent to that of the upper elementary grades."[149] Despite earning high grades in the ESL classes, then, "they proceeded to junior college where much the same pattern repeated itself."[150] Bilingual education was proposed by some as an alternative, one which would give greater stress to subject-matter content. This, however, was rejected for at least two reasons. For one, although funds were available, eligibility required that students be low income, but the Punjabi did not qualify on this standard. For the other, as Bradfield observed, "the general attitude of the school officials seems to be, 'Let them learn English and become Americanized as soon as possible.'"[151] (Bradfield was referring to schools in Yuba City, CA, one of the main locations of Punjabis. I do not know if it is Valleyside.)

A great cultural gulf separated the Sikh and the non-Sikh communities. In El Centro, the county seat of Imperial County, Chakravorti observed in the late 1960s, "All members of the first generation [of Sikhs] speak and read Punjabi; none in the second generation can speak or read Punjabi."[152] The privilege of using one's mother tongue was not accorded to young Punjabis. Bradfield reported that in Yuba City, she had not encountered anyone outside the Sikhs' community "who seemed to have more than a superficial understanding of their presence, history, and culture."[153] Meanwhile, in that same town, an Indian mother braced herself before visiting her son's school:

> Tomorow in my blue skirt I will go
> to see the teacher, my tongue
> stiff and swollen
> in my unwilling mouth, my few
> English phrases. She will pluck them
> from me, nail shut my lips. My son
> will keep sitting in the last row
> among the red words that drink his voice.[154]

"Nail shut my lips" is how the Asian Indian community viewed the Anglo response to their grievances.

The marginality of many Asian Indians was expressed in personal names and manner of speech. Frequently, names were changed by the children:

> This is . . . very common behavior among children, for their names are often mispronounced in school and they do not want to seem different. Thus they will use their anglicized names when they are in school with white playmates and their Indian names when they are among Asian Indians. . . . [With reference to an 11-year-old girl] when she is with her Indian friends, she speaks English with an Indian accent, and when she is in school she speaks English with an American accent. She unconsciously switches back and forth with ease. . . .[155]

Aggarwal observed a time factor at work in renaming: "Second generation Indians start to feel 'back-to-India' sentiments once they reach the college level. . . . Many drop the Americanized versions of their names in favor of their given names. For example, Roger reverts to Raj. . . ."[156] When D. S. Saund, an Indian who had become a naturalized citizen in 1949, ran for Congress in 1956 as a Democrat, his name was advertised as "D.S. Saund." His Republican opponent, however, referred to him in newspaper ads as "Dilip Singh in big letters and Saund in small letters."[157] Saund was elected and reelected for a second term. (He was a farmer with a Ph.D. in mathematics from Berkeley.)

CONCLUDING REMARKS

The easiest way for a group to succeed in the United States is to have succeeded elsewhere first. This was the case for most contemporary Asian Indians. In 1990, nearly four out of five of them were immigrants, the majority having entered the country since 1965. Their greatest assets were advanced education and capital resources, both originating in India rather than the United States. All the Asian Indians in the United States constitute less than one tenth of 1% of India's population, a most unrepresentative sample, far more so than the Punjabis of pre-World War I times.

In general, little can be learned about Asian Indian school experiences because the schools rarely publish separate materials on them. Also, Asian Indians are the most scattered geographically of all sizable minorities and thus are least likely for that reason alone to constitute concentrations of schooling problems.

NOTES

[1] F. E. Keay and D. D. Karve, *A History of Education in India and Pakistan,* 4th ed. (Oxford University Press, 1964), p. 162.

[2] Ibid., p. 162.

[3] Hermann Kulke and Dietmar Rothermund, *A History of India* (Barnes and Noble, 1986), pp. 43–44.

[4] P. N. Chopra, B. N. Puri, and M. N. Das, *A Social, Cultural and Economic History of India*, vol. 1 (Macmillan India, 1974), pp. 157, 162.

[5] D. N. Jha, "Higher Education in Ancient India," p. 1 in Moonis Raza, ed., *Higher Education in India. Retrospect and Prospect* (Association of Indian Universities, 1991).

[6] Keay and Karve, *A History of Education in India and Pakistan*, p. 79.

[7] Chopra, Puri, and Das, *A Social, Cultural and Economic History of India*, vol. 2, p. 148.

[8] Ibid., p. 147.

[9] Ibid., p. 149.

[10] Ibid., vol. 1, p. 168.

[11] Keay and Karve, *A History of Education in India and Pakistan*, p. 77.

[12] Ibid., p. 136.

[13] Chopra, Puri, and Das, *A Social, Cultural and Economic History of India*, vol. 2, p. 146.

[14] Ibid., p. 153.

[15] Ibid., p. 157.

[16] Keay and Karve, *A History of Education in India and Pakistan*, p. 77.

[17] See Muzaffar Alam, "Higher Education in Medieval India," pp. 13, 15 in Moonis Raza, ed., *Higher Education in India. Retrospect and Prospect* (Association of Indian Universities, 1991).

[18] Keay and Karve, *A History of Education in India and Pakistan*, p. 109.

[19] Ibid., p. 111.

[20] P. N. Chopra, B. N. Puri, and M. N. Das, *A Social, Cultural and Economic History of India*, vol. 3, p. 223.

[21] Rudolf C. Heredia, "Education and Mission. School as Agent of Evangelisation," *Economic and Political Weekly* 30 (September 16, 1995), p. 2334.

[22] Ibid., p. 2334.

[23] "Macaulay's Minute on Education (1835)," p. 4 in J. C. Aggarwal, ed., *Landmarks in the History of Modern Indian Education*, 2nd revised ed. (Vikas Publishing House, 1993).

[24] Ibid., p. 11.

[25] Ibid., p. 11.

[26] S. N. Mukerji, *History of Education in India. Modern Period*, 5th ed. (Acharya Book Depot, 1966), p. 76.

[27] Ibid., p. 75.

[28] See "Resolution of March 7, 1835," in Aggarwal, *Landmarks*, pp. 13–14.

[29] "Wood's Despatch (1854)," in ibid., p. 16.

[30] Ibid., p. 17.

[31] Ibid., p. 11.

[32] Chopra, Puri, and Das, *A Social, Cultural and Economic History of India*, vol. 3, p. 271.

[33] Mukerji, *History of Education in India*, p. 186.

[34] Ibid., p. 188.

[35] Chopra, Puri, and Das, *A Social, Cultural and Economic HIstory of India*, vol. 3, p. 269.

[36] Ibid., pp. 245–246.

[37] Mukerji, *History of Education in India*, p. 134.

[38] Ibid., p. 135.

[39] Ibid., 196.

[40] Chopra, Muri, and Das, *A Social, Cultural and Economic History of India*, vol. 3, p. 282.

[41] Mukerji, *History of Education in India: Modern Period*, p. 241.

[42] Ibid., pp. 230, 232.

[43] Aparna Baso, "Higher Education in Colonial India," p. 23 in Moonis Raza, ed., *Higher Education in India. Retrospect and Prospect* (Association of Indian Universities, 1991).

[44] Kulke and Rothermund, *A History of India*, p. 251.

[45] Mukerji, *History of Education in India: Modern Period*, p. 102.

[46]Mozammel Haque, "Muslim Education in Bengal: Problems and Progress (1871–1900), *Islam and the Modern Age*, 14 (August 1983), p. 166.

[47]Ibid., p. 175.

[48]Abdul Rashid Khan, "The All-India Muslim Educational Conference. Sole Educational Representative Organization of Indian Muslims 1906–1947," *Journal of the Pakistan Historical Society*, 42 (July 1994), pp. 303–310.

[49]See Haque, "Muslim Education in Bengal," p. 172.

[50]Khan, "The All-India Muslim Educational Conference," p. 307.

[51]*Progress of Education in India, 1927–32*, quoted in Alan Peshkin, "Education, the Muslim Elite, and the Creation of Pakistan," *Comparative Education Review*, 6 (October 1962), p. 257.

[52]Erik Komarov, "Specificities of Emergence of Modern Social Classes in India in the 19th and Early 20th Centuries," p. 154 in Joachim Heidrich, ed., *Changing Identities. The Transformation of Asian and African Societies Under Colonialism* (Verlag das Arabische Buch, 1994).

[53]Ibid., p. 156.

[54]See ibid., pp. 159–160.

[55]Ibid., p. 160.

[56]See Aggarwal, ed., *Landmarks in the History of Modern Indian Education*, pp. 51–57.

[57]See ibid., pp. 77–83.

[58]Amartya Sen, "Beyond Liberalization: Social Opportunity and Human Capability," *The Other Side*, No. 126 (November 1994), pp. 15–16. Emphasis in original.

[59]Jandhyala B. G. Tilak, "Urban Bias and Rural Neglect in Education: A Study on Rural-Urban Disparities in Education in Andhra Pradesh," *Margin*, 17 (October 1984), p. 62.

[60]R. Radhakrishnan and R. Akila, "India's Educational Efforts: Rhetoric and Reality," *Economic and Political Weekly*, 28 (November 27, 1993), p. 2617.

[61]Krishna Kumar, *Political Agenda of Education. A Study of Colonialist and Nationalist Ideas* (Sage, 1991), p. 109. Kumar commented: "Equal opportunity for education could hardly mean anything without equal rights to a childhood free from economic responsibility."

[62]Marc Galanter, *Competing Equalities. Law and the Backward Classes in India* (University of California Press, 1984), p. 61.

[63]Sen, "Beyond Liberalization," p. 18. Emphasis in original.

[64]Radhakrishnan and Akila, "India's Educational Efforts," p. 1619.

[65]C. Upendranadh, "Structural Adjustment and Education. Issues Related to Equity," *Economic and Political Weekly*, 28 (October 30, 1993), p. 2417.

[66]Ibid., p. 2418.

[67]Mathew Zachariah, "The Durability of Academic Secondary Education in India," *Comparative Education Review*, 14 (June 1970), p. 158.

[68]Radhakrishnan and Akila, "India's Educational Efforts," p. 2613.

[69]Upendranadh, "Structural Adjustment and Education," p. 2415.

[70]Sen, "Beyond Liberalization," p. 11. See also Jean Drèze and Jackie Loh, "Literacy in India and China," *Economic and Political Weekly*, 30 (November 11, 1995), pp. 2868–2878.

[71]E. T. Mathew, "Educated Unemployment in Kerala. Some Socio-Economic Aspects," *Economic and Political Weekly*, 30 (February 11, 1995), p. 325. See also Sen, "Beyond Liberalization," p. 11.

[72]Keay and Karve, *A History of Education in India and Pakistan*, pp. 223–224.

[73]A. C. Minocha, "Making a Mess of Higher Education. Madhya Pradesh Disbands Uchcha Skirsha Amedan Ayog," *Economic and Political Weekly*, 29 (February 19, 1994), p. 411.

[74]Savita R. Pagnis and Susan Verghese, "The Role of Higher Education in the Empowerment of Women," p. 178 in C. Chakrapani and S. Vijaya Kumar, eds., *Changing Status and Role of Women in Indian Society* (M D Publications, 1994).

[75]Moonis Raza and Yash Aggarwal, "Higher Education in Contemporary India. Nature of

Quantitative Growth," pp. 33, 39 in Moonis Raza, ed., *Higher Education in India. Retrospect and Prospect* (Association of Indian Universities, 1991).

[76] Moonis Raza and Yash Aggarwal, "Higher Education in Contemporary India. Stagewise Structure and Facultywise Spectrum," pp. 45–46 in Moonis Raza, ed., *Higher Education in India. Retrospect and Prospect* (Association of Indian Universities, 1991).

[77] Ibid., p. 45.

[78] Maureen Woodhall, *Student Loans in Higher Education: 2. Asia* (UNESCO, 1991), p. 56.

[79] Ibid., p. 61.

[80] Upendranadh, "Structural Adjustment and Education," p. 2415.

[81] Khanne, "Recent Developments in Indian Higher Education," p. 97 in Moonis Raza, ed., *Higher Education in India. Retrospect and Prospect* (Association of Indian Universities, 1991).

[82] Vinay Dharmadhikari, "Education for India's Development: Two New Strategies," *The Other Side*, No. 123 (August 1994), p. 18.

[83] Khanne, "Recent Developments in Indian Higher Education," p. 104.

[84] Keith Bradsher, "Skilled Workers Watch Their Jobs Migrate Overseas," *New York Times*, August 28, 1995.

[85] Aggarwal, *Landmarks in the History of Modern Indian Education*, p. 407.

[86] Ibid., p. 413.

[87] Ibid., p. 414.

[88] Ibid., p. 418.

[89] K. G. Rastogi, "India's National Policy on Education," *Asian Literacy and Reading Bulletin* (December 1987), p. 7.

[90] Upendrandh, "Structural Adjustment and Education," p. 2417.

[91] Sen,"Beyond Liberalization," p. 17.

[92] Ibid., p. 16. Emphasis in original.

[93] Pradip Maiti and Manabendu Chattopadhysay, "Trends in Level of Living in Urban India," *Economic and Political Weekly*, 28 (November 13, 1993), p. 2550.

[94] John F. Burns, "India Repels an Invasion of Money," *New York Times*, September 24, 1995.

[95] Sarvepalli Gopal, "The English Language in India Since Independence, and its Future Role," p. 205 in John Grigg, ed., *Nehru Memorial Lectures 1966–1991* (Oxford University Press, 1992). Gopal delivered his lecture in 1988. See also Robert J Baumgardner, ed., *South Asian English: Structure, Use and Users* (University of Illinois Press, 1996), p. 1, who wrote that there are 25 million "users of English" in India. This would mean fewer than 3% of the population.

[96] Ibid., p. 202.

[97] Ibid., p. 202.

[98] Peggy Mohan, "Market Forces and Language in Global India," *Economic and Political Weekly*, 30 (April 22, 1995), p. 888.

[99] Hans R. Dua, "Hindi Language Spread Policy and Its Implication: Achievements and Prospects," *International Journal of the Sociology of Language*, No. 107 (1994), pp. 115–143.

[100] Sadhna Saxena and Kamal Mahendroo, "Politics of Language," *Economic and Political Weekly*, 28 (November 6, 1993), p. 2446.

[101] See Aggarwal, *Landmarks in the History of Modern Indian Education*, p. 82.

[102] Ibid., pp. 78–81.

[103] K. S. Chalam, "Caste Reservations and Equality of Opportunity in Education," *Economic and Political Weekly*, 25 (October 13, 1990), p. 2333. See also S. Bandyopadhyay, "Toward a Corporate Pluralist Society: Caste and Colonial Policy of Protective Discrimination in Bengal, 1911–1937," *Calcutta Historical Journal*, 11 (July 1986–June 1987), pp. 69–117.

[104] J. V. Naik, "Intellectual Basis and Ideological Premises of Maharashtrian Response to British Colonial Rule," p. 247 in Joachim Heidrich, ed., *Changing Identities. The Transformation of Asian and African Societies under Colonialism* (Das Arabische Buch, 1994).

[105] Chalam, "Caste Reservations and Equality of Opportunity in Education," p. 2333.

[106]Upendranadh, "Structural Adjustment and Education," p. 2418.

[107]Raza and Aggarwal, "Higher Education in Contemporary India. Systemic Inequities and Disparities," p. 64.

[108]See Galanter, *Competing Equalities*, p. 63.

[109]Vimal P. Shah and B. S. Vaishnav, "Social Class and Educational and Occupational Attainments of the Scheduled Caste Postmatric Scholars in an Urban Setting," p. 106 in Abraham Yogev and Sally Tomlinson, eds., *International Pespectives on Education and Society. Affirmative Action and Positive Policies in the Education of Ethnic Minorities* (JAI Press, 1989).

[110]Kumar, *Political Agenda of Education*, p. 107.

[111]Chalam, "Caste Reservations and Equality of Opportunity in Education," p. 2337.

[112]John R. Wood, "Reservations in Doubt: The Backlash against Affirmative Action in Gujarat, India," *Pacific Affairs*, 60 (1987) p. 421.

[113]Ibid., p. 425.

[114]For a left critique of the affirmative-action approach embodied in reservations, see Ruth Glass, "Divided and Degraded: The Downtrodden Peoples of India," *Monthly Review*, 34 (July–August 1982), pp. 101–127.

[115]Chan, *Asian Americans. An Interpretive History* (Twayne, 1991), p. 3.

[116]Premdatta Varma, *The Asian Indian Community's Struggle for Legal Equality in the United States* (Doctoral dissertation, University of Cincinnati, 1989), p. 105.

[117]Ibid., pp. 146–147. See also Jogesh C. Misrow, *East Indian Immigration on the Pacific Coast* (R and E Research Associates, 1971, orig. 1915), p. 32.

[118]John R. Wunder, "South Asians, Civil Rights and the Pacific Northwest: The 1907 Bellingham Anti-Indian Riot and Subsequent Citizenship and Deportation Struggles," *Western Legal History*, 4 (Winter-Spring 1991), p. 64.

[119]Varma, *The Asian Indian Community's Struggle*, pp. 99–100.

[120]Ibid., p. 93, footnote 42.

[121]Chan, *Asian Americans*, p. 109. See also Salim Khan, *A Brief History of Pakistanis in the Western United States* (Master's thesis, California State University, Sacramento, 1981), p. 33.

[122]Karen I. Leonard, "Pioneer Voices from California. Reflections on Race, Religion, and Ethnicity," p. 123 in N. Gerald Barrier and Verne A. Dusenberg, eds., *The Sikh Diaspora. Migration and the Experience Beyond Punjab* (South Asia Books, 1989).

[123]Ibid., p. 128.

[124]Karen I. Leonard, *Making Ethnic Choices. California's Punjabi Mexican Americans* (Temple University Press, 1991).

[125]Gary R. Hess,"The Forgotten Asian Americans: The East Indian Community in the United States," *Pacific Historical Review*, 43 (1974), p. 591.

[126]Joan M. Jensen, *Passage from India. Asian Indian Immigrants in North America* (Yale University Press, 1988), pp. 41, 45.

[127]Karen I. Leonard,"Historical Constructions of Ethnicity: Research on Punjabi Immigrants in California," *Journal of American Ethnic History* 12 (Summer 1993), p. 7.

[128]Varma, *The Asian Indian Community's Struggle*, p. 235.

[129]Surinder M. Bhardwaj and N. Madhusudena Rao, "Asian Indians in the United States: A Geographic Appraisal," pp. 198–199 in Colin Clarke, Ceri Peach, and Steven Vertovec, eds., *South Asians Overseas. Migration and Ethnicity* (Cambridge University Press, 1990).

[130]U.S. Bureau of the Census, 1 Table 5, "India," package of tables for "The Foreign-Born Population: 1994," *Current Population Survey*, Series P 20–486, p. 270.

[131]1 Table 6, "India," package of tables for "The Foreign-Born Population: 1994," *Current Population Survey*, Series P 20–486, p. 297.

[132]Saran, *The Asian Indian Experience in the United States* (Schenkman, 1985), p. 29.

[133]Priya Agarwal, *Passage from India: Post-1965 Indian Immigrants and Their Children* (Yuvati Publications, 1991), p. 45.

[134] Arthur W. Helweg and Usha M. Helweg, *An Immigrant Success Story. East Indians in America* (University of Pennsylvania Press, 1990), pp. 60–61.

[135] Edward A. Gargan, "India Among the Leaders in Software for Computers," *New York Times,* December 29, 1993.

[136] Wilawan Kanjanapan, "The Immigration of Asian Professionals to the United States: 1988– 1990," *International Migration Review,* 19 (Spring 1995), p. 16.

[137] U.S. Bureau of the Census, 1 Table 6, "India," package of tables for "The Foreign-Born Population: 1994," *Current Population Survey,* Series P 20–486, p. 297.

[138] Ibid., p. 297.

[139] Maxine P. Fisher, *The Indians of New York City. A Study of Immigrants from India* (South Asia Books, 1980), p. 21.

[140] Helweg and Helweg, *An Immigrant Success Story,* p. xiii.

[141] Leonard, *Making Ethnic Choices,* p. 194.

[142] Bruce La Brack, "Immigration Law and the Revitalization Process: The Case of the California Sikhs," p. 64 in S. Chandrasekhar, ed., *From India to America* (Population Review Book, 1982).

[143] Leonard, "Historical Constructions of Ethnicity," p. 8.

[144] Margaret A. Gibson and Parminder K. Bhachu, "The Dynamics of Educational Decision Making: A Comparative Study of Sikhs in Britain and the United States," p. 69 in Margaret A. Gibson and John U. Ogbu, *Minority Status and Schooling. A Comparative Study of Immigrant and Involuntary Minorities* (Garland, 1991).

[145] Margaret A. Gibson, "Collaborative Educational Ethnography: Problems and Profits," *Anthropology and Education Quarterly,* 16 (Summer 1985), p. 130.

[146] Ibid., p. 130.

[147] Ibid., p. 126.

[148] Ibid., p. 129.

[149] Ibid., p. 129.

[150] Ibid., p. 130.

[151] Helen H. Bradfield, *The East Indians of Yuba City: A Study in Acculturation* (Master's thesis, Sacramento State College, 1971), p. 94.

[152] Robindra C. Chakravorti, *The Sikhs of El Centro: A Study in Social Integration* (Doctoral dissertation, University of Minnesota, 1968), p. 84.

[153] Bradfield, *The East Indians of Yuba City,* p. 109.

[154] Chitra Banerjee Divakaruni, "Yuba City School," p. 120 in The Women Of South Asian Descent Collective, ed., *Our Feet Walk the Sky. Women of the South Asian Diaspora* (Aunt Lute Books, 1993).

[155] Helweg and Helweg, *An Immigrant Success Story,* pp. 155–156.

[156] Aggarwal, *Passage from India,* p. 37.

[157] Saund, *Congressmen from India* (Dutton, 1960), pp. 101–102.

CHAPTER FOURTEEN

Cross-Group Issues

This chapter concludes the book by examining some critical issues that are broader than one or another geographical area. The model-minorities issue is the first of these. During the latter part of the 1960s, a population expert, William Petersen, wrote of Japanese Americans as a model minority. The press, however, extended the concept to all Asian-Americans, thus further diluting an already flimsy concept. Advocates contended that Asian-Americans were the most successful American minority, a standard for all other minorities. Advanced beyond the majority even, Asian-Americans were hailed by many as leaders in education, in community cohesion, family relations, occupational attainment, family income, citizenship, self-dependence, and more.[1] Claims like these were almost never made by Asian-Americans themselves. As Kashima observed, the model-minority image "for the most part . . . is a perspective from the outside looking in."[2] Frequently, its adherents urged African-Americans to be heedful of the Asians' modelled behavior rather than depend so exclusively on political action and demonstrative tactics. Many conservative White political figures, publishers, and journalists, unsympathetic to the African-American-led civil rights movement, promoted the model-minority image. Although few African-Americans were convinced by the argument, many Whites seemed to accept it. Indeed, the entire model-minority thesis appeared to be prepared more for the benefit of Whites than of anyone else.

Among Whites, its greatest appeal was the feature of self-congratulation. Embedded in the concept of model minority was that of the model majority. By this was meant a large group who held power in the society but whose members not only restrained themselves from oppressing minorities but stood ready to accord every group its just due. By conceiving itself so loftily, a majority established itself as a paragon of balanced judgment with respect to each and every minority. In turn, a minority that insisted on the remediation of historic injustices and labelled the majority an oppressor was itself regarded as unjust and incapable of serving as a model to other minorities. Only the model majority could exercise a proper judgment on minorities. A minority's readiness to accept that judgment and act on it was the surest sign of superiority to other minorities. (See "concluding remarks" to Chapter 3; see also Table 14.1.)

Numerous Asian-American researchers criticized the concept of Model Minority. They found it highly deficient in factual basis. The myth alleged, for example, that many Asian-Americans had largely achieved income parity with Whites, and that a far larger percentage had a higher education—both showing the vitality of equal opportunities in this country.[3] Here and there, income equality was achieved, but more frequently, higher income resulted from more members of the family working. Individual incomes lagged. Also, most Asian-Americans found that their greater education did not result in earnings equal to those produced by equally educated Whites. This was not equal opportunity nor was it American in origin. In 1990, 66% of Asian-Americans were foreign-born and most adults among them had gained their education overseas.

TABLE 14.1
Two Groups of Minorities in the United States

Asian-Americans:	Immigration or conquest	Exclusion from schools	Legal segregation	Quotas in higher education	English compelled	Compulsory-ignorance laws
Chinese	I	Y	Y	N	Y	N
Japanese	I	N	Y	N	Y	N
Koreans	I	N	Y	N	Y	N
Filipinos	C	N	N	N	Y	N
Vietnamese	I	N	N	N	Y	N
Cambodians	I	N	N	N	Y	N
Laotians-Hmong	I	N	N	N	Y	N
Hong Kongers	I	N	N	N	Y	N
Taiwanese	I	N	N	N	Y	N
Micronesians	C	N	N	N	Y	N
Polynesians	C	N	N	N	Y	N
Asian Indians	I	N	N	N	Y	N
Classic Minorities:						
African Americans	E	Y	Y	Y	Y	Y
Mexican-Americans	C	N	Y	Y	Y	N
Puerto Ricans	C	N	N	N	Y	N
American Indians	C	Y	Y	Y	Y	N

C = Conquest; E = Enslavement; I = Immigration; N = No; Y = Yes

Education was a prime asset of the Model Minority thesis. Asian-Americans, it was said, had achieved greatly in education despite the discrimination they had suffered. Although this was undeniable, at the same time the thesis tended to speak of Asian-Americans as a monolithic whole. Asian-American was equated with high academic achievement. In the schools and colleges, unfortunately, teachers and administrators assumed that no serious instructional problems existed among Asian-American students. As we saw in earlier chapters, however, this is not the case.

In the mid-1980s, schools in and around New York's Chinatown contained numerous students who were seriously deficient in reading. On the other hand, throughout the United States, Koreans tend to live in suburbs and attend schools that are predominantly White. In these largely middle-class schools, academic achievement is relatively high. In central cities such as Chicago, many Koreans live in poorer areas and attend schools that give their students a less advanced preparation. Filipinos in Hawaii attend the poorest schools whereas in California, this is less so. During the years since 1975, students from Vietnamese, Cambodian, and Hmong families—one group poorer than the other—met with failure in many schools. Inappropriate educational approaches by school officials led to high dropout rates and gang formation. Samoans, as we saw earlier, had been universally literate in their own language before the end of the 19th century. Yet, in schools on the American mainland nearly a century later, they were among the lowest academic achievers. In chapter 8, we saw how Hmong children in two Wisconsin schools were deprived of an equal education by manipulation of ESL regulations.

Hsia, in the most comprehensive work on the subject, wrote of the "unequivocal evidence that Asian Americans, particularly newcomers, do not do well on tests that measure English verbal abilities or achievement in vocabulary, reading, and writing."[4] She also referred more than once to the 25% of Asian-American students who have difficulty in the English language. This record is not precluded to hold even with the same ethnic group that produces many valedictorians in American high schools.

It is, however, especially in higher education that numerous Asian-American students fail to operate at the lofty levels projected by the Model Minority myth. Their SAT scores, for example, were higher than those for other minorities as well as Whites; but they also varied with family income as they do for all groups.[5] A widespread misimpression suggested that Asian-American students constituted a disproportionately large percentage of enrollment in the most selective institutions. In 1992, 289,000 or 43.1% of Asian-American collegians were enrolled in community colleges. This did not include another 100,000 nonresident alien Asian-Americans who were also in community colleges.[6] It is not known whether Asian-Americans succeeded in expanding the small contingent of community-college students who ever advanced to a 4-year institution.

California enrolls about 310,000—or 40%—of the country's Asian-American higher-education enrollment.[7] They are not, however, primarily found on the flagship campuses of the University of California.[8] This is not surprising because, as Suzuki wrote, "the vast majority of Asian students are not super-bright, highly motivated over-achievers who come from well-to-do families."[9] According to the state higher-education master plan, UC enrolls students from the top one eighth of high-school graduating classes and CSU from the top one third. Students from the bottom two thirds ordinarily qualify only for community colleges.

During the mid-1980s, CSU began a decade-long process of opinion polling of its students on various aspects of their campus experiences. Asian-American students were the least positive about the educational content of those experiences. As this continued to be the case, the central administration appointed a committee to investigate the reasons for the dissatisfaction. In 1990, the committee made its first report; 4 years later, a second report—the final one—was completed. An additional source of information was a series of three public hearings held from October to December of 1989, prior to the committee's first report. Giving testimony at these hearings were students, teachers, staff, and local campus administrators, as well as some informed persons outside CSU. All in all, CSU came under closer scrutiny in these proceedings than any other higher-education institution serving Asian-American students.

Perhaps the single topic that was most persistently discussed was the English writing examination that had to be passed before graduation. The president of CSU Fullerton reported that only 20% of native English speakers failed the exam whereas 65% of nonnative speaking-students did so.[10] At San Jose State University, another CSU campus, the figures were 6% and nearly 50%.[11] Given an English Placement Test at CSU Fresno during January 1989, nearly 60% of Asians failed, marginally more than non-Hispanic Blacks at the same school.[12] Undergraduate Asians at CSU Hayward made up 47% of repeat takers on the Writing Skills Graduation Test whereas 59% of graduate repeat test takers were Asians.[13] An associate dean at San Francisco State University testified that, "I have encountered Asian-American students who cannot write simple sentences but who have managed to get through college thus far by primarily taking courses which only require multiple-choice exams."[14]

Communication difficulties permeated work of the entire university. As a faculty member of the Computer Science Department at CSU Fullerton stated, Asian-Americans made up over three out of four students with "serious writing problems."[15] But the difficulties went beyond writing. Not only have a number of companies ceased recruiting on one campus because of poor writing by students, but many Asian-American students are unable to participate effectively in campus interviews.[16] Job seeking after graduation is extremely difficult for these students.[17] One faculty member reported that "students who are not very good at language and get an entry-level job discover after four or five years, that they are not promoted."[18] At CSU Fresno, a year and a half after graduation, 18 graduates out of 26 who had registered with a campus center for aid in seeking employment were working as technicians and still searching for a job in their advanced specialty.[19]

Students and others pointed to the linkage between the so-called Model Minority and academic problems. "Very often the 'Model Minority' has been tossed around to hide the benign neglect that has been bestowed upon the Asian students."[20] A leader of the Asian Student Union at San Francisco State complained, "There is no help. There is no help other than your classmates, the people in your organizations, your clubs or whatever."[21] Similar terms were used to describe the plight of Cambodian students at CSU Long Beach. "And we are here, minority of minority, who need help the most and we don't get help."[22] Even when helpers were willing to give aid, one witness explained, too often they were not trained to do so. This applied to English teachers as well as others.[23]

About a year after the three public hearings were held, in 1990, the Asian-Pacific American Advisory Committee released its report that included 29 recommendations. These related to actions requested of the individual campuses and the central administration. In 1994, after nearly 4 more years, the Committee issued a follow-up report reviewing whatever progress had been recorded since 1990.

There was little progress to report. With respect to the Graduate Writing Assessment Requirements, a subject of frequent student complaint, the Committee wrote flatly that "the students were not provided support" in preparing for writing exams.[24] To two specific recommendations on ESL programs, "no responses were made by the 20 campuses." (Four campuses seem not to have responded to any questions or recommendations.) On the entire issue of ESL programs, the Committee wrote:

> [The responses present] a bleak picture of the resources available to students with ESL needs. . . . Many of the CSU campuses have yet to respond to the needs of ESL students. . . . Most campuses have yet to develop appropriate assistance and support for these [GWAR] students. General support for ESL students is also dismal. Only seven of the sixteen campuses that responded to the survey reported offering ESL classes in the regular curriculum. However, three of those campuses offered only two classes each.[25]

The Committee also recorded that it was "disturbed that campuses maintained a seemingly insurmountable barrier without providing programs for English language improvement."[26] Only a single campus—San Francisco State—had a "fully operational program which is responsive to the needs of ESL students."[27] "Despite the dire situation presented by the 1990 . . . report and at the urging of the Board of Trustees," added the Committee, "campus response to the needs of ESL students has been non-existent or [is] only now just beginning to occur."[28]

Committee findings in other parts of the 1994 report were not inconsistent with those just reviewed. Under the title "Campus Climate and Racial Harassment," the Committee reported:

> [Asian-American] students appeared to be more alienated from campus life, experienced more stress, and felt less support than other students. . . . [They] reported more personal experiences of racism and harassment than other students without perceived mechanisms for remedy or support.[29]

On two campuses—Fresno and Dominguez Hills—"a substantial proportion (37 percent . . . and 28 percent . . .) reported feeling uncomfortable on campus because of their race or felt racial discrimination frequently or occasionally."[30] Few concerns of Asian-Americans were specially provided for in the ordinary personal counseling structures of CSU. The Committee reported its feeling of discouragement over the lack of Asian-American mental-health providers.

In the area of curriculum and instruction, the Committee in 1990 had made seven recommendations. Now, 4 years later, the Committee recorded its observation:

> In general, major changes in instruction and curriculum have not been made at the campus level. Budgetary constraints were most often cited as the reason or excuse given for lack of progress in this area. . . . CSU campuses can make critical changes that are not costly to create curricula that included the history, culture, and experiences of Asian Pacific Americans.[31]

By using the word *excuse,* the Committee expressed its skepticism of the plea of financial stringency. The Committee expressed "great concern" over CSU's "minimal record" in the area of Asian-American studies.[32] Once more, San Francisco State was cited as an outstanding exception. In the field of faculty and staff affirmative action, the Committee pointed to severe underrepresentation of Asian-American women on the faculties as well as to glass-ceiling effects in senior and executive management positions.

In one degree or another, problems of CSU could be found elsewhere in higher education, as indicated in earlier chapters. At the University of Massachusetts, Boston, for example, isolation from faculty and staff marked the Asian-Americans' school days. Similarly, a minimum of help was afforded them in course work, advising, and mentoring. Problems in writing English were prominent among Southeast Asians at the University of Minnesota, even in professional schools.

Although more than two out of five Asian-American students attended community colleges, little about their day-to-day problems appears in educational research literature. Chu studied Asian-American students at the Los Angeles Community College. In 1989, 758 students were classified as high, medium, or low achievers by grade point averages. They represented five Asian-American groups: Chinese, Japanese, Koreans, Filipinos, and Vietnamese. Koreans ranked highest, followed by Chinese and Filipinos. At or even below average were

Vietnamese and Japanese. (The Japanese numbered less than 5% of the total and may not have been representative.) According to the Chinese, half of their number was eligible to attend the University of California or CSU.[33] On the other hand, two thirds of the Japanese were not eligible for these alternative institutions. Academic progress of students who had been in the United States for less than 10 years depended in part on their coming from middle- and upper class families and the quality of their previous schooling. Many of the students in the study planned to transfer to a university after completion of their course work, but no attempt was made to ascertain how many did so.[34] At the City College of San Francisco—a community college—ESL classes were very crowded and waiting lists are long. An actual wait of a year for class openings is not unusual.[35] Angie Fa, the head of the college's Asian-American Studies program, commented on the price the college was paying for the myth of the Model Minority: "The perception is that without any help, without any programs, without any culturally relevant curriculum, the Asian-American students are going to make it."[36]

During the 1980s, few institutions came to bear the distinguishing mark of Asian-Americans as much as higher education. By decade's end, slightly over a half of their collegians attended universities.[37] Between 1981 and 1990, Asian-Americans enrolled in higher education rose from 1.6 to 5.1% of the whole.[38] On the most selective campuses, by 1990, they constituted some 12% of all freshmen.[39] At elite institutions, they were enrolled in disproportionately large numbers, "by a factor of 2.8 at the elite collegs and more than 4 at the elite universities."[40] The elite institutions easily accommodated such numbers. Between 1981 and 1990, the percentage of freshmen in the most selective colleges and universities expanded from 10.7 to 16.2%. In private universities, the enrollment of men rose from 11.6 to 20.3% whereas the enrollment of women increased from 13.0 to 23.2%; in public universities, the figures were a rise of 8.2 to 21.7% and from 10.2 to 23.9%.[41] Solmon and Wingard reported that the share of Asians in "very highly selective private institutions, the most elite group of institutions" between 1976 and 1984 rose from 1.4 to 2.5%.[42] These figures are not inconsistent with the earlier figures.

Thousands of Asian-American youth did not get anywhere near higher education. Many in community colleges did not transfer to senior institutions. Dropouts from higher education were numerous as Asian-American students failed to receive appropriate instructional assistance. Inhospitability from faculty and staff cooled down a zeal for learning. These darker aspects of the Asian-American experience, however, were overshadowed by far more extensive discussions of a small minority of Asian-American students in the elite universities. This was not to say, however, that no serious problems existed in these rarefied precincts. The source of these problems, however, was the institutions' administrations, who feared the wrath of Whites as Asian-American collegians occupied increasingly the most treasured places in the country's higher education. During the mid-1980s, it became clearer by the day that public and private elite institutions were dampening the enrollment of Asian-Americans by means of a quota.[43] As Woo put it, "Whenever ethnic minorities begin seriously to threaten the status of dominant groups, admissions criteria are strategically redefined. . . . Insofar as academic standards and qualifications have been redefined, the outcome has largely favored white majority applicants."[44] Institutions practicing such discrimination almost always denied the charge initially but later yielded largely in apology or silence.

Neither in the common schools nor in higher education could the reality of the Model Minority be found. Instead, it was the compounding of privilege that prevailed. Class advantages, both imported and native-born, traversed well-trodden paths throughout American education. During the 1960s, a vigorous civil rights movement had helped create a legislative climate in which the Immigration Act of 1965 became a reality, much to the advantage of Asian-Americans and others. During the following generation, a new Asian-America flourished. By the 1990s, however, unresolved internal challenges such as poverty and new threats such as anti-immigrant sentiments and outright violence endangered Asian-America anew. The older civil rights movement was supplemented by creation of new organizations within the Asian-American community, mechanisms that had not existed before the 1960s.

During the late 1980s and early 1990s, violence against Asian-Americans became common.[45] Schools were among the sites of physical attacks.[46] Wherever hate violence struck, it left terror in its wake because the victims were usually randomly selected and thus entire communities felt menaced. One survey reported, "In Los Angeles in 1993, there were 43 killings of Asian Pacific American merchants within 3 months. In Washington, D.C., in 1993, there were 9 killings of Asian Pacific American merchants, 4 in September alone."[47] Law enforcement officers were frequently the aggressors. "In New York City, the number of incidents of police brutality directed against Asian Pacific Americans is alarming. Many of these incidents arise from traffic disputes. . . ."[48] During 1994, the number of anti-Asian hate crimes increased by 35% over the preceding year.[49] In Los Angeles-area high schools, violent confrontations between Chinese and Chicano students were reported.

In 1990, Congress enacted the Hate Crimes Statistics Act, but in the next 5 years a still-incomplete picture of violence against Asian-Americans emerged. The legislation had many weaknesses regarding coverage, jurisdiction, accuracy of data, underreporting, and police training.[50]

Virtually without exception, Asian-Americans were not the initiators of physical hate violence. Defensive or retaliatory attacks did occur occasionally. Legal authorities failed frequently even to act on complaints. Even in schools, often teachers and administrators were unable or unwilling to stop violence against Asian-American students. Few complaints about such failures were lodged by educational institutions and organizations, despite the serious educational consequences of hate crimes and violence.[51] Neither did leading educational journals review a major report in 1992 by the U.S. Commission for Civil Rights, *Civil Rights Issues Facing Asian-Americans in the 1990s*, although more than one fourth of the entire report dealt with education. It was not clear whether the federal Department of Education made any public comment on the report.

Between 1996 and 2050, the number of Asian-American students is predicted to rise from 4 to 9%.[52] Sometime between 2030 and 2040, the number of school-age non-Hispanic White children is expected to be less than 50%. By 2030, almost one fourth of all school-age children wil be Hispanics. "These trends," stated an official of the Census Bureau, "are so substantial, it would take tremendous social changes to stop them."[53] Historically, however, parallel changes have occurred before. In 1882, the immigration of Chinese was abruptly reversed by passage of the Chinese Exclusion Act. By the late 1980s and early 1990s, little-noticed but significant social changes were underway to change the trends.

Without benefit of any new legislative changes, the Immigration and Naturalization Service (INS) reported a sharp drop in the number of legal immigrants during 1994 and 1995. The inflow fell by over 20%, from 904,262 in 1993 to 720,461 in 1995. A *New York Times* story noted that the decline "was the largest two-year drop in legal immigration since the 1930s and is part of an overall trend in immigration during the last four years."[54] Since 1974, over 800,000 Vietnamese had left their country for the United States and elsewhere. By mid-1996, however, only 35,000 remained in refugee camps and almost none of these qualified any longer as refugees under United States law.[55] Meanwhile, a backlog of married children and siblings of U.S. citizens and resident aliens was on a waiting list for visas, some for years. According to INS, "more than 70 percent of the 260,414 married children awaiting entry and the nearly 1.6 million siblings are Asian."[56] Immigration from South Korea dropped sharply during 1990 to 1994, from some 25,500 to about 10,800 a year.[57] In 1994 alone, for every two newcomers from South Korea, there was an additional one who moved back to South Korea, a pattern comparable with that of many Europeans earlier in this century.

Changes within the organization of U.S. health services also affected immigration levels toward the close of the century. During the years 1965 to 1994, the number of physicians per 100,000 population grew from 139 to 252 or from 266,045 to 660,582.[58] Although doctors' incomes increased over this period, by the end of it, their incomes had begun to slip. This was attributed to the growth of managed health care, particularly Health Maintenance Organizations (HMOs). Many influential sectors of the medical community contended that the unfavorable financial trends would continue or worsen unless the physician supply was reduced.

One fifth of all practicing physicians in the United States are graduates of foreign medical schools. Many were trained in India and the Philippines, as pointed out in earlier chapters. In the United States, they were admitted on a commitment to practice in underserved areas such as inner city hospitals, AIDS clinics, rural areas, state psychiatric hospitals, and Medicaid patients. Numbering nearly 150,000, they have become a vital sector of American medicine. Federal and other public funds help finance their employment. Proposals to reduce drastically their numbers increased as the financial status of medical practitioners declined.

In a 2-month period during 1995 and 1996, two reports by prestigious national organizations addressed these issues. The Pew Health Professions Commission declared in November 1995 that by decade's end, half of the presently available hospital beds would be closed. Surpluses of specialized health personnel would mount rapidly over present levels. These would include 100,000 to 150,000 doctors, 200,000 to 300,000 nurses, and 40,000 pharmacists.[59] Over the next decade, advised the Commission, U.S. medical schools should reduce intake of students by 20 to 25%. In addition, reductions were recommended in the number of positions for graduates of foreign medical schools. Congress was urged to require that foreign graduates of American medical schools return to their own countries after graduation.

The second report in January 1996 issued by the Institute of Medicine—an arm of the National Academy of Sciences—disagreed with the Pew Commission. It held that closing down some medical schools and reducing intake of new students was unnecessary at present. It agreed, however, on the timeliness of cutting the number of hospital residencies open to graduates of foreign medical schools. The Institute reported that the number of foreigners serving in residencies or fellowship-training programs increased between 1988 and 1993 from 12,433 to 22,706. During those same years, graduates of American medical schools numbered 17,500.[60]

Although the number of physicians did not approach a majority of any subgroup of Asian-Americans, they constituted perhaps the single most economically successful occupational group and often were among the community's leadership. Family and old-school connections with institutions of higher education back home were widespread in Korea, the Philippines, and India. Frequently, special training schools, including medical schools, were built to produce graduates who could readily emigrate to the United States. These connections were being strained by the new situation in the United States.

Engineers constituted another group of Asian-Americans whose future was coming under threat during the late 1980s and early 1990s. As in the health field, so, too, in engineering a slump had begun and spread in those years. At the same time, the immigration of foreign-born scientists and engineers rose; from 1985 to 1993, their numbers were 39,000 and 82,000.[61] (By no means were these mainly Asians.) Unemployment among scientists and engineers deepened. Between 1991 and 1994, four giant firms announced planned layoffs of 221,000.[62] Over the period 1968 to 1995, the median salary of engineers with 10 or more years of experience fell by some 13% in constant dollars. Central to this trend was the ending of the Cold War and the consequent decline in defense contracting with the major employers of scientific and engineering personnel. Meanwhile, U.S. high-technology firms hired new personnel. Many of these were foreign-born persons who had completed their professional education in the United States. "Recently arrived Asian engineers earn 22 percent less than native-born Caucasians, when everything [else] is held constant. . . . [They] may have indeed become a group of 'high tech coolie' for economic exploitation by employers in engineering industries."[63] This differential existed even though many of the Asian engineers had the same educational qualifications as Caucasian engineers. Tang also found that these Asian-born engineers had barely half the likelihood of ever becoming managers as compared with American-born Whites.[64] Increasing numbers of such thwarted engineers left their jobs to form high-tech firms in Silicon Valley. Nearly always, however, these companies were subcontractors rather than prime producers.[65] Exceedingly few Asian-Americans were employed in the highest managerial posts of the largest established firms.

Clearly, the long-term prospects for Asian immigration were declining. Although between 1990 and 1994 the Asian-American population grew by 4.5% a year, the excess of births over deaths accounted only for 14% of the growth.[66] Reductions in immigration struck at the major source of population expansion. William Tamayo, a lawyer, did not hesitate to label certain immigration-reform measures as anti-Asian (and anti-Hispanic).[67]

As medicine, engineering, and science become less attractive careers, more Asian-American students will seek opportunities in the social sciences and humanities. During the next generation, the language issue will recede in importance as most Asian-Americans are born in the United States. The present generation of younger Asian-Americans, however, will have received an education almost as strictly governed by social class as their parents' education had been in the old country. Here, as there, those who prospered could manage to gain schooling equivalent with their class position. The others were left to their own devices.

Asian-Americans as a whole were the target of extensive institutional discrimination from their earliest years in the United States. Schooling was one of the prime areas of such action. For some 14 years, Chinese children were excluded altogether from public schools in California. This resulted from the refusal of the state legislature to make any educational provision for them. In many cases, Chinese and Japanese children were segregated in so-called Oriental schools by state law and practice. Sometimes, they were allowed to attend White schools but were grouped in separate rooms. In at least one case, an urban high school was segregated by floor. Asian-American children were often compelled to attend inferior facilities, especially when these were segregated. Special-language needs went largely unattended as school systems stressed the need to bypass mother tongues rather than foster mastery of English. Especially during the first century or so of Asian-American schooling (1850–1965) this resulted in grave academic difficulties among many Asian-American children. Both during and after this initial period, public schools were deeply reluctant to employ Asian-American teachers and other school staff.

Chinese Americans contested these measures and other forms of discrimination by whatever means available. Including lawsuits against schools, immigration rights, and citizenship cases, Chan wrote, "tens of thousands of Asians sought justice through legal action."[68] Many of these efforts were aided greatly by the existence of Constitutional Amendments and Congressional enactments that flowed from the Civil War. Thus, the 14th Amendment (1868), the Civil Rights Act of 1870, and the Civil Rights Act of 1871—passed primarily to protect the rights of former slaves—were utilized by Chinese Americans and other Asian-Americans. (Nearly a century later, efforts to pass the Civil Rights Act of 1964 helped create an atmosphere that produced the 1965 Immigration Act that clearly benefited Asian-Americans and others.)

School segregation was a familiar feature of Asian-American education during the years before 1965. Because of the sharp economic differentiation within Asian groups, the segregation was distributed unevenly. In the 1980s and after, segregation increased on the whole. According to Orfield, half of Asian-American students attended mostly White schools, but another 40% were in schools enrolling from 50 to 90% minority students.[69] On the West Coast, however, the segregation is more striking:

> In California there are 78 [school] districts with more than 15,000 students. In two-fifths (44%) of these larger systems most of the Asian students attend predominantly minority schools and in 31% of the large districts, most Asian students study in schools where the majority of the students are poor. About two dozen large districts, in other words, are beginning to show serious patterns of racial and economic isolation.[70]

These trends are consistent with the increasing residential concentration of Asian-Americans during the 1980s.

According to a Harris Poll in 1989, a majority of Asians favored the use of busing for racial balance and only 38% opposed the policy.[71] Also, Asian parents whose children were being bused for desegregation were asked about their experience. Seventy percent replied "very satisfactory" and another 29% "fairly satisfactory." In Wausau and La Crosse, Wisconsin, Hmong parents strongly favored desegregation plans that affected many of their children (see chapter 8). In San Francisco during 1971 and 1975, 64 and 73% of Orientals opposed busing (see chapter 2). At the same time, in 1971, Chinese parents had kept their children out of school in protest at the desegregation plan. Within 8 weeks, however, two thirds or more of the absentees had returned to the desegregated schools. In 1995 and 1996, the Chinese American community in San Francisco was split over the issue of Chinese student admission to Lowell High School, widely regarded as the city's best. Chinese Americans constituted 41.3% of enrollment, along with 24.9% other Asians, 17.3% Whites, 12.8% Hispanics, 4.5% African-American, and 0.2% Native Americans. According to a federal court order, no single group can occupy more than 40% of the places. In an attempt to keep within these bounds, Chinese American children were being required to meet higher admission standards. Chinese for Affirmative Action, the oldest Chinese civil rights organization in the city, opposed any action to overturn the court order.[72]

It is noteworthy how readily some Asian-Americans participated in community struggles over school desegregation. Whether in two small Wisconsin towns or a large city such as San Francisco, Hmong and Chinese Americans hardly hesitated to take public positions on extremely stressful issues. Also notable was the viewpoint adopted by some Chinese Americans in San Francisco that they should not press for maximum enrollment of their community's children out of deference to non-Asian minorities who had fewer opportunities to gain a first-class education. Of course, many in the community disagreed with this approach.

Because the word *minority* is commonly used to cover a very broad range of experiences, it may be useful to discover how well the term applies to Asian-Americans and certain classic minorities in the present context. The listing on p. 314, entitled "Two Groups of Minorities in the United States," deals primarily with education. How do the two groups differ?

The four classic minorities all shared the experience of state violence in their introduction into American society. Most were excluded from public schools for long periods. During much of their history, their schools were segregated by law. They could attend mainstream higher education only by means of a strict quota. All were compelled to use English in the schools and were punished if they continued to use their native language. Of the classic minorities, only the African-Americans were subjected to compulsory-ignorance laws in most Southern colonies and states between 1740 and 1865. These measures forbade the teaching of reading and writing to slaves. Apparently, nowhere else in the world were such laws enacted.

Among Asian-Americans, almost all were free immigrants to the United States. Only the Chinese Americans suffered outright exclusion from public schools between 1871 and 1884. Legally segregated schools were the rule for Chinese Americans until the late 1940s. Most Japanese American children, however, attended nonsegregated schools. None of the Asian-American groups confronted quotas in the colleges and universities they attended. During the mid-1980s and early 1990s, however, the issue of overrepresentation strongly suggested efforts to restrict the presence of Asian-Americans in elite institutions of higher education. All Asian-American groups had to set aside their mother tongue in schools. Because the compulsory-ignorance laws were identified with

TABLE 14.2

Characteristics of Various Groups of California Students, 1980 and 1994

	Asian		Black		Latino		White	
	1980	1994	1980	1994	1980	1994	1980	1994
Public K–12 Enrollments	7.1	11.3	9.9	8.5	25.8	37.0	56.4	42.4
Public High School Graduates	6.2	15.2	8.5	7.5	16.0	29.6	58.3	46.9
California Community College								
First-time Freshmen	5.6	16.1	10.0	8.3	13.7	27.7	69.0	46.5
New Transfer Students at CSU	7.3	20.1	6.1	7.1	10.0	20.3	75.1	50.9
New Transfer Students at UC	10.7	30.5	3.7	3.9	7.4	15.6	77.1	48.6
California State University								
CSU Eligible* H.S. Graduates	12.4	21.7	3.2	5.1	9.5	16.2	73.5	53.5
First-time Freshmen	10.1	23.6	8.4	8.9	11.4	27.1	68.9	39.3
Baccalaureate Degree Recipients	8.8	17.4	5.3	4.9	7.2	14.3	77.4	62.3
Graduate Program Enrollments	7.9	13.5	5.5	6.1	7.8	14.9	77.7	64.5
University of California								
UC Eligible* H.S. Graduates	14.3	27.5	2.5	3.1	6.7	7.4	75.3	56.3
First-time Freshmen	16.3	38.4	4.2	4.7	6.3	16.6	72.8	39.2
Baccalaureate Degree Recipients	12.6	29.2	2.8	3.8	4.8	12.2	79.1	53.8
Graduate Program Enrollments	9.6	19.6	3.9	4.6	5.6	9.3	80.4	65.7

*Composition of Eligible High School Graduates is based on estimated eligibility rates for the Classes of 1983 and 1990.

Note: From California Postsecondary Education Commission, 1996.

slavery, which ended in 1865, and because no Asians were enslaved in the United States, no formal bar against educating them ever existed.

A number of Asian-Americans experienced certain educational and civic deprivations before arriving in the United States. The Filipino Americans, for example, suffered from severe social-class discrimination in schooling matters. Colonialism under the Spanish, Americans, and the Japanese laid heavy burdens on those Filipinos least able to shoulder them. The Koreans, Cambodians, Vietnamese, and Laotians, as well as the people of Hong Kong and Taiwan, the Pacific peoples, and those of India were severely handicapped by colonialist discrimination. Segregation was the rule under various colonial occupiers. Language dominance usually followed political domination.

As the myth of the model minority spread in the United States, little note was taken of these negative aspects of Asian-American experiences. If, after all, even the model minority had its enduring problems, it could not serve as an exemplar to the most afflicted. How successful had Asian-Americans been in the field of education? To a large degree, especially wherever social class factors are at work. In the most selective colleges and universities, Asian-American students are present in proportions far beyond their representation in the general population. In California, for example, the representation of Asian-Americans among first-time freshmen rose from 16.3% in 1980 to 38.4% in 1994 at the University of California (see Table 14.2). During the same years, they made up only 6.2 and 15.2% of all public high-school graduates in the state.

As in American higher education as a whole, attendance in highly selective institutions is strongly correlated with income/social class, whatever the ethnic group. But Asian-American attendance exceeds even the record of White, upper-middle class groups. At the same time, as we have seen, many educational problems of Asian-Americans remain unattended.

NOTES

[1] Examples of this literature include two items by William Petersen: "Success Story: Japanese American Style," *New York Times Magazine,* January 9, 1966 and *Japanese Americans. Oppression and Success* (Random House, 1971); and Louis Winnick, "America's 'Model Minority'," *Commentary,* (August 1990), pp. 22–29.

[2] Tetsuden Kashima, "Japanese American Internees Return, 1945 to 1955: Readjustment and Social Amnesia," *Phylon,* 41 (Summer 1980), p. 115.

[3] Lewis C. Solmon and Tamara L. Wingard, "The Changing Demographics: Problems and Opportunities," p. 32 in Philip G. Altbach and Kofi Lomotey, eds., *The Racial Crisis in American Higher Education* (SUNY Press, 1991).

[4] Jayjia Hsia, *Asian Americans in Higher Education and at Work* (Lawrence Erlbaum Associates, 1988), p. 70.

[5] Dana Y. Takagi, "The Retreat from Race," *Socialist Review,* 22 (October–December 1992), p. 186.

[6] *Digest of Education Statistics, 1994* (GPO, 1994), p. 207.

[7] Norimitsu Orishi, "Affirmative Action: Choosing Sides," *New York Times, Education Life,* March 31, 1996, p. 28. These figures are for 1994.

[8] Jayjia Hsia and Marsha Hirano-Nakanishi, "The Demographics of Diversity. Asian Americans and Higher Education," *Change,* 4 (November–December 1989), p. 27.

[9] Bob H. Suzuki, "Asian Americans as the 'Model Minority' Outdoing Whites? Or Media Hype?" *Change,* 4 (November–December 1989), p. 18.

[10] Jewell Plummer Cobb in Asian Pacific American Education Advisory Committee, *Enriching California's Future: Asian Pacific Americans in the CSU. Public Hearing Issues Summary and Testimony.* Vol. 2 (Office of the Chancellor, The California State University, November 1990), p. 38. Because this volume is not continuously paged, the present writer inserted page numbers on all 596 pages, beginning with the third leaf.

[11] Ray Lou, "Model Minority? Getting Behind the Veil," *Change,* (November–December 1989), p. 17.

[12] Raul Z. Moreno in *Enriching California's Future,* vol. 2, p. 243.

[13] Judy K. Sakaki in ibid., p. 425.

[14] Jim Okutsu in ibid., p. 551.

[15] Martin Katz in ibid., p. 105.

[16] Mary Kay Tirrell and Vickie Hellenas in ibid., pp. 64, 230.

[17] Judy K. Sakaki in ibid., p. 427.

[18] Tirrell in ibid., p. 67.

[19] Hellenas in ibid., pp. 229, 231.

[20] Susan Sung in ibid., p. 482.

[21] Margaret Wong in ibid., p. 567.

[22]Him Chhim in ibid., p. 145.

[23]Peter Masters in ibid., p. 191.

[24]Asian Pacific American Education Advisory Committee, The California State University, *Asian Pacific Americans in the CSU: A Follow-Up Report* (Office of the Chancellor, CSU, August 1994), p. 9.

[25]Ibid., p. 10.

[26]Ibid., p. 10.

[27]Ibid., p. 12.

[28]Ibid., p. 12.

[29]Ibid., p. 13.

[30]Ibid., p. 14.

[31]Ibid., p. 15.

[32]Ibid., p. 17.

[33]Lap Tak Chu, *Factors Discriminating the Academically High, Average, and Low-Achievers Among Junior College Asian-American Students* (Doctoral dissertation, UCLA, 1991), p. 63.

[34]Ibid., p. 127.

[35]Denise K. Magner, "College's Asian Enrollment Defies Stereotype," *Chronicle of Higher Education* (February 10, 1993), p. A34.

[36]Ibid., p. A34.

[37]Paul W. Kingston, "The Pursuit of Inclusion: Recent Trends in Minority Enrollments in Higher Education," *Educational Policy*, 6 (December 1991), pp. 386–387.

[38]Ibid., p. 383.

[39]Ibid., p. 387.

[40]Ibid., p. 389.

[41]Ibid., p. 389.

[42]Solmon and Wingard, "The Changing Demographics: Problems and Opportunities," p. 32.

[43]A good starting point on this entire issue is Dana Y. Takagi, *The Retreat from Race. Asian-American Admissions and Racial Politics* (Rutgers University Press, 1992). See also chapter 5, U.S. Commission on Civil Rights, *Civil Rights Issues Facing Asian Americans in the 1990s* (The Commission, February 1992). An example of the inhospitability on one campus of the University of California can be found in Alexander W. Astin and others, *The UCLA Campus Climate for Diversity* (Higher Education Research Institute, Graduate School of Education, University of California, Los Angeles, March 1991).

[44]Deborah Woo, "The 'Overrepresentation' of Asian Americans: Red Herrings and Yellow Perils," *Sage Race Relations Abstracts*, 15 (May 1990), p. 4.

[45]See chapter 2, "Bigotry and Violence Against Asian Americans," pp. 22–48 in *Civil Rights Issues Facing Asian Americans in the 1990s* (U.S. Commission on Civil Rights, February 1991); NOTE, "Racial Violence Against Asian Americans," *Harvard Law Review*, 106 (June 1993), pp. 1926–1943; Mike Davis, "Who Killed Los Angeles? Part Two: The Verdict is Given," *New Left Review*, No. 199 (May–June 1993), pp. 29–54; Kathryn Imahara and others, *Audit of Violencee Against Asian Pacific Americans, 1993* (National Asian Pacific American Legal Consortium, April 1994); and Kenneth B. Noble, "Attacks Against Asian Americans Are Rising," *New York Times*, December 13, 1995.

[46]See Jack Levin and Jack McDevitt, *Hate Crimes. The Rising Tide of Bigotry and Bloodshed* (Plenum Press, 1993), esp. pp. 115–135. See also U.S. Commission on Civil Rights, *Civil Rights Issues Facing Asian Americans in the 1990s*, pp. 88–89.

[47]Imahara and others, *Audit of Violence*, p. 21.

[48]Ibid., p. 23. See also William Tamayo's statement that over the past 10 years, "there has been an increase of violence by immigration officers," in U.S. Commission on Civil Rights, *Round Table Conference on Asian Civil Rights. Issues for the 1990s*, vol. 3 (The Commission, 1989), p. 191.

[49]Noble, "Attacks Against Asian Americans Are Rising." For a listing of such cases of violence,

see U.S. Commission on Civil Rights, *Civil Rights Issues Facing Asian Americans in the 1990s*, pp. 25–31.

[50]See U.S. Commission on Civil Rights, *Civil Rights Issues Facing Asian Americans in the 1990s*, pp. 47–48.

[51]See ibid., pp. 88–99.

[52]Census Bureau estimate in *Education Week*, March 27, 1996, p. 3.

[53]Ibid., p. 3.

[54]Eric Schmitt, "Senate Judiciary Committee Advances Immigration Bill," *New York Times*, March 29, 1996, p. A10.

[55]Seth Mydans, "New Boat People Exodus: Back to Vietnam," *New York Times*, April 17, 1996, p. 1.

[56]Steven A. Holmes, "Anti-Immigrant Mood Moves Asians to Organize," *New York Times*, January 3, 1996, p. 1.

[57]Pam Belluck, "Healthy Korean Economy Draws Immigrants Home," *New York Times*, August 22, 1995.

[58]Milt Freudenheim, "Doctors' Incomes Fall as Managed Care Grows," *New York Times*, November 17, 1995.

[59]Carol Jouzaitis, "Glut of Doctors, Nurses Predicted by Commission," *Chicago Tribune*, November 17, 1995. See also Esther B. Fein, "Medical Schools Are Urged to Cut Admissions by 20%," *New York Times*, November 17, 1995.

[60]Warren E. Leary, "Cut in Programs Is Pushed To Halt U.S. Doctor Surplus," *New York Times*, January 24, 1996, p. A13.

[61]Michael S. Teitelbaum, "Too Many Engineers, Too Few Jobs," *New York Times*, March 19, 1996, p. A15.

[62]Ibid.

[63]Joyce Tang, "Asian American Engineers: Earnings, Occupational Status, and Promotions," p. 15 in paper presented at the 86th annual meetings of the American Sociological Association in August, 1991.

[64]Ibid., p. 17.

[65]See Edward Jang-Woo Park, "Asians Matter: Asian American Entrepreneurs in the High Technology Industry in Silicon Valley," pp. 155–177 in Bill Ong Hing and Ronald Lee, eds., *The State of Asian Pacific America: Reframing the Immigration Debate. A Public Policy Report* (LEAP Asian Pacific American Public Policy Institute and UCLA Asian American Studies Center, 1996).

[66]Larry Hajime Shinagawa, "The Impact of Immigration on the Demography of Asian Pacific Americans," p. 61 in ibid.

[67]See William R. Tamayo, "Asian Americans and Present U.S. Immigration Policies: A Legacy of Asian Exclusion," pp. 1105–1130 in Hyung-chan Kim, ed., *Asian Americans and the Supreme Court* (Greenwood, 1992).

[68]Sucheng Chan, *Asian Americans. An Interpretive HIstory* (Twayne, 1991), p. 90. See also Charles J. McClain, *In Search of Equality. The Chinese Struggle Against Discrimination in Nineteenth-Century America* (University of California Press, 1994).

[69]Gary Orfield with assistance from Diane Glass, *Asian Students and Multiethnic Desegregation* (Harvard Project on School Desegregation, October 1994), p. 11.

[70]Ibid., p. 29.

[71]Ibid., p. 7.

[72]See ibid., p. 7; Peter Schmidt, "Chinese-American Parents in S. F. Win Round in Court," *Education Week* (October 11, 1995); Jane Meredith Adams, "Education Tables Are Turned," *Chicago Tribune*, January 1, 1996, p. 15; and "New Admissions Policy Offered For San Francisco's Top School," *New York Times*, January 11, 1996, p. A9.

Index

Note: Page references followed by n. and a number refer to numbered footnotes.